Hymns

for

Worship

EDITORS
R. J. Stevens and Dane K. Shepard

PUBLISHER
Guardian of Truth Foundation
420 Old Morgantown Road
Bowling Green, KY 42102
(800) 428–0121

ISBN 0–9620615–0–6

PRINTED IN THE U.S.A.
Ninth Printing
May, 1998

FOREWORD

Sing unto God, sing praises to His name (Psalm 68:4). A hymn is a song in praise or honor of God. **Hymns For Worship Revised** has been designed to praise and glorify God, edify His people, and encourage true, spiritual worship. Traditional favorites have been included along with old and new hymns and gospel songs. We express our gratitude to the many editors and song writers whose contributions to worship in hymnals and songs have helped make this book possible.

The special features of this revised edition are:

Topical arrangement: Most of the songs have been arranged in sections according to a general topic. These sections and topics are found in the Table of Contents. They are flexible and more specific categories can be found in the Topical Index.

Format: Each song has been printed to make the text and music easy to read and follow.

Scripture Index: An appropriate scripture has been included with each song in the book. The scripture references with the corresponding song numbers are listed in the index.

Shaped notes: "Shaped notes" are an extension of the syllable singing method using the "moveable do" system. They have been included in this edition to aid in a-cappella, congregational singing.

Pitch and directing guide: A guide with the pitch and meter is located in the upper, left side of each song, giving the key, directing pattern, and the starting syllables of the melody (i.e. Ab-3-MI).

Topical Index: To help in the selection of songs in varying keys and meters within the same category, the key and directing pattern have been listed after each title (i.e. E-4).

Topical Index guide: To aid in finding songs in the same topical category, each song has been assigned one or two index-guide symbols such as A-1, B-2, C-3, etc. These letters and numbers have been placed in the upper, right side of each song and correspond with a specific subject heading in the Topical Index.

Extra numbered pages: Numbered, blank pages have been provided at the end of the book for the addition of other songs not included in this edition.

Our sincere desire is that **Hymns For Worship Revised** will bring praise to God and draw people closer to Him in worship and devotion. **To God be the glory!** is our prayer.

R. J. Stevens
Dane K. Shepard
Editors

CONTENTS

THE HYMNS

INDEXES

0 Sing And Rejoice In The Savior's Birth

Eb-2-DO
C. E. C.

For unto you is born this day in the city of David
a Savior, which is Christ the Lord. Luke 2:11

C-1, P-2

C. E. Couchman
arr. R. J. Stevens

1. Glo - ry! Glo - ry! Sing al - le - lu - ia! Sing glo - ry to
2. Shep - herds, do not fear. I bring glad ti - dings: A Sav - ior is
3. Low - ly man - ger bed, low - ly the vir - gin who cra - dles His

God. Glo - ry fills the earth — An - gels re - joice in the
here. Joy, joy for Christ the Lord! Je - sus, Im - man - u - el, the
head. Hail! Hail, King of kings! Glo - ry to God for the

CHORUS

Sav - ior's birth.
Son of God. Have you heard? A child is born! Wel - come,
ran - som He brings.

rit. *a tempo*

star, that lights e - ter - nal morn. Glo - ry sent to earth;

CODA

Sing and re - joice in the Sav - ior's birth. Al - le - lu - ia!

Holy, Holy, Holy

1

Holy, holy, holy is the Lord of hosts. Isa. 6:3

Eb-4-DO
Reginald Heber

P-2, W-5
John B. Dykes

1. Ho - ly, ho - ly, ho - ly, Lord God Al - might - y!
2. Ho - ly, ho - ly, ho - ly! All the saints a - dore Thee,
3. Ho - ly, ho - ly, ho - ly! Tho' the dark - ness hide Thee,
4. Ho - ly, ho - ly, ho - ly, Lord God Al - might - y!

Ear - ly in the morn - ing our song shall rise to Thee;
Cast - ing down their gold - en crowns a - round the glass - y sea;
Tho' the eye of sin - ful man Thy glo - ry may not see,
All Thy works shall praise Thy name in earth, and sky, and sea;

Ho - ly, ho - ly, ho - ly! Mer - ci - ful and Might - y!
Cher - u - bim and ser - a - phim fall - ing down be - fore Thee,
On - ly Thou art ho - ly; there is none be - side Thee,
Ho - ly, ho - ly, ho - ly! Mer - ci - ful and Might - y!

God o - ver all, and blest e - ter - nal - ly.
Who wert, and art, and ev - er more shalt be.
Per - fect in pow'r, in love, and pu - ri - ty.
God o - ver all, and blest e - ter - nal - ly.

2 Hallelujah! Praise Jehovah!

Praise ye Him, sun and moon; praise Him all His hosts. Psa. 148:3

G-4-SOL
Psalm 148, Arr.

P-2
Wm. J. Kirkpatrick

1. Hal - le - lu - jah, praise Je - ho - vah! From the heav-ens praise His
2. Let them prais - es give Je - ho - vah! They were made at His com-
3. All ye fruit - ful trees and ce - dars, All ye hills and moun-tains

name; Praise Je - ho - vah in the high - est; All His an - gels
mand; Them for - ev - er He es - tab - lished: His de - cree shall
high, Creep-ing things and beasts and cat - tle, Birds that in the

praise pro-claim. All His hosts to - geth - er praise Him, Sun and
ev - er stand. From the earth, O praise Je - ho - vah, All ye
heav-ens fly, Kings of earth, and all ye peo - ple, Princ - es

moon and stars on high; Praise Him, O ye heav'n of heav - ens,
floods, ye drag - ons all, Fire and hail and snow and va - pors,
great, earth's judg-es all; Praise His name, young men and maid - ens,

CHORUS

3

Lift Your Voice In Praise

F-4-DO

Dane Shepard and
Linda Coffey

*They shall lift up their voice, they shall sing for the majesty
of the Lord . . . Isa. 24:14*

C-6, P-2

Dane Shepard

1. Lord, God of all the earth, We praise Thy holy
2. Lord, God, Thy grace and pow'r De - liv - ers us from
3. Lord, God of faith and love, We give our hearts to

name; The King of kings and Lord of lords,
sin; The Lamb of God and Prince of peace,
Thee; The Liv - ing Word, the great I AM,

CHORUS

Shall ev - er be the same.
The vic - to - ry shall win. How won - der - ful, how
Our hope shall ev - er be.

glo - ri - ous Is Christ our King a - bove. Let us all re -

joice, O lift your voice In praise of His grace and love.

Blessed Assurance

4

Let us draw near with a true heart in full assurance of faith . . . Heb. 10:22

D-3-MI

F. J. Crosby

A-1, T-1

Mrs. J. F. Knapp

1. Bless - ed as - sur - ance, Je - sus is mine! Oh, what a
2. Per - fect sub - mis - sion, per - fect de - light, Vi - sions of
3. Per - fect sub - mis - sion, all is at rest, I, in my

fore - taste of glo - ry di - vine! Heir of sal - va - tion, pur - chase of
rap - ture now burst on my sight, An - gels de - scend - ing, bring from a -
Sav - ior am hap - py and blest, Watch - ing and wait - ing, look - ing a -

Fine CHORUS

God, Born of His Spir - it, washed in His blood.
bove, Ech - oes of mer - cy, whis - pers of love. This is my
bove, Filled with His good - ness, lost in His love.

D.S.- Prais - ing my Sav - ior all the day long.

sto - ry, this is my song, Prais - ing my Sav - ior

D. S.

all the day long; This is my sto - ry, this is my song;

5 How Great Thou Art

Bb-4-SOL
S. K. H.

For Thou art great, and doest wondrous things: Thou art God alone. Psa. 86:10

P-2
Stewart K. Hine

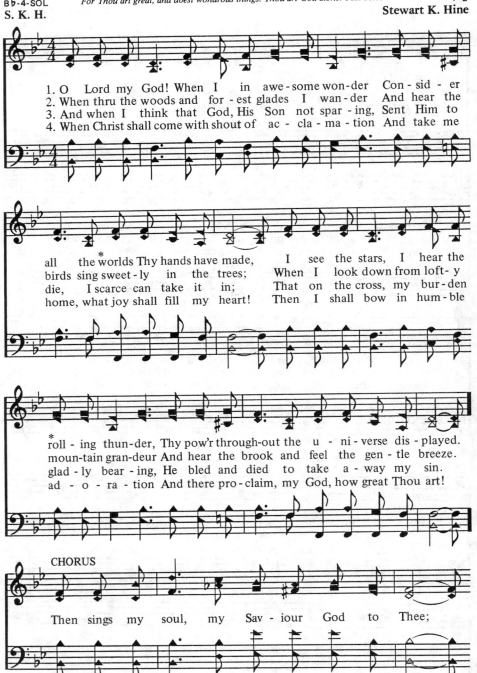

1. O Lord my God! When I in awe - some won - der Con - sid - er
2. When thru the woods and for - est glades I wan - der And hear the
3. And when I think that God, His Son not spar - ing, Sent Him to
4. When Christ shall come with shout of ac - cla - ma - tion And take me

all the *worlds Thy hands have made, I see the stars, I hear the
birds sing sweet - ly in the trees; When I look down from loft - y
die, I scarce can take it in; That on the cross, my bur - den
home, what joy shall fill my heart! Then I shall bow in hum - ble

roll - ing thun - der, Thy pow'r through-out the u - ni - verse dis - played.
moun-tain gran-deur And hear the brook and feel the gen - tle breeze.
glad - ly bear - ing, He bled and died to take a - way my sin.
ad - o - ra - tion And there pro - claim, my God, how great Thou art!

CHORUS

Then sings my soul, my Sav - iour God to Thee;

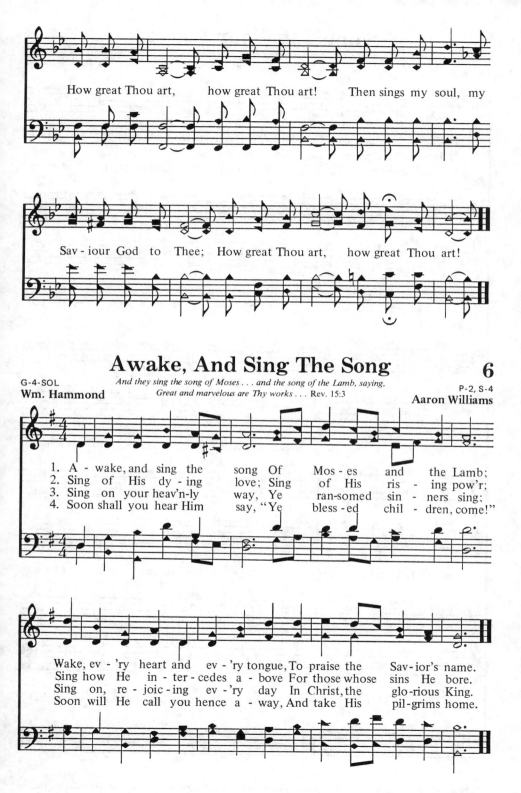

How great Thou art, how great Thou art! Then sings my soul, my

Sav - iour God to Thee; How great Thou art, how great Thou art!

Awake, And Sing The Song 6

G-4-SOL
Wm. Hammond

*And they sing the song of Moses . . . and the song of the Lamb, saying,
Great and marvelous are Thy works . . . Rev. 15:3*

P-2, S-4
Aaron Williams

1. A - wake, and sing the song Of Mos - es and the Lamb;
2. Sing of His dy - ing love; Sing of His ris - ing pow'r;
3. Sing on your heav'n-ly way, Ye ran-somed sin - ners sing;
4. Soon shall you hear Him say, "Ye bless - ed chil - dren, come!"

Wake, ev - 'ry heart and ev - 'ry tongue, To praise the Sav-ior's name.
Sing how He in - ter - cedes a - bove For those whose sins He bore.
Sing on, re - joic-ing ev - 'ry day In Christ, the glo-rious King.
Soon will He call you hence a - way, And take His pil-grims home.

7 Saints Lift Your Voices

F-3-DO
D. M. A.

But they that wait upon the Lord shall . . .
mount up with wings as eagles. Isa. 40:31

Donald M. Alexander
Arr. by R. J. Stevens

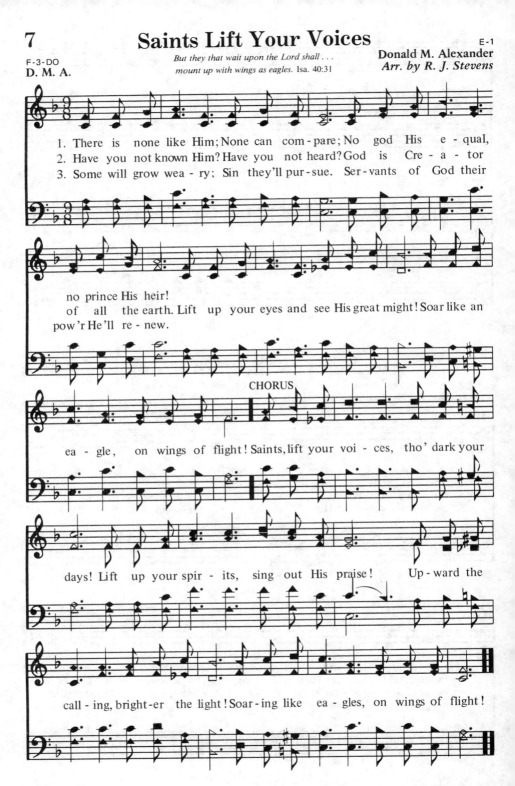

1. There is none like Him; None can com-pare; No god His e-qual,
2. Have you not known Him? Have you not heard? God is Cre - a - tor
3. Some will grow wea - ry; Sin they'll pur-sue. Ser-vants of God their

no prince His heir!
of all the earth. Lift up your eyes and see His great might! Soar like an
pow'r He 'll re - new.

CHORUS

ea - gle, on wings of flight! Saints, lift your voi - ces, tho' dark your

days! Lift up your spir - its, sing out His praise! Up - ward the

call - ing, bright-er the light! Soar-ing like ea - gles, on wings of flight!

Glory To His Name

Ab-4-MI

Having made peace through the blood of His cross . . . to reconcile all things . . .
Col. 1:20

E. A. Hoffman

J. H. Stockton

1. Down at the cross where my Sav - ior died, Down where for
2. I am so won - drous - ly saved from sin, Je - sus so
3. Oh, pre - cious foun - tain that saves from sin, I am so
4. Come to this foun - tain so rich and sweet; Cast thy poor

cleans - ing from sin I cried, There to my heart was the
sweet - ly a - bides with - in, There at the cross where He
glad I have en - tered in; There Je - sus saves me and
soul at the Sav - ior's feet; Plunge in to - day and be

D. S.-There to my heart was the

Fine CHORUS

blood ap - plied; Glo - ry to His name.
took me in; Glo - ry to His name.
keeps me clean; Glo - ry to His name.
made com - plete; Glo - ry to His name.

Glo - ry to His

blood ap - plied; Glo - ry to His name.

D. S.

name, Glo - ry to His name;

9

Our God, He Is Alive

And God said . . . I AM THAT I AM. Ex. 3:14

D♭-4-SOL
A. W. D.

P-2, T-1
A. W. Dicus

1. There is, be-yond the az-ure blue, a God, concealed from
2. There was, a long, long time a-go, a God whose voice the
3. Se-cure, is life from mor-tal mind, God holds the germ with-
4. Our God, whose Son up-on a tree, a life was will-ing

hu-man sight, He tint-ed skies with heav-'nly hue and
proph-ets heard, He is the God that we should know, who
in His hand, Tho' men may search, they can-not find, for
there to give, That He from sin might set man free, and

CHORUS

framed the worlds with His great might.
speaks from His in-spir-ed Word.
God a-lone does un-der-stand.
ev-er-more with Him could live.

There is a

There is a God,

God,
He is a-live,

He is a-live, in Him we

in Him we live, and we sur-vive; From dust our
live, and we sur-vive;

God cre-at-ed man, He is our
From dust our God cre-at-ed man,

rit.

God, the great I AM.
He is our God, the great I AM.

We Thank Thee, Lord

10

G-3-MI   *Blessed be the Lord, who daily loadeth us with benefits, even the God of our salvation.*   H-5, T-2

Albert H. Hutchinson   Psa. 68:19   **Robert N. Quaile, 1903**

1. For all the bless-ings of the year, For all the friends we
2. For life and health, those com-mon things, Which ev-'ry day and
3. For love of Thine which nev-er tires, Which all our bet-ter

hold so dear, For peace on earth, both far and near, We thank Thee, Lord.
hour brings, For home, where our af-fec-tion clings, We thank Thee, Lord.
thought in-spires, And warms our lives, with heav'n-ly fires, We thank Thee, Lord.

11 Our King Immanuel

F-4-SOL
James Rowe

And they shall call His name Immanuel, which being interpreted is, God with us.
Matt. 1:23

C-6, P-2
Samuel W. Beasley

1. See! the Mon-arch of mon-archs Come in maj-es-ty!
2. Like the waves of the o-cean Rolls His praise to-day,
3. O the joy that will thrill us Some glad day on high,

Let us bow down and wor-ship Him Who do-eth all things
For His won-der-ful love has helped So man-y to ex-
When we see Him in glo-ry, where Ce-les-tial prais-es

well; He leads the na-tions out of sin And caus-es foes to
cel; He sends the cap-tives, free from chains, All sing-ing on their
swell; Where cher-u-bim and ser-a-phim Now join us when we

flee: All hail, Our King Im-
way:
cry: All hail our King Im-man-u-el!

CHORUS

man-u-el! O hon-or His name for-ev-er
O hon-or His name For-

12 He's My King

A♭-4-DO

Blessed be the King that cometh in the name of the Lord . . . and glory in the highest.
Luke 19:38

C-6, P-2

James Rowe

James D. Vaughan

1. All day long of Je-sus I am sing-ing, He my song of
2. Streams of love a-round my soul are flow-ing, From His heart, love's
3. In His light, I'm go-ing home to glo-ry, With the souls who

joy will ev-er be; All the while He keeps my heart-bells
ev-er-last-ing spring; That is why my faith in Him I'm
trust His sav-ing grace; Go-ing home to sing and tell His

CHORUS

ring-ing, For His love is ev-'ry-thing to me. He's my
show-ing, That is why an end-less song I sing.
sto-ry, In the bless-ed sun-shine of His face. He's my pre-cious

King, and O I dear-ly love Him; He's my King, no
King, He's my glo-rious King,

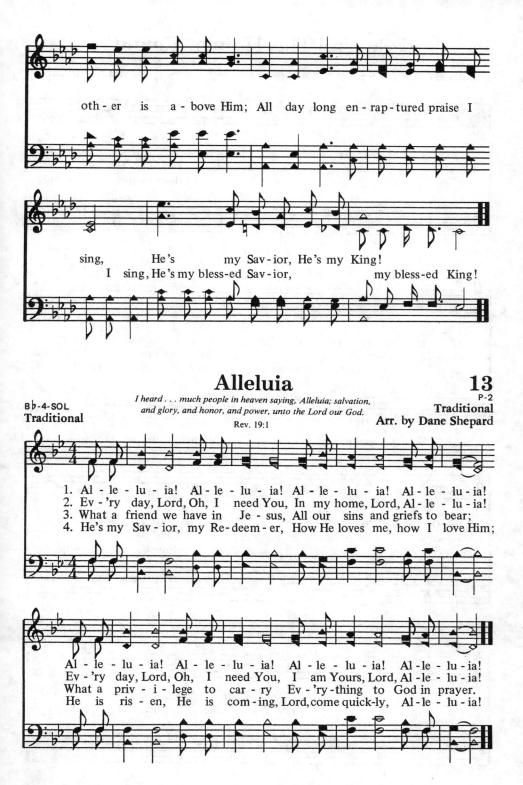

oth-er is a-bove Him; All day long en-rap-tured praise I

sing, He's my Sav-ior, He's my King!
I sing, He's my bless-ed Sav-ior, my bless-ed King!

Alleluia

I heard . . . much people in heaven saying, Alleluia; salvation,
and glory, and honor, and power, unto the Lord our God.

Rev. 19:1

13
P-2

Bb-4-SOL
Traditional

Traditional
Arr. by Dane Shepard

1. Al - le - lu - ia! Al - le - lu - ia! Al - le - lu - ia! Al - le - lu - ia!
2. Ev - 'ry day, Lord, Oh, I need You, In my home, Lord, Al - le - lu - ia!
3. What a friend we have in Je - sus, All our sins and griefs to bear;
4. He's my Sav - ior, my Re - deem - er, How He loves me, how I love Him;

Al - le - lu - ia! Al - le - lu - ia! Al - le - lu - ia! Al - le - lu - ia!
Ev - 'ry day, Lord, Oh, I need You, I am Yours, Lord, Al - le - lu - ia!
What a priv - i - lege to car - ry Ev - 'ry-thing to God in prayer.
He is ris - en, He is com - ing, Lord, come quick-ly, Al - le - lu - ia!

14   O Spread The Tidings 'Round

C-3-SOL

How beautiful are the feet of them that preach the gospel of peace,
and bring glad tidings of good things! Rom. 10:15

P-2, S-5

F. Bottome, Arr. L. O. S.   Wm. J. Kirkpatrick

1. O spread the ti - dings 'round, wher - ev - er man is found, Wher -
2. Lo, the great King of kings, with heal - ing in His wings, To
3. O bound - less love di - vine! how shall this tongue of mine To

ev - er hu - man hearts and hu - man woes a - bound; Let ev - 'ry
ev - 'ry cap - tive soul a full de - liv - 'rance brings; And thro' the
wond'ring mor - tals tell the match - less grace di - vine — That I, in

D. S.—name, the sweet-est heard; His will re-demp-tion brings; O spread the

Fine

Chris-tian tongue pro-claim the joy - ful sound: Our Lord is Lord of lords.
va - cant cells the song of tri-umph rings; Our Lord is King of kings.
earth's de-cline should in His im - age shine! In Him, the Word of heav'n.

ti - dings 'round, wher-ev - er man is found—The Lord is King of kings.

CHORUS   *D. S.*

Of lords, He is the Lord! Di - vine, the liv - ing Word! His

I Am His Child

15

Praise ye the Lord . . . for He is good: His mercy endureth for ever. Psa. 106:1

A- 1, P-2

C-3- DO
D. M. A.

Donald M. Alexander
Arr. by R. J. Stevens

1. Must I live a life of sin-ning Just to know God will for-
2. Must I be in heav-en with Him Just to know the Lord is
3. Must my pray'rs be loud-ly spo-ken Just to know the Fa-ther
4. Must I see the King leave heav-en Just to keep my hope-ful

give me? Must I then be bro-ken-heart-ed Just to
reign-ing? Must I see His acts of pow-er Just to
hears me? Must I die with no-one know-ing Just to
yearn-ing? Must I watch with per-fect vis-ion Just to

CHORUS

know that He can cheer me?
know that He is with me? Praise the Lord! I am for-
know the Fa-ther sees me?
know that He's re-turn-ing?

giv-en! And my Fa-ther up in heav-en knows and

hears and will be with me; Praise the Lord! I am His child!

16

D-2-DO
M. L.
Tr. F. H. Hedge
P-2, W-1
Martin Luther, 1529

A Mighty Fortress

He is my refuge and my fortress: my God, in Him will I trust.
Psa. 91:2

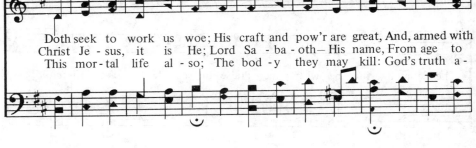

1. A might-y for-tress is our God, A bul-wark nev-er fail - ing; Our help-er He, a - mid the flood Of mor-tal ills pre-vail - ing. For still our an -cient foe Doth seek to work us woe; His craft and pow'r are great, And, armed with

2. Did we in our own strength con - fide Our striv-ing would be los - ing; Were not the right One on our side The Man of God's own choos - ing. Dost ask who that may be? Christ Je - sus, it is He; Lord Sa - ba - oth— His name, From age to

3. And tho' this world, with e - vil filled, Should threat-en to un-do us; We will not fear, for God hath willed His truth to tri - umph through us. Let goods and kin - dred go, This mor-tal life al - so; The bod-y they may kill: God's truth a-

cru - el hate, On earth is not his e - qual.
age the same, And He must win the bat - tle.
bid - eth still, His king - dom is for - ev - er.

Sun Of My Soul

17

The Lord is my light and my salvation: whom shall I fear? Psa. 27:1

F-3-DO
John Keble, 1820

F-2, P-5
Peter Ritter

1. Sun of my soul, Thou Sav - ior dear, It is not
2. When the soft dews of kind - ly sleep My wea - ried
3. A - bide with me from morn till eve, For with - out
4. Come near and bless us when we wake, Ere thru the

night if Thou be near; O may no earth - born
eye - lids gen - tly steep, Be my last tho't, how
Thee I can - not live; A - bide with me when
world our way we take; Till in the o - cean

cloud a - rise To hide Thee from Thy ser - vant's eyes!
sweet to rest For - ev - er on my Sav - ior's breast.
night is nigh, For with - out Thee I dare not die.
of Thy love, We lose our - selves in heav'n a - bove.

18 The Great Redeemer

*In whom we have redemption through His blood
the forgiveness of sins, according to the riches of His grace. Eph. 1:7*

D-4-SOL
Frances Foster

Samuel W. Beazley

1. How I love the great Re - deem-er Who is do - ing so much for me;
2. He has pur-chased my re - demp-tion, Rolled my bur-den of sin a - way,
3. Glo - ry be to Him for - ev - er! End - less prais - es to Christ the Lamb!

With what joy I tell the sto - ry Of the love that makes men free. Till my
And is walk - ing on be - side me, Grow-ing dear -er day by day. That is
He has filled my life with sun-shine, He has made me what I am. O that

earth - ly life is end - ed, I will send .... songs a - bove, ...
why I sing His prais - es, That is why .... joy is mine, ...
ev - 'ry one would know Him, O that all .... would a - dore! ....

Then be - side the crys - tal sea More and more my soul shall be Prais - ing
That is why for - ev - er more On the ev - er - last-ing shore I shall
O that all would trust the love Of the might - y Friend a - bove And be

Je - sus and His love.
sing of love di - vine. He is ev - 'ry-thing to me, to me, He is
His for - ev - er more.

19 Heavenly Sunlight

G-3-SOL

I am the light of the world: he that followeth Me shall not walk in darkness . . .
John 8:12

F-2, J-1

Henry J. Zelley, 1899

George H. Cook, 1899

1. Walk-ing in sun-light, all of my jour-ney; O - ver the moun-tains
2. Shad-ows a - round me, shad-ows a - bove me, Nev - er con-ceal my
3. In the bright sun-light, ev - er re - joic - ing, Press-ing my way to

thru the deep vale; Je - sus has said, "I'll nev - er for-
Sav - ior and Guide; He is the light in Him is no
man - sions a - bove; Sing - ing His prais - es, glad - ly I'm

sake thee", Prom - ise di - vine that nev - er can fail.
dark - ness, Ev - er I'm walk - ing close to His side.
walk - ing, Walk - ing in sun - light, sun - light of love.

CHORUS

Heav - en - ly sun - light, heav - en - ly sun - light; Flood-ing my soul with

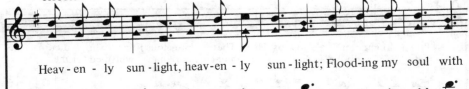

glo - ry di - vine: Hal - le - lu - jah, I am re -

joic - ing, Sing - ing His prais - es, Je - sus is mine.

O God, Our Help In Ages Past   20

Lord, Thou hast been our dwelling place in all generations. Psa. 90:1

C-4-SOL

Isaac Watts

G-3, P-5

William Croft

1. O God, our help in a - ges past, Our hope for years to come,
2. Un - der the shad - ow of Thy throne Still may we dwell se - cure;
3. Be - fore the hills in or - der stood, Or earth re - ceived her frame,
4. O God, our help in a - ges past, Our hope for years to come,

Our shel - ter from the storm - y blast, And our e - ter - nal home!
Suf - fi - cient is Thine arm a - lone, And our de - fense is sure.
From ev - er - last - ing Thou art God, To end - less years the same.
Be Thou our guide while life shall last, And our e - ter - nal home.

21 Praise The Lord

A-4-SOL

P-2

J. Kempthorne

Praise ye the Lord. Praise ye the Lord from the heavens: Praise Him in the heights.
Praise ye Him, all His angels. Psa. 148: 1, 2

Lowell Mason

1. Praise the Lord, ye heav'ns, a - dore Him! Praise Him, an - gels,
2. Praise the Lord, for He hath spo - ken; Worlds His might - y
3. Praise the Lord, for He is glo - rious; Nev - er shall His
4. Praise the God of our sal - va - tion; Hosts on high, His

in the height; Sun and moon re - joice be - fore Him;
voice o - beyed; Laws which nev-er shall be bro - ken,
prom-ise fail; God hath made His saints vic - to - rious:
pow'r pro-claim; Heav'n and earth, and all cre - a - tion,

1. Sun and moon re - joice be - fore Him;
REFRAIN

Praise Him, all ye stars of light.
For their guid - ance He hath made.
Sin and death shall not pre - vail.
Laud and mag - ni - fy His name.

Hal - le -

Praise Him, all ye stars of light.
A - men.

lu -jah! A - men, Hal - le - lu - jah! A - men, A - men, A - men.

He Is In Our Midst

G-4-SOL
G. B. S.

*Sing and rejoice . . . for lo, I come,
and I will dwell in the midst of thee, saith the Lord. Zech. 2:10*

J-1, P-2
Glenda B. Schales
Arr. by Dane Shepard

1. Draw from the springs of sal - va - tion, Give thanks to His great and
2. Call on His name with thanks - giv - ing. Yes joy - ous - ly praise His

ho - ly name. Make known His deeds a - mong the peo - ple, Make known His
name in song. Thru love He au - thored our sal - va - tion, Thru love He

CHORUS

ex - al - ted way. Praise the Lord And shout for
did give His Son. praise the Lord shout and cry for

joy for the Ho - ly One is in our midst. Praise the Lord
joy praise the Lord

And shout for joy for He is in our midst.
shout and cry for

23 Great Is Thy Faithfulness

His compassions fail not. They are new every morning: great is Thy faithfulness.
Lam. 3:22,23

D-3-MI

P-2, P-5

Thomas O. Chisholm

Wm. M. Runyan

1. Great is Thy faith-ful-ness, O God my Fa-ther, There is no
2. Sum-mer and win-ter, and spring-time and har-vest, Sun, moon and
3. Par-don for sin and a peace that en-dur-eth, Thine own dear

shad-ow of turn-ing with Thee; Thou chang-est not, Thy com-
stars in their cours-es a-bove Join with all na-ture in
pres-ence to cheer and to guide; Strength for to-day and bright

pas-sions, they fail not; As Thou hast been Thou for-ev-er wilt be.
man-i-fold wit-ness To Thy great faith-ful-ness, mer-cy, and love.
hope for to-mor-row, Bless-ings all mine, with ten thou-sand be-side!

CHORUS

Great is Thy faith-ful-ness! Great is Thy faith-ful-ness! Morn-ing by

morn-ing new mer-cies I see; All I have need-ed Thy hand hath pro-

vid - ed; Great is Thy faith - ful - ness, Lord, un - to me! A - men.

For The Beauty Of The Earth 24

Ab-4-DO
Folliott S. Pierpoint

*Every good gift and every perfect gift is from above,
and cometh down from the Father . . .* **Arranged from Conrad Kocher**
Jas. 1:17

P-2, T-2

1. For the beau - ty of the earth, For the glo - ry of the skies,
2. For the joy of hu - man love, Broth-er, sis - ter, par - ent, child,
3. For Thy church that ev - er - more Lift - eth ho - ly hands a - bove,

For the love which from our birth O - ver and a - round us lies,
Friends on earth, and friends a - bove, For all gen - tle tho'ts and mild,
Of - f'ring up on ev - 'ry shore Her pure sac - ri - fice of love,

Lord of all, to Thee we raise This our hymn of grate - ful praise.

25
Wonderful Jesus

I will extol Thee, my God, O King; and I will bless Thy name for ever . . . Psa. 145:1

G-3-MI

James Rowe

P-2

J. P. Denton

1. Won - der - ful Je - sus! glo - ri - ous friend! He will be
2. Won - der - ful Je - sus! show - ing the way In - to the
3. Won - der - ful Je - sus! all thru the night He will en-

with me un - to the end, Cheer - ing, up - hold - ing, keep - ing me
bless - ed king - dom of day; Guid - ing my foot - steps, hold - ing con-
fold me, giv - ing me light; Then when the morn - ing breaks on the

strong, Fear - less and loy - al, shield - ing from wrong.
trol, Mak - ing me hap - py, keep - ing me whole.
shore, This He will whis - per, "Mine ev - er - more."

CHORUS

Won - der - ful Je - sus! mar - vel - ous King! Ev - er His

praise my spir - it shall sing, When I be - hold His

glo - ri -fied face, How I shall praise His won- der- ful grace!

Jesus, Thou Joy Of Loving Hearts 26

Eb-3-MI
Bernard of Clairvaux
Tr. Ray Palmer

We also joy in God, through our Lord Jesus Christ,
by whom we have now received the atonement. Rom. 5:11

P-2
Henry P. Smith

1. Je - sus, Thou joy of lov - ing hearts, Thou fount of life,
2. Thy truth un-changed hath ev - er stood; Thou sav - est those
3. On Thee we feed, Thou liv - ing bread, And long to feast
4. O Je - sus, ev - er with us stay, Make all our mo -

Thou light of men, From all the bliss that earth
That on Thee call; To them that seek Thee Thou
up - on Thee still; We drink of Thee, Thou foun-
ments calm and bright; Chase the dark night of sin

im - parts We turn un - filled to Thee a - gain.
art good; To them that find Thee, all in all.
tain - head, Whose streams each thirst - ing soul can fill.
a - way, Shed o'er the world Thy ho - ly light.

27 Joyful, Joyful We Adore Thee

J-1, P-2

G-4-MI
Henry van Dyke

But let all those that put their trust in Thee rejoice . . .
let them also that love Thy name be joyful in Thee. Psa. 5:11

Ludwig van Beethoven
Arr. by Edward Hodges

1. Joy-ful, joy-ful, we a-dore Thee, God of glo-ry, Lord of love:
2. All Thy works with joy surround Thee, Earth and heav'n re-flect Thy rays,
3. Thou art giv-ing and for-giv-ing, Ev-er bless-ing, ev-er blest,
4. Mor-tals join the might-y cho-rus, Which the morn-ing stars be-gan;

Hearts un-fold like flowers be-fore Thee, Open-ing to the sun a-bove,
Stars and an-gels sing a-round Thee, Cen-ter of un-bro-ken praise;
Well-spring of the joy of liv-ing, O-cean-depth of hap-py rest!
Fa-ther love is reign-ing o'er us, Broth-er love binds man to man.

Melt the clouds of sin and sad-ness; Drive the dark of doubt a-way;
Field and for-est, vale and mountain, Flow-ery mead-ow, flash-ing sea,
Thou our Fa-ther, Christ our bro-ther, All who live in love are Thine;
Ev-er sing-ing, march we on-ward, Vic-tors in the midst of strife;

Giv-er of im-mor-tal glad-ness, Fill us with the light of day!
Chant-ing bird and flow-ing foun-tain Call us to re-joice in Thee.
Teach us how to love each oth-er, Lift us to the joy di-vine.
Joy-ful mu-sic leads us sun-ward In the tri-umph song of life.

Is It For Me?

F-3-DO
Frances R. Havergal

Ye rejoice with joy unspeakable . . . receiving the end of your faith,
even the salvation of your souls. 1 Pet. 1:8,9

C-10, P-2
T. C. O'Kane

1. Is it for me, dear Sav - ior, Thy glo - ry and Thy rest—
2. Is it for me, Thy wel - come, Thy gra - cious "En - ter in"—
3. O Sav - ior, pre - cious Sav - ior, My heart is at Thy feet;
4. I'll be with Thee for - ev - er, And nev - er grieve Thee more;

CHORUS

For me, so weak and sin - ful? O shall I be so blest?
For me Thy "Come, ye bless - ed," For me so full of sin?
I bless Thee, and I love Thee, And Thee I long to meet.
Dear Sav - ior, I must praise Thee, And love Thee ev - er - more.

O Sav - ior, my Re - deem - er, What can I but a - dore, And

mag - ni - fy and praise Thee, And love Thee ev - er more?

29 How Good Is The God We Adore

G-2-SOL

Joseph Hart
Verses 3 & 4, Avis B. Christiansen

For Thou, Lord, art good, and ready to forgive;
Psa. 86:5

P-2

Homer Hammontree

1. How good is the God we a-dore, Our faith-ful, un-
2. How bound-less the grace He hath shown In giv-ing Him-
3. How glo-rious to walk in the light He send-eth from
4. 'Tis Je - sus, the First and the Last, Whose Spir-it shall

change- a - ble Friend, Whose love is as great as His pow'r And
self on the tree For sin - ners con-demned and un-done, Un-
heav - en a - bove, To lean on His in - fi - nite might And
guide us safe home; We'll praise Him for all that is past And

CHORUS

knows neith-er meas-ure nor end.
wor - thy of mer - cy so free!
rest in His un - fail - ing love! How great is Thy good-ness, O
trust Him for all that's to come.

Lord! How grand and how glo - rious Thy name! In earth and in

heav-en a-dored, Re-deem-er and Sav-ior of men!

All Things Praise Thee

30

The heavens declare the glory of God; and the firmament showeth His handiwork.
Psa. 19:1

A-4-DO
G. W. Conder

P-2
Conrad Kocher

1. All things praise Thee, Lord most high, Heav'n and earth, and sea and sky;
2. All things praise Thee—night to night Sings in si-lent hymns of light;
3. All things praise Thee: heav'n's high shrine Rings with mel-o-dy di-vine;

All were for Thy glo-ry made, That Thy great-ness, thus dis-played,
All things praise Thee—day by day Chants Thy pow'r in burn-ing ray;
Low-ly bend-ing at Thy feet, Ser-aph and arch-an-gel meet;

Should all wor-ship bring to Thee; All things praise Thee—Lord, may we!
Time and space are prais-ing Thee; All things praise Thee—Lord, may we!
This their high-est bliss, to be Ev-er prais-ing—Lord, may we!

31 What A Savior

But God commendeth His love toward us, in that,
while we were yet sinners, Christ died for us. Rom. 5:8

Db-4-DO
M. P. D.

C-10, S-1
Marvin P. Dalton

1. Once I was stray-ing in sin's dark val-ley, No hope with-in could I see; God sent from heav-en a lov-ing Sav-ior To save a poor lost soul like me.
2. He left the Fa-ther, with all His rich-es, With calm-ness sweet and se-rene, Came down from heav-en and gave His life-blood, To make the vil-est sin-ner clean.
3. Death's chill-y wa-ters I'll soon be cross-ing, His hand will lead me safe o'er; I'll join the cho-rus in that great cit-y, And sing up there for-ev-er-more.

CHORUS

O what a Sav-ior, O hal-le-lu-jah, His heart was bro-ken on Cal-va-ry; His hands were nail-scarred, His side was

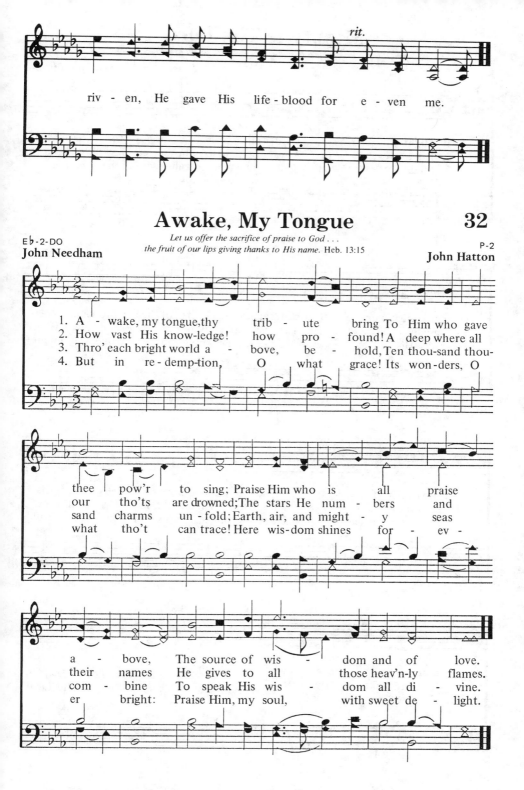

rit.

riv - en, He gave His life-blood for e - ven me.

Awake, My Tongue

32

Let us offer the sacrifice of praise to God . . .
the fruit of our lips giving thanks to His name. Heb. 13:15

Eb-2-DO
John Needham

P-2
John Hatton

1. A - wake, my tongue, thy trib - ute bring To Him who gave
2. How vast His know-ledge! how pro - found! A deep where all
3. Thro' each bright world a - bove, be - hold, Ten thou-sand thou-
4. But in re - demp-tion, O what grace! Its won-ders, O

thee pow'r to sing; Praise Him who is all praise
our tho'ts are drowned; The stars He num - bers and
sand charms un - fold; Earth, air, and might - y seas
what tho't can trace! Here wis-dom shines for - ev -

a - bove, The source of wis - dom and of love.
their names He gives to all those heav'n-ly flames.
com - bine To speak His wis - dom all di - vine.
er bright: Praise Him, my soul, with sweet de - light.

33 Mighty Is The Lord

E♭-4-SOL
J. E.

Praise Him for His mighty acts: praise Him according to His excellent greatness.
Psa. 150:2

P-2

Johnny Elmore

1. Might-y is the Lord, our God, give praise to His great
2. Ho-ly is the Lord of Hosts, whose reign shall nev-er
3. Might-y is our God, Je-ho-vah, won-drous is His

name, great name; Saints of earth, and hosts of heav'n pro-claim a-
cease, ne'er cease; He can save the fall-en race and give His
grace, His grace; He is build-ing now in heav'n, that we might

broad His fame; Come re-joic-ing, shout "Ho-san-na"
ser-vants peace; All the earth should sing His prais-es,
have a place; How He makes us want to serve Him,

that all men might see; Might - y is the Lord
for He makes us free; Might-y, Might - y is the Lord
His own peo-ple be;

34 Worthy Art Thou

B♭-3-SOL
T. S. T.

Worthy is the Lamb that was slain to receive power, and riches, and wisdom, and strength, and honor, and glory, and blessing. Rev. 5:12

Tillit S. Teddlie

P-2

1. Wor-thy of praise is Christ our Re-deem-er, Wor-thy of
2. Lift up the voice in praise and de-vo-tion, Saints of all
3. Lord, may we come be-fore Thee with sing-ing, Filled with Thy

glo-ry, hon-or and pow'r! Wor-thy of all our souls ad-o-
earth be-fore Him should bow; An-gels in heav-en wor-ship Him
spir-it, wis-dom and pow'r; May we as-cribe Thee glo-ry and

ra-tion, Wor-thy art Thou! Wor-thy art Thou!
say-ing, Wor-thy art Thou!
hon-or, Wor-thy art Thou!

CHORUS

Wor-thy of rich-es, bless-ings and hon-or, Wor-thy of wis-dom,

glo-ry and pow'r! Wor-thy of earth and heav-en's thanks-

giv - ing Wor - thy art Thou! Wor - thy art Thou!
Wor - thy art Thou! art Thou!

O Worship The King

35

A-3-SOL
Robert Grant

Our Lord Jesus Christ . . . the King of kings,
and Lord of lords . . . to whom be honor and power . . . 1 Tim. 6:14-16

C-6, P-2

J. Michael Haydn

1. O wor - ship the King, all - glo - rious a - bove, And grate - ful - ly
2. Thy boun - ti - ful care, what tongue can re - cite? It breathes in the
3. Frail chil - dren of dust, and fee - ble as frail, In Thee do we

sing His won - der - ful love; Our Shield and De - fend - er, the
air, it shines in the light; It streams from the hills, it de -
trust, nor find Thee to fail; Thy mer - cies, how ten - der! how

An - cient of Days, Pa - vil - ioned in splen - dor and gird - ed with praise.
scends to the plain, And sweet - ly dis - tills in the dew and the rain.
firm to the end! Our Mak - er, De - fend - er, Re - deem - er, and Friend!

36 Each Step I Take

Hold up my goings in Thy paths, that my footsteps slip not. Psa. 17:5

Eb-4-SOL
W. E. M.

F-2, G-3
W. Elmo Mercer

1. Each step I take my Sav-ior goes be-fore me, And with His
2. At times I feel my faith be-gin to wa-ver, When up a-
3. I trust in God, no mat-ter come what may, For life e-

lov-ing hand He leads the way. And with each breath I whis-per
head I see a chas-m wide, It's then I turn and look up
ter-nal is in His hand, He holds the key that o-pens

"I a-dore Thee;" Oh, what joy to walk with Him each day.
to my Sav-ior, I am strong when He is by my side.
up the way, That will lead me to the prom-ised land.

CHORUS

Each step I take I know that He will guide me; To high-er ground He

ev-er leads me on. Un-til some day the last step will be

tak - en, Each step I take just leads me clos - er home.

Revive Us Again

Wilt Thou not revive us again: that Thy people may rejoice in Thee? Psa. 85:6

37

G-3-SOL

William P. MacKay, 1863

H-4, P-2

John J. Husband, 1820

1. We praise Thee, O God! for the Son of Thy love,
2. We praise Thee, O God! for Thy Spir - it of light,
3. All glo - ry and praise to the Lamb that was slain,

For Je - sus who died, and is now gone a - bove.
Who has shown us our Sav - ior, and scat - tered our night.
Who has borne all our sins, and has cleansed ev - 'ry stain.

CHORUS

Hal - le - lu - jah! Thine the glo - ry, Hal - le - lu - jah! A - men!

Hal - le - lu - jah! Thine the glo - ry, Re - vive us a - gain.

38 King Most High

I will praise the Lord according to His righteousness:
and I will sing praise to the name of the Lord most high. Psa. 7:17

F-4-DO
James R. Cope

C-6, P-2
R. J. Stevens

1. From the earth from the sky breaks
2. Hum-ble birth held no worth till
3. Words He gave me to say, by
4. Dark-est pow'r He o'er-came, life

1. From the earth from the sky

forth the joy-ful cry, "Our Lord is King most high!" Cru-ci-fied,..
an-gel voice sang forth, "A King is born this day!" Then the earth
works He led the way—This Lord and King to be. Then a-lone,
for me He re-gained; A pro-phet ne'er to die; Priest for-e'er

He re-vived, that's why He's King most high.
was a-ware its hope had come to stay.
blood a-toned, His life He gave for me.
on His throne: Lord, God my King most high.

1. cru-ci-fied He re-vived

CHORUS

My Lord is great and good, and He will hear my cry;
My Lord

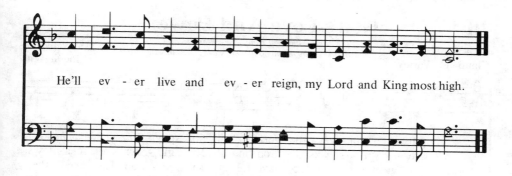

He'll ev - er live and ev - er reign, my Lord and King most high.

God Of Our Fathers

39

F-2-DO

The Lord of hosts is with us; the God of Jacob is our refuge. Psa. 46:7

P-2, P-5

Daniel C. Roberts

George W. Warren

1. God of our fa - thers, whose al - might - y hand Leads forth in beau -
2. Thy love di - vine hath led us in the past; In this free land
3. Re - fresh Thy peo - ple on their toil - some way; Lead us from night

ty all the star - ry band Of shin - ing worlds in splen - dor thro' the
by Thee our lot is cast; Be Thou our rul - er, guard - ian, guide and
to nev - er - end - ing day; Fill all our lives with love and grace di -

skies, Our grate - ful songs be - fore Thy throne a - rise.
stay, Thy word our law, Thy path our cho - sen way.
vine, And glo - ry, laud and praise be ev - er Thine. A - men.

40 God's Love And Power

The invisible things of Him . . . are clearly seen,
being understood by the things that are made . . . Rom. 1:20

L-5, P-2

R. J. Stevens and
Joe Stevens

Bb-4-SOL
Claude E. Worley

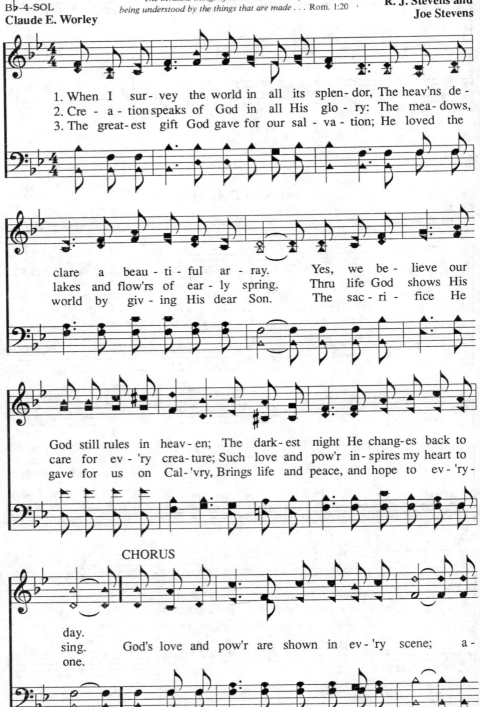

1. When I sur-vey the world in all its splen-dor, The heav'ns de-
2. Cre - a - tion speaks of God in all His glo - ry: The mea - dows,
3. The great-est gift God gave for our sal - va - tion; He loved the

clare a beau - ti - ful ar - ray. Yes, we be - lieve our
lakes and flow'rs of ear - ly spring. Thru life God shows His
world by giv - ing His dear Son. The sac - ri - fice He

God still rules in heav - en; The dark - est night He chang-es back to
care for ev - 'ry crea-ture; Such love and pow'r in-spires my heart to
gave for us on Cal - 'vry, Brings life and peace, and hope to ev - 'ry-

CHORUS

day.
sing. God's love and pow'r are shown in ev - 'ry scene; a-
one.

dorn-ing truth on which we can re-ly. When time is o'er, all

earth will then pro-claim Christ, Lord of lords and King most high.

Fairest Lord Jesus

41

Thou art fairer than the children of men. Psa. 45:2

E-4-DO

German Hymn, 1677

C-6, P-2

Arr. Richard S. Willis, 1850

1. Fair - est Lord Je - sus! Ru - ler of all na - ture! O
2. Fair are the mead - ows, Fair - er still the wood - lands, Robed
3. Fair is the sun - shine, Fair - er still the moon - light, And

Thou of God and man the Son! Thee will I cher - ish,
in the bloom-ing garb of spring; Je - sus is fair - er,
all the twin - kling star - ry host: Je - sus shines bright - er,

Thee will I hon - or, Thou, my soul's glo - ry, joy, and crown.
Je - sus is pur - er, Who makes the woe - ful heart to sing.
Je - sus shines pur - er, Than all the an - gels heav'n can boast;

42 Blessed In Christ

Thou art worthy, O Lord, to receive glory and honour and power. Rev. 4:11

B♭-3-MI

Donald M. Alexander

R. J. Stevens

1. Bless-ed in Christ, with bless-ings a-bun-dant, I can thru Him face
2. Bless-ed in Christ, a glo-ri-ous fu-ture, Now that He cleansed the
3. Bless-ed in Christ, with mar-vel-ous pow-er! Dai-ly I live, my

liv-ing each day. Tho' pres-sures mount and stress-es sur-round
sins from my past. Each day I'm ris-ing, no-bler I'm liv-
Lord to o-bey. Pow-er a-bove my ask-ing or think-

me, I go to my Fa-ther, thru Je-sus I pray.
ing, Thru grace and mer-cy He'll save me at last.
ing Will cheer my heart and lift me a-way!

CHORUS

Fa-ther I praise Thee for Thy in-ter-ven-tion! Je-sus I

praise Thee for Thy re-demp-tion! Spir-it I praise Thee for

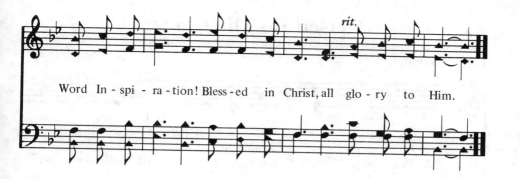

Word In - spi - ra - tion! Bless -ed in Christ, all glo - ry to Him.

God Is The Fountain Whence

43

F-3-DO

O Lord . . . the fountain of living waters, Heal me, O Lord, and I shall be healed.

Jer. 17:13,14

Benjamin Beddome

Lowell Mason

P-2

1. God is the foun - tain whence Ten thou - sand bless - ings
2. The com - forts He af - fords Are nei - ther few nor
3. He fills my heart with joy, My lips at - tunes for

flow; To Him my life, my health,
small; He is the source of fresh
praise; And to His glo - ry I'll

and friends, And ev - 'ry good I owe.
de - lights, My por - tion and my all.
de - vote The rem - nant of my days.

44 To God Be The Glory

A♭-3-SOL

Fanny J. Crosby

Give unto the Lord glory and strength. Give unto the Lord the glory due unto His name. Psa. 29:1,2

P-2

W. H. Doane

1. To God be the glo - ry, great things He hath done, So
2. O per - fect re-demp-tion, the pur-chase of blood, To
3. Great things He hath taught us, great things He hath done, And

loved He the world that He gave us His Son, Who yield - ed His
ev - 'ry be - liev - er the prom-ise of God; The vil - est of-
great our re - joic - ing thro' Je - sus the Son; But pur - er and

D. S.-come to the

life an a - tone-ment for sin, And o-pened the Life-gate that
fend - er who tru - ly be - lieves, When bur - ied with Je - sus a
high - er and great - er will be Our won - der, our trans-port,when

Fa - ther thru Je - sus the Son, And give Him the glo - ry great

Fine CHORUS

all may go in.
par-don re - ceives. Praise the Lord, praise the Lord, Let the earth hear His
Je - sus we see.

things He hath done.

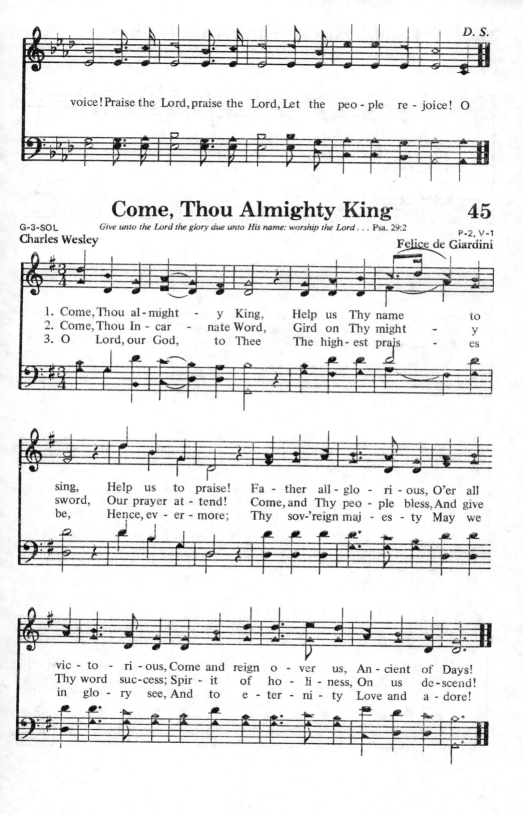

Come, Thou Almighty King   **45**

G-3-SOL   *Give unto the Lord the glory due unto His name: worship the Lord . . . Psa. 29:2*   P-2, V-1

Charles Wesley   Felice de Giardini

voice! Praise the Lord, praise the Lord, Let the peo-ple re-joice! O

1. Come, Thou al-might - y King,   Help us Thy name   to
2. Come, Thou In-car - nate Word,   Gird on Thy might - y
3. O Lord, our God,   to Thee   The high-est prais - es

sing,   Help us to praise! Fa - ther all - glo - ri - ous, O'er all
sword,   Our prayer at - tend! Come, and Thy peo - ple bless, And give
be,   Hence, ev - er - more; Thy sov'reign maj - es - ty May we

vic - to - ri - ous, Come and reign o - ver us, An - cient of Days!
Thy word suc-cess; Spir - it of ho - li - ness, On us de - scend!
in glo - ry see, And to e - ter - ni - ty Love and a - dore!

46

Hark! The Herald Angels Sing

G-4-SOL
Charles Wesley

And suddenly there was . . . a multitude of the heavenly host praising God . . .
Luke 2:13

C-1, P-2
Mendelssohn

1. Hark! the her - ald an - gels sing, "Glo - ry to the
2. Mild, He lays His glo - ry by, Born that man no
3. Hail the heav'n - born Prince of Peace! Hail the Son of

new - born King! Peace on earth and mer - cy mild, God and
more may die; Born to raise the sons of earth, Born to
Right-eous - ness! Light and life to all He brings, Ris'n with

sin - ners rec - on - ciled!" Joy - ful, all ye na - tions, rise;
give them sec - ond birth. Veiled in flesh the God - head see;
heal - ing in His wings. Christ, by high - est heav'n a - dored,

Join the tri - umph of the skies; With th' an - gel - ic host pro-claim,
Hail th' in-car - nate De - i - ty; Pleased as man with men to dwell,
Christ, the ev - er - last - ing Lord; Come, De - sire of na-tions, come,

Christ is born in Beth - le - hem! With th' an - gel - ic
Je - sus, our Im - man - u - el! Pleased as man with
Fix in us Thy hum - ble home; Come, De - sire of

host pro - claim, Christ is born in Beth - le - hem!
men to dwell, Je - sus, our Im - man - u - el!
na - tions, come, Fix in us Thy hum - ble home.

God Is So Good

For the Lord is good; His mercy is everlasting . . . Psa. 100:5

47

E♭-2-DO

T-1
Unknown

1 God is so good, God is so good,
2. Je - sus is real, Je - sus is real,
3. He saved my soul, He saved my soul,
4. I praise His name, I praise His name,

God is so good, He's so good to me!
Je - sus is real, He's so real to me!
He saved my soul And He made me whole!
I praise His name, He's so good to me!

48 On Zion's Glorious Summit

Ab-4-SOL
John Kent

Holy, holy, holy, Lord God Almighty, which was and is and is to come. Rev. 4:8

H-2, P-2
Robert Skene

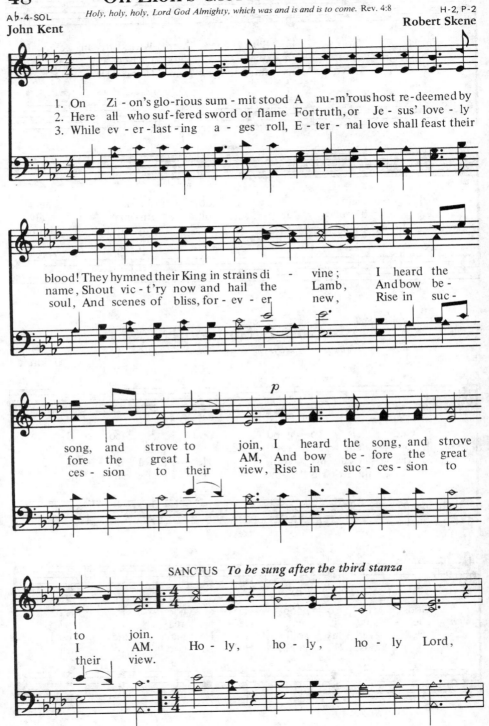

1. On Zi - on's glo - rious sum - mit stood A nu - m'rous host re - deemed by blood! They hymned their King in strains di - vine; I heard the song, and strove to join, I heard the song, and strove to join.

2. Here all who suf - fered sword or flame For truth, or Je - sus' love - ly name, Shout vic - t'ry now and hail the Lamb, And bow be - fore the great I AM, And bow be - fore the great I AM.

3. While ev - er - last - ing a - ges roll, E - ter - nal love shall feast their soul, And scenes of bliss, for - ev - er new, Rise in suc - ces - sion to their view, Rise in suc - ces - sion to their view.

p

SANCTUS *To be sung after the third stanza*

Ho - ly, ho - ly, ho - ly Lord,

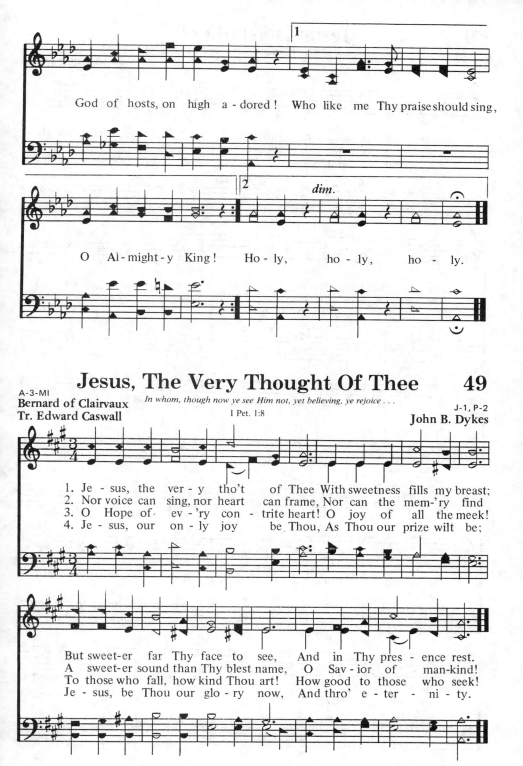

God of hosts, on high a - dored! Who like me Thy praise should sing,

dim.

O Al - might - y King! Ho - ly, ho - ly, ho - ly.

Jesus, The Very Thought Of Thee 49

A-3-MI
Bernard of Clairvaux
Tr. Edward Caswall

In whom, though now ye see Him not, yet believing, ye rejoice . . .
I Pet. 1:8

J-1, P-2
John B. Dykes

1. Je - sus, the ver - y tho't of Thee With sweetness fills my breast;
2. Nor voice can sing, nor heart can frame, Nor can the mem - 'ry find
3. O Hope of ev - 'ry con - trite heart! O joy of all the meek!
4. Je - sus, our on - ly joy be Thou, As Thou our prize wilt be;

But sweet-er far Thy face to see, And in Thy pres - ence rest.
A sweet-er sound than Thy blest name, O Sav - ior of man-kind!
To those who fall, how kind Thou art! How good to those who seek!
Je - sus, be Thou our glo - ry now, And thro' e - ter - ni - ty.

50 Jesus Is Wonderful

And His name shall be called Wonderful, Counselor, the Mighty God . . . Isa. 9:6

F-4-DO
M. D.

P-2, T-1
Merrill Dunlop

1. Je - sus is won - der - ful! Sav - ior di - vine; Je - sus is
2. Je - sus is won - der - ful! He is my King; Je - sus is
3. Je - sus is won - der - ful! Bless - ings, I know, A - long my

CHORUS

won - der - ful—And He is mine! Yes, Je - sus is won - der - ful,
won - der - ful—Of Him I sing! Yes, He is my Lord and King,
dai - ly path He doth be - stow. Yes,

Je - sus is mine— He is the One that I love;
Sav - ior di - vine— He is the One that I love; I love.

Bless - ings, I know, He doth be - stow— Com - ing from

heav - en a - bove; (a - bove;) Je - sus is won - der - ful,

Je - sus is mine,— He is the One that I love.

Our Father And Our God

51

Grace be to you, and peace, from God our Father, and from the Lord Jesus Christ . . .
Eph. 1:2

F-4-SOL
Dee Bowman

P-2
R. J. Stevens

1. Our God and Fa - ther, Lord and King, The
2. Our Might - y Coun - s'ler, glo - r'ous Lord, The
3. Our Lord, Cre - a - tor, Sav - ior Friend, On
4. Our grace - ful Mas - ter, great art Thou, Be -

heav'ns and earth Thy glo - ry sing: With loud ho - sa - nas
Spir - it guides us thru Thy Word; We hum - bly serve in
Thee our strength and hope de - pend; We praise Thy Son whom
fore Thy throne in faith we bow; We wor - ship Thee with

praise they bring Our Fa - ther and our God.
one ac - cord Our Fa - ther and our God.
Thou didst send, Our Fa - ther and our God.
prais - es now, Our Fa - ther and our God. A - men.

52 # God Is Our Loving Father

L-5, P-2

Eb-4-SOL
E. W. S.

The earth is the Lord's, and the fulness thereof;
The world, and they that dwell therein. Ps. 24:1

Eugene W. Sikes
Arr. by R. J. Stevens

1. Our God, Cre-a-tor of the u-ni-verse, Our God, the Lord of all the earth, We praise and mag-ni-fy His glo-rious name; He is all the world to you and me.
2. Let ev-'ry knee be-fore Him hum-bly bow; He reigns su-preme-ly o-ver all. Through Him all things cre-a-ted now ex-ist; He holds the scep-ter in His hand.
3. For God so loved us, e-ven sin-ners; He gave His on-ly son to die, And on the cross our debt was glad-ly paid; Je-sus died that you and I might live.
4. And at the time of my de-par-ture, As it must come for ev-'ry man, Let not my loved ones weep in sor-row; My soul is in my Fa-ther's hands.

Fine CHORUS

But lis-ten
But lis-ten
But lis-ten
For lis-ten

D.S. lov-ing Fa-ther of us all.

to the won-drous sto-ry, the ver-y tho't will thrill

D.S.

your soul, That God, the Rul-er of the world is the

Christ, The Lord, Is Risen Today   53

Db-4-DO

Now is Christ risen from the dead, and become the first fruits of them that slept.
1 Cor. 15:20

C-8, P-2

Charles Wesley, 1739

Lyra Davidica, 1708

1. Christ, the Lord, is ris'n to-day, Hal — — le - lu - jah!
2. Vain the stone, the watch, the seal, Hal — — le - lu - jah!
3. Lives a - gain our glo-rious King, Hal — — le - lu - jah!

Sons of men and an-gels say, Hal — le - lu - jah!
Christ hath burst the gates of hell, Hal — le - lu - jah!
Where, O death, is now thy sting? Hal — le - lu - jah!

Raise your joys and tri-umphs high Hal — le - lu - jah!
Death in vain for - bids His rise, Hal — le - lu - jah!
Once He died our souls to save, Hal — le - lu - jah!

Sing, ye heav'ns; thou earth, re - ply, Hal — le - lu - jah!
Christ hath o - pened par - a - dise, Hal — le - lu - jah!
Where's thy vic - t'ry, boast-ing grave? Hal — le - lu - jah!

54

Praise Him! Praise Him!

I will sing praises unto my God . . . Psa. 146:2

A♭-2-MI   P-2

Fanny J. Crosby, 1869   Chester G. Allen, 1869

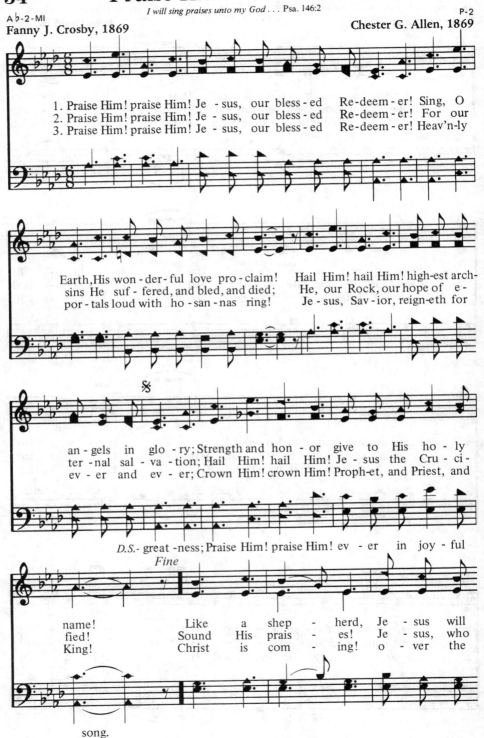

1. Praise Him! praise Him! Je - sus, our bless - ed Re-deem - er! Sing, O
2. Praise Him! praise Him! Je - sus, our bless - ed Re-deem - er! For our
3. Praise Him! praise Him! Je - sus, our bless - ed Re-deem - er! Heav'n-ly

Earth, His won - der - ful love pro - claim! Hail Him! hail Him! high-est arch-
sins He suf - fered, and bled, and died; He, our Rock, our hope of e -
por - tals loud with ho - san - nas ring! Je - sus, Sav - ior, reign-eth for

an - gels in glo - ry; Strength and hon - or give to His ho - ly
ter - nal sal - va - tion; Hail Him! hail Him! Je - sus the Cru - ci -
ev - er and ev - er; Crown Him! crown Him! Proph-et, and Priest, and

D.S.- great -ness; Praise Him! praise Him! ev - er in joy - ful

Fine

name! Like a shep - herd, Je - sus will
fied! Sound His prais - es! Je - sus, who
King! Christ is com - ing! o - ver the

song.

guard His chil - dren; In His arms He car - ries them all day
bore our sor - rows, Love un - bound - ed, won - der - ful, deep and
world vic - to - rious, Pow'r and glo - ry un - to the Lord be -

REFRAIN

D. S.

long:
strong: Praise Him! praise Him! tell   of   His   ex - cel - lent
long:

The Lord Is In His Holy Temple

55

D-3-DO

But the Lord is in His holy temple: let all the earth keep silence before Him. Hab. 2:20

W-5

Habakkuk 2:20

Wm. J. Kirkpatrick

The   Lord   is   in   His   ho - ly   tem - ple: Let

all   the   earth   keep   si - lence   be - fore   Him; Keep

p   *rall.*

si - lence,   keep   si - lence,   Keep   si - lence   be - fore   Him.

56 All Creatures Of Our God And King

Eb-3-DO

Francis of Assisi, 1225
Paraphrased by William H. Draper, 1926

All Thy works shall praise Thee, O Lord; and Thy saints shall bless Thee. Psa. 145:10

P-2

17th Century

1. All crea-tures of our God and King, Lift up your voice and
2. Thou rush-ing wind that art so strong, Ye clouds that sail in
3. Thou flow-ing wa-ter, pure and clear, Make mu-sic for thy
4. And all ye men of ten-der heart, For-giv-ing oth-ers
5. Let all things their Cre-a-tor bless, And wor-ship Him in

with us sing   Al-le-lu-ia! Al-le-lu-ia! Thou
heav'n a-long, O   praise Him! Al-le-lu-ia! Thou
Lord to hear. Al-le-lu-ia! Al-le-lu-ia! Thou
take your part. O   sing ye! Al-le-lu-ia! Ye
hum-ble-ness. O   praise Him! Al-le-lu-ia! Praise,

burn-ing sun with gold-en beam, Thou sil-ver moon with
ris-ing morn, in praise re-joice; Ye lights of eve-ning
fire so mas-ter-ful and bright, That giv-est man both
who long pain and sor-row bear, Praise God and on Him
praise the Fa-ther, Praise the Son, And praise the Spir-it,

soft-er gleam,
find a voice,
warmth and light, O praise Him, O praise Him! Al-le-
cast your care!
Three in One!

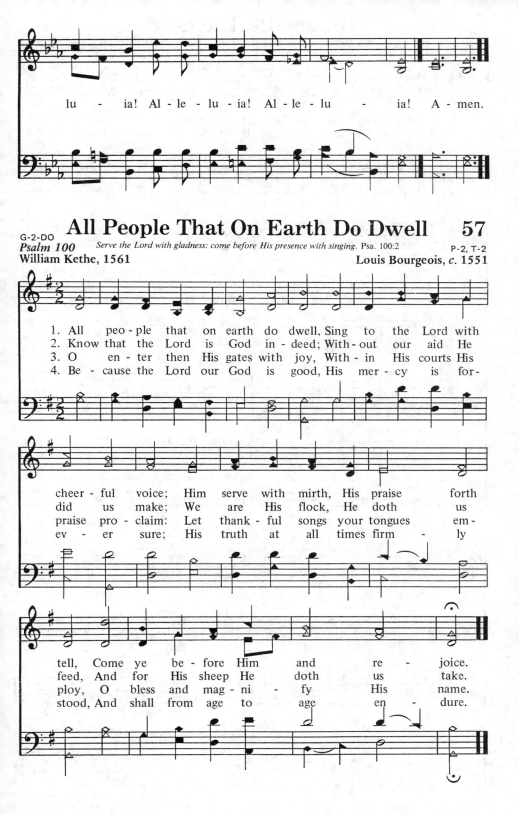

All People That On Earth Do Dwell   57

G-2-DO
Psalm 100
William Kethe, 1561

Serve the Lord with gladness: come before His presence with singing. Psa. 100:2

P-2, T-2
Louis Bourgeois, *c.* 1551

lu - ia! Al - le - lu - ia! Al - le - lu - ia! A - men.

1. All   peo - ple   that   on   earth   do   dwell, Sing   to   the   Lord   with
2. Know   that   the   Lord   is   God   in - deed; With - out   our   aid   He
3. O   en - ter   then   His   gates   with   joy,   With - in   His   courts   His
4. Be - cause   the   Lord   our   God   is   good, His   mer - cy   is   for -

cheer - ful   voice;   Him   serve   with   mirth,   His   praise   forth
did   us   make;   We   are   His   flock,   He   doth   us
praise   pro - claim: Let   thank - ful   songs   your   tongues   em -
ev - er   sure;   His   truth   at   all   times   firm - ly

tell,   Come   ye   be - fore   Him   and   re - joice.
feed,   And   for   His   sheep   He   doth   us   take.
ploy,   O   bless   and   mag - ni - fy   His   name.
stood,   And   shall   from   age   to   age   en - dure.

58
Blessed Be The Lord

E-2-DO

D. K. S.

Blessed be the Lord for evermore. Amen, and Amen. Psa. 89:52

P-2

Dane K. Shepard

1. Bless - ed be the Lord for - ev - er, Ex - alt - ed be His
2. Bless the Lord, for He is wor - thy - He reigns on heav - en's
3. Bless - ed be the Lord, our Sav - ior: The life, the truth, the

name; All the earth and high - est heav - ens His pow'r and
throne; Wor - ship now in truth and spir - it, and hon - or
way; He's the ris - en King of glo - ry, He'll come a -

CHORUS

love pro - claim. (pro - claim.)
Him a - lone. (a - lone.) Praise the Lord, our King a - bove,
gain one day. (one day.)

Bless His name, pro - claim His love; Bless - ed be the

Lord for - ev - er, and ev - er - more. A - men. (A - men.)

I Will Pray

59

Evening, and morning and at noon, will I pray . . . Psa. 55:17

Bb-3-MI

A. Cummings

P-3

J. H. Penney

1. Fa - ther, in the morn - ing Un - to Thee I pray;
2. At the bus - y noon - tide, Pressed with work and care,
3. When the eve - ning shad - ows Chase a - way the light,
4. Thus in life's glad morn - ing, In its bright noon - day,

1. Un - to Thee I pray;

Let Thy lov - ing kind - ness Keep me thru this day.
Then I'll wait with Je - sus, Till He hears my pray'r.
Fa - ther, then I'll pray Thee, Bless Thy child to - night.
In the shad - owy eve - ning, Ev - er will I pray.

Keep me thru this day.

CHORUS

I will pray, I will pray, Ev - er will I
I will pray, I will pray, Ev - er will I

pray; Morn - ing, noon and eve - ning Un - to Thee I'll pray.
pray; Un - to Thee I'll pray.

60 Lead Me Gently Home, Father

D-4-MI
W. L. T.

For Thou art my rock and my fortress; therefore . . . lead me, and guide me. Psa. 31:3

D-1

Will L. Thompson

Duet

1. Lead me gent - ly home, Fa - ther, Lead me gent - ly home,
2. Lead me gent - ly home, Fa - ther, Lead me gent - ly home,
3. Lead me gent - ly home, Fa - ther, Lead me gent - ly home,

When life's toils are end - ed, and part - ing days have come;
In life's dark - est hours, Fa - ther, when life's trou - bles come,
In temp - ta - tion's hour, Fa - ther, when sore tri - als come;

Sin no more shall tempt me, Ne'er from Thee I'll roam,
Keep my feet from wan - d'ring, Lest from Thee I roam,
Be Thou near to keep me, Take me as Thine own,

rit. *p*

If Thou'lt on - ly lead me, Fa - ther, Lead me gent - ly home.
Lest I fall up - on the way - side, Lead me gent - ly home.
For I can - not live with - out Thee, Lead me gent - ly home.

CHORUS

Lead me gent - ly home, Fa - ther, lead me gent - ly
Lead me gent - ly home, Fa - ther Lead me gent - ly home, Fa - ther,

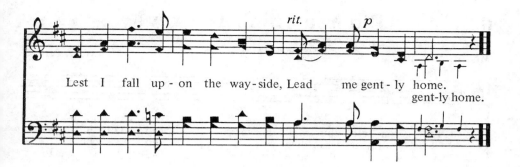

Lest I fall up - on the way-side, Lead me gent - ly home.
gent-ly home.

Dear Lord And Father Of Mankind 61

D-4-MI

John G. Whittier

*And the peace of God . . . shall keep your hearts
and minds through Christ Jesus.* Phil. 4:7

D-1, P-3

Frederick C. Maker

1. Dear Lord and Fa - ther of man - kind, For - give our
2. In sim - ple trust like theirs who heard, Be - side the
3. O Sab - bath rest by Gal - i - lee, O calm of
4. Drop Thy still dews of qui - et - ness, Till all our

fool - ish ways; Re - clothe us in our right - ful mind, In
Syr - ian sea, The gra - cious call - ing of the Lord, Let
hills a - bove, Where Je - sus knelt to share with Thee The
striv - ings cease; Take from our souls the strain and stress, And

pur - er lives Thy ser - vice find, In deep - er rev - 'rence, praise.
us, like them, with - out a word Rise up and fol - low Thee.
si - lence of e - ter - ni - ty, In - ter - pret - ed by love!
let our or - dered lives con - fess The beau - ty of Thy peace.

62 Did You Think To Pray?

*In everything by prayer and supplication with thanksgiving
let your requests be made known unto God.* Phil. 4:6

F-4-MI

E-1, P-3

Mrs. M. A. Kidder

W. O. Perkins

1. Ere you left your room this morn - ing, Did you think to
2. When your heart was filled with an - ger, Did you think to
3. When sore tri - als came up - on you, Did you think to

pray? In the name of Christ, our Sav - ior, Did you
pray? Did you plead for grace, my broth - er, That you
pray? When your soul was bowed in sor - row, Balm of

D. S. – So when

Fine CHORUS

sue for lov - ing fa - vor, As a shield to - day?
might for - give an - oth - er Who had crossed your way? O how
Gil - ead did you bor - row At the gates of day?

life seems dark and drear - y, Don't for - get to pray.

D. S.

pray - ing rests the wea - ry! Prayer will change the night to day;

I Need Thee Every Hour

63

Ab-3-DO

D-1

O Lord, hear me: for I am poor and needy. Psa. 86:1

Annie S. Hawks

Robert Lowry

1. I need Thee ev-'ry hour, Most gra - cious Lord;
2. I need Thee ev-'ry hour, Stay Thou near by;
3. I need Thee ev-'ry hour, In joy or pain;
4. I need Thee ev-'ry hour, Most Ho - ly One;

No ten - der voice like Thine Can peace af - ford.
Temp - ta - tions lose their pow'r When Thou art nigh.
Come quick - ly and a - bide, Or life is vain.
O make me Thine in - deed, Thou bless - ed Son!

CHORUS

I need Thee, O I need Thee; Ev - 'ry hour I need Thee!

O bless me now, my Sav - ior: I come to Thee! A - men.

64 Everlasting Love

F-4-DO
D. K. S.

I have loved thee with an everlasting love;
Therefore with loving-kindness have I drawn thee. Jer. 31:3

L-4
Dane K. Shepard

1. Je - sus waits pa-tient-ly for me; I'm not all that— I should—
2. O— Lord, I— hum - bly pray, Fill my heart with Your mer-cy each

be. He's with me each day, ans-wers when I pray, and be-
day; Then grace I will know and my life will show Your com-

stows ev - er - last - ing love. Now I praise Him for all that He's
plete, ev - er - last - ing love. Now I praise You for all that You've

done for me, His sav - ing grace sets me free; He suf-
done for me, Once I was blind – now I see; You emp-

fered and died, now He's glo - ri - fied, And pro - claims ev - er-
tied Your-self, left Your throne a - bove, And brought me ev - er-

last - ing love.   You are love, ev - er - last - ing love.

last - ing   love;

O Master, Let Me Walk With Thee   65

E-3-MI

He that loseth his life for My sake shall find it. Matt. 10:39

D-1, W-4

W. Gladden, 1879

H. P. Smith, 1874

1. O Mas-ter, let me walk with Thee In low-ly paths of ser - vice free; Tell me Thy se-cret; help me bear The strain of toil, the fret of care.

2. Help me the slow of heart to move By some clear, win-ning word of love; Teach me the way-ward feet to stay, And guide them in the home-ward way.

3. Teach me Thy pa-tience! still with Thee In clos-er, dear-er com - pa - ny, In work that keeps faith sweet and strong, In trust that tri-umphs o - ver wrong.

4. In hope that sends a shin-ing ray Far down the fu-ture's broad - 'ning way, In peace that on-ly Thou canst give, With Thee, O Mas-ter, let me live.

66 God Bless You, Go With God

The Lord bless thee, and keep thee ... and be gracious unto thee ...
and give thee peace. Num. 6:24-26

B♭-4-MI
W. R.

C-14, E-1
Warren Roberts

This is my dai - ly prayer, God bless you, go with
God, Hold fast His might - y hand, thru - out the
day; His grace your heart sus - tain, His pow'r re-
lieve your pain, Your prayer be not in vain,
as you trav - el His way. In spite of

all the lies, that some may hurl, Christ is the

on - ly hope of all the world; God bless you,

go with God, thru all e - ter - ni - ty,

1
My prayer will al - ways be, May you go with God.

2
May you go with God, May you go with God.

67 I Need Thee Ever Near Me

E♭-2-MI

Have mercy upon me, O Lord; for I am weak . . . Psa. 6:2

P-3

Harry Presley

R. J. Stevens

1. Lord, wilt Thou lift my fee - ble hand? Deep is the dark - ness
2. Wilt Thou Thy might - y hand ex - tend, Lift me from grief to
3. When all my earth - ly friends are gone, Lord wilt Thou walk be -
4. Do not for - sake me Lord, I pray; Dark is the way and

o'er me. Give me the strength to firm - ly stand Thru all that
glad - ness? Wilt Thou my faint - ing soul at - tend, Lord, wilt Thou
side me? I can - not find my way a - lone, O Sav - ior
lone - ly. Keep Thou my feet lest I should stray, Shed forth Thy

CHORUS

lies be - fore me.
share my sad - ness?
wilt Thou guide me?   O Lord hide not Thy bless - ed face,
love up - on me.

I need Thee ev - er near me! As I ap - proach Thy

throne of grace, Wilt Thou in mer - cy hear me?

Lord, We Come Before Thee Now   68

G-2-DO   *O come, let us worship and bow down: let us kneel before the Lord our maker.*   W-5

W. Hammond   Psa. 95:6   **C. H. A. Malan**

Slowly

1. Lord, we come be - fore Thee now; At Thy feet we
2. Lord, on Thee our souls de - pend: In com - pas - sion
3. Grant that all may seek and find Thee a God su -

hum - bly bow: O do not our suit dis - dain; Shall we
now de - scend; Fill our hearts with Thy rich grace, Tune our
preme - ly kind; Heal the sick, the cap - tive free; Let us

seek Thee, Lord in vain? Shall we seek Thee, Lord in vain?
lips to sing Thy praise, Tune our lips to sing Thy praise.
all re - joice in Thee, Let us all re - joice in Thee.

69 What A Friend We Have In Jesus

In whom we have boldness and access with confidence by faith in Him. Eph. 3:12

F-4-SOL
C-5

Geo. Scriven

C. C. Converse

1. What a Friend we have in Je-sus, All our sins and griefs to bear;
2. Have we tri-als and temp-ta-tions? Is there trou-ble an-y-where?
3. Are we weak and heav-y la-den, Cumbered with a load of care?

What a priv-i-lege to car-ry Ev-'ry-thing to God in prayer.
We should nev-er be dis-cour-aged, Take it to the Lord in prayer.
Pre-cious Sav-ior, still our ref-uge —Take it to the Lord in prayer.

O what peace we of-ten for-feit, O what need-less pain we bear,
Can we find a friend so faith-ful, Who will all our sor-rows share?
Do thy friends de-spise, for-sake thee? Take it to the Lord in prayer;

All be-cause we do not car-ry Ev-'ry-thing to God in prayer.
Je-sus knows our ev-'ry weak-ness: Take it to the Lord in prayer.
In His arms He'll take and shield thee, Thou wilt find a sol-ace there.

One Step At A Time

For we walk by faith, not by sight. II Cor. 5:7

70

Ab-4-SOL
T. J. Shelton

C-12, F-3
J. H. Rosecrans

1. One step at a time, dear Savior, I cannot take
2. One step at a time, dear Savior, I am not walk-
3. One step at a time, dear Savior, Oh, guard my fal-

an-y-more; The flesh is so weak and hope-less, I
ing by sight; Keep step with my soul, dear Sav-ior, I
ter-ing feet! Keep hold of my hand, dear Sav-ior, Till

D.S.-step at a time, dear Sav-ior, Till

Fine CHORUS

know not what is be-fore.
walk by faith in Thy might. One step at a time, dear
I my jour-ney com-plete.

hope grows strong-er in me.

D. S.

Sav-ior, Till faith grows strong-er in Thee; One
in Thee;

71 God Answers Prayer Today

If we ask anything according to His will, He heareth us . . . I John 5:14

A-4-MI

J. B. L. & R. J. S.

J. Brent Lewis
Arr. by R. J. Stevens

P-3

1. We pray for strength that our de-sires may be ful-filled, But weak-ness
2. We thank our Fa-ther for the bless-ings we've re-ceived, O what a
3. As days grow short and life be-gins to fade a-way, We see God's

comes and hum-bles us to do God's will. We pray for health that
joy to know He hears when we be-lieve. We do not seek from
wis-dom as He an-swers when we pray. Our heav'n-ly Fa-ther

we can do some great-er thing, Yet bur-dens come; To Him we
Him earth's wealth or world-ly fame, We seek Him first; In Je-sus
knows our ev'-ry care and need, He knows what's best; His will we

CHORUS

al-ways cling.
bless-ed name. God an-swers prayer to-day, But in the
must give heed.

wis - est way, He knows what's best for us, from day to day.

Be With Me, Lord

72

For He hath said, I will never leave thee, nor forsake thee. Heb. 13:5

E♭-4-MI

T. O. Chisholm

C-14, D-1

L. O. Sanderson

1. Be with me, Lord, I can - not live with-out Thee, I dare not
2. Be with me, Lord, and then if dan - gers threat-en, If storms of
3. Be with me, Lord, no oth - er gift or bless-ing, Thou couldst be-
4. Be with me, Lord, when lone - li - ness o'er-takes me, When I must

try to take one step a - lone; I can - not bear the loads of
-tri - al burst a - bove my head; If lash - ing seas leap ev - 'ry
stow could with this one com-pare; A con-stant sense of Thy a-
weep a - mid the fires of pain, And when shall come the hour of

life, un - aid - ed, I need Thy strength to lean my - self up - on.
where a - bout me, They can - not harm or make my heart a - fraid.
bid - ing pres-ence, Wher-e'er I am to feel that Thou art near.
"my de - part - ure" For "worlds un-known," O Lord, be with me there.

73 Sweet Hour Of Prayer

D-2-DO
Wm. W. Walford, 1845

And this is the confidence that we have in Him, that, if we ask anything
according to His will, He heareth us. 1 John 5:4

P-3
Wm. B. Bradbury, 1861

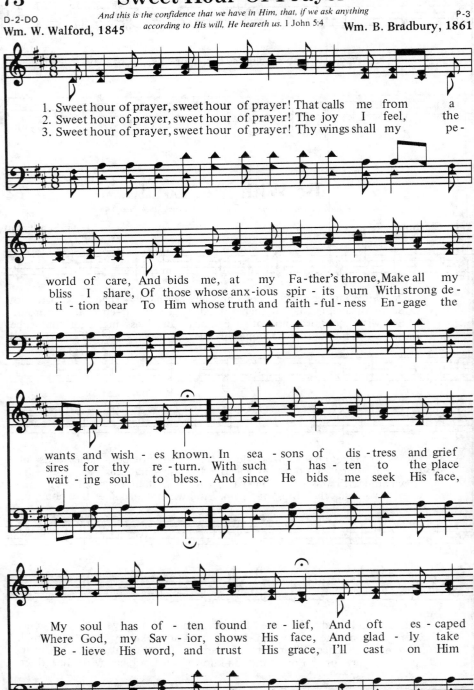

1. Sweet hour of prayer, sweet hour of prayer! That calls me from a world of care, And bids me, at my Father's throne, Make all my wants and wishes known. In seasons of distress and grief My soul has often found relief, And oft escaped

2. Sweet hour of prayer, sweet hour of prayer! The joy I feel, the bliss I share, Of those whose anxious spirits burn With strong desires for thy return. With such I hasten to the place Where God, my Savior, shows His face, And gladly take

3. Sweet hour of prayer, sweet hour of prayer! Thy wings shall my petition bear To Him whose truth and faithfulness Engage the waiting soul to bless. And since He bids me seek His face, Believe His word, and trust His grace, I'll cast on Him

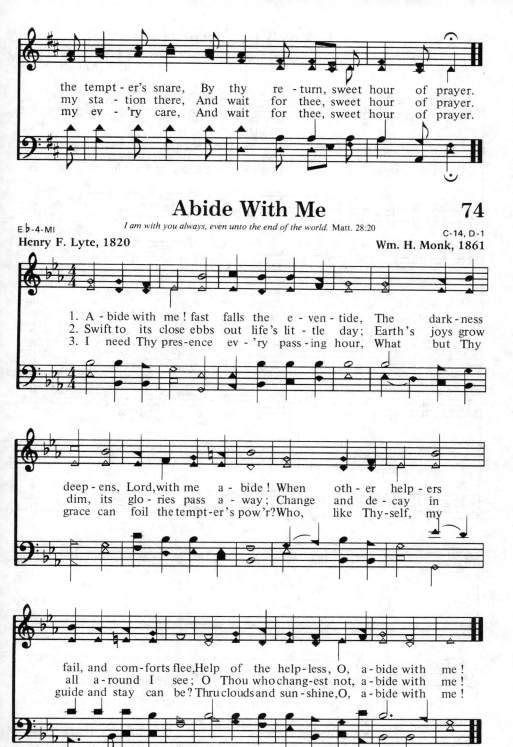

the tempt - er's snare, By thy re - turn, sweet hour of prayer.
my sta - tion there, And wait for thee, sweet hour of prayer.
my ev - 'ry care, And wait for thee, sweet hour of prayer.

Abide With Me

74

I am with you always, even unto the end of the world. Matt. 28:20

E♭-4-MI

Henry F. Lyte, 1820

C-14, D-1

Wm. H. Monk, 1861

1. A - bide with me! fast falls the e - ven - tide, The dark - ness
2. Swift to its close ebbs out life's lit - tle day; Earth's joys grow
3. I need Thy pres - ence ev - 'ry pass - ing hour, What but Thy

deep - ens, Lord, with me a - bide! When oth - er help - ers
dim, its glo - ries pass a - way; Change and de - cay in
grace can foil the tempt - er's pow'r? Who, like Thy - self, my

fail, and com - forts flee, Help of the help - less, O, a - bide with me!
all a - round I see; O Thou who chang - est not, a - bide with me!
guide and stay can be? Thru clouds and sun - shine, O, a - bide with me!

75 I Am The Vine

D-3-DO
K. S.

I am the vine and ye are the branches . . . without Me ye can do nothing. John 15:5

E-1, S-5

Arr. by Knowles Shaw

1. "I am the vine and ye are the branch-es," Bear pre-cious fruit for
2. "Now ye are clean thru words I have spo-ken, Liv-ing in Me, much
3. Yes, by your fruits the world is to know you, Walk-ing in love as

Je-sus to-day; Branch-es in Him no fruit ev-er
fruit ye shall bear; Dwell-ing in you, My prom-ise un-
chil-dren of day; Fol-low your Guide, He pass-eth be-

CHORUS

bear-ing, Je-sus hath said, "He tak-eth a-way."
bro-ken, Glo-ry in heav'n with Me ye shall share." "I am the
fore you, Lead-ing to realms of glo-ri-ous day.

vine and ye are the branch-es; I am the vine, be

faith-ful and true; Ask what ye will, your pray'r shall be

grant - ed, The Fa - ther loved Me, so I have loved you."

Closer To Thee 76

Bb-2-SOL
A. T.

Thou art my refuge and my portion in the land of the living. Psa. 142:5

D-1, F-2
Austin Taylor

1. Clos - er to Thee, near to Thy side, Clos - er dear Lord,
2. Clos - er to Thee, near to Thy breast, Clos - er to Thee;
3. Clos - er to Thee, hap - py and free, Grant me, O Lord,

I would a - bide; Hold me in Thy em - brace,'Neath ev - 'ry
Lord, let me rest; Guide me when I would stray, Keep me from
ev - er to be; Hear me in ev - 'ry cry, Stand near when

smile of grace, Grant me, Thy child, a place Clos - er to Thee.
sin each day, Draw me, dear Lord, I pray, Clos - er to Thee.
I must die, Then take me home on high, Clos - er to Thee.

77   I Must Tell Jesus

Eb-3-DO
E. A. H.

C-5, C-15
E. A. Hoffman

Casting all your care upon Him; for He careth for you. 1 Pet. 5:7

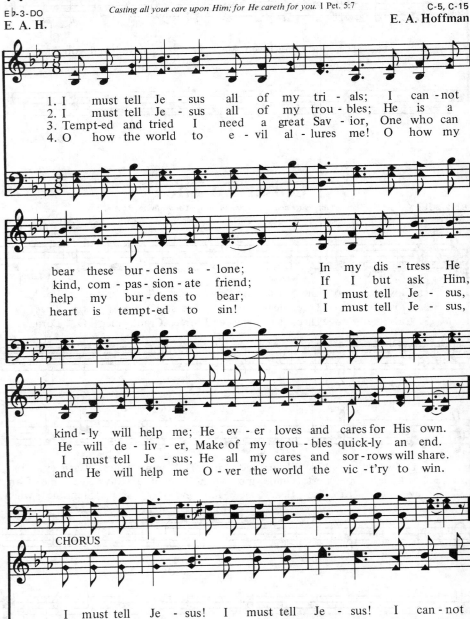

1. I must tell Jesus all of my tri - als; I can - not
2. I must tell Jesus all of my trou - bles; He is a
3. Tempt-ed and tried I need a great Sav - ior, One who can
4. O how the world to e - vil al - lures me! O how my

bear these bur - dens a - lone;   In my dis - tress He
kind, com - pas - sion - ate friend;   If I but ask Him,
help my bur - dens to bear;   I must tell Je - sus,
heart is tempt-ed to sin!   I must tell Je - sus,

kind - ly will help me; He ev - er loves and cares for His own.
He will de - liv - er, Make of my trou - bles quick-ly an end.
I must tell Je - sus; He all my cares and sor - rows will share.
and He will help me O - ver the world the vic -t'ry to win.

CHORUS

I must tell Je - sus! I must tell Je - sus! I can - not

bear my bur-dens a - lone; I must tell Je - sus!

I must tell Je - sus! Je - sus can help me, Je - sus a - lone.

My God, My Father, Though I Stray 78

D-4-SOL

Thy will be done in earth as it is in heaven. Matt. 6:10

D-1

Charlotte Elliott, 1834

Arthur S. Sullivan

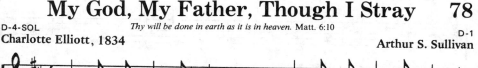

1. My God, my Fa - ther, tho' I stray Far from my home, on life's rough
2. Tho' dark my path, and sad my lot, Let me be still and mur-mur
3. Re - new my will from day to day; Blend it with Thine, and take a-
4. Then, when on earth I breathe no more The prayer oft mixed with tears be -

way, O teach me from my heart to say, "Thy will be done!"
not, Or breathe the prayer di - vine - ly taught, "Thy will be done!"
way, All that now makes it hard to say, "Thy will be done!"
fore, I'll sing up - on a hap-pier shore, "Thy will be done!" A - men.

79 The Garden Of Prayer

The Lord hath heard my supplication: the Lord will receive my prayer. Psa. 6:9

D-2-MI

Eleanor Allen Schroll

J. H. Fillmore

1. There's a gar-den where Je-sus is wait-ing, There's a
2. There's a gar-den where Je-sus is wait-ing, And I
3. There's a gar-den where Je-sus is wait-ing, And He

place that is won-drous-ly fair; For it glows with the
go with my bur-den and care, Just to learn from His
bids you come meet with Him there, Just to bow and re-

light of His pres-ence: 'Tis the
lips words of com-fort, In the beau-ti-ful gar-den of prayer.
ceive a new bless-ing, In the

CHORUS

O the beau-ti-ful gar-den, the gar-den of prayer, O the

beau-ti-ful gar-den of prayer; There my Sav-ior a-waits, and He

81 Jesus, Lover Of My Soul

For Thou hast been . . . a strength to the needy in his distress,
a refuge from the storm . . . Isa. 25:4

F-2-MI

Charles Wesley, 1740

L-4

S. B. Marsh

1. Je - sus, Lov - er of my soul, Let me to Thy bos - om fly,
2. Oth - er ref - uge have I none, Hangs my help-less soul on Thee;
3. Plen-teous grace with Thee is found, Grace to cov - er all my sin;

While the near - er wa - ters roll, While the tem - pest still is high;
Leave, O leave me not a - lone, Still sup - port and com-fort me;
Let the heal - ing streams a - bound, Make and keep me pure with - in;

Hide me, O my Sav - ior, hide, Till the storm of life is past;
All my trust on Thee is stayed; All my help from Thee I bring;
Thou of life the foun - tain art; Free - ly let me take of Thee;

Safe in - to the ha - ven guide, O re - ceive my soul at last.
Cov - er my de - fense-less head With the shad - ow of Thy wing.
Spring Thou up with - in my heart, Rise to all e - ter - ni - ty.

Our Fellowship

82

E-4-DO
Craig A. Roberts

*That ye also may have fellowship with us: and truly our fellowship
is with the Father, and with His Son Jesus Christ. 1 John 1:3*

F -2, U -1
Kelly R. Hersey
R. J. Stevens

1. O Fa-ther, watch-ing o-ver me, And lead-ing me thru life,
2. O Fa-ther, Thou spared not Thy Son, But bought us with His blood;
3. Past chil-dren of Thy cov-e-nant, From ev'-ry age and land,

So ma-ny times I call to Thee In sor-row, guilt and strife. And
From ma-ny na-tions, made Thou one U-nit-ed bro-ther-hood. Wher-
As-cend-ed up-ward, tri-um-phant, And joined a might-y band. One

faith-ful, Lord, art Thou near-by To an-swer ev'-ry prayer. Pro-
e'er we ga-ther in His name, A com-mon love we share, At
day, we hope to sing with them The hymn com-posed be-yond, And

tect me Lord, lest I de-ny Our fel-low-ship, Thy care.
home, in dis-tant land, the same Com-mun-ion ev'-ry-where!
with Thy con-gre-ga-tion, form An e-ver-last-ing bond.

83 In The Hour Of Trial

Db-4-MI

James Montgomery, 1834

Let us therefore come boldly unto the throne of grace, that we may obtain mercy, and find help in time of need. Heb. 4:16

D-1

Spencer Lane, 1875

1. In the hour of tri - al, Je - sus, plead for me.
2. With for - bid - den pleas - ures Would this vain world charm;
3. Should Thy mer - cy send me Sor - row toil and woe;

Lest by base de - ni - al, I de - part from Thee.
Or its sor - did treas - ures Spread to work me harm;
Or should pain at - tend me On my path be - low;

When Thou see'st me wa - ver, With a look re - call,
Bring to my re - mem - brance Sad Geth-sem - a - ne,
Grant that I may nev - er Fail Thy hand to see,

rall.

Nor for fear or fa - vor Suf - fer me to fall.
Or, in dark - er sem - blance, Cross-crown'd Cal - va - ry.
Grant that I may ev - er Cast my care on Thee.

Tarry With Me

Eb-3-DO

Mrs. C. S. Smith

Yea, though I walk through the valley of the shadow of death,
I will fear no evil: for Thou art with me. Psa. 23:4

D-1

Knowles Shaw

1. Tar - ry with me, O my Sav - ior, For the day is
2. Deep - er, deep - er grow the shad - ows, Pal - er now the
3. Tar - ry with me, O my Sav - ior; Lay my head up -

pass - ing by; See, the shades of eve - ning gath - er,
glow - ing west; Swift the night of death ad - vanc - es:
on Thy breast Till the morn - ing; then a - wake me,

And the night is draw - ing nigh.
Shall it be the night of rest?
Morn-ing of e - ter - nal rest.

CHORUS

Tar - ry with me, bless - ed Sav - ior; Leave me not till morn - ing light; For I'm lone - ly here with - out Thee: Tar - ry with me thru the night.

85 Sowing The Seed Of The Kingdom

The seed is the word of God. Luke 8:11

D-4-DO
F. A. F.

S-5
Fred A. Fillmore

1. Are you sow-ing the seed of the king-dom, broth-er, In the
2. Are you sow-ing the seed of the king-dom, broth-er, In the
3. Are you sow-ing the seed of the king-dom, broth-er, All a -

morn-ing bright and fair? Are you sow-ing the seed of the king-dom,
still and sol-emn night? Are you sow-ing the seed of the king-dom,
long the fer-tile way? Are you sow-ing the seed of the king-dom,

CHORUS

broth-er, In the heat of the noon-day's glare? For the
broth-er, For a har - vest pure and white? For the
broth-er? You must reap at the last great day!

har - vest time is com-ing on, (com-ing on,) And the reap-ers'

work will soon be done; (soon be done;) Will your sheaves be man-y?

will you gar - ner an - y, For the gath - 'ring at the har - vest home?

Hear Now Our Prayers

86

P-3

Give ear to my prayer, O God . . . Psa. 55:1

Db-4-SOL
Claude E. Worley

**R. J. Stevens and
Tim Stevens**

1. O Lord, Di - vine and Ho - ly, We praise Thy glo - rious name,
2. For - give our fool - ish fol - lies And flesh - ly lures to sin,
3. Let not our ser - vice fal - ter Or fail Thy coun - sel keep,

And wor - ship thru the a - ges, Thy mer - cy to pro - claim.
For we re - pent in sor - row And strive Thy praise to win.
As we be - hold the fu - ture and pray Thy will to meet.

CHORUS

Hear now our prayers and plead - ings, O Lord in heav'n a - bove,

For we are weak and lone - ly With - out Thy help and love.

87

F-2-MI

Katharina von Schlegel
Tr. by **Jane L. Borthwick**

Be Still My Soul

Be still, and know that I am God. Psa. 46:10

C-15

Jean Sibelius

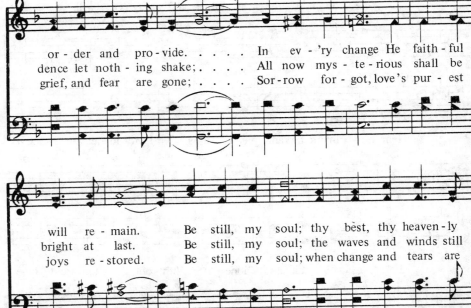

1. Be still, my soul; the Lord is on thy side.... Bear pa-tient-
2. Be still, my soul; thy God doth un-der-take... To guide the
3. Be still, my soul. The hour is has-tening on ... When we shall

ly the cross of grief or pain; Leave to thy God to
fu-ture as He has the past. Thy hope, thy con-fi-
be for-ev-er with the Lord; When dis-ap-point-ment,

or-der and pro-vide. .... In ev-'ry change He faith-ful
dence let noth-ing shake;.... All now mys-te-rious shall be
grief, and fear are gone; .... Sor-row for-got, love's pur-est

will re-main. Be still, my soul; thy best, thy heaven-ly
bright at last. Be still, my soul; the waves and winds still
joys re-stored. Be still, my soul; when change and tears are

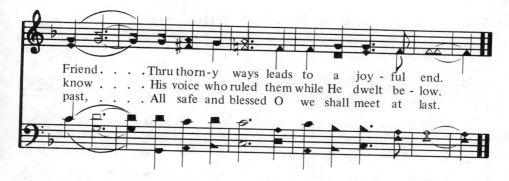

Friend. . . . Thru thorn-y ways leads to a joy - ful end.
know . . . . His voice who ruled them while He dwelt be - low.
past, ... All safe and blessed O we shall meet at last.

O Savior, Let Me Walk With Thee   88

Cause me to know the way wherein I should walk . . . Psa. 143:8

Db-4-DO
T. P. S.

P-3

Timothy Paul Stevens

1. O Sav - ior, let me walk with Thee a - long life's
2. O Sav - ior, let me talk with Thee and thank Thee
3. O Sav - ior, let me be with Thee in that sweet

rug - ged way; Please hold my hand that I may
for Thy love; O help me Lord, for - give Thou
home on high; I'm long - ing for Thy face to

see Thy guid - ing light each day.
me from Thy throne in heav'n a - bove. A - men.
see in the sweet land by and by.

89 Jesus, Savior, Pilot Me

Bb-3-MI

He commandeth even the winds and water, and they obey Him. Luke 8:25

G-3

Edward Hopper

John E. Gould

1. Je - sus, Sav - ior, pi - lot me O - ver life's tem -
2. As a moth - er stills her child, Thou canst hush the
3. When at last I near the shore, And the fear - ful

pes - tuous sea; Un - known waves be - fore me roll,
o - cean wild; Bois-t'rous waves o - bey Thy will
break-ers roar 'Twixt me and the peace - ful rest,

Hid - ing rock and treach -'rous shoal; Chart and
When Thou say'st to them, "Be still!" Won - drous
Then, while lean - ing on Thy breast, May I

com - pass came from Thee: Je - sus, Sav - ior, pi - lot me.
Sov -'reign of the sea, Je - sus, Sav - ior, pi - lot me.
hear Thee say to me, "Fear not, I will pi - lot thee."

O Lord, Our Lord

90

F-4-DO

M. Lynwood Smith

O Lord our Lord, how excellent is Thy name in all the earth!
Who hast set Thy glory above the heavens. Psa. 8:1

C-6, D-1

C. C. Stafford

1. O Lord, Our Lord, How ex-cel-lent and might-y;
2. O Lord, Our Lord, Who dwell-eth in the heav-en;
3. O Lord, Our Lord, In mer-cy look up-on me;

How high and ho-ly is Thy won-drous Name.
In-cline Thine ear and hear my fee-ble plea.
I am un-wor-thy of Thy ten-der love.

O how ex-alt-ed is Thy might-y glo-ry,
Help me to serve Thee till my work is fin-ished,
O Ho-ly One, for-give me of my sin-ning,

Far up a-bove and o'er the earth's do-main.
Then take me home, O Lord, to live with Thee.
And help me dai-ly look to Thee a-bove. A-men.

91
Lord, Help Me

Help me, O Lord my God: O save me according to Thy mercy. Psa. 109:26

D-4-MI
Melvin Stanton

D-1
Tillit S. Teddlie

1. Lord, help me lift my heart to Thee; Lord, raise my eyes that I may
2. Lord, help me yield my life to Thee; Lord, break my will that I may
3. Lord, help me have a pa-tient heart; Lord, grant me peace when far a-

see Be - yond this mount and vale of tears, Far a - bove all these
be Ful - ly com-mit - ted to Thy ways, Serv-ing glad - ly thru
part From friends I love, with foes I stand; Help me wait, and to

D. S.-In that sweet par - a -

Fine CHORUS

clouds of fears.
out my days. Lord, I sur-ren-der all to Thee! Glad-ly Thy
un - der-stand.

dise of love.

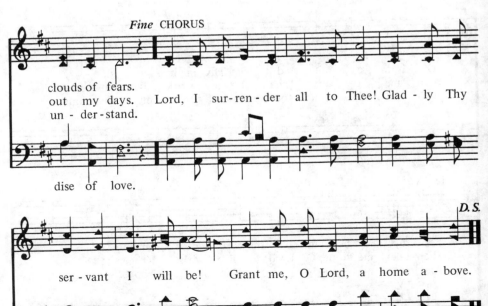

D. S.

ser - vant I will be! Grant me, O Lord, a home a - bove.

Others

92

Eb-3-SOL

C. D. Meigs

Look not every man on his own things, but every man also on the things of others.
Phil. 2:4

W-4

Elizabeth McE. Shields

1. Lord, help me live from day to day In such a self-for-
2. Help me in all the work I do To ev-er be sin-
3. Let "Self" be cru-ci-fied and slain And bur-ied deep: and

get-ful way That e-ven when I kneel to pray My prayer shall
cere and true, And know that all I'd do for you Must needs be
all in vain May ef-forts be to rise a-gain, Un-less to

CHORUS *ad lib.*

be for Oth-ers.
done for Oth-ers. Oth-ers, Lord, yes, oth-ers, Let this my mot-
live for Oth-ers.

rit.

to be, Help me to live for oth-ers, That I may live like Thee.

93

C-4-MI
I. B. S.
(A. A. W.)

My God And I

If a man love Me . . . My Father will love him, and We will come unto him,
and make Our abode with him. John 14:23

F-2
I. B. Sergei
(Austris A. Wihtol)

1. My God and I go in the field to-geth-er, We
2. He tells me of the years that went be-fore me, When
3. My God and I will go for aye to-geth-er, We'll

walk and talk as good friends should and do; We clasp our hands, our
heav'n-ly plans were made for me to be, When all was but a
walk and talk as good friends should and do; This earth will pass, and

voic-es ring with laugh-ter, My God and I walk
dream of dim con-cep-tion, To come to life, earth's
with it com-mon tri-fles, But God and I will

thru the mead-ow's hue; We clasp our hands, our voic-es ring with
ver-dant glo-ry see; When all was but a dream of dim con-
go un-end-ing-ly; This earth will pass, and with it com-mon

laugh-ter, My God and I walk thru the mead-ow's hue.
cep - tion, To come to life, earth's ver-dant glo-ry see.
tri - fles, But God and I will go un - end - ing - ly.

Savior, Breathe An Evening Blessing 94

Bb-2-SOL
James Edmeston, 1820

Thou shalt not be afraid for the terror by night;
nor for the arrow that flieth by day. Psa. 91:5

C-14, D-1
Geo. C. Stebbins, 1878

Slowly

1. Sav - ior, breathe an eve - ning bless - ing Ere re - pose our
2. Tho' de - struc - tion walk a - round us, Tho' the ar - rows
3. Tho' the night be dark and drear - y, Dark - ness can - not
4. Should swift death this night o'er - take us, And our couch be -

spir - its seal; Sin and want we come con - fess - ing:
past us fly, An - gel guards from Thee sur - round us:
hide from Thee; Thou art He who, nev - er wea - ry,
come our tomb, May the morn in heav'n a - wake us,

Thou canst save and Thou canst heal.
We are safe if Thou art nigh.
Watch - est where Thy peo - ple be.
Clad in bright and death - less bloom. A - men.

95   'Tis The Blessed Hour Of Prayer

Eb-3-DO   P-3

Peter and John went up together . . . at the hour of prayer . . . Acts 3:1

Fanny J. Crosby, 1880   Wm. H. Doane, 1880

1. 'Tis the bless-ed hour of prayer, when our hearts low-ly bend,
2. 'Tis the bless-ed hour of prayer, when the Sav-ior draws near,
3. At the bless-ed hour of prayer, trust-ing Him, we be-lieve

And we gath-er to Je-sus, our Sav-ior and Friend; If we
With a ten-der com-pas-sion His chil-dren to hear; When He
That the bless-ing we're need-ing we'll sure-ly re-ceive; In the

come to Him in faith, His pro-tec-tion to share,
tells us we may cast at His feet ev-'ry care, What a
full-ness of this trust we shall lose ev-'ry care,

balm for the wea-ry! O how sweet to be there!

CHORUS

Bless-ed hour of prayer, bless-ed hour of prayer,

Our Heavenly Father Understands   96

A♭-4-SOL
B. E. S.

If we ask anything according to His will, He heareth us . . . we know that we have the petitions that we desired . . . I John 5:15

C-15
Broadus E. Smith

1. I need the prayers of those who love me, I need the prayers of
2. I can-not walk the straight and nar-row, With-out my Sav-ior's
3. He'll hold your hand when you are dy-ing, Give strength to cross the

those who care; I need the help of ev-'ry Chris-tian, To take God's
guid-ing hand; He'll light the way and make it fair-er, For all the
Jor-dan wide; He'll help you an-swer at the judg-ment, If in His

CHORUS

mes-sage ev-'ry-where.
faith-ful in this land. He an-swers prayer for all the faith-ful, He
love you will a-bide.

holds the fu-ture in His hand; He'll guide us safe-ly o-ver

Jor - dan, Our heav-'nly Fa-ther un-der-stands, un-der-stands.

97 O To Be Like Thee

D-3-DO

But we all . . . beholding as in a glass the glory of the Lord, are changed into the same
image from glory to glory . . . II Cor. 3:18

C-13, L-2

Thomas O. Chisholm, 1897

Wm. J. Kirkpatrick, 1897

1. O to be like Thee! bless-ed Re-deem-er: This is my
con-stant long-ing and pray'r; Glad-ly I'll for-feit all of earth's
treas-ures, Je-sus, Thy per-fect like-ness to wear.

2. O to be like Thee! full of com-pas-sion, Lov-ing, for-
giv-ing, ten-der and kind, Help-ing the help-less, cheer-ing the
faint-ing, Seek-ing the wan-d'ring sin-ner to find.

3. O to be like Thee! low-ly in spir-it, Ho-ly and
harm-less, pa-tient and brave; Meek-ly en-dur-ing cru-el re-
proach-es, Will-ing to suf-fer, oth-ers to save.

4. O to be like Thee! Lord, I am com-ing, Now to re-
ceive th'a-noint-ing di-vine; All that I am and have I am
bring-ing; Lord, from this mo-ment all shall be Thine.

CHORUS

O to be like Thee! O to be like Thee! bless-ed Re-
deem-er, pure as Thou art; Come in Thy sweet-ness,

come in Thy full-ness; Stamp Thine own im - age deep on my heart.

Take My Life, And Let It Be 98

G-3-DO

For ye are bought with a price: therefore glorify God in your body . . . I Cor. 6:20

C-16

Frances R. Havergal, 1874

Mozart

1. Take my life, and let it be Con - se-
2. Take my hands, and let them move At the
3. Take my voice, and let me sing Al - ways,
4. Take my will, and make it Thine: It shall
5. Take my love, my Lord, I pour At Thy

crat - ed, Lord, to Thee; Take my mo - ments
im - pulse of Thy love; Take my feet and
on - ly, for my King; Take my lips, and
be no long - er mine; Take my heart — it
feet its treas - ure store; Take my self and

and my days, Let them flow in cease - less praise.
let them be Swift and beau - ti - ful for Thee.
let them be Filled with mes - sag - es from Thee.
is Thine own: It shall be Thy roy - al throne.
I will be Ev - er, on - ly, all for Thee!

99 Savior, Lead Me Lest I Stray

Lead me, O Lord, in Thy righteousness . . . Psa. 5:8

Db-4-SOL
F. M. D.

G-3
Frank M. Davis

1. Sav - ior, lead me, lest I stray, Gen - tly
2. Thou the ref - uge of my soul, When life's
3. Sav - ior, lead me, then at last, When the
1. Sav - ior, lead me, lest I stray, Gen -

lead me all the way; I am safe when
storm - y bil - lows roll; I am safe when
storm of life is past; To the land of
tly lead me all the way; I am

by Thy side, I would in Thy love a -
Thou art nigh, All my hopes on Thee re -
end - less day, Where all tears are wiped a -
safe when by Thy side, I would

CHORUS

bide.
ly. Lead me, lead me, Sav - ior,
way. Sav - ior,
in Thy love a - bide.

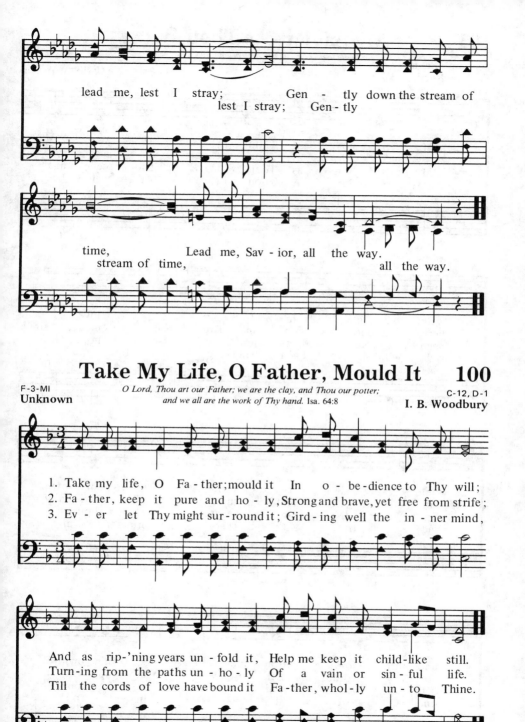

lead me, lest I stray; Gen - tly down the stream of
lest I stray; Gen - tly

time, Lead me, Sav - ior, all the way.
stream of time, all the way.

Take My Life, O Father, Mould It   100

F-3-MI
Unknown

*O Lord, Thou art our Father; we are the clay, and Thou our potter;
and we all are the work of Thy hand. Isa. 64:8*

C-12, D-1
I. B. Woodbury

1. Take my life, O Fa - ther; mould it In o - be - dience to Thy will;
2. Fa - ther, keep it pure and ho - ly, Strong and brave, yet free from strife;
3. Ev - er let Thy might sur - round it; Gird - ing well the in - ner mind,

And as rip - 'ning years un - fold it, Help me keep it child-like still.
Turn - ing from the paths un - ho - ly Of a vain or sin - ful life.
Till the cords of love have bound it Fa - ther, whol - ly un - to Thine.

101

My Savior, As Thou Wilt

Teach me to do Thy will; for Thou art my God. Psa. 143:10

D-4-SOL

Benjamin Schmolke
Tr. Jane Borthwick

C-16

Carl von Weber

1. My Sav - ior, as Thou wilt! O may Thy
2. My Sav - ior, as Thou wilt! If need - y
3. My Sav - ior, as Thou wilt! Tho' seen thro'
4. My Sav - ior, as Thou wilt! All shall be

will be mine; In - to Thy hand of love I
here and poor, Give me Thy peo - ple's bread, Their
man - y a tear, Let not my star of hope Grow
well with me; Each chang - ing fu - ture scene I

would my all re - sign; Thro' sor - row
por - tion rich and sure; The man - na
dim or dis - ap - pear; Since Thou on
glad - ly trust with Thee; Straight to my

and thro' joy, Con - duct me as Thine own,
of Thy word, Let my soul feed up - on,
earth hast wept And sor - rowed oft a - lone,
home a - bove I trav - el calm - ly on,

And help me still to say, "My Lord, Thy will be done."
And, if all else should fail, "My Lord, Thy will be done."
If I must weep with Thee, "My Lord, Thy will be done."
And sing, in life or death, "My Lord, Thy will be done."

Dear Lord, Hear My Prayer 102

Thou hast heard my voice: hide not Thine ear at my cry . . . Lam. 3:56

Db-2-DO

P-3

Carri Mullins Hawkins

Tim Stevens

1. Dear Lord, grant me Thy lov-ing care, And lis-ten to
2. Dear Lord, I pray on bend-ed knee, In mer-cy hear
3. Dear Lord, when my short life is o'er, O take me home

my earn-est prayer. O keep me in Thy per-fect way,
my hum-ble plea. My soul lift up from Sa-tan's snare
for-ev-er more, To dwell with Thee in heav'n a-bove,

In Je-sus' Ho-ly name, I pray.
To live for Christ whose name I wear. A-men. A-men.
And share in praise Thy end-less love.

103 Out Of Self And Into Thee

A♭-4-DO

Jessie H. Brown

Whosoever shall lose his life for
My sake shall find it. Matt. 16:25

C-16

R. J. Stevens

1. Out of sad-ness, in-to glad-ness, Sav-ior, Thou hast bid-den me;
2. Out of ter-ror, out of er-ror, Out of all that dark-ness brings,
3. Out of seem-ing, out of dream-ing, Out of earth's un-cer-tain-ty,

In-to bless-ing, all pos-sess-ing, Out of self and in-to Thee.
In-to un-ion and com-mun-ion With the Ho-ly King of Kings.
In-to sure-ness and se-cure-ness, Out of self and in-to Thee.

CHORUS

Out of self and in-to Thee; Lord, Thy won-drous love I see,

rit.

Let me dai-ly far-ther flee, Out of— self and in-to Thee.

Take My Hand, Precious Lord

104

There shall Thy hand lead me, and Thy right hand shall hold me. Psa. 139:10

T. A. D.

D-1

Thomas A. Dorsey

A♭-3-MI

1. When my way grow-eth drear, pre-cious Lord, lin-ger
2. When the shad-ows ap-pear, and the night draw-eth
3. Pre-cious Lord, take my hand, lead me on, let me

near, When my life is al-most gone;
near, And the day is past and gone;
stand, I am tired, I am weak, I am worn;

Hear my cry, hear my call, hold my hand lest I fall;
At the riv-er I stand, guide my feet, hold my hand;
Thru the storm, thru the night, lead me on to the light;

rit.

Take my hand, pre-cious Lord, lead me home.

105 I Am Thine, O Lord

Let us draw near with a true heart . . . Heb. 10:22

Ab-4-MI
Fanny J. Crosby, 1875

C-16, D-1
Wm. H. Doane, 1875

1. I am Thine, O Lord; I have heard Thy voice, And it told Thy
2. Con-se-crate me now to Thy ser-vice, Lord, By the pow'r of
3. O the pure de-light of a sin-gle hour That be-fore Thy
4. There are depths of love that I can-not know Till I cross the

love to me, But I long to rise in the arms of faith,
grace di-vine; Let my soul look up with a stead-fast hope,
throne I spend, When I kneel in prayer, and with Thee, my God,
nar-row sea; There are heights of joy that I may not reach

CHORUS

And be clos-er drawn to Thee. Draw me near - er,
And my will be lost in Thine.
I com-mune as friend with friend. near - er, near - er,
Till I rest in peace with Thee.

near-er, bless-ed Lord, To the cross where Thou hast died, Draw me nearer,

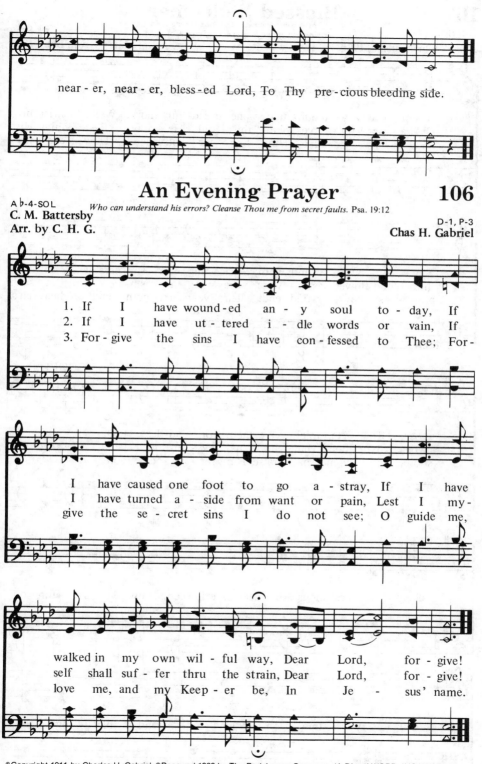

near-er, near-er, bless-ed Lord, To Thy pre-cious bleeding side.

An Evening Prayer

106

A ♭-4-SOL
Who can understand his errors? Cleanse Thou me from secret faults. Psa. 19:12

C. M. Battersby
Arr. by C. H. G.

D-1, P-3
Chas H. Gabriel

1. If I have wound-ed an-y soul to-day, If
2. If I have ut-tered i-dle words or vain, If
3. For-give the sins I have con-fessed to Thee; For-

I have caused one foot to go a-stray, If I have
I have turned a-side from want or pain, Lest I my-
give the se-cret sins I do not see; O guide me,

walked in my own wil-ful way, Dear Lord, for-give!
self shall suf-fer thru the strain, Dear Lord, for-give!
love me, and my Keep-er be, In Je-sus' name.

107 Blessed Redeemer

D-3-SOL

In Whom we have redemption through
His blood, even the forgiveness of sins. Col. 1:14

R-1, C-17

Avis B. Christiansen, 1920

Harry Dixon Loes, 1920

1. Up Cal-v'ry's moun-tain, one dread-ful morn, Walked Christ my
2. "Fa-ther, for-give them!" thus did He pray, E'en while His
3. O how I love Him, Sav-ior and Friend! How can my

Sav-ior, wea-ry and worn; Fac-ing for sin-ners death on the
life-blood flowed fast a-way; Pray-ing for sin-ners while in such
prais-es ev-er find end! Thro' years un-num-bered on heav-en's

CHORUS

cross, That He might save them from end-less loss.
woe— No one but Je-sus ev-er loved so. Bless-ed Re-
shore, My tongue shall praise Him for-ev-er-more.

deem-er, pre-cious Re-deem-er! Seems now I see Him on

Cal-va-ry's tree! Wound-ed and bleed-ing, for

sin-ners plead-ing—Blind and un-heed-ing, dy-ing for me!

Something For Jesus

108

G-4-MI

S. D. Phelps

What doth the Lord require of thee, but to do justly, and to love mercy,
and to walk humbly with thy God? Mic. 6:8

D-1

Robert Lowry

1. Sav - ior, Thy dy - ing love Thou gav - est me, Nor should I
2. Give me a faith-ful heart—Like - ness to Thee— That each de -
3. All that I am and have—Thy gifts so free— In joy, in

aught with - hold, Dear Lord, from Thee: In love my soul would bow,
part - ing day Hence-forth may see Some work of love be - gun,
grief, thru life, Dear Lord, for Thee! And when Thy face I see,

My heart ful - fil its vow, Some of-f'ring bring Thee now, Something for Thee.
Some deed of kind - ness done, Some wand'rer sought and won, Something for Thee.
My ransomed soul shall be, Thru all e - ter - ni - ty, Something for Thee.

109 Higher Ground

A♭-3-SOL
Johnson Oatman, Jr., 1898

I press toward the mark for the prize of the high calling of God in Christ Jesus.
Phil. 3:14

D-1, H-2
Charles H. Gabriel, 1898

1. I'm press-ing on the up-ward way, New heights I'm
2. My heart has no de-sire to stay Where doubts a-
3. I want to live a-bove the world, Tho' Sa-tan's
4. I want to scale the ut-most height, And catch a

gain-ing ev-'ry day; Still pray-ing as I on-ward bound,
rise and fears dis-may; Tho' some may dwell where these a-bound,
darts at me are hurled; For faith has caught the joy-ful sound,
gleam of glo-ry bright; But still I'll pray till heav'n I've found,

CHORUS

"Lord, plant my feet on high-er ground."
My prayer, my aim is high-er ground.
The song of saints on high-er ground. Lord, lift me
"Lord, lead me on to high-er ground."

up and let me stand, By faith, on heav-en's ta-ble-land, A high-er

plane than I have found; Lord, plant my feet on high-er ground.

My Jesus, I Love Thee

We love Him, because He first loved us. 1 John 4:19

F-4-DO

D-1, L-4

Wm. R. Featherstone, 1862

Adoniram J. Gordon, 1876

1. My Je - sus, I love Thee, I know Thou art mine,
2. I love Thee, be - cause Thou hast first lov - ed me,
3. I'll love Thee in life, I will love Thee in death,
4. In man - sions of glo - ry and end - less de - light,

For Thee all the fol - lies of sin I re - sign;
And pur - chased my par - don on Cal - va - ry's tree;
And praise Thee as long as Thou lend - est me breath;
I'll ev - er a - dore Thee in heav - en so bright;

My gra - cious Re - deem - er, my Sav - ior art Thou;
I love Thee for wear - ing the thorns on Thy brow;
And say when the death - dew lies cold on my brow;
I'll sing with the glit - ter - ing crown on my brow;

If ev - er I loved Thee, my Je - sus, 'tis now.

111 Clay In The Potter's Hand

Eb-2-MI

O Lord, Thou art our Father; we are the clay, and Thou our potter;
and we all are the work of Thy hand. Isa. 64:8

D-1

Mr. & Mrs. C. W.

Clyde Williams

With feeling

1. O Lord, you know my strength in-deed is small, Lest Thou should lead,
2. Thou art the Pot - ter, I am the clay, Make of my life
3. Fa-ther, we pray for pow-er to be strong, Let not our lives

I'm prone to slip and fall; Guide and di - rect, o'er e - vil help
as pleas - es Thee each day; Weave in - to beau - ty as You have
be marred by sin, and wrong; Lead to Thy throne, by love take full

me stand, Make me as clay in the pot - ter's hand.
it planned, Make me as clay in the pot - ter's hand.
com-mand, Make us as clay in the pot - ter's hand.

CHORUS

Mold me, make me, as You'd have me be, Take me, use me,

that the lost may see; Guard me, guide me, thru this

pil - grim land, Make me as clay, in the pot-ter's hand.

Teach Me Thy Way 112

Teach me Thy way, O Lord, and lead me in a plain path . . . Psa. 27:11

F-3-MI

B. M. R.

D-1, G-3

B. Mansell Ramsey

1. Teach me Thy way, O Lord, Teach me Thy way! Thy guid - ing
2. When I am sad at heart, Teach me Thy way! When earth - ly
3. When doubts and fears a - rise, Teach me Thy way! When storms o'er-
4. Long as my life shall last, Teach me Thy way! Wher - e'er my

grace af - ford—Teach me Thy way!   Help me to walk a-right,
joys de - part, Teach me Thy way!   In hours of lone - li -ness,
spread the skies, Teach me Thy way!   Shine thru the cloud and rain,
lot be cast, Teach me Thy way!   Un - til the race is run,

More by faith, less by sight; Lead me with heav'n-ly light, Teach me Thy way!
In times of dire dis-tress, In fail - ure or suc - cess, Teach me Thy way!
Thru sor-row, toil and pain; Make Thou my path-way plain, Teach me Thy way!
Un - til the jour-ney's done, Un-til the crown is won, Teach me Thy way!

113 Where No One Stands Alone

The Lord stood with me, and strengthened me . . . and I was delivered . . . II Tim. 4:17

Db-3-DO
M. L.

D-1
Mosie Lister

1. Once I stood in the night with my head bowed low,
2. Like a king I may live in a pal-ace so tall,

In the dark-ness as black as could be; And my heart
With great rich-es to call my own; But I don't

felt a-lone and I cried, "O Lord, Don't hide Your face from
know a thing in this whole wide world That's worse than be-ing a-

CHORUS

me." "Hold my hand all the way, Ev-'ry hour, ev-'ry day,
lone.

From here to the great un-known. Take my

hand; Let me stand Where no one stands a - lone."

Close To Thee

Thou art my refuge and my portion . . . Psa. 142:5

114

G-3-SOL

Fanny J. Crosby

D-1

Silas J. Vail

1. Thou, my ev - er - last - ing por - tion, More than friend or life to me;
2. Not for ease or world - ly pleas - ure, Nor for fame my pray'r shall be;
3. Lead me thru the vale of shad - ows, Bear me o'er life's fit - ful sea;

All a - long my pil - grim jour - ney, Sav - ior, let me walk with Thee.
Glad - ly will I toil and suf - fer, On - ly let me walk with Thee.
Then the gate of life e - ter - nal May I en - ter, Lord with Thee.

CHORUS

D. S.

Close to Thee, close to Thee, Close to Thee, close to Thee;

115 In The Desert Of Sorrow And Sin

If any man thirst, let him come unto Me, and drink. John 7:37

D-1

C-4-DO

H. R. Trickett

Fred A. Fillmore

1. In the des - ert of sor - row and sin, Lo! I faint as I
2. In my weak - ness I turn to the fount, From the Rock that was
3. O Thou God of com - pas - sion, I pray, Let me ev - er a-

jour - ney a - long; With the war - fare with - out and with - in, See my
smit - ten for me; And I drink, and I joy - ful - ly count All my
bide in Thy sight; Let me drink of the fount day by day, Till I

CHORUS

strength and my hope near - ly gone. I thirst, let me
tri - als a bless - ing to be.
join Thee in man - sions of light. I thirst, let me

drink, Of the life - giv - ing stream let me
drink, let me drink,

drink; 'Tis the Rock, cleft for
drink; let me drink. 'Tis the Rock,

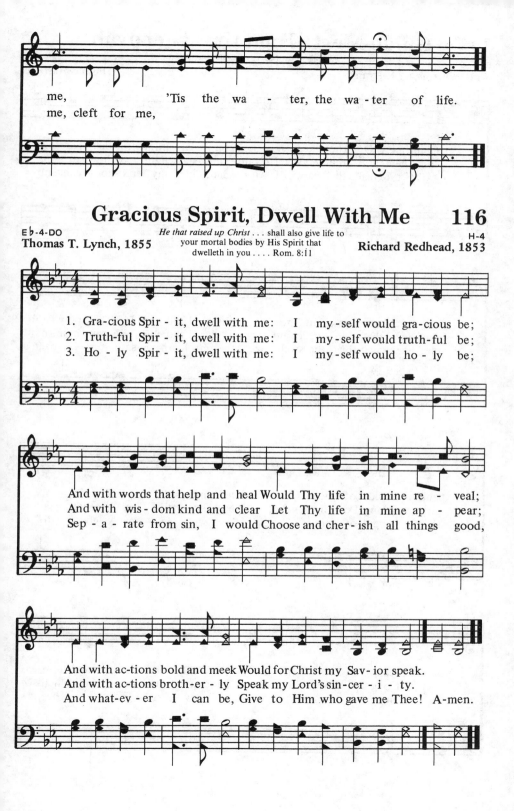

me,   'Tis the wa - ter, the wa-ter of life.
me, cleft for me,

Gracious Spirit, Dwell With Me   116

E♭-4-DO

He that raised up Christ . . . shall also give life to
Thomas T. Lynch, 1855   *your mortal bodies by His Spirit that*   Richard Redhead, 1853
dwelleth in you . . . . Rom. 8:11

H-4

1. Gra-cious Spir-it, dwell with me: I my-self would gra-cious be;
2. Truth-ful Spir-it, dwell with me: I my-self would truth-ful be;
3. Ho-ly Spir-it, dwell with me: I my-self would ho-ly be;

And with words that help and heal Would Thy life in mine re - veal;
And with wis-dom kind and clear Let Thy life in mine ap - pear;
Sep-a-rate from sin, I would Choose and cher-ish all things   good,

And with ac-tions bold and meek Would for Christ my Sav-ior speak.
And with ac-tions broth-er-ly Speak my Lord's sin-cer-i-ty.
And what-ev-er I can be, Give to Him who gave me Thee! A-men.

117 Guide Me, O Thou Great Jehovah

For Thy name's sake lead me and guide me. Psa. 31:3

D-3-SOL

Wm. Williams, 1745; trans.

D-1, G-3

Thomas Hastings

1. Guide me, O Thou great Je - ho - vah, Pil - grim thru this bar - ren
2. O - pen now the crys - tal foun - tain, Whence the heal - ing wa - ters
3. When I tread the verge of Jor - dan, Bid my anx - ious fears sub -

land; I am weak, but Thou art might - y, Hold me with Thy pow'r - ful
flow; Let the fier - y, cloud - y pil - lar, Lead me all my jour - ney
side; Bear me thru the swell - ing cur - rent, Land me safe on Ca - naan's

p

hand; Bread of heav - en, Feed me till I want no
thru; Strong De - liv - 'rer, Be Thou still my strength and
side; Songs of prais - es I will ev - er give to

f   *rit.*

more: Bread of heav - en, Feed me till I want no more.
shield: Strong De - liv - 'rer, Be Thou still my strength and shield.
Thee; Songs of prais - es I will ev - er give to Thee.

Take Time To Be Holy

118

Be ye holy for I am holy. 1 Pet. 1:16

F-2-MI
W. D. Longstaff

D-1, H-3
Geo. C. Stebbins

1. Take time to be ho - ly, Speak oft with thy Lord;
2. Take time to be ho - ly, The world rush - es on;
3. Take time to be ho - ly, Be calm in thy soul;

A - bide in Him al - ways, And feed on His word.
Spend much time in se - cret With Je - sus a - lone.
Each tho't and each mo - tive Be - neath His con - trol.

Make friends of God's chil - dren; Help those who are weak,
A - bid - ing in Je - sus, Like Him thou shalt be;
Thus led by His Spir - it To foun - tains of love,

For - get - ting in noth - ing His bless - ings to seek.
Thy friends in thy con - duct His like - ness shall see.
Thou soon shall be fit - ted For serv - ice a - bove.

119 Only In Thee

Bb-3-MI

Who hath blessed us with all spiritual blessings in heavenly places in Christ. Eph. 1:3

C-16, D-1

T. O. Chisholm

Chas. H. Gabriel

1. On - ly in Thee, O Sav - ior mine,   Dwell-eth my
2. On - ly in Thee a ra - diance bright,   Shines like a
3. On - ly in Thee, dear Sav - ior, slain,   Los - ing Thy

soul   in peace di - vine,   Peace that the world, tho'
bea - con in the night,   Guid - ing my pil - grim
life   my own to gain,   Trust - ing, I'm cleansed from

all com - bine,   Nev - er can take from me.
bark a - right,   O - ver life's track - less sea.
ev' - ry stain;   Thou art my on - ly plea.

Pleas - ures of earth so seem - ing - ly sweet,   Fail at the
On - ly in Thee, when trou - bles mo - lest,   When with temp-
On - ly in Thee, my heart will de - light,   Till in that

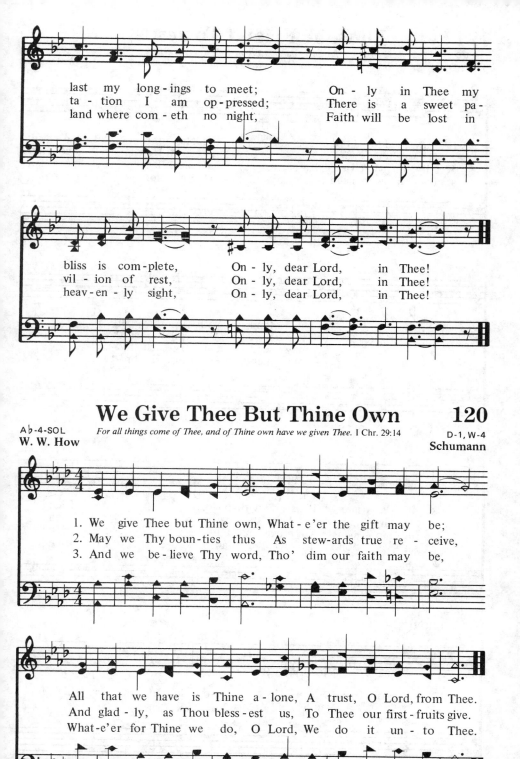

last my long-ings to meet;
ta-tion I am op-pressed;
land where com-eth no night,

On-ly in Thee my
There is a sweet pa-
Faith will be lost in

bliss is com-plete,
vil-ion of rest,
heav-en-ly sight,

On-ly, dear Lord, in Thee!
On-ly, dear Lord, in Thee!
On-ly, dear Lord, in Thee!

We Give Thee But Thine Own   120

For all things come of Thee, and of Thine own have we given Thee. I Chr. 29:14

Ab-4-SOL
W. W. How

D-1, W-4
Schumann

1. We give Thee but Thine own, What-e'er the gift may be;
2. May we Thy boun-ties thus As stew-ards true re-ceive,
3. And we be-lieve Thy word, Tho' dim our faith may be,

All that we have is Thine a-lone, A trust, O Lord, from Thee.
And glad-ly, as Thou bless-est us, To Thee our first-fruits give.
What-e'er for Thine we do, O Lord, We do it un-to Thee.

121 I'll Be A Friend To Jesus

F-4-DO

J. W. D.

D-1

J. W. Dennis

Then all the disciples forsook Him, and fled.
And they that had laid hold on Jesus led Him away . . . Matt. 26:56,57

1. They tried my Lord . . . . and Mas - ter, With no one
2. The world may turn . . . . a-gainst Him, I'll love Him
3. I'll do what He . . . . . . may bid me; I'll go where
4. To all who need . . . . . . a Sav - ior, My Friend I

to . . . . de - fend; With - in the halls . . . .
to . . . . the end, And while on earth . . . . . .
He . . . . may send; I'll try each fly - . . . .
rec - - - om - mend, Be - cause He bro't . . . .

. . . of Pi - late He stood with-out . . . . a friend.
. . . I'm liv - ing, My Lord shall have . . . . a friend.
. . . ing mo - ment To prove that I'm . . . . His friend.
. . . sal - va - tion, Is why I am . . . . His friend.

CHORUS

I'll be a friend to Je - sus, My life for
I'll be a friend to Je - sus,

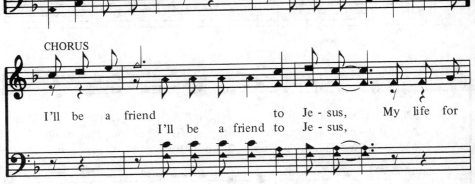

Him   I'll spend;   I'll be a friend . . . . . .
My life for Him I'll spend;   I'll be a

. . . to Je - sus,   Un - til my years   shall end.
friend to Je - sus,   Un - til my years shall end.

Now The Day Is Over   122

I will both lay me down in peace, and sleep: for Thou, Lord,
only makest me dwell in safety. Psa. 4:8

A-4-SOL
Sabine Baring-Gould, 1865

D-1
Joseph Barnby, 1868

1. Now the day is   o - ver,   Night is draw-ing   nigh, . .
2. Je - sus, give the   wea - ry,   Calm and sweet re - pose; . .
3. When the morn - ing   wak - ens,   Then may I a - rise, . . .

. . . Shad - ows of the ev - 'ning   Steal a - cross the sky.
. . . With Thy ten-d'rest bless - ing   May our eye - lids close.
. . . Pure and fresh and sin - less   In Thy ho - ly eyes. A - men.

ev'ning Steal a - cross   the sky

123 The Ninety And Nine

*Doth he not leave the ninety and nine, and goeth into the mountains and
seeketh that which is gone astray? Matt. 18:12*

G-2-SOL
Elizabeth C. Clephane

C-11, E-1
Ira D. Sankey

1. There were nine-ty and nine that safe - ly lay In the shel-ter
2. "Lord, Thou hast here Thy nine-ty and nine, Are they not e-
3. But none of the ran-somed ev - er knew How deep were the
4. "Lord, whence are those blood-drops all the way That marks out the
5. But all thru the moun-tains, thun - der-riv'n And up from the

of the fold, But one was out on the hills a - way,
nough for Thee?" But the Shep-herd made an - swer: "This of mine
wat - ers crossed Nor how dark was the night that the Lord passed thru
moun-tain's track?" "They were shed for one who had gone a - stray
rock - y steep, There a - rose a glad cry to the gate of heav'n,

Far off from the gates of gold; A - way on the
Has wan-dered a - way from me, And al-though the
Ere He found His sheep that was lost. Far out in the
Ere the Shep-herd could bring him back." "Lord, whence are Thy
"Re - joice, I have found my sheep." And the an - gels

moun - tains wild and bare, A - way from the ten - der
road be rough and steep, I go to the des - ert to
des - ert He heard its cry, 'Twas sick and help - less and
hands so rent and torn? They're pierced to - night by
e - choed a - round the throne, "Re - joice, for the Lord brings

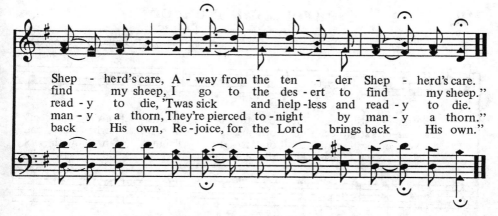

Shep - herd's care, A - way from the ten - der Shep - herd's care.
find my sheep, I go to the des - ert to find my sheep."
read - y to die, 'Twas sick and help - less and read - y to die.
man - y a thorn, They're pierced to - night by man - y a thorn."
back His own, Re - joice, for the Lord brings back His own."

Nearer My God To Thee 124

It is good for me to draw near to God: I have put my trust in the Lord . . . Psa. 73:28

G-4-MI

Sarah F. Adams, 1841

D-1

Lowell Mason

1. Near - er, my God, to Thee, Near - er to Thee;
2. Tho' like a wan - der - er, The sun gone down,
3. Or if, on joy - ful wing, Cleav - ing the sky,

Fine

E'en tho' it be a cross That rais - eth me,
Dark - ness be o - ver me, My rest a stone,
Sun, moon and stars for - got, Up - ward I fly,

D. S.—Near - er, my God, to Thee, Near - er, to Thee!

D. S.

Still all my song shall be, Near - er, my God, to Thee!
Yet in my dreams I'd be, Near - er, my God, to Thee!
Still all my song shall be, Near - er, my God, to Thee!

125
Nearer, Still Nearer

D-4-MI
L. N. M.

And I . . . will draw all men unto Me. John 12:32

D-1, F-2

Leila N. Morris, 1898

1. Near-er, still near-er, close to Thy heart, Draw me, my
2. Near-er, still near-er, noth-ing I bring, Naught as an
3. Near-er, still near-er, Lord, to be Thine, Sin with its
4. Near-er, still near-er, while life shall last, Till safe in

Sav-ior, so pre-cious Thou art; Fold me, O fold me close
off-'ring to Je-sus my King; On-ly my sin-ful, now
fol-lies, I glad-ly re-sign; All of its pleas-ures, pomp
glo-ry, my an-chor is cast; Thro' end-less a-ges, ev-

to Thy breast, Shel-ter me safe in that ha-ven of
con-trite heart, Grant me the cleans-ing Thy blood doth im-
and its pride, Give me but Je-sus, my Lord, cru-ci-
er to be, Near-er, my Sav-ior, still near-er to

rest, Shel-ter me safe in that ha-ven of rest.
part, Grant me the cleans-ing Thy blood doth im-part.
fied, Give me but Je-sus, my Lord, cru-ci-fied.
Thee, Near-er, my Sav-ior, still near-er to Thee.

Open My Eyes, That I May See   126

Open Thou mine eyes, that I may behold wondrous things out of Thy law. Psa. 119:18

Ab-2-DO
C. H. S.

D-1
Chas. H. Scott

1. O-pen my eyes, that I may see Glimp-ses of truth Thou hast for me;
2. O-pen my ears, that I may hear Thy word of truth Thou sendest clear;
3. O-pen my mouth, and let me bear Glad-ly the warm truth ev-'ry-where;

Place in my hands the won-der-ful key That shall un-clasp, and
And while the wave-notes fall on my ear, Ev-'ry-thing false will
O - pen my heart, and let me pre-pare Love with Thy chil - dren

REFRAIN

set me free. Si-lent-ly now I wait for Thee, Read-y, my God, Thy
dis - ap-pear. Si-lent-ly now I wait for Thee, Read-y, my God, Thy
thus to share. Si-lent-ly now I wait for Thee, Read-y, my God, Thy

will to see: O-pen my eyes, il - lu-mine me, Sav -ior di - vine!
will to see: O-pen my ears, il - lu-mine me, Sav -ior di - vine!
will to see: O-pen my heart, il - lu-mine me, Sav -ior di - vine!

127 This Is My Father's World

The heavens declare the glory of God; and the firmament showeth His handiwork. Psa. 19:1

Eb-4-DO
Maltbie D. Babcock, 1901

T-1
Franklin L. Sheppard, 1915

1. This is my Fa - ther's world, And to my lis - t'ning
2. This is my Fa - ther's world, The birds their car - ols
3. This is my Fa - ther's world, O let me ne'er for -

ears, All na - ture sings, and round me rings The mu - sic
raise, The morn - ing light, the lil - y white, De - clare their
get That though the wrong seems oft so strong, God is the

of the spheres. This is my Fa - ther's world, I
Mak - er's praise. This is my Fa - ther's world, He
Rul - er yet. This is my Fa - ther's world, In

rest me in the thought Of rocks and trees, of
shines in all that's fair; In the rust - ling grass I
bat - tle we must trod; Je - sus who died shall be

skies and seas— His hand the won- ders wrought.
hear Him pass, He speaks to me ev-'ry-where.
sat - is - fied, The king - dom turns back to God. A - men.

Take My Life, And Let It Be 128

A-3-SOL
Present your bodies a living sacrifice . . . to the Lord . . . Rom. 12:1
C-16, D-1
Miss Frances E. Havergal
Arr. by R. M. McIntosh

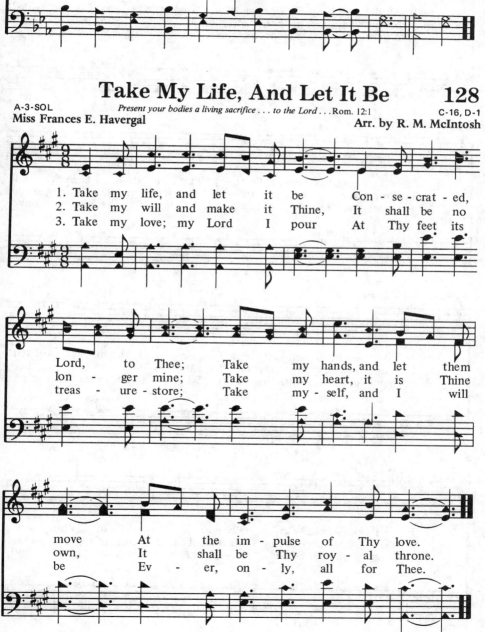

1. Take my life, and let it be Con - se - crat - ed,
2. Take my will and make it Thine, It shall be no
3. Take my love; my Lord I pour At Thy feet its

Lord, to Thee; Take my hands, and let them
lon - ger mine; Take my heart, it is Thine
treas - ure - store; Take my - self, and I will

move At the im - pulse of Thy love.
own, It shall be Thy roy - al throne.
be Ev - er, on - ly, all for Thee.

129 All The Way My Savior Leads Me

Ab-3-MI

Fanny J. Crosby, 1875

I will instruct thee and teach thee in the way which thou shalt go:
I will guide thee with Mine eye. Psa. 32:8

G-3

Robert Lowry, 1875

1. All the way my Sav-ior leads me: What have I to ask be-side?
2. All the way my Sav-ior leads me, Cheers each winding path I tread,
3. All the way my Sav-ior leads me: O the full-ness of His love!

Can I doubt His ten-der mer-cy, Who thru life has been my Guide?
Gives me grace for ev-'ry tri-al, Feeds me with the liv-ing bread;
Per-fect rest to me is prom-ised In my Fa-ther's house a-bove;

Heav'n-ly peace, di-vin-est com-fort, Here by faith in Him to dwell!
Tho' my wea-ry steps may fal-ter, And my soul a-thirst may be,
When my spir-it, clothed im-mor-tal, Wings its flight to realms of day,

For I know, what-e'er be-fall me, Je-sus do-eth all things well;
Gush-ing from the Rock be-fore me, Lo! a spring of joy I see;
This my song thru end-less a-ges: Je-sus led me all the way!

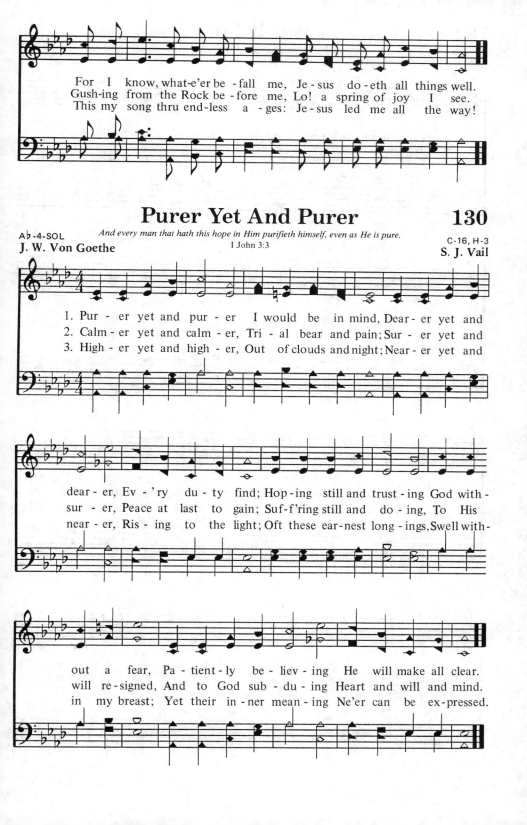

For I know, what-e'er be-fall me, Je-sus do-eth all things well.
Gush-ing from the Rock be-fore me, Lo! a spring of joy I see.
This my song thru end-less a-ges: Je-sus led me all the way!

Purer Yet And Purer

130

A♭-4-SOL

J. W. Von Goethe

And every man that hath this hope in Him purifieth himself, even as He is pure.
I John 3:3

C-16, H-3

S. J. Vail

1. Pur-er yet and pur-er   I would be in mind, Dear-er yet and
2. Calm-er yet and calm-er, Tri-al bear and pain; Sur-er yet and
3. High-er yet and high-er, Out of clouds and night; Near-er yet and

dear-er, Ev-'ry du-ty find; Hop-ing still and trust-ing God with-
sur-er, Peace at last to gain; Suf-f'ring still and do-ing, To His
near-er, Ris-ing to the light; Oft these ear-nest long-ings, Swell with-

out a fear, Pa-tient-ly be-liev-ing He will make all clear.
will re-signed, And to God sub-du-ing Heart and will and mind.
in my breast; Yet their in-ner mean-ing Ne'er can be ex-pressed.

131 Jesus Is Mine

Eb-2-SOL

Mrs. Catherine J. Bonar

I count all things but loss for the excellency of the knowledge of Christ Jesus my Lord. Phil. 3:8

C-16, D-1

T. E. Perkins

1. Fade, fade, each earth-ly joy, Je - sus is mine! Break
2. Tempt not my soul a - way, Je - sus is mine! Here
3. Fare - well, mor-tal - i - ty, Je - sus is mine! Wel-

ev - 'ry ten - der tie, Je - sus is mine!
would I ev - er stay, Je - sus is mine!
come, e - ter - ni - ty, Je - sus is mine!

Dark is the wil - der - ness, Earth has no rest - ing place,
Per - ish - ing things of clay, Born but for one brief day,
Wel - come, oh, loved and blest, Wel - come sweet scenes of rest,

Je - sus a - lone can bless, Je - sus is mine!
Pass from my heart a - way, Je - sus is mine!
Wel - come, my Sav - iour's breast, Je - sus is mine!

O Jesus, I Have Promised

132

G-4-MI

D-1, W-4

John E. Bode

If any man serve Me, let him follow Me; and where I am,
there shall also My servant be. John 12:26

Arthur H. Mann

1. O Je - sus, I have prom - ised To serve Thee to the end;
2. O let me feel Thee near me: The world is ev - er near;
3. O Je - sus, Thou hast prom - ised To all who fol - low Thee,

Be Thou for ev - er near me, My Mas - ter and my Friend:
I see the sights that daz - zle, The tempt - ing sounds I hear;
That where Thou art in glo - ry There shall Thy ser - vant be;

I shall not fear the bat - tle If Thou art by my
My foes are ev - er near me, A - round me and with -
And Je - sus, I have prom - ised To serve Thee to the

side, Nor wan - der from the path - way If Thou wilt be my Guide.
in; But, Je - sus, draw Thou near - er, And shield my soul from sin.
end: O give me grace to fol - low My Mas - ter and my Friend.

133 The Banner Of The Cross

Bb-4-MI
David W. Whittle, 1887

Thou hast given a banner to them that fear Thee,
that it may be displayed because of the truth.
Psa. 60:4

W-1
James McGranahan, 1887

1. There's a roy - al ban - ner giv - en for dis - play
2. O - ver land and sea, wher - ev - er man may dwell,
3. When the Great Com - mand - er, from the vault - ed sky,

To the sol - diers of the King; As an en - sign fair we
Make the glo - rious ti - dings known; Of the crim - son ban - ner
Sounds the res - ur - rec - tion day, Then be - fore our King the

lift it up to - day, While as ran - somed ones we sing.
now the sto - ry tell, While the Lord shall claim His own.
faint and foe shall die And the saints shall march a - way.

CHORUS

March - ing on! march - ing on! For
March - ing on and on! march - ing on, and on! For

Christ count ev - 'ry - thing but loss For the
Christ count ev - 'ry - thing, ev - 'ry - thing but loss, For the

King of kings toil and sing 'Neath the ban-ner of the cross.
King of kings, we'll toil and sing Be - neath the ban-ner of the cross.

Father Of Mercies

134

F-3-MI

Blessed be God . . . the Father of Mercies, and the God of all comfort. II Cor. 1:3

D-1, T-2

F. W. Faber, *et al.*

Traditional Melody

1. Fa - ther of mer - cies, day by day My love to Thee grows
2. Fa - ther of mer - cies, God of love, Whose gen - tle gifts all
3. Fa - ther of mer - cies, may our hearts Ne'er o - ver - look Thy

more and more; Thy gifts are strewn up - on my way Like sands up -
crea - tures share, The roll - ing sea - sons as they move Pro - claim to
boun-teous care; But what our Fa - ther's hand im - parts Still own in

on the great sea - shore, Like sands up - on the great sea - shore.
all Thy con - stant care, Pro - claim to all Thy con - stant care.
grate-ful praise and prayer, Still own in grate - ful praise and prayer.

135 More Like Jesus

F-2-SOL
J. M. S.

Let this mind be in you, which was also in Christ Jesus. Phil. 2:5

C-13, D-1
J. M. Stillman

1. I want to be more like Je - sus, And fol - low Him
2. I want to be kind and gen - tle To those who are
3. I want to be meek and low - ly, Like Je - sus, our

day by day; I want to be true and faith - ful, And
in dis - tress; To com - fort the bro - ken - heart - ed With
Friend and King; I want to be strong and ear - nest, And

ev - 'ry com - mand o - bey.
sweet words of ten - der - ness.
souls to the Sav - ior bring.

CHORUS

More and more like

Je - sus, I would ev - er be; . . . . More and
ev - er be;

more like Je - sus, My Sav - ior who died for me.

O Sacred Head

136

C-4-MI

Bernard of Clairvaux
Tr. J. W. Alexander

And when they had woven a crown of thorns, they put it upon His head . . .
and smote Him on the head. Matt. 27:29,30

D-1

Hans Hassler, 1601
Harmonized by Bach, 1729

1. *mp* { O sa-cred head, now wound - ed, With grief and shame
Now scorn-ful - ly sur - round - ed With thorns, Thine on-

2. *mf* { What lan-guage shall I bor - row To thank Thee, dear-
For this Thy dy - ing sor - row, Thy pit - y with-

weighed down;
ly crown; } How art Thou pale with an - -
est Friend, } O make me Thine for ev - -
out end? }

guish, With sore a - buse and scorn; How does that vis-
er; And, should I faint - ing be, Lord, let me nev-

age lan - guish, Which once was bright as morn!
er, nev - er Out - live my love to Thee.

137 Safe In The Arms Of Jesus

Hold Thou me up, and I shall be safe. Psa. 119:117

G-4-MI

Fanny J. Crosby

C-15

Wm. H. Doane

1. Safe in the arms of Je - sus, Safe on His gen - tle
2. Safe in the arms of Je - sus, Safe from cor - rod - ing
3. Je - sus, my heart's dear ref - uge, Je - sus has died for

D. S.—Safe on His gen - tle

breast, There by His love o'er-shad - ed, Sweet - ly my
care, Safe from the world's temp-ta - tions, Sin can - not
me; Firm on the Rock of A - ges, Ev - er my

breast, There by His love o'er-shad - ed, Sweet - ly my

Fine

soul shall rest. Hark! 'tis the voice of an - gels, Borne in a
harm me there. Free from the blight of sor - row, Free from my
trust shall be. Here let me wait with pa - tience, Wait till the

soul shall rest.

song to me, O - ver the fields of glo - ry, O - ver the
doubts and fears; On - ly a few more tri - als, On - ly a
night is o'er; Wait till I see the morn - ing Break on the

CHORUS

jas - per sea.
few more tears!   Safe   in   the   arms   of   Je - sus,
gold - en shore.

Prince Of Peace! Control My Will   138

Unto us a Son is given . . . the Prince of Peace.
Of the increase of His government and peace there shall be no end . . . Isa. 9:6,7

D-3-MI

Mary A. S. Barber

D-1, P-1

W. T. Porter

1. Prince of peace! con - trol   my   will,   Bid   this
2. Thou hast bo't me with   Thy blood,   O -   pened
3. May Thy will, not mine   be   done;   May   Thy
4. Sav - ior, at Thy feet   I   fall;   Thou   my

strug - gling heart   be   still;   Bid   my fears and doubt - ings
wide   the gate   of   God;   Peace   I ask, but peace must
will   and mine   be   one;   Chase these doubt - ings from my
Life,   my God,   my   All;   Let Thy hap - py ser - vant

cease—   Hush   my spir - it   in - to peace.
be,   Lord,   in be - ing one with Thee.
heart;   Now   Thy per - fect peace im - part.
be   One   for ev - er - more with Thee.   A - men.

139
Deeper And Deeper

E♭-2-MI
O. J. S.

Looking unto Jesus the author and finisher of our faith;
who for the joy set before Him endured the cross . . . Heb. 12:2

C-16, D-1
Oswald J. Smith

1. In - to the heart of Je - sus, deep - er and deep-er I go,
2. In - to the will of Je - sus, deep - er and deep-er I go,
3. In - to the cross of Je - sus, deep - er and deep-er I go,
4. In - to the joy of Je - sus, deep - er and deep-er I go,

Seek - ing to know the rea - son why He should love me so,
Pray - ing for grace to fol - low, seek - ing His way to know,
Fol - low-ing thro' the gar - den fac - ing the dread - ed foe,
Ris - ing with soul en - rap - tured far from the world be - low,

Why He should stoop to lift me up from the mir - y clay,
Bow - ing in full sur - ren - der low at His bless - ed feet,
Drink-ing the cup of sor - row, sob - bing with bro - ken heart:
Joy in the place of sor - row, peace in the midst of pain,

rall.

Sav - ing my soul, mak - ing me whole, Tho' I had wan-dered a - way.
Bid-ding Him take, break me and make, Till I am mold-ed and meet.
"O Sav-ior, help! dear Sav-ior, help! Grace for my weak-ness im - part."
Je - sus will give, Je - sus will give; He will up-hold and sus - tain.

Savior Divine, Dwell In My Heart 140

E♭-2-SOL
G. C. T.

With my whole heart have I sought Thee . . . Thy word have I hid in mine heart . . .
Psa. 119:10,11

C-13, D-1
Grant Colfax Tullar

1. Lord, in Thy mer-cy, lend ear to my plea, Turn not a-
2. Test me and try me, O Sav-ior di-vine! Let me be
3. Dwell in me, Sav-ior, nor ev-er de-part! Ful-ly Thine

way, nor de-ny; May Thy word ev-er dwell rich-ly in me,
filled with Thy love; Then from my heart shall Thy glo-ry-light shine,
own I would be; Naught but Thy wis-dom shall rule in my heart,

CHORUS

Hear Thou and an-swer my cry.
Light-ing the path-way a-bove.   Lord, I would keep soul and
Till Thy dear face I shall see.

bod-y for Thee, No room for self or for sin shall there be; Fit for Thy

dwell-ing, for Thee set a-part—Sav-ior di-vine, dwell in my heart.

141 His Yoke Is Easy

Take My yoke upon you, and learn of Me . . .
for My yoke is easy, and My burden is light. Matt. 11:29,30

Db-2-SOL
D. S. Warner

T-1
B. E. Warren

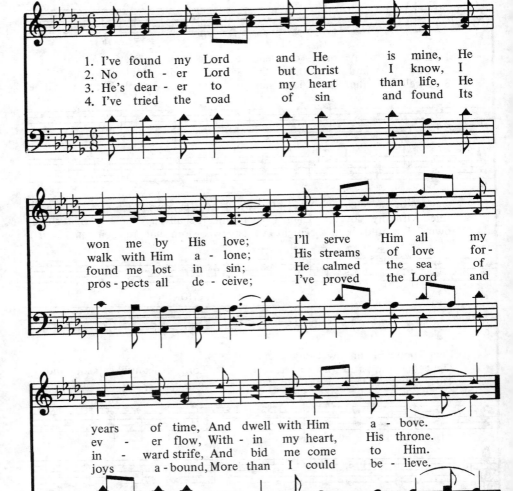

1. I've found my Lord and He is mine, He
2. No oth - er Lord but Christ I know, I
3. He's dear - er to my heart than life, He
4. I've tried the road of sin and found Its

won me by His love; I'll serve Him all my
walk with Him a - lone; His streams of love for -
found me lost in sin; He calmed the sea of
pros - pects all de - ceive; I've proved the Lord and

years of time, And dwell with Him a - bove.
ev - er flow, With - in my heart, His throne.
in - ward strife, And bid me come to Him.
joys a - bound, More than I could be - lieve.

CHORUS

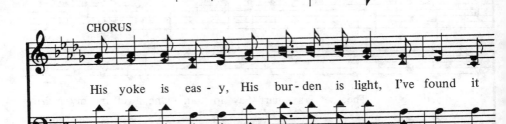

His yoke is eas - y, His bur - den is light, I've found it

so,   I've found it so: His   ser - vice is   my

sweet-est de - light, His bless - ings ev - er flow.

More Love To Thee, O Christ 142

I pray that your love may abound yet more and more . . . Phil. 1:9

A♭-4-SOL

Elizabeth Prentiss, 1856

D-1, L-3

William H. Doane, 1870

1. More love to Thee, O Christ, More love to Thee! Hear Thou the
2. Once earth-ly joy I craved, Sought peace and rest; Now Thee a-
3. Then shall my lat-est breath Whis - per Thy praise; This be the

prayer I make, On bend - ed knee; This is my ear - nest plea,
lone I seek, Give what is best; This all my prayer shall be,
part - ing cry My heart shall raise, This still its prayer shall be,

More love, O Christ, to Thee, More love to Thee! More love to Thee.

143 Glorious Things Of Thee Are Spoken

Glorious things are spoken of thee, O city of God. Psa. 87:3

F-4-DO

John Newton

K-1

F. J. Haydn

1. Glo-rious things of thee are spo - ken, Zi - on, cit - y of our God! He whose word can - not be bro - ken Formed thee for His own a - bode: On the Rock of a - ges found - ed, What can shake thy sure re - pose?

2. See, the streams of liv - ing wa - ters, Spring - ing from e - ter - nal love, Well sup - ply thy sons and daugh - ters, And all fear of want re - move: Who can faint while such a riv - er Ev - er flows their thirst t' as-suage?

3. Sav - ior, since of Zi - on's cit - y I, thro' grace, a mem - ber am, Let the world de - ride or pit - y, I will glo - ry in Thy name. Fad - ing is the world-ling's pleas - ure, All his boast - ed pomp and show;

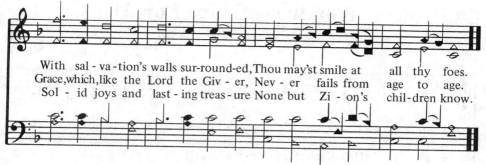

With sal - va - tion's walls sur-round-ed, Thou may'st smile at all thy foes.
Grace, which, like the Lord the Giv - er, Nev - er fails from age to age.
Sol - id joys and last - ing treas - ure None but Zi - on's chil-dren know.

My Faith Looks Up To Thee 144

Looking to Jesus the author and finisher of our faith. Heb. 12:2

E♭-4-DO

Ray Palmer, 1830

D-1, F-1

Lowell Mason, 1832

1. My faith looks up to Thee, Thou Lamb of Cal - va - ry,
2. May Thy rich grace im - part Strength to my faint - ing heart,
3. While life's dark maze I tread, And grief a - round me spread,

Sav - ior di - vine; Now hear me while I pray, Take all my
My zeal in - spire; As Thou hast died for me, O may my
Be Thou my guide; Bid dark - ness turn to day, Wipe sor - row's

sins a - way, O let me from this day Be whol - ly Thine!
love to Thee Pure, warm, and change-less be, A liv - ing fire!
tears a - way, Nor let me ev - er stray From Thee a - side.

145 Wondrous Grace For All

For the grace of God that bringeth salvation
hath appeared to all men... Tit. 2:11

G-2-SOL
W. R. B.

E-1, G-2
Wilma Reese Bell
Arr. by R. J. Stevens

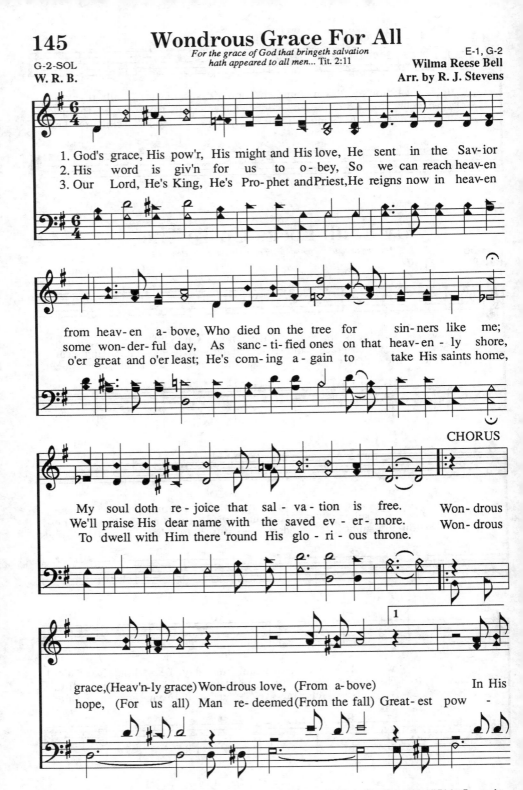

1. God's grace, His pow'r, His might and His love, He sent in the Sav-ior
2. His word is giv'n for us to o-bey, So we can reach heav-en
3. Our Lord, He's King, He's Pro-phet and Priest, He reigns now in heav-en

from heav-en a-bove, Who died on the tree for sin-ners like me;
some won-der-ful day, As sanc-ti-fied ones on that heav-en-ly shore,
o'er great and o'er least; He's com-ing a-gain to take His saints home,

CHORUS

My soul doth re-joice that sal-va-tion is free. Won-drous
We'll praise His dear name with the saved ev-er-more. Won-drous
To dwell with Him there 'round His glo-ri-ous throne.

1

grace, (Heav'n-ly grace) Won-drous love, (From a-bove) In His
hope, (For us all) Man re-deemed (From the fall) Great-est pow -

Word that mortals have heard. Oh, what grace, wondrous grace for all.

Have Thine Own Way, Lord   146

Eb-3-MI
We are the clay, and Thou our potter; and we shall be the work of Thy hand. Isa. 64:8
B-1, D-1
Adelaide Pollard, 1902
Geo. C. Stebbins, 1907

Slowly

1. Have Thine own way, Lord! Have Thine own way! Thou art the
2. Have Thine own way, Lord! Have Thine own way! Search me and
3. Have Thine own way, Lord! Have Thine own way! Hold o'er my

Potter; I am the clay.   Mold me and make me
try me, Master, to-day!   Whit-er than snow, Lord,
be-ing Ab-so-lute sway!   Fill with Thy Spir-it

Af-ter Thy will, While I am wait-ing, Yield-ed and still.
Wash me just now, As in Thy pres-ence Hum-bly I bow.
Till all shall see Christ on-ly, al-ways, Liv-ing in me!

147

E-4-MI

Day By Day

C-12, C-15

Carolina Sandell Berg *Blessed be the Lord who daily loadeth us with benefits . . .*
Trans. by A. L. Skoog
Psa. 68:19

Oscar Ahnfelt

1. Day by day and with each pass-ing moment, Strength I find to
2. Ev-'ry day the Lord Him-self is near me With a spe-cial
3. Help me then in ev-'ry trib-u-la-tion So to trust Thy

meet my tri-als here; Trust-ing in my Fa-ther's wise be-stow-ment,
mer-cy for each hour; All my cares He fain would bear, and cheer me,
prom-is-es, O Lord, That I lose not faith's sweet con-so-la-tion

I've no cause for wor-ry or for fear. He whose heart is kind
He whose name is Coun-sel-lor and Pow'r. The pro-tec-tion of
Of-fered me with-in Thy ho-ly Word. Help, me, Lord, when toil

be-yond all meas-ure Gives un-to each day what He deems best. Lov-ing
His child and treas-ure Is a charge that on Him-self He laid; "As your
and trou-ble meet-ing, E'er to take, as from a fa-ther's hand, One by

ly, its part of pain and pleas - ure, Min-gling toil with peace and rest.
days, your strength shall be in meas - ure," This the pledge to me He made.
one, the days, the moments fleet - ing, Till I reach the prom-ised land.

Thou Art The Way

148

I am the way, the truth, and the life;
no man cometh unto the Father, but by Me. John 14:6

Bb-3-DO

George W. Doane

D-1, R-2

James Welch

1. Thou art the Way: to Thee a - lone From sin and
2. Thou art the Truth: Thy word a - lone True wis - dom
3. Thou art the Life: the rend - ing tomb Pro - claims Thy

death we flee; And he who would the
can im - part; Thou on - ly canst in -
con - qu'ring arm; And those who put their

Fa - ther seek, Must seek Him, Lord, by Thee.
struct the mind, And pu - ri - fy the heart.
trust in Thee Nor death nor hell shall harm.

149 I Will Sing The Wondrous Story

Eb-3-MI

On the sea of glass . . . and they sing . . . the song of the Lamb . . . Rev. 15:2, 3

S-1, S-4

Francis H. Rowley, 1886

Peter P. Bilhorn, 1887

1. I will sing the won-drous sto - ry Of the Christ who died for me,
2. I was lost, but Je - sus found me, Found the sheep that went a-stray,
3. He will keep me till the riv - er Rolls its wa - ters at my feet;

How He left His home in glo - ry For the cross of Cal - va - ry.
Threw His lov - ing arms a-round me, Drew me back un - to His way.
Then He'll bear me safe - ly o - ver, Where the loved ones I shall meet.

CHORUS

Yes, I'll sing the won-drous sto - ry
Yes, I'll sing the won-drous sto - ry
Sing it with the saints in glo - ry,
Sing it with the saints in glo - ry,

Of the Christ who died for me,
Of the Christ who died for me,

Gath-ered by the crys - tal sea.

Gath-ered by the crys - tal sea.

Purer In Heart, O God

150

Blessed are the pure in heart: for they shall see God. Matt. 5:8

G-4-MI

Mrs. A. L. Davison

D-1, H-3

J. H. Fillmore

1. Pur - er in heart, O God, Help me to be; May I de-
2. Pur - er in heart, O God, Help me to be; Teach me to
3. Pur - er in heart, O God, Help me to be; That I Thy

vote my life Whol - ly to Thee. Watch Thou my way-ward feet,
do Thy will Most lov - ing - ly. Be Thou my Friend and Guide,
ho - ly face One day may see. Keep me from se - cret sin,

Guide me with coun-sel sweet; Pur - er in heart, Help me to be.
Let me with Thee a - bide; Pur - er in heart, Help me to be.
Reign Thou my soul with - in; Pur - er in heart, Help me to be.

151 Christ, We Do All Adore Thee

C-4-DO

P-2

Th. Baker

*Unto Him that loved us, and washed us from our sins in His own blood . . .
be glory and dominion for ever . . . Rev. 1:5,6*

Th. Dubois

Christ, we do all a - dore Thee, and we do praise Thee for -

ev - er; Christ, we do all a - dore Thee, and we do

praise Thee for - ev - er, for on the ho - ly cross hast Thou the

world from sin re - deem - ed; Christ, we do all a - dore Thee,

and we do praise Thee for - ev - er: Christ, we do all a - dore Thee!

By Christ Redeemed

152

For as often as ye eat this bread, and drink this cup,
ye do show the Lord's death till He come.
I Cor. 11:26

E♭-4-MI

Geo. Rawson, Arr., 1857

From A. H. Troyte's Chant

L-1

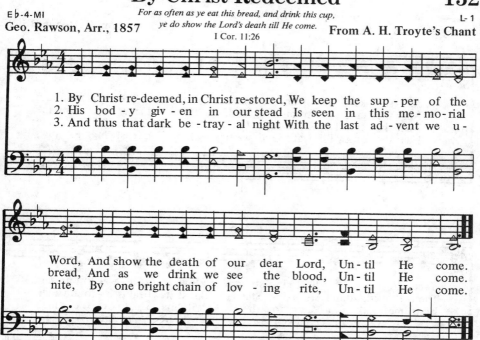

1. By Christ re-deemed, in Christ re-stored, We keep the sup-per of the
2. His bod-y giv-en in our stead Is seen in this me-mo-rial
3. And thus that dark be-tray-al night With the last ad-vent we u-

Word, And show the death of our dear Lord, Un-til He come.
bread, And as we drink we see the blood, Un-til He come.
nite, By one bright chain of lov-ing rite, Un-til He come.

'Tis Set, The Feast Divine

153

For as often as ye eat this bread, and drink this cup,
ye do show the Lord's death till He come. I Cor. 11:26

E♭-3-DO

Vana R. Raye

L. O. Sanderson

L-1

1. 'Tis set, the feast di-vine— The bread, the fruit of the vine—
2. May we the Lord dis-cern, His death our ho-ly con-cern;

And saints com-mune be-fore the shrine, In the sup-per of the Lord.
We feast in faith, His com-ing yearn, In the sup-per of the Lord.

154 Near The Cross

154

F-2-MI

Fanny J. Crosby, 1869

God forbid that I should glory, save in the cross . . . Gal. 6:14

C-17

Wm. H. Doane, 1869

1. Je - sus, keep me near the cross: There a pre-cious foun-tain,
2. Near the cross, a trem-bling soul, Love and mer - cy found me;
3. Near the cross! O Lamb of God, Bring its scenes be - fore me;
4. Near the cross I'll watch and wait, Hop - ing, trust-ing, ev - er,

Free to all, a heal - ing stream, Flows from Cal - v'ry's mountain.
There the Bright and Morn-ing Star Sheds its beams a - round me.
Help me walk from day to day With its shad - ow o'er me.
Till I reach the gold - en strand, Just be - yond the riv - er.

CHORUS

In the cross, in the cross, Be my glo - ry ev - er,

Till my rap - tured soul shall find Rest be - yond the riv - er.

Wonderful Love Of Jesus

Christ also hath loved us, and hath given Himself for us . . . Eph. 5:2

C-2-SOL
E. D. Mund

L-4
E. S. Lorenz

1. In vain in high and ho - ly lays My soul her grate - ful voice would
2. A joy by day, a peace by night, In storms a calm, in dark - ness
3. My hope for par - don when I call, My trust for lift - ing when I

raise; For who can sing the wor - thy praise Of the
light; In pain a balm, in weak - ness might Is the won - der - ful love of
fall; In life, in death, my all in all, Is the

Je - sus.

REFRAIN

Won - der - ful love! won - der - ful love!

Won - der - ful love of Je - sus! Won - der - ful love!

won - der - ful love! Won - der - ful love of Je - sus!

156 Tell Me The Story Of Jesus

Eb-4-MI

The Son of man came not to be ministered unto, but to minister and
to give His life a ransom for many. Matt. 20:28

E-1

Fanny J. Crosby, 1880

John R. Sweney, 1880

1. Tell me the sto-ry of Je-sus, Write on my heart ev-'ry word;
2. Fast-ing a-lone in the des-ert, Tell of the days that are passed,
3. Tell of the cross where they nailed Him, Writhing in anguish and pain;

Cho. - Tell me the sto-ry of Je-sus, Write on my heart ev-'ry word;

Fine

Tell me the sto-ry most pre-cious, Sweet-est that ev-er was heard.
How for our sins He was tempt-ed, Yet was tri-um-phant at last.
Tell of the grave where they laid Him, Tell how He liv-eth a-gain.

Tell me the sto-ry most pre-cious, Sweetest that ev-er was heard.

Tell how the an-gels, in cho-rus, Sang as they wel-comed His birth,
Tell of the years of His la-bor, Tell of the sor-row He bore,
Love in that sto-ry so ten-der, Clear-er than ev-er I see;

D. C. for Chorus

"Glo-ry to God in the high-est! Peace and good tid-ings to earth."
He was de-spised and af-flict-ed, Home-less, re-ject-ed and poor.
Stay, let me weep while you whis-per, Love paid the ran-som for me.

At The Cross

157

Surely He hath borne our griefs, and carried our sorrows . . .
He was bruised for our iniquities.
Isa. 53:4,5

E-4-DO

Isaac Watts, 1707; Ref., R.E.H., 1885

R. E. Hudson, 1885

C-4, C-17

1. A - las, and did my Sav - ior bleed, And did my Sov - 'reign die;
2. Was it for crimes that I have done, He groaned up - on the tree?
3. Well might the sun in dark - ness hide, And shut His glo - ries in,
4. But drops of grief can ne'er re - pay The debt of love I owe:

Would He de - vote that sa - cred head For such a one as I?
A - maz - ing pit - y, grace un - known! And love be - yond de - gree!
When Christ, the might - y Mak - er, died For man the crea - ture's sin.
Here, Lord, I give my - self a - way, 'Tis all that I can do!

CHORUS

At the cross, at the cross where I first saw the light, And the

bur-den of my heart rolled a - way, It was there by
rolled a - way,

faith I re - ceived my sight, And now I am hap-py all the day!

158 Nailed To The Cross

F-4-MI

Mrs. Frank A. Breck

C-3, C-17

Grant Colfax Tullar

Duet ad lib.

Having forgiven you all trespasses; blotting out the handwriting of ordinances . . . nailing it to the cross.

Col 2:13,14

1. There was One who was will - ing to die in my stead, That a
2. He is ten - der and lov - ing and pa - tient with me, While He
3. I will cling to my Sav - ior and nev - er de - part, I will

soul so un - wor - thy might live, And the path to the cross He was
cleans-es my heart of its dross, But "there's no con - dem - na - tion," I
joy - ful - ly jour - ney each day, With a song on my lips and a

will - ing to tread, All the sins of my life to for - give.
know I am free, For my sins are all nailed to the cross.
song in my heart, That my sins have been tak - en a - way.

CHORUS *pp*

They are nailed to the cross, they are nailed to the cross, O how

much He was will-ing to bear! With what an-guish and loss, Je-sus

went to the cross! But He car-ried my sins with Him there.

When My Love To Christ Grows Weak 159

C-3-MI
Surely He hath borne our griefs . . . He was wounded for our transgressions . . .
D-1, G-1

J. R. Wreford
and with His stripes we are healed. Isa. 53:4,5
Mrs. Jos. F. Knapp

1. When my love to Christ grows weak, When for deep-er faith I seek,
2. There I walk a-mid the shades, While the ling-'ring twi-light fades,
3. When my love for man grows weak, When for strong-er faith I seek,
4. There be-hold His ag-o-ny, Suf-fered on the bit-ter tree;
5. Then to life I turn a-gain, Learn-ing all the worth of pain;

Then in tho't I go to Thee, Gar-den of Geth-sem-a-ne!
See that suff-'ring, friend-less One, Weep-ing, pray-ing there a-lone.
Hill of Cal-va-ry! I go To thy scenes of fear and woe.
See His an-guish, see His faith, Love tri-umph-ant still in death.
Learn-ing all the might that lies In a full self-sac-ri-fice.

160 One Day

DƄ-3-SOL
J. Wilbur Chapman

C-4, R-2
Charles H. Marsh

1. One day when heav-en was filled with His prais-es, One day when
2. One day they led Him up Cal-va-ry's moun-tain, One day they
3. One day the grave could con-ceal Him no long-er, One day the
4. One day the trum-pet will sound for His com-ing, One day the

sin was as black as could be, Je-sus came forth to be
nailed Him to die on the tree, Suf-fer-ing an-guish, de-
stone rolled a-way from the door; Then He a-rose, o-ver
skies with His glo-ry will shine; Won-der-ful day, my be-

born of a vir-gin—Dwelt a-mong men, my ex-am-ple is
spised and re-ject-ed; Bear-ing our sins, my Re-deem-er is
death He had con-quered; Now is as-cend-ed, my Lord ev-er-
lov-ed ones bring-ing; Glo-ri-ous Sav-ior, this Je-sus is

CHORUS

He!
He!
more!
mine!

Liv-ing, He loved me; dy-ing, He saved me; Bur-ied, He

car - ried my sins far a - way; Ris - ing, He jus - ti - fied

free-ly for-ev-er: One day He's com-ing—oh, glo-ri-ous day!

Hallelujah! What A Savior! 161

He is . . . a man of sorrows, and acquainted with grief. Isa. 53:3

C-4-SOL
P. P. B., 1875

L-1, P-2
Philip P. Bliss

1. "Man of Sor - rows," what a name | For the Son of God who came
2. Bear - ing shame and scoff-ing rude, | In my place con-demned He stood,
3. Guilt - y, vile and help-less we; | Spot-less Lamb of God was He;
4. Lift - ed up was He to die, | "It is fin -ished," was His cry;
5. When He comes, our glo-rious King, | All His ransomed home to bring,

Ru - ined sin-ners to re-claim! Hal-le-lu-jah! what a Sav-ior!
Sealed my par-don with His blood; Hal-le-lu-jah! what a Sav-ior!
"Full a-tone-ment!" can it be? Hal-le-lu-jah! what a Sav-ior!
Now in heav'n ex-alt-ed high, Hal-le-lu-jah! what a Sav-ior!
Then a-new this song we'll sing, Hal-le-lu-jah! what a Sav-ior!

162 Night, With Ebon Pinion

Eb-2-MI
L. H. Jameson

G-1
J. P. Powell

And being in agony He prayed more earnestly:
and His sweat was as it were great drops of blood . . . Luke 22:44

1. Night, with eb - on pin - ion, Brood - ed o'er the vale;
2. Smit - ten for of - fens - es Which were not His own,
3. "Ab - ba, Fa - ther, Fa - ther, If in - deed it may,

All a - round was si - lent, Save the night-wind's wail, When
He, for our trans-gres - sions, Had to weep a - lone, No
Let this cup of an - guish Pass from Me, I pray; Yet,

Christ, the Man of Sor - rows, In tears and sweat as blood,
friend with words to com - fort, Nor hand to help was there,
if it must be suf - fer'd, By Me Thine on - ly Son,

Pros - trate in the gar - den, Raised His voice to God.
When the Meek and Low - ly Hum - bly bowed in pray'r.
Ab - ba, Fa - ther, Fa - ther, Let Thy will be done."

In Remembrance

This do in remembrance of Me. Luke 22:19

163

Ab-4-SOL
Rue Porter

L-1
Will W. Slater

1. On this Lord's Day we as-sem-ble, 'Round the ta - ble
2. We re-call His bro-ken bod-y, As we look up-
3. And this crim-son cup re-minds us, Of that dread scene
4. There in ag-o - ny He suf-fered, On the cross for

of the Lord; Hap-py hearts are made to trem-ble,
on this bread; "Give ye thanks, di - vide, and eat it,
long a - go; When He died in pain and an-guish,
you and me; Now, up-on the Throne He's reign-ing,

REFRAIN

When we hear His bless-ed word.
In My mem-o - ry," He said.
There His blood was made to flow. Thanks to God for
Bless-ed Lamb of Cal - va - ry.

such a Sav-ior, Now en-throned in heav'n a - bove; Thanks for

this ex - alt-ed fa - vor, Blest me-mo-rial of His love.

164 The Depth Of God's Love

But God commendeth His love toward us, in that, while we were yet sinners,
Christ died for us. Rom. 5:8

Bb-2-MI
T. S. T.

L-5

Tillit S. Teddlie

1. Oh the depth and the rich - es of God's sav - ing grace Flow-ing
2. How my heart hum - bly bows in His pres-ence to - day, When I
3. Oh what mar - ve - lous mer - cy, what in - fi - nite love! What im -

down from the cross for me! There the debt for my sins by the
think of His ag - o - ny, By His stripes I am freed from the
meas - ur - able grace I see! By His blood I am cleansed; I am

CHORUS

Sav - ior was paid In His suff'-ring on Cal - va - ry! Oh the
bond-age of sin Thru His suff'-ring on Cal - va - ry! Oh the
hap - py and free Thru His suff'-ring on Cal - va - ry! Oh the

depth of such won - der - ful love, Flow-ing bound-less and
rich - es and depth

full and free! And the debt for my
debt on the cross

sins was all paid In His suff'-ring on Cal - va - ry!

Thus Remember Me

165

Ab-3-SOL
Vana R. Raye

This do in remembrance of Me . . . I Cor. 11:24

L-1
L. O. Sanderson

1. Je - sus, on the night be - trayed, Honor -'d
2. Je - sus, giv - en in our stead, Blest the
3. Lord, we thank Thee for the bread, And the

God as He blest the bread, And to His dis -
fruit of the vine, and said: "This, my blood, for
cup from the name - less dread; Help us to dis -

ci - ples said: "Thus re - mem - ber me."
you is shed; So, re - mem - ber me."
cern our head; And re - mem - ber Thee.

166 He Loved Me So

F-4-SOL
J. G. D.

C-1, L-4
J. G. Dailey

Unto Him that loved us, and washed us
from our sins in His own blood . . . to Him be glory . . . Rev. 1:5,6

1. Why did my Sav-ior come to earth, And to the hum-ble go? Why did He choose a low-ly birth?
2. Why did He drink the bit-ter cup Of sor-row pain and woe? Why on the cross be lift-ed up?
3. Till Je-sus comes I'll sing His praise, And then to glo-ry go, And live with Him thru end-less days,

CHORUS

Be-cause He loved me so! He loved me so; He loved, He loved me so, He loved me so; He loved, He loved me so; He gave His pre-cious life for me, for me, Be-cause He loved me so.

We Saw Thee Not

167

E-3-DO

C-8, F-1

*Whom having not seen, ye love; in whom, though
now ye see Him not, yet believing, ye rejoice . . . I Pet. 1:8*

Anne Richter

Knowles Shaw

1. We saw Thee not when Thou didst come To this poor world of sin and death;
2. We saw Thee not when lift - ed high, A - mid that wild and sav - age crew;
3. We gazed not in the o - pen tomb, Where once Thy mangled body lay;
4. We walked not with the chos - en few, Who saw Thee from the earth ascend;

Nor yet be - held Thy cot - tage home, In that de - spis - ed Naz - a - reth;
Nor heard we that im - plor - ing cry, "For - give, they know not what they do!"
Nor saw Thee in that "up - per room," Nor met Thee on the o - pen way;
Who raised to heav'n their wond'ring view, then low to earth all pros - trate bend;

REFRAIN

But we be - lieve Thy foot-steps trod Its streets and plains, Thou Son of God:
But we be - lieve the deed was done, That shook the earth and veiled the sun;
But we be - lieve that an - gels said, "Why seek the liv - ing with the dead?"
But we be - lieve that hu - man eyes Be - held that jour-ney to the skies;

But we be - lieve Thy footsteps trod Its streets and plains, Thou Son of God.
But we be - lieve the deed was done, That shook the earth and veiled the sun;
But we be - lieve that an - gels said, "Why seek the liv - ing with the dead?"
But we be - lieve that hu - man eyes Be - held that jour-ney to the skies.

168 Beneath The Cross Of Jesus

And being found in fashion as a man, He humbled Himself, and became obedient unto death, even the death of the cross. Phil. 2:8

Db-4-SOL

Elizabeth C. Clephane, 1872

C-16, C-17

Fredrick C. Maker, 1881

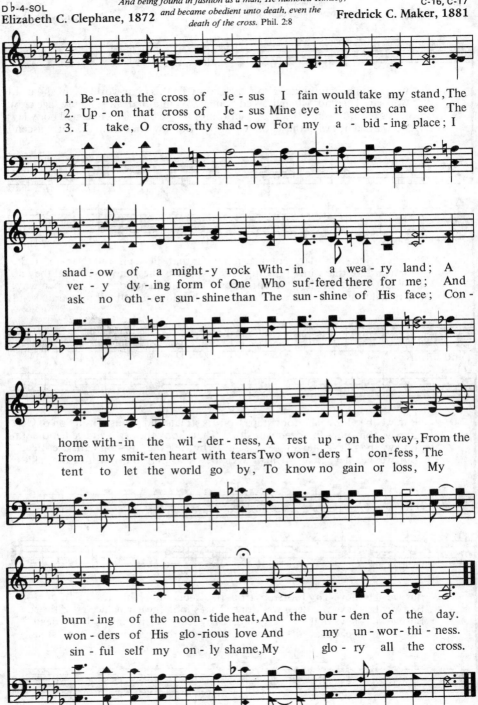

1. Be - neath the cross of Je - sus I fain would take my stand, The shad - ow of a might - y rock With - in a wea - ry land; A home with - in the wil - der - ness, A rest up - on the way, From the burn - ing of the noon - tide heat, And the bur - den of the day.

2. Up - on that cross of Je - sus Mine eye it seems can see The ver - y dy - ing form of One Who suf - fered there for me; And from my smit - ten heart with tears Two won - ders I con - fess, The won - ders of His glo - rious love And my un - wor - thi - ness.

3. I take, O cross, thy shad - ow For my a - bid - ing place; I ask no oth - er sun - shine than The sun - shine of His face; Con - tent to let the world go by, To know no gain or loss, My sin - ful self my on - ly shame, My glo - ry all the cross.

O Lord, We Give Our Hearts To Thee 169

Harry Presley

As often as ye eat this bread and drink this cup,
ye do show the Lord's death till He come . . . 1 Cor. 11:26

R. J. Stevens

1. O Lord, we give our hearts to Thee, To do Thy will we humbly seek To- geth- er in Thy mem- o- ry, Up- on the first day of the week.

2. Lord, con- se- crate this bread we break Thy bo- dy of- fered on the tree- As we by faith Thy bo- dy take, And eat com- mun- ing now with Thee.

3. Bless Thou this cup, O pre- cious Vine, Thy blood to wash our sins a- way. Lord, wilt Thou grace this feast di- vine, And drink a- new with us to- day.

CHORUS

O, Lord, that we might all dis- cern By faith Thy death to ev- er see, And speak to all of Thy re- turn, In our re- mem- brance, Lord, of Thee.

170 In Gethsemane Alone

My soul is exceeding sorrowful, even unto death: tarry ye here, and watch with Me.
Matt. 26:38

B♭-4-SOL
S. E. R.

G-1, L-4
S. E. Reed

1. Oh, what won-drous love I see Free - ly shown for you and me,
2. "Tar - ry here," He told the three, "Tar - ry here and watch for Me;"
3. Long in an-guish deep was He, Weep-ing there for you and me,

By the One who did a - tone! Just to show His match-less grace,
But they heard no bit - ter moan; For the three dis - ci - ples slept
For our sin to Him was known; We should love Him ev - er - more

rit.

Je - sus suf-fered for the race,
While my lov - ing Sav - ior wept In Geth-sem - a - ne, a - lone.
For the an - guish that He bore

REFRAIN

Oh, what love, match-less love, Oh, what love . . . . .
Oh, what love, match-less love, Oh, what

. . . . for me was shown! His for - ev - er I will be
love

For the love He gave to me, When He suf-fered all a - lone.

The Lord's Supper 171

A♭-4-MI
T. S. T.

*Take, eat: this is My body . . . This cup is the new testament
in My blood: this do ye . . . in remembrance of Me.* 1 Cor. 11:24,25

L-1
Tillit S. Teddlie

1. When we meet in sweet com-mun-ion Where the feast di - vine is spread;
2. "God so loved" what wondrous measure! Loved and gave the best of heav'n;
3. Feast di - vine, all else sur-pass-ing, Pre-cious blood for you and me;

Hearts are brought in clos - er un - ion While par - tak - ing of the bread.
Bought us with that match-less treas-ure, Yea, for us His life was giv'n.
While we sup, Christ gen - tly whis - pers:"Do this in my mem-o - ry."

D. S. —While we feast Christ gen - tly whis - pers:"Do this in my mem-o - ry."

CHORUS

Pre-cious feast, all else sur-pass-ing, Wondrous love for you and me;

172 Precious Communion

Db-4-SOL
Claude E. Worley

And upon the first day of the week when the disciples came together to break bread... Acts 20:7

L-1
**R. J. Stevens and
Paula Stevens Ladd**

1. Pre - cious Com- mun- ion: The feast of our dear Lord, Shows
2. Pre - cious Com- mun- ion: Each first day of the week, The
3. Pre - cious Com- mun- ion: We all re - mem - ber Him Who

forth the sac - ri - fice He made; His bo - dy and His blood.
bread and cup bring to our mind The fel - low - ship we keep.
gave His life up - on the cross, Re - deem - ing us from sin.

CHORUS

In this com - mun - ion, We hon - or Christ as King, And

wor - ship Him as Lord of lords Un - til He comes a - gain.

In True Communion

173

G-4-SOL
L-1
D. O. & R. J. S.

Dusty Owens
Arr. M. Garrett & R. J. Stevens

The cup . . . is it not the communion of the blood of Christ?
The bread . . . the body of Christ? 1 Cor. 10:16

1. We ga-ther now on this Lord's Day, To eat the bread and drink the cup; Re-mem-ber-ing the life He gave, In true com-mun-ion now we sup. Thank you, Lord, you died for me; Help me, Lord, to be like Thee.

2. We hear by faith the plead-ing Son; "Oh Fa-ther pass this cup from me, Tho' not my will but Thine be done;" That night in Gar-den's ag-o-ny. Bless us, Lord, as oft we show Sin-cere faith from here be-low.

3. We share His bo-dy and His blood, With qui-et heart our mind dis-cerns The Christ whose side flowed crim-son flood, His death we show 'til He re-turns. Lord, be with us in this place; Keep us safe-ly in Thy grace.

174 Christ Arose

C-4-SOL
R. L., 1874

C-4, C-8
Robert Lowry

Ye seek Jesus, which was crucified. He is not here: for He is risen . . . Matt. 28:5,6

Slowly

1. Low in the grave He lay — Je-sus, my Sav-ior! Wait-ing the
2. Vain-ly they watch His bed — Je-sus, my Sav-ior! Vain-ly they
3. Death can-not keep his prey — Je-sus, my Sav-ior! He tore the

com-ing day —
seal the dead — Je-sus, my Lord! Up from the grave He a-
bars a-way —

CHORUS *Quickly*

rose   With a might-y tri-umph o'er His foes; . . . . .
He a-rose   He a-

. . . . He a-rose a Vic-tor from the dark do-main, And He
rose,

lives for-ev-er with His saints to reign: He a-rose! . . . .
He a-

... He a - rose! Hal - le - lu - jah! Christ a - rose!
rose! He a - rose!

The Breaking Of Bread 175

And upon the first day of the week, when the disciples
came together to break bread . . . Acts 20:7

Eb-4-MI
Ellis Crum

L-1
William M. Sherwin

1. Dear Lord, we break the bread, In mem - o - ry, Of that great
2. Bless Thou the cup, dear Lord, To us this day, May we with
3. Our Sav - ior now doth reign, In heav'n a - bove, Death's pow'r He

sac - ri - fice on Cal - va - ry; This we do each Lord's day
hearts pre - pared His Word o - bey; We now His death pro - claim,
o - ver came, such match - less love; To heav'n He did as - cend,

As Christ hast said, Bless all dis - ci - ples now who break the bread.
In His own way, Un - til He comes a - gain, We keep this day.
There He's en - throned, He is our dear - est friend, For us a - toned.

176 In The Glory Of His Cross

God forbid that I should glory, save in the cross of our Lord . . . Gal. 6:14

Bb-4-MI
Don Alexander

C-17, L-1
R. J. Stevens

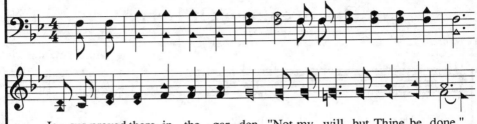

1. On a hill out-side the cit-y, God the Fa-ther gave His Son;
2. Pre-cious blood of Je-sus flowed there To re-deem my soul from sin;
3. Walk-ing dai-ly with my Sav-ior As He goes out-side the gate;
4. Christ is com-ing in His glo-ry, Ev-'ry eye will plain-ly see;

Je-sus prayed there in the gar-den, "Not my will but Thine be done."
Je-sus laid down His own bod-y, Then He took it up a-gain.
Dai-ly trust-ing, al-ways pray-ing, As I la-bor here and wait.
What a day for those who serve Him! With the Lord we'll ev-er be.

With His blood He en-tered glo-ry, Now He hears my ev-'ry prayer;
For it pleased the Lord to bruise Him, So that He could take my place;
Grant me love to share the gos-pel With the sin-ful who are lost;
In e-ter-nal hab-i-ta-tions, 'Round the Fa-ther's throne a-bove,

I will glo-ry, all my glo-ry, In the glo-ry of His care.
I will glo-ry, all my glo-ry, In the glo-ry of His grace.
I will glo-ry, all my glo-ry, In the glo-ry of His cross.
We will glo-ry, all our glo-ry, In the glo-ry of His love.

Upon The First Day Of The Week 177

Upon the first day of the week . . . the disciples came together to break bread.
Acts 20:7

Bb-4-SOL
J. H. Childress

L-1, W-5
B. M. Taylor

Slow

1. Up-on the first day of the week, Our Sav-ior came forth from the
2. Up-on the first day of the week, Dis-ci-ples met to break the
3. Up-on the first day of the week, Let each of us lay by in
4. Up-on this day "be-lov-ed" John, Saw Christ, and heard His trum-pet

grave, He died, was bur-ied, then a-rose, To reign, to tri-umph,
bread, And drink the cup in mem-o-ry Of Him whose blood for
store, As blessed and pros-pered by the Lord, The King of kings whom
voice; We, too, in spir-it wor-ship Him, With pray'r and song our

CHORUS

and to save!
us was shed! Though oth-ers may for-sake the Lord, (for-sake the Lord.)
we a-dore!
hearts re-joice!

Yet, we are here Thy truth to seek; (to seek,) Thy ho-ly

rit.

pres-ence com-forts us, (dear Lord,) Up-on the first day of the week.

178 True Worship

F-4-MI
T. S. T.

They that worship Him must worship Him in spirit and in truth. John 4:24

W-5
Tillit S. Teddlie

1. Oft we come to - geth - er, Oft we sing and pray;
2. May we keep in mem - 'ry, All that Thou hast said,
3. May we all in spir - it All with one ac - cord,

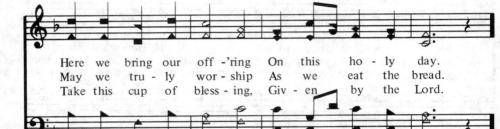

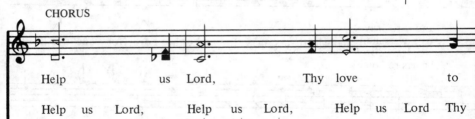

Here we bring our off - 'ring On this ho - ly day.
May we tru - ly wor - ship As we eat the bread.
Take this cup of bless - ing, Giv - en by the Lord.

CHORUS

Help us Lord, Thy love to

Help us Lord, Help us Lord, Help us Lord Thy

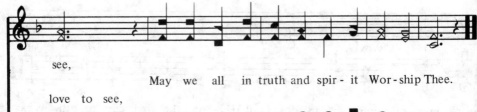

see,   May we all in truth and spir - it Wor - ship Thee.

love to see,

Lead Me To Calvary

179

Eb-4-MI

Jennie Evelyn Hussey, 1921

And when they were come to the place, which is called Calvary, there they crucified Him . . . Luke 23:33

G-1, L-1

Wm. J. Kirkpatrick, 1921

1. King of my life, I crown Thee now, Thine shall the glo-ry be;
2. Show me the tomb where Thou wast laid, Ten-der-ly mourned and wept;
3. Let me like Ma-ry, thru the gloom, Come with a gift to Thee;
4. May I be will-ing, Lord, to bear Dai-ly my cross for Thee;

Lest I for-get Thy thorn-crown'd brow, Lead me to Cal-va-ry.
An-gels in robes of light ar-rayed Guard-ed Thee whilst Thou slept.
Show to me now the emp-ty tomb, Lead me to Cal-va-ry.
E-ven Thy cup of grief to share, Thou hast borne all for me.

CHORUS

Lest I for-get Geth-sem-a-ne; Lest I for-get Thine ag-o-ny;

Lest I for-get Thy love for me, Lead me to Cal-va-ry.

180 Wonderful Story Of Love

C-2-DO
J. M. D.

L-4, W-3
J. M. Driver

Hereby perceive we the love of God, because He laid down His life for us . . .
1 John 3:16

1. Won-der-ful sto-ry of love, Tell it to me a - gain,
2. Won-der-ful sto-ry of love, Tho' you are far a - way,
3. Won-der-ful sto-ry of love, Je - sus pro-vides a rest,

Won-der-ful sto-ry of love, Wake the im-mor-tal strain;
Won-der-ful sto-ry of love, Still He doth call to - day,
Won-der-ful sto-ry of love, For all the pure and blest;

An-gels with rap-ture an-nounce it, Shep-herds with won-der re - ceive it;
Call-ing from Cal - va - ry's moun-tain, Down from the crys - tal bright foun-tain,
Rest in those man-sions a - bove us With those who've gone on be - fore us,

Sin - ner, O won't you be - lieve it?
E'en from the dawn of cre - a - tion, Won-der-ful sto-ry of love.
Sing-ing the rap - tur - ous cho - rus,

Won - der - ful, Won - der - ful,
Won - der - ful sto - ry of love, Won - der - ful sto - ry of love,

Won - der - ful,
Won - der - ful sto - ry of love, Won - der - ful sto - ry of love.

In Memory Of The Savior's Love   181

For as often as ye eat this bread and drink this cup,
ye do show the Lord's death till He come. 1 Cor. 11:26

F-4-DO
Thos. Cotterill, 1805   L-1
Este's Psalter, 1592

1. In mem - 'ry of the Sav - ior's love We keep the sa - cred feast,
2. By faith we take the bread of life With which our souls are fed,
3. Be - neath His ban - ner thus we sing The won - ders of His love;

Where ev - 'ry hum - ble, con - trite heart Is made a wel - come guest.
The cup in to - ken of His blood That was for sin - ners shed.
And here an - tic - i - pate by faith The heav'n - ly feast a - bove.

182 I Believe In Mount Calvary

And when they were come to the place, which is called Calvary, there they crucified Him . . .

Bb-3-SOL

F-1, T-1

William J. Gaither, Gloria Gaither, Dale Oldham

Luke 23:33

William J. Gaither

1. There are things as we trav - el this earth's shift-ing sands That trans-
2. I be - lieve that the Christ who was slain on that cross Has the
3. I be - lieve that this life with its great mys-ter - ies Sure - ly

cend all the rea - son of man; But the things that mat - ter
pow - er to change lives to - day; For He changed me com-plete-ly,
some-day will come to an end; But faith will con - quer

the most in this world, They can nev - er be held in our hand.
a new life is mine, That is why by the cross I will stay.
the dark - ness and death And will lead me at last to my friend.

CHORUS

I be - lieve in a hill called Mount Cal-v'ry, I'll be - lieve what-

ev - er the cost; And when time has sur - ren - dered and

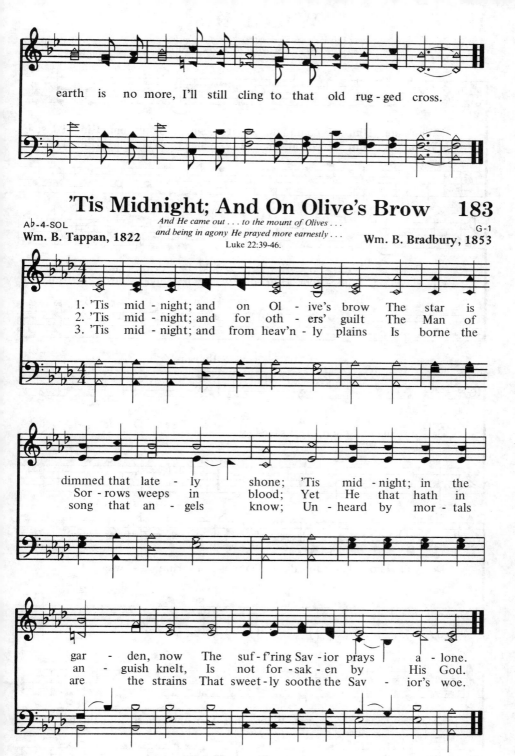

earth is no more, I'll still cling to that old rug-ged cross.

'Tis Midnight; And On Olive's Brow 183

Ab-4-SOL
Wm. B. Tappan, 1822

And He came out . . . to the mount of Olives . . .
and being in agony He prayed more earnestly . . .
Luke 22:39-46.

G-1
Wm. B. Bradbury, 1853

1. 'Tis mid-night; and on Ol-ive's brow The star is
2. 'Tis mid-night; and for oth-ers' guilt The Man of
3. 'Tis mid-night; and from heav'n-ly plains Is borne the

dimmed that late-ly shone; 'Tis mid-night; in the
Sor-rows weeps in blood; Yet He that hath in
song that an-gels know; Un-heard by mor-tals

gar-den, now The suf-f'ring Sav-ior prays a-lone.
an-guish knelt, Is not for-sak-en by His God.
are the strains That sweet-ly soothe the Sav-ior's woe.

184 Without Him

F-3-SOL
Mylon R. LeFevre

C -10, T -1
Mylon R. LeFevre

At that time ye were without Christ . . . having
no hope, and without God in the world. Eph. 2:12

1. With - out Him I could do noth - ing, With - out Him I'd sure-
2. With - out Him I would be dy - ing, With - out Him I'd be

ly fail; With - out Him I would be drift - ing Like a
en - slaved; With - out Him life would be hope - less, But with

Refrain

ship with - out a sail.
Je - sus, thank God, I'm saved.
Je - sus, O Je - sus!

Do you know Him to - day? Do not turn Him a - way. O Je -

sus, O Je - sus, With - out Him, how lost I would be.

Jesus Is Lord Of All

185

F-2-MI

C-6, T-1

But for us there is but...One Lord Jesus Christ,
by Whom are all things, and we by Him. 1 Cor. 8:6

Gloria & William Gaither

William J. Gaither

1. All my to-mor-rows, all my past – Je-sus is Lord of
2. All of my con-flicts, all my thoughts– Je-sus is Lord of
3. All of my long-ings, all my dreams– Je-sus is Lord of

all.   I've quit my strug-gles, con-tent-ment at last!
all.   His love wins the bat-tles I could not have fought;
all.   All of my fail-ures His pow-er re-deems;

CHORUS

Je-sus is Lord of all.
Je-sus is Lord of all.   King of kings, Lord of lords,
Je-sus is Lord of all.

Je-sus is Lord of all;   All my pos-ses-sions and

all my life, Je-sus is Lord of all.

186 I Stand Amazed

Ab-4-SOL
C. H. G.

Christ also hath loved us, and hath given Himself for us an offering and a sacrifice . . .
Eph. 5:2

L-1, L-4
Chas H. Gabriel, 1905

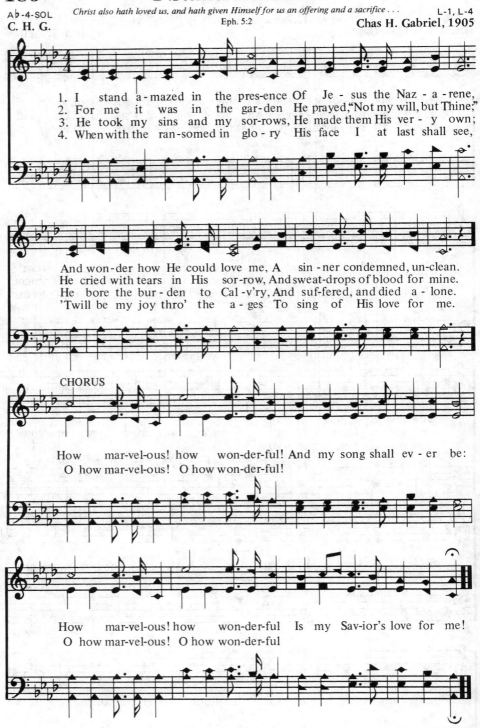

1. I stand a-mazed in the pres-ence Of Je - sus the Naz - a -rene,
2. For me it was in the gar-den He prayed,"Not my will, but Thine;"
3. He took my sins and my sor-rows, He made them His ver - y own;
4. When with the ran-somed in glo - ry His face I at last shall see,

And won-der how He could love me, A sin -ner condemned, un-clean.
He cried with tears in His sor-row, And sweat-drops of blood for mine.
He bore the bur - den to Cal -v'ry, And suf-fered, and died a - lone.
'Twill be my joy thro' the a - ges To sing of His love for me.

CHORUS

How mar-vel-ous! how won-der-ful! And my song shall ev - er be:
O how mar-vel-ous! O how won-der-ful!

How mar-vel-ous! how won-der-ful Is my Sav-ior's love for me!
O how mar-vel-ous! O how won-der-ful

Lord, Make Calvary Real To Me

187

F-4-DO
M. D.

But we see Jesus, Who was made a little lower than the angels for the suffering of death . . . Heb. 2:9

C-4, L-1
Merrill Dunlop

1. Show me the cross of Cal-va-ry, O-pen my eyes to see
2. Show me the cross of Cal-va-ry, O-pen my ears to Thy plea:
3. Low at the cross of Cal-va-ry, Bowed is my heart as I see

Thy dy-ing form in ag-o-ny—
"Fa-ther, for-give them!"—can it be? Lord, make it real to
Grace that can save e-ter-nal-ly—

CHORUS *Faster*

me. Lord, make Cal-va-ry real to me! Je-sus,

dy-ing in ag-o-ny, Thy great sac-ri-fice

let me see: Lord, make Cal-va-ry real to me!

188
There Stands A Rock

G-4-MI

Thou art my Rock and my fortress. Psa. 71:3

C-9

S. S. Journal

T. C. O'Kane

1. There stands a Rock on shores of time, That rears to
2. That Rock's a cross, its arms out - spread, Ce - les - tial
3. That Rock's a tow'r, whose loft - y height, Il - lumed with

heav'n its head sub - lime; That Rock is cleft, and
glo - ry bathes its head; To its firm base my
heav'n's un - cloud - ed light, Opes wide its gates be -

they are blest Who find with - in this cleft a rest.
all I bring, And to the cross of A - ges cling.
neath the dome, Where saints find rest with Christ at home.

CHORUS

Some build their hopes on the ev - er - drift - ing sand, Some on their

fame or their treas - ure or their land; Mine's on the Rock that for-

ev - er shall stand, Je - sus, the "Rock of A - ges."

When I Survey The Wondrous Cross   189

What things were gain to me, those I counted loss for Christ. Phil. 3:7

F-2-DO

Isaac Watts, 1707

L-1

Gregorian. Arr. L. Mason, 1824

1. When I sur - vey the won - drous cross On which the
2. For - bid it, Lord, that I should boast, Save in the
3. See, from His head, His hands, His feet, Sor - row and
4. Were the whole realm of na - ture mine, That were a

Prince of glo - ry died, My rich - est gain I
death of Christ, my Lord; All the vain things that
love flow min - gled down; Did e'er such love and
pres - ent far too small; Love so a - maz - ing,

count but loss And pour con - tempt on all my pride.
charm me most I sac - ri - fice them to His blood.
sor - row meet, Or thorns com - pose so rich a crown?
so di - vine, De - mands my soul, my life, my all.

190 We're Marching To Zion

Come to Zion with songs in everlasting joy . . . Isa. 35:10

G-2-DO
Isaac Watts, 1707

U-1, W-1
Robert Lowry, 1867

1. Come, we that love the Lord, And let our joys be known, Join
2. Let those re-fuse to sing Who nev-er knew our God; But
3. Then let our songs a-bound, And ev-'ry tear be dry; We're

in a song with sweet ac-cord, Join in a song with sweet ac-cord,
chil-dren of the heav'n-ly King, But chil-dren of the heav'n-ly King,
march-ing thru Im-man-uel's ground, We're marching thru Im-man-uel's ground,

And thus sur - round the throne, And thus sur-round the throne.
May speak their joys a-broad, May speak their joys a-broad.
To fair - er worlds on high, To fair - er worlds on high.

(1) And thus sur-round the throne, And thus sur-round the throne.

CHORUS

We're march - ing to Zi - on, beau-ti-ful, beau-ti-ful Zi - on; We're
We're march-ing on to Zi - on,

march-ing up-ward to Zi - on, The beau-ti-ful cit-y of God.
Zi - on, Zi - on,

Heaven Holds All To Me

191

But now they desire a better country, that is, an heavenly. Heb. 11:16

Ab-2-MI
T. S. T.

H-2, R-3
Tillit S. Teddlie

1. Earth holds no treas-ures but per-ish with us-ing, How-ev-er
2. Out on the hills of that won-der-ful coun-try, Hap-py, con-
3. Why should I long for the world and its sor-rows, When in that

pre-cious they be; Yet there's a coun-try to which I am
tent-ed and free, An-gels are wait-ing and watch-ing my
home o'er the sea Mil-lions are sing-ing the won-der-ful

CHORUS

go-ing, Heav-en holds all to me.
com-ing, Heav-en holds all to me. Heav-en holds all to
sto-ry? Heav-en holds all to me.

p

me, Bright-er its glo-ry will be; Joy with-out
to me,

mf *rit.*

meas-ure will be my treas-ure, Heav-en holds all to me.

192 Won't It Be Wonderful There?

Bb-2-MI
James Rowe

And there shall be no more death, neither sorrow, nor crying,
neither shall there be any more pain. Rev. 21:4

H-2
Homer F. Morris

1. When with the Sav-ior we en-ter the glo-ry-land, Won't it be wonder-ful there? End-ed the trou-bles and cares of the sto-ry-land, Won't it be won-der-ful there?
2. Walk-ing and talk-ing with Christ, the su-per-nal One, Won't it be wonder-ful there? Prais-ing, a-dor-ing the match-less e-ter-nal One, Won't it be won-der-ful there?
3. There where the tem-pest will nev-er be sweep-ing us, Won't it be wonder-ful there? Sure that for-ev-er the Lord will be keep-ing us, Won't it be won-der-ful there?

REFRAIN

Won't it be won-der-ful there, won-der-ful there, Hav-ing no bur-dens to bear? o-ver there? Joy-ous-ly sing-ing with heart-bells all

ring-ing, O won't it be won-der-ful there?
won-der-ful there?

I Am Bound For The Promised Land 193

F-4-DO

Samuel Stennett

But now they desire a better country . . . an heavenly . . .
for He hath prepared for them a city. Heb. 11:16

H-2, T-1

Arr. by R. M. McIntosh

1. On Jor - dan's storm - y banks I stand,
2. O'er all those wide ex - tend - ed plains
3. When shall I reach that hap - py place,

CHORUS— I am bound for the prom - ised land, prom - ised land,

And cast a wish - ful eye, To Ca - naan's
Shines one e - ter - nal day, There God the
And be for - ev - er blest? When shall I

I am bound for the prom - ised land; O who will

Fine

fair and hap - py land, Where my pos - ses - sions lie.
Son for - ev - er reigns And scat - ters night a - way.
see the Fa - ther's face, And in His bos - om rest?

come and go with me? I am bound for the prom - ised land.

194 When We All Get To Heaven

C-4-SOL

When He shall come to be glorified in His saints, and to be admired in all of them in that day. II Thess. 1:10

H-2, S-4

Mrs. J. G. W.

Mrs. J. G. Wilson

1. Sing the won-drous love of Je - sus, Sing His mer - cy
2. While we walk the pil - grim path - way, Clouds will o - ver -
3. Let us then be true and faith - ful, Trust-ing, serv - ing

and His grace; In the man - sions, bright and bless - ed,
spread the sky; But when trav - 'ling days are o - ver
ev - 'ry day; Just one glimpse of Him in glo - ry

CHORUS

He'll pre - pare for us a place.
Not a shad - ow, not a sigh.
Will the toils of life re - pay.
1. for us a place.

When we all get to

When we all

heav - en, What a day of re - joic - ing that will be!

What a day of re - joic - ing that will be!

When we all see Je - sus, We'll

When we all

sing and shout the vic - to - ry.
and shout the vic - to - ry.

Beyond The Sunset

195

E♭-4-SOL
Virgil P. Brock

For now is our salvation nearer than when we believed.
The night is far spent, the day is at hand. Rom. 13:11,12

H-2
Blanche K. Brock

1. Be - yond the sun - set, O bliss - ful morn - ing, When with our
2. Be - yond the sun - set, no clouds will gath - er, No storms will
3. Be - yond the sun - set, a hand will guide me To God the
4. Be - yond the sun - set, O glad re - un - ion With our dear

Sav - ior heav'n is be - gun. Earth's toil - ing end - ed, O glor - ious
threat - en, no fears an - noy; O day of glad-ness, O day un -
Fa - ther, whom I a - dore; His glor - ious pres - ence, His words of
loved ones who've gone be - fore; In that fair home-land we'll know no

dawn - ing, Be - yond the sun - set, when day is done.
end - ing, Be - yond the sun - set, e - ter - nal joy!
wel - come, Will be my por - tion on that fair shore.
part - ing; Be - yond the sun - set for ev - er - more. A - men.

196   How Beautiful Heaven Must Be

G-2-SOL   H-2
A. S. Bridgewater   A. P. Bland

And there shall be no more death, neither sorrow, nor crying . . .
and the Lamb is the light thereof. Rev. 21:4,23

1. We read of a place that's called heav-en, It's made for the
2. In heav-en, no droop-ing nor pin-ing, No wish-ing for
3. The an-gels so sweet-ly are sing-ing, Up there by the

pure and the free; These truths in God's word He has giv - en, How
else-where to be; God's light is for - ev - er there shin - ing, How
beau - ti - ful sea; The song of re - demp-tion is ring - ing, How

CHORUS

beau - ti - ful heav - en must be.
beau - ti - ful heav - en must be.   How beau - ti - ful heav - en must
beau - ti - ful heav - en must be.

be,   Sweet home of the hap - py and free; Fair ha - ven of
must be,

rest for the wea - ry, How beau - ti - ful heav - en must be.

Beautiful Isle Of Somewhere

197

A-2-MI

Jessie B. Pounds

And on either side of the river, was there the tree of life . . .
and their shall be no night there. Rev. 22:2,5

H-2

J. S. Fearis

1. Some-where the sun is shin-ing, Somewhere the song-birds dwell;
2. Some-where the day is long-er, Somewhere the task is done;
3. Some-where the load is lift-ed, Close by an o-pen gate;

Hush then, thy sad re-pin-ing, God lives, and all is
Some-where the heart is strong-er, Some-where the crown is
Some-where the clouds are rift-ed, Some-where the an-gels

CHORUS

well.
won.
wait.

Some - where, Some - where,
Some-where, beau-ti-ful, beau-ti-ful Isle,

Beau-ti-ful Isle of Some-where! Land of the true,

where we live a-new, Beau-ti-ful Isle of Some-where!

198 An Empty Mansion

Eb-2-DO

In My Father's house are many mansions . . . I go to prepare a place for you.

H-2, R-3

Mrs. J. B. Karnes

John 14:2

C. A. Luttrell

1. Here I la-bor and toil as I look for a home, Just an
2. Ev-er thank-ful am I that my Sav-ior and Lord Prom-ised
3. When my la-bor and toil-ing have end-ed be-low And my

hum-ble a-bode a-mong men, While in heav-en a man-sion
un-to the wea-ry sweet rest; Noth-ing more could I ask than
hands shall lie fold-ed in rest, I'll ex-change this old home for

is wait-ing for me And a gen-tle voice plead-ing "come in."
a man-sion a-bove, There to live with the saved and the blest.
a man-sion up there And in-vite the arch-an-gel as guest.

CHORUS

There's a man-sion now emp-ty, just wait-ing for me, At the

end of life's trou-ble-some way, And I know that the Sav-ior

will wel-come me there Near the door of that man-sion some day.

Where The Roses Never Fade 199

F-4-MI
E. J. & J.

The tree of life . . . yielded her fruit every month:
and the leaves of the tree were for the healing of the nations. Rev. 22:2

H-2, R-3
Elsie, Jack & Jim

1. I am go-ing to a cit-y Where the streets with gold are laid,
2. In this world we have our trou-bles, Sa-tan's snares we must e-vade;
3. Saved ones gone to be with Je-sus, In their robes of white ar-rayed,

Fine

Where the tree of life is bloom-ing, And the ros-es nev-er fade.
We'll be free from all temp-ta-tions Where the ros-es nev-er fade.
Now are wait-ing for my com-ing Where the ros-es nev-er fade.

D. S. – I am go-ing to a cit-y Where the ros-es nev-er fade.

D. S.

Here they bloom but for a sea-son, Soon their beau-ty is de-cayed;

200 In That Home Of The Soul

A♭-4-SOL
J. W. G.

In Thy presence is fulness of joy; at Thy right hand there are pleasures for evermore.
Psa. 16:11

H-2
Jas. W. Gaines

1. Soon the toils of life will cease, Then no sor-row we shall
2. There the Sav-ior we shall see, And His glo-ry ev-er
3. While the a-ges on-ward roll, 'Round the shin-ing throne we'll

know, In that home of the soul; There we'll
share, In that home of the soul; Re-u-
sing, With the

dwell in joy and peace, Robed in gar-ments white as snow,
nit-ed we shall be, With the ran-somed o-ver there,
an-gels we'll ex-tol, Christ who was our Lord, and King,

In that home of the soul. Bless-ed
In that home

REFRAIN

thought, there to dwell, In that home
Bless - ed tho't, ev - er dwell, In that home,

of the soul; End - less praise we shall
of the soul; End - less praise

swell, In that home of the soul.
glad - ly swell, In that home of the soul.

A Charge To Keep I Have 201

C-3-SOL
Walk worthy of the vocation wherewith ye are called. Eph. 4:1
C-16, L-6
Charles Wesley, 1762
Lowell Mason, 1832

1. A charge to keep I have, A God to glo - ri - fy;
2. To serve the pres - ent age, My call - ing to ful - fill—
3. Help me to watch and pray, And on Thy - self re - ly,

A nev - er - dy - ing soul to save, And fit it for the sky.
O may it all my pow'rs en - gage To do my Mas - ter's will!
As - sured if I my trust be - tray, I shall for ev - er die.

202 Beyond This Land Of Parting

G-4-SOL

H-2

Mrs. M. B. C. Slade

A. B. Everett

And the city had no need of the sun . . . for the glory of God did lighten it . . . Rev. 21:23

1. Be - yond this land of part - ing, los - ing and leav - ing, Far be-
2. Be - yond this land of toil - ing, sow - ing and reap - ing, Far be-
3. Be - yond this land of wait - ing, seek - ing and sigh - ing, Far be-

yond the loss - es, dark - en - ing this, And far be - yond the tak - ing
yond the shad - ows dark - en - ing this, And far be - yond the sigh - ing,
yond the sor - rows dark - en - ing this, And far be - yond the pain and

REFRAIN

and the be - reav - ing Lies the sum - mer - land of bliss. Land be - yond,
moan - ing and weeping, Lies the sum - mer - land of bliss. Land be - yond,
sick - ness and dy - ing, Lies the sum - mer - land of bliss.

so fair and bright! Land be - yond, where is no night! Sum - mer-
so fair and bright! Land be - yond, where is no night!

land, God is its Light, O hap - py sum - mer - land of bliss!
Sum - mer - land,

Above The Bright Blue

A-2-MI

C. E. P., Alt.

H-2

Then we which are alive . . . shall be caught up together with them in the clouds,
to meet the Lord in the air . . . I Thess. 4:17

Chas. Edw. Pollock

1. There's a beau-ti-ful place called heav-en, It is hid-den a-
2. This land of sweet rest a-waits us, Some day it will
3. We know not when He shall call us, Wheth-er soon, the glad

bove the bright blue, Where the good, who from earth-ties are riv-en,
break on our view, 'Tis prom-ised by Christ the Re-deem-er,
sum-mons shall be, But we know, when we pass o'er the riv-er,

CHORUS

Live and love an e-ter-ni-ty thru.
To His fol-low-ers faith-ful and true.   A-bove the bright blue, the
The glo-ry of Je-sus we'll see.

beau-ti-ful blue, Je-sus is wait-ing for me and for you;

Heav-en is there, not far from our sight, Beau-ti-ful cit-y of light.

204 Never Grow Old

Eb-2-DO
J. C. M.

And God shall wipe away all tears from their eyes;
and there shall be no more death . . . Rev. 21:4

H-2
Jas. C. Moore

1. I have heard of a land on the far a-way strand,'Tis a
2. In that beau-ti-ful home where we'll nev-er-more roam, We shall
3. When our work here is done and the life-crown is won, And our

beau-ti-ful home of the soul; Built by Je-sus on high,
be in the sweet by and by; Hap-py praise to the King
trou-bles and tri-als are o'er; All our sor-row will end,

where we nev-er shall die, 'Tis a land where we nev-er grow
thru e-ter-ni-ty sing, 'Tis a land where we nev-er shall
and our voic-es will blend, With the loved ones who've gone on be-

CHORUS

old. Nev-er grow old, Nev-er grow old, In a
die. where we'll
fore.

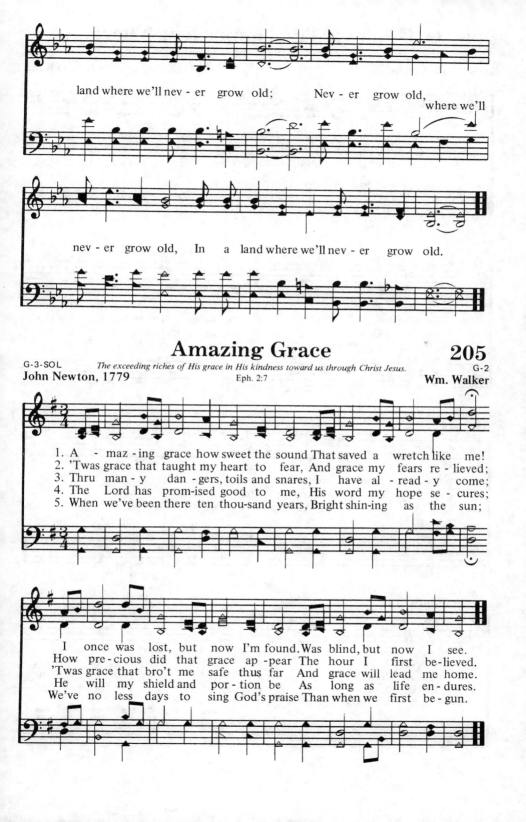

land where we'll nev - er grow old; Nev - er grow old, where we'll

nev - er grow old, In a land where we'll nev - er grow old.

Amazing Grace

205

G-3-SOL

The exceeding riches of His grace in His kindness toward us through Christ Jesus.

G-2

John Newton, 1779

Eph. 2:7

Wm. Walker

1. A - maz - ing grace how sweet the sound That saved a wretch like me!
2. 'Twas grace that taught my heart to fear, And grace my fears re - lieved;
3. Thru man - y dan - gers, toils and snares, I have al - read - y come;
4. The Lord has prom-ised good to me, His word my hope se - cures;
5. When we've been there ten thou-sand years, Bright shin-ing as the sun;

I once was lost, but now I'm found, Was blind, but now I see.
How pre - cious did that grace ap -pear The hour I first be - lieved.
'Twas grace that bro't me safe thus far And grace will lead me home.
He will my shield and por - tion be As long as life en - dures.
We've no less days to sing God's praise Than when we first be - gun.

206 O Think Of The Home Over There

They desire a better country, that is, a heavenly . . .
for He hath prepared for them a city. Heb. 11:16

A-4-SOL

D. W. C. Huntington

H-2

T. C. O'Kane

1. O think of a home o - ver there, By the side of the riv-
2. O think of the saints o - ver there, Who be - fore us the jour-
3. I'll soon be at home o - ver there, For the end of my jour-

er of light, Where the saints all im - mor - tal and
ney have trod, Of the songs that they breathe on the
ney I see; o - ver there, All the saints and the an - gels up

fair Are robed in their gar-ments of white.
air, In their home in the pal - ace of God.
there Are watch-ing and wait-ing for me.
o - ver there.

CHORUS

O - ver there, o - ver there, O think of the
O - ver there, o - ver there, O think of the
O - ver there, o - ver there, I'll soon be at
O - ver there, o - ver there,

home o - ver there,   O - ver there,
saints o - ver there,   O - ver there,
home o - ver there,   O - ver there,
            o - ver there,   O - ver there,

o - ver there, o - ver there, O think of a home o - ver there.
o - ver there, o - ver there, O think of the saints o - ver there.
o - ver there, o - ver there, I'll soon be at home o - ver there.

My Lord, My Truth, My Way   207

I Am the Way, the Truth and the Life . . . John 14:6

C-3-SOL

Charles Wesley

D-1

George Kingsley

1. My Lord, my Truth, my Way, My sure, un - err - ing Light, On
2. My Wis - dom and my Guide, My Coun - sel - or Thou art; O
3. Teach me the hap - py art In all things to de - pend On

Thee my fee - ble steps I stay, Which Thou wilt guide a - right.
nev - er let me leave Thy side, Or from Thy paths de - part!
Thee: O nev - er, Lord, de - part, But love me to the end!

208 Sing To Me Of Heaven

Every several gate was of one pearl: and the street of the city was pure gold . . .
Rev. 21:21

G-4-SOL
Ada Powell

H-2, S-4
B. B. Beall

1. Sing to me of heav-en, sing that song of peace, From the toils that
2. Sing to me of heav-en, as I walk a-lone, Dreaming of the
3. Sing to me of heav-en, ten-der-ly and low, Till the shad-ows

bind me it will bring re-lease; Bur-dens will be lift-ed that are
com-rades that so long have gone; In a fair-er re-gion, 'mong the
o'er me rise and swift-ly go; When my heart is wea-ry, when the

press-ing so, Show-ers of great bless-ing o'er my heart will flow.
an-gel throng, They are hap-py as they sing that old, sweet song.
day is long, Sing to me of heav-en, sing that old, sweet song.

REFRAIN

Sing to me of heav-en, let me fond-ly
Sing to me of heav-en, let me fond-ly

dream Of its gold-en glo-ry, of its pearl-y gleam;
dream Of its gold-en glo-ry, of its pearl-y gleam;

Sing to me when shad-ows of the eve - ning fall,
Sing to me when shad-ows of the eve-ning fall,

Sing to me of heav - en, Sweet-est song of all.
Sing to me of heav - en, Sing the sweet-est song of all.

Christ For The World We Sing 209

G-3-SOL

God was in Christ, reconciling the world unto Himself . . .

S-4, S-5

Samuel Wolcott

and hath committed unto us the word of reconciliation. II Cor. 5:19

Felice De Giardini

1. Christ for the world! we sing; The world to Christ we bring,
2. Christ for the world! we sing; The world to Christ we bring,
3. Christ for the world! we sing; The world to Christ we bring,

With lov - ing zeal; The poor and them that mourn, The faint and
With fer - vent prayer; The way - ward and the lost, By rest - less
With one ac - cord, With us the work to share, With us re -

o - ver-borne, Sin - sick and sor - row-worn, Whom Christ doth heal.
pas -sions tossed, Re - deemed at count-less cost From dark de - spair.
proach to dare, With us the cross to bear, For Christ our Lord.

210

Eb-4-SOL
W. W. S.

C-15, H-2

Alone At Eve

For our citizenship is in heaven: from whence also
we look for the Savior, the Lord Jesus Christ. Phil. 3:20

Will W. Slater

1. Walk-ing a-lone at eve and view-ing the skies a-far,
2. Sit-ting a-lone at eve and dream-ing the hours a-way,
3. Clos-ing my eyes at eve and think-ing of heav-en's grace,

Bid-ding the dark-ness come to wel-come each sil-ver star;
Watch-ing the shad-ows fall-ing now at the close of day;
Long-ing to see my Lord, yes, meet-ing Him face to face;

I have a great de-light in the won-der-ful scenes a-bove,
God in His mer-cy comes with His word He is draw-ing near,
Trust-ing Him as my all where-so-ev-er my foot-steps roam,

D.S.- Rest for a wea-ry soul once re-deemed by the Sav-ior's love,

Fine

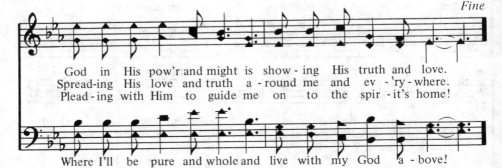

God in His pow'r and might is show-ing His truth and love.
Spread-ing His love and truth a-round me and ev-'ry-where.
Plead-ing with Him to guide me on to the spir-it's home!

Where I'll be pure and whole and live with my God a-bove!

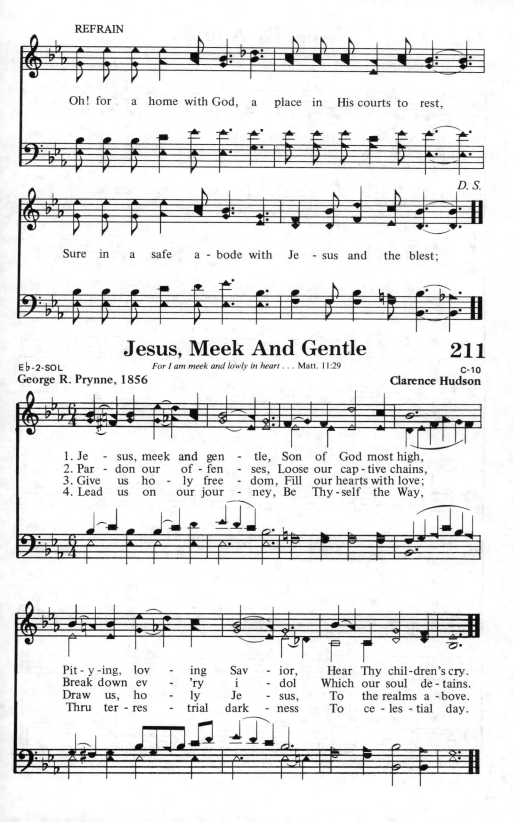

REFRAIN

Oh! for a home with God, a place in His courts to rest,

D. S.

Sure in a safe a - bode with Je - sus and the blest;

Jesus, Meek And Gentle

211

For I am meek and lowly in heart . . . Matt. 11:29

E♭-2-SOL

C-10

George R. Prynne, 1856

Clarence Hudson

1. Je - sus, meek and gen - tle, Son of God most high,
2. Par - don our of - fen - ses, Loose our cap - tive chains,
3. Give us ho - ly free - dom, Fill our hearts with love;
4. Lead us on our jour - ney, Be Thy - self the Way,

Pit - y - ing, lov - ing Sav - ior, Hear Thy chil - dren's cry.
Break down ev - 'ry i - dol Which our soul de - tains.
Draw us, ho - ly Je - sus, To the realms a - bove.
Thru ter - res - trial dark - ness To ce - les - tial day.

212 Sweet By And By

G-4-DO

I go and prepare a place for you, I will come again, and receive you . . . John 14:3

H-2

S. Fillmore Bennett

Joseph P. Webster

1. There's a land that is fair-er than day, And by faith we can see it a-far; For the Sav-ior waits o-ver the way, To pre-pare us a dwell-ing place there.

2. We shall sing on that beau-ti-ful shore The me-lo-di-ous songs of the blest, And our spir-its shall sor-row no more, Not a sigh for the bless-ings of rest.

3. To our boun-ti-ful Fa-ther a-bove, We will of-fer our trib-ute of praise, For the glo-ri-ous gift of His love, And the bless-ings that hal-low our days.

REFRAIN

In the sweet by and by, We shall meet on that beau-ti-ful shore, In the sweet by and by, We shall meet on the beau-ti-ful shore.

In the sweet, In the sweet by and by,

Here We Are But Straying Pilgrims 213

G-4-DO

And confessed that they were strangers and pilgrims on the earth. Heb. 11:13

C-12, H-2

I. N. Carman

W. O. Perkins

Unison

1. Here we are but stray-ing pil-grims; Here our path is oft-en dim;
2. Here our feet are oft-en wea-ry On the hills that throng our way;
3. Here our souls are oft-en fear-ful Of the pil-grim's lurk-ing foe;

But to cheer us on our jour-ney, Still we sing this way-side hymn:
Here the tem-pest dark-ly gath-ers, But our hearts with-in us say:
But the Lord is our de-fend-er, And He tells us we may know:

CHORUS

Yon-der o-ver the roll-ing riv-er, Where the shin-ing

man-sions rise, Soon will be our home for ev-er, And the

smile of the bless-ed Giv-er Glad-dens all our long-ing eyes.

214

No Tears In Heaven

F-4-DO
R. S. A.

And God shall wipe away all tears . . . and there shall
be no more death, neither sorrow, nor crying . . . Rev. 21:4

C-15, H-2
Robert S. Arnold

1. No tears in heav-en, no sor-rows giv-en, All will be glo-ry in that land; There'll be no sad-ness, all will be glad-ness, When we shall join that hap-py band.

2. Glo-ry is wait-ing, wait-ing up yon-der, Where we shall spend an end-less day; There with our Sav-ior, we'll be for-ev-er, Where no more sor-row can dis-may.

3. Some morn-ing yon-der, we'll cease to pon-der O'er things this life has bro't to view; All will be clear-er, saved ones be dear-er, In heav'n where all will be made new.

CHORUS

No tears, in heav-en fair, no tears, no tears up there, Sor-row and

pain will all have flown; No tears, in heav-en fair,

no tears, no tears up there, No tears in heav-en will be known.

Lord, Dismiss Us In Thy Care 215

F-4-DO
J. D. Tant

*Now the God of peace be
with you all. Amen.* Rom. 15:33

C-14
Jefferson David Tant
Arr. by R. J. Stevens

1. Lord, dis-miss us in Thy care, Help us all Thy love to share.
2. Send us forth in-to the world, With the flag of truth un-furled.
3. Bless us as we leave this place, We all thank Thee for Thy grace.

Bless us now, O gra-cious Lord, Hav-ing fed up-on Thy word.
Help us now Thy light to give, That the lost with Thee might live.
Bring us back, we pray O Lord, Keep us all in one ac-cord.

216
O That Will Be Glory

Ab-2-SOL
C. H. G.

When He shall appear, we shall be like Him; for we shall see Him as He is. 1 John 3:2

H-2

Chas. H. Gabriel

1. When all my la-bors and tri-als are o'er, And I am
2. When, by the gift of His in-fi-nite grace, I am ac-
3. Friends will be there I have loved long a-go; Joy like a

safe on that beau-ti-ful shore, Just to be near the dear
cord-ed in heav-en a place, Just to be there and to
riv-er a-round me will flow; Yet just a smile from my

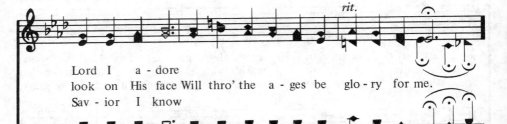

rit.

Lord I a-dore
look on His face Will thro' the a-ges be glo-ry for me.
Sav-ior I know

CHORUS

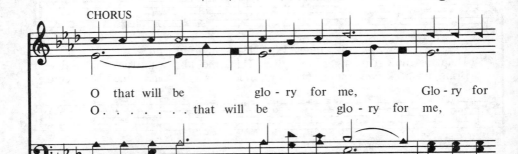

O that will be glo-ry for me, Glo-ry for
O. . . . . . . that will be glo-ry for me,

me, glo - ry for me; When by His grace I shall
Glo - ry for me, glo - ry for me; . . . . . .

look on His face, That will be glo - ry, be glo - ry for me.

Happy The Home When God Is There 217

Ab-3-MI
Henry Ware, Jr.
Alt. Bryan J. Leech

*I call to remembrance the . . . faith that is in thee, which dwelt
first in thy grandmother . . . and thy mother. II Tim. 1:5*

H-5
John B. Dykes

1. Hap - py the home when God is there And love fills ev - 'ry - one,
2. Hap - py the home where God's strong love Is start - ing to ap - pear,
3. Hap - py the home where pray'r is heard And praise is ev - 'ry - where,
4. Lord, let us in our homes a - gree This bless - ed peace to gain;

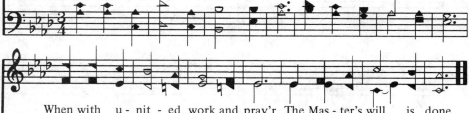

When with u - nit - ed work and pray'r The Mas - ter's will is done.
Where all the chil - dren hear His fame And par - ents hold Him dear.
Where par - ents love the sa - cred Word And its true wis - dom share.
U - nite our hearts in love to Thee, And love to all will reign.

218 Just Over In The Glory-Land

Bb-4-SOL

James W. Acuff

A great multitude . . . stood before the throne . . . saying,
Salvation to our God . . . and unto the Lamb. Rev. 7:9,10

H-2

Emmett S. Dean

1. I've a home pre-pared where the saints a-bide, Just o-ver
2. I am on my way to those man-sions fair, Just o-ver
3. With the blood-washed throng I will shout and sing, Just o-ver

in the glo-ry-land; And I long to be by my Sav-ior's
in the glo-ry-land; There to sing God's praise, and His glo-ry
in the glo-ry-land; Glad ho-san-nas to Christ, the Lord and

CHORUS

side, Just o-ver in the glo-ry-land. Just o- -
share, Just o-ver in the glo-ry-land.
King, Just o-ver in the glo-ry-land. o-ver,

- -ver in the glo-ry-land, I'll join the hap-py
o-ver yes, join

an-gel band, Just o-ver in the glo-ry-land; Just o- -
o-ver,

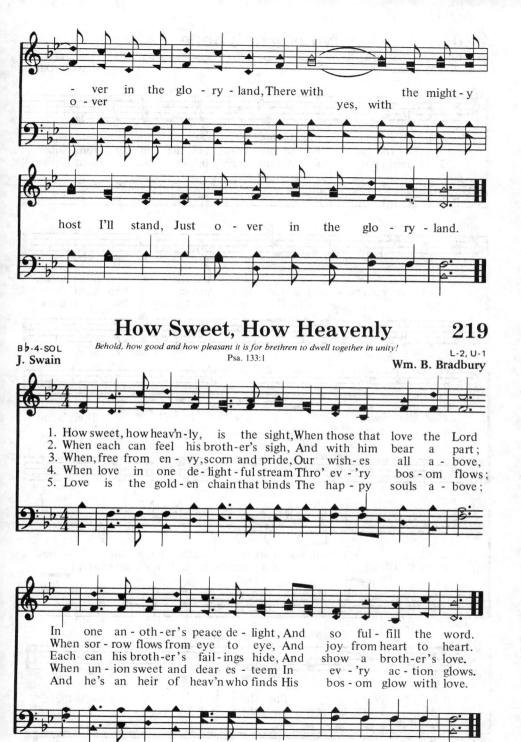

- ver in the glo - ry - land, There with the might - y
o - ver yes, with

host I'll stand, Just o - ver in the glo - ry - land.

How Sweet, How Heavenly 219

B♭-4-SOL
J. Swain
Behold, how good and how pleasant it is for brethren to dwell together in unity!
Psa. 133:1
L-2, U-1
Wm. B. Bradbury

1. How sweet, how heav'n-ly, is the sight, When those that love the Lord
2. When each can feel his broth-er's sigh, And with him bear a part;
3. When, free from en - vy, scorn and pride, Our wish-es all a - bove,
4. When love in one de - light - ful stream Thro' ev - 'ry bos - om flows;
5. Love is the gold - en chain that binds The hap - py souls a - bove;

In one an - oth - er's peace de - light, And so ful - fill the word.
When sor - row flows from eye to eye, And joy from heart to heart.
Each can his broth - er's fail - ings hide, And show a broth - er's love.
When un - ion sweet and dear es - teem In ev - 'ry ac - tion glows.
And he's an heir of heav'n who finds His bos - om glow with love.

220

No Night There

Eb-3-DO

And the city lieth foursquare . . . there shall be no night there. Rev. 21:16,25

C-15, H-2

John R. Clements

Hart P. Danks

1. In the land of fade-less day Lies the "cit - y four-square,"
2. All the gates of pearl are made, In the "cit - y four-square,"
3. There they need no sun-shine bright, In that "cit - y four-square,"

It shall nev - er pass a - way, And there is "no night there."
All the streets with gold are laid, And there is "no night there."
For the Lamb is all the light, And there is "no night there."

CHORUS *mf*

God shall "wipe a - way all tears;" There's no
God shall "wipe a - way all tears;"

death, no pain, nor fears; And they count not
There's no death, no pain, nor fears; And they count not time

time by years, For there is "no night there."
by years, by years, For there is "no night there."

The Unclouded Day

The tree of life . . . yielding her fruit every month . . . Rev. 22:2

G-4-SOL
J. K. A.

H-2
J. K. Alwood

1. O they tell me of a home far be-yond the skies, O they
2. O they tell me of a home where the Saints have gone, O they
3. O they tell me that He smiles on His chil-dren there, And His

tell me of a home far a - way; O they tell me of a home
tell me of that land far a - way, Where the tree of life
smile drives their sor-rows all a - way; And they tell me that no tears

D.S.- O they tell me of a home,
Fine

where no storm clouds rise, O they tell me of an un-cloud-ed day.
in e - ter - nal bloom Sheds its fra-grance thru the un-cloud-ed day.
ev - er come a - gain, In that love - ly land of un-cloud-ed day.

where no storm-clouds rise, O they tell me of an un-cloud-ed day.

CHORUS

D. S.

O the land of cloud-less day, O the land of an un-cloud-ed sky;

222 After The Shadows

Ab-3-MI
James Rowe

For our light affliction, which is but for a moment, worketh for us a far more exceeding and eternal weight of glory. II Cor. 5:17

A-1, C-15
Samuel W. Beazley

1. Af - ter the mid night, morn - ing will greet us; Af - ter the sad - ness, joy will ap - pear; Af - ter the temp - est, sun-light will meet us; Af - ter the jeer - ing, praise we shall hear.

2. Af - ter the bat - tle, peace will be giv - en; Af - ter the weep-ing, song there will be; Af - ter the jour - ney there will be heav - en, Bur - dens will fall and we shall be free.

3. Shad-ows and sun-shine all thru the sto - ry, Tear-drops and pleas-ure, day af - ter day; But when we reach the king-dom of glo - ry, Tri - als of earth will van - ish a - way.

CHORUS

Af - ter the shad - ows, there will be sun - shine;
Af - ter the shad - ows, there will be sun-shine;

Af - ter the frown, the soul-cheer-ing smile;
Af - ter the frown, the soul-cheer-ing

rit.

... Cling to the Sav - ior, love Him for-
smile; Cling to the Sav - ior,

ev - er; All will be well in a lit - tle while.
love Him for - ev - er;

Peace, Perfect Peace

223

Thou wilt keep him in perfect peace, whose mind is stayed on Thee. Isa. 26:3

C-4-SOL

Edward H. Bickersteth, 1875

George T. Caldbeck, 1877

C-15, P-1

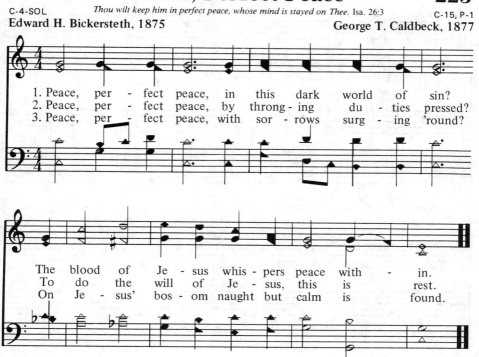

1. Peace, per - fect peace, in this dark world of sin?
2. Peace, per - fect peace, by throng - ing du - ties pressed?
3. Peace, per - fect peace, with sor - rows surg - ing 'round?

The blood of Je - sus whis - pers peace with - in.
To do the will of Je - sus, this is rest.
On Je - sus' bos - om naught but calm is found.

224 There's A Rainbow In The Cloud

This is the token of the covenant which I make between Me and you . . .
I do set My bow in the clouds . . . Gen. 9:12, 13

F-4-MI
A. H.

H-2, H-6
Alton Howard
Arr. by P. West

1. As I jour-ney here mid the toil and tears, There's a rain-bow..
2. Af-ter storm and rain, fields of gold-en grain,
3. When the storms all pass, comes a bright-er day,

.........in the cloud;   He will safe-ly lead,
                               Win-ter's cold and pain,
There's a rain-bow   in the cloud; In that Cit-y fair

I must have no fear, There's a rain-bow   in the
sum-mer's har-vest grain,
there's a crown to wear,   There's a rain-bow

CHORUS

cloud.   There's a rain-bow   that is
      in the cloud.   There's a rain-bow

shin-ing,   There's a rain-bow
      that is shin-ing,   There's a rain-bow

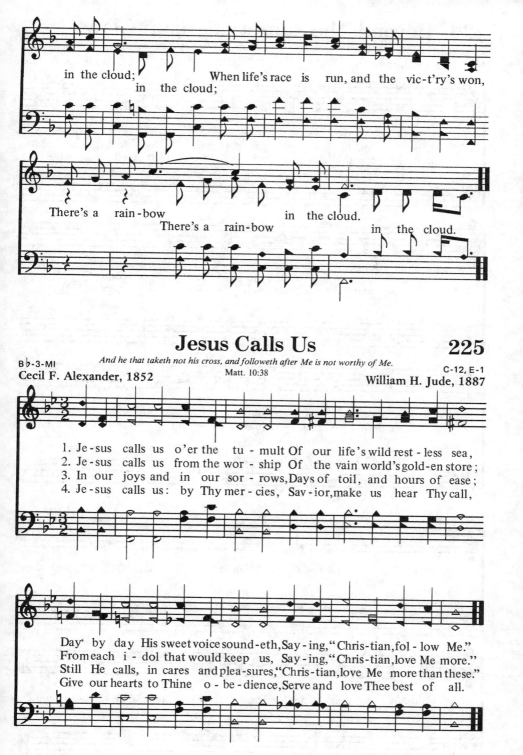

in the cloud; When life's race is run, and the vic-t'ry's won,
in the cloud;

There's a rain-bow in the cloud.
There's a rain-bow in the cloud.

Jesus Calls Us

225

B♭-3-MI

Cecil F. Alexander, 1852

And he that taketh not his cross, and followeth after Me is not worthy of Me.
Matt. 10:38

C-12, E-1

William H. Jude, 1887

1. Je-sus calls us o'er the tu-mult Of our life's wild rest-less sea,
2. Je-sus calls us from the wor-ship Of the vain world's gold-en store;
3. In our joys and in our sor-rows, Days of toil, and hours of ease;
4. Je-sus calls us: by Thy mer-cies, Sav-ior, make us hear Thy call,

Day by day His sweet voice sound-eth, Say-ing, "Chris-tian, fol-low Me."
From each i-dol that would keep us, Say-ing, "Chris-tian, love Me more."
Still He calls, in cares and plea-sures, "Chris-tian, love Me more than these."
Give our hearts to Thine o-be-dience, Serve and love Thee best of all.

226 Beyond The Sunset's Radiant Glow

Then we . . . shall be caught up . . . to meet the Lord in the air:
and so shall we ever be with the Lord. 1 Thess. 4:17

Eb-4-DO
Josephine Pollard

H-2
W. O. Perkins

1. Be - yond the sun - set's ra - diant glow   There is   a bright - er
2. Be - yond the sun - set's pur - ple rim,   Be - yond the twi - light,
3. Be - yond this des - ert, dark and drear,   The gold - en cit - y

world, I know, Where gold - en glo - ries ev - er shine,—   Be -
deep and dim, Where clouds and dark - ness nev - er come,   My
will ap - pear; And morn - ing's love - ly beams a - rise   Up -

CHORUS

yond the tho't of day's de - cline.
soul shall find its heav'n - ly home. Be - yond the sun - set's ra - diant
on my man - sion in the skies.

glow,   There is   a bright - er world, I know; Be - yond the
ra - diant glow,

sun - set I may spend De - light - ful days that nev - er end.

There Is A Habitation

227

Eb-4-DO

H-2

That great city . . . having the glory of God . . . had a wall great and high,
and had twelve gates . . . Rev. 21:10-12

L. H. Jameson

J. H. Rosecrans

1. There is a hab - i - ta - tion, Built by the liv - ing God,
2. A cit - y with foun - da - tions Firm as th'e - ter - nal throne,
3. No night is there, no sor - row, No death and no de - cay;
4. With - in its pearl - y por - tals, An - gel - ic ar - mies sing,

For all of ev - 'ry na - tion, Who seek that grand a - bode.
No wars, nor des - o - la - tions Shall ev - er move a stone.
No yes - ter - day, no mor - row—But one e - ter - nal day.
With glo - ri - fied im - mor - tals, The prais - es of its King.

CHORUS

O Zi - on, Zi - on, I long thy gates to see;
O Zi - on, love - ly Zi - on, O

O Zi - on, Zi - on, When shall I dwell in thee?
love - ly Zi - on, love - ly Zi - on,

228 The Christian's Welcome Home

C-4-SOL
C. E. P.

Then the King shall say . . . Come, ye blessed of My Father,
inherit the kingdom prepared for you . . . Matt. 25:34

H-2
Chas. Edw. Pollock

1. How sweet will be the wel - come home, (wel - come home,) When
2. When we the love - ly prom - ised land (prom-ised land) With
3. If we are faith - ful we shall gain, (safe - ly gain,) The

this short life is o'er; When pain and sor - row, grief and
spir - it eyes shall see; We'll join the ho - ly an - gel
land of prom - ised rest; Where with the Sav - ior we shall

CHORUS

care, (grief and care,) Shall trou - ble us no more. Wel - come
band, (an - gel band,) In praise, dear Lord, to Thee.
live, (we shall live,) And be for - ev - er blest.

home, sweet wel - come home, My
Wel - come home, sweet wel - come home, My

home, sweet home, Wel - come home, sweet
home, my heav'n-ly home, sweet home, Wel - come home,

wel - come home,
sweet wel-come home,
The Chris-tian's wel - come home.

No, Not One

229

F-4-MI
There is a friend that sticketh closer than a brother. Prov. 18:24
Johnson Oatman, Jr.

C-5
George C. Hugg

1. There's not a friend like the low - ly Je - sus,
   None else could heal all our soul's dis - eas - es,
2. No friend like Him is so high and ho - ly,
   And yet no friend is so meek and low - ly,
3. There's not an hour that He is not near us,
   No night so dark but His love can cheer us,

D.C.- There's not a friend like the low - ly Je - sus,

Fine CHORUS

No, not one! no, not one!
No, not one! no, not one!
Je - sus knows all a -

No, not one! no, not one!

D. C.

bout our strug-gles; He will guide till the day is done;

230 This World Is Not My Home

G-4-DO
A. E. B.

Lay not up for yourselves treasures upon earth . . .
but lay up for yourselves treasures in heaven . . . Matt. 6:19,20

H-2
Albert E. Brumley

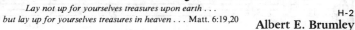

1. This world is not my home, I'm just a pass-ing thru. My
2. They're all ex-pect-ing me, and that's one thing I know, My
3. Just up in glo-ry-land we'll live e-ter-nal-ly, The

treas-ures are laid up some-where be-yond the blue; The an-gels
Sav-ior par-doned me and now I on-ward go; I know He'll
saints on ev-'ry hand are shout-ing vic-to-ry, Their songs of

beck-on me from heav-en's o-pen door,
take me thru tho' I am weak and poor, And I can't feel at home
sweet-est praise drift back from heav-en's shore,

Fine CHORUS

in this world an-y-more. O Lord, you know I have no friend like

you, If heav-en's not my home, then Lord what will I do?

The an-gels beck-on me from heav-en's o-pen door,

Soldiers Of Christ, Arise

231

G-4-DO

Charles Wesley, 1749

Be strong in the Lord . . . Put on the whole armor of God, that ye may be able to stand . . . Eph. 6:10,11

E-1, W-1

Wm. B. Bradbury

1. Sol - diers of Christ, a - rise   And put your ar - mor on;
2. Strong in the Lord of hosts   And in His might-y pow'r;
3. Stand, then, in His great might,   With all His strength en-dued;
4. Leave no un-guard-ed place,   No weak-ness of the soul;
5. That hav-ing all things done,   And all your con-flicts past,

1. a - rise, ...

1. Sol - diers of Christ, a - rise And put your ar - mor on;

Strong in the strength which God   sup - plies,
Who in the strength of   Je - sus   trusts,
But take, to arm you for   the   fight,
Take ev - 'ry vir - tue, ev - 'ry   grace,
You may o'er-come thru Christ   a - lone,

1. Strong in the strength which God sup - plies,

Strong in the strength which God sup-plies Thru His   be - lov - ed   Son.
Who in the strength of Je - sus trusts, Is more   than con - quer - or.
But take, to arm you for the fight, The pan - o - ply of   God.
Take ev - 'ry vir - tue, ev - 'ry grace, And for - ti - fy the   whole.
You may o'er-come thru Christ a - lone, And stand   en - tire at   last.

232
F-2-SOL

When All Of God's Singers Get Home

Luther G. Presley
Cho. V. O. S.

I heard a great voice of much people in heaven, saying,
Hallelujah . . . unto the Lord our God. Rev. 19:1

H-2, S-4
Virgil O. Stamps

1. What a song of de-light in that cit-y so bright Will be
2. As we sing here on earth, songs of sad-ness or mirth, 'Tis a
3. Hav-ing o-ver-come sin, "hal-le-lu-jah a-men" Will be

waft-ed 'neath heav-en's fair dome, How the ran-somed will raise
fore-taste of rap-ture to come; But our joy can't com-pare
heard in that land o'er the foam, Ev-'ry heart will be light

hap-py songs in His praise,
with the glo-ry up there, When all of God's sing-ers get home.
and each face will be bright, God's sing-ers get home.

Fine

CHORUS

When all of God's sing-ers get home, Where nev-er a sor-row
When all of God's sing-ers get home,

will come; There'll be "no place like home,"
or heart-aches will come; There'll be no place like heav-en my home,

D.S.

The Greatest Of All Is Love

233

E♭-2-SOL

And now these three remain: faith, hope and love.
But the greatest of these is love. I Cor. 13:13

M. Roy Stevens
Lanier Stevens

L-3

R. J. Stevens

1. We are walk-ing by faith and not by sight, Will-ing to serve
2. We are filled with the hope of heav-en's grace, Long-ing to see
3. We have learned to love Him with all our heart, Try-ing each day

our Lord a-right, Know-ing the will of God a-bove; That the
our Sav-ior's face, Know-ing some day when He shall come; He has
to do our part, Lov-ing our neigh-bor and our God, Thus ful-

CHORUS

great-est of all is love.
prom-ised to bear us home. The great-est of all is
fill-ing our Sav-ior's word.

love, sent down from the Fa-ther a-bove. Now a-bid-eth

faith and hope and love; But the great-est of all is love.

234

The Sands Of Time

F-4-MI

And that, knowing the time . . . for now is our salvation nearer . . .
The night is far spent, the day is at hand. Rom 13:11, 12

Anne R. Cousin

H-2

D'Urhan-Rimbault

1. The sands of time are sink - ing, The dawn of heav - en breaks;
2. O Christ, He is the foun - tain, The deep, sweet well of love;
3. The King there in His beau - ty With - out a veil is seen;

The sum - mer morn I've sighed for, The fair, sweet morn a - wakes;
The streams on earth I've tast - ed, More deep I'll drink a - bove;
It were a well-spent jour - ney, Tho' sev'n deaths lay be - tween;

Dark, dark hath been the mid - night, But day - spring is at hand,
There to an o - cean full - ness His mer - cy doth ex - pand,
The Lamb with His fair ar - my Doth on Mount Zi - on stand,

And glo - ry, glo - ry dwell - eth In Im - man - uel's land.
And glo - ry, glo - ry dwell - eth In Im - man - uel's land.
And glo - ry, glo - ry dwell - eth In Im - man - uel's land.

Immortally Arrayed

235

Eb-2-DO
Harry Presley

Earnestly desiring to be clothed upon with our house which is from heaven . . . .
II Cor. 5:2

F-4, H-2
R. J. Stevens

1. When life on earth for me is past, O Sav-ior take my
2. When I shall cease to walk life's road, Let me come home to
3. When all my la - bors are com-plete, And I can work no

hand. Lord grant that I might firm - ly stand up - on the
Thee; Take me in - to Thy blest a - bode To dwell e -
more; O Sav - ior guide my wea - ry feet Thru death to

CHORUS

gold - en strand.
ter - nal - ly.   For soon my jour - ney here must
hea - ven's door.

end, My earth - ly life must fade. Lord grant that

I might then a - scend Im - mor - tal - ly ar - rayed.

236 I Have Heard Of A Land

F-3-DO

And the street of the city was pure gold . . . there shall be no night there.

Mrs. F. A. F. White

Rev. 21:21,25

H-2

Mark M. Jones

1. I have heard of a land On a far - a - way strand, In the
2. There are ev - er - green trees That bend low in the breeze, And their
3. There's a home in that land, At the Fa - ther's right hand, There are

Bi - ble the sto - ry is told, Where cares nev - er come,
fruit - age is bright - er than gold; There the throne of God stands,
mansions whose joys are un - told; And per - en - ni - al spring,

Nev - er dark - ness nor gloom,
In that fair - est of lands, And noth - ing shall ev - er grow old.
Where the saints ev - er sing,

CHORUS

In that beau - ti - ful land, On the far a - way strand, No storms

with their blasts ev - er frown; The street, I am told, is

paved with pure gold, And the sun, it shall nev - er go down.

Let The Lower Lights Be Burning 237

Bb-3-SOL
P. P. B.
S-5

Philip P. Bliss

Let your light so shine before men, that they may see your good works . . . Matt. 5:16

1. Bright-ly beams our Fa-ther's mer-cy From the light-house ev - er-more;
2. Dark the night of sin has set-tled, Loud the an - gry bil-lows roar;
3. Trim your fee - ble lamp, my bro-ther; Some poor sea-man tem-pest tossed;

Fine

But to us He gives the keep-ing Of the lights a - long the shore.
Ea - ger eyes are watch-ing, long-ing, For the lights a - long the shore.
Try - ing now to make the har - bor, In the dark-ness may be lost.

D. S.–Some poor faint-ing, strug-gling sea - man, You may res - cue, you may save.

CHORUS

D. S.

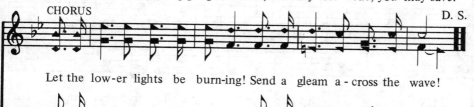

Let the low-er lights be burn-ing! Send a gleam a - cross the wave!

238   God Shall Wipe Away All Tears

F-2-MI

And God shall wipe away all tears from their eyes. Rev. 7:17

C-15, H-2

J. R. Baxter, Jr.

Wesley H. Daniel

1. When we reach that home and lay our bur-dens down,
2. When the pearl-y gates un-fold for you and me, God shall
3. When we sweet-ly sing with all that ran-somed throng,

wipe a-way all tears;   When we join the saints and
When we see the Christ who
No more part-ings come to

wear a robe and crown,
set the cap-tive free,   God shall wipe a-way all tears.
mar that hap-py song,

CHORUS

God shall wipe a-way all the tears from ev-'ry eye,

Give us joy for all our fears;   When we meet Him in that

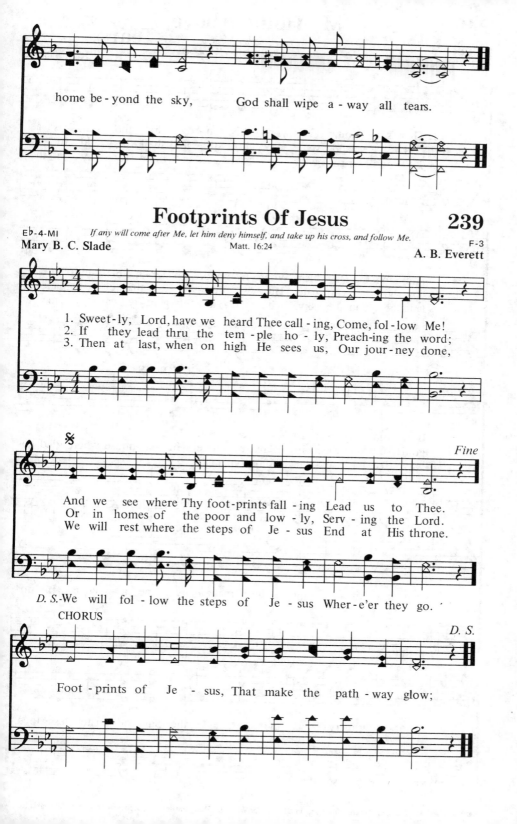

home be - yond the sky, God shall wipe a - way all tears.

Footprints Of Jesus

239

Eb-4-MI

Mary B. C. Slade

If any will come after Me, let him deny himself, and take up his cross, and follow Me.

Matt. 16:24

F-3

A. B. Everett

1. Sweet-ly, Lord, have we heard Thee call - ing, Come, fol-low Me!
2. If they lead thru the tem - ple ho - ly, Preach-ing the word;
3. Then at last, when on high He sees us, Our jour - ney done,

Fine

And we see where Thy foot-prints fall - ing Lead us to Thee.
Or in homes of the poor and low - ly, Serv - ing the Lord.
We will rest where the steps of Je - sus End at His throne.

D. S.-We will fol - low the steps of Je - sus Wher-e'er they go.

CHORUS

D. S.

Foot - prints of Je - sus, That make the path - way glow;

240 My Home Above

A♭-4-SOL
Harry Presley

We have a building of God...
eternal in the heavens... II Cor. 5:1

H-2
R. J. Stevens

1. There's a home be-yond this bo-dy for the soul, 'Tis a man-sion for the blest, Where from God e-ter-nal bless-ings ev-er flow And the saved for-ev-er rest.
2. 'Tis a land some day my spir-it shall be-hold In a joy be-yond com-pare; How I long to see that cit-y made of gold And to meet my Sav-ior there.
3. I will rise with Je-sus ev-er-more to stay In the land be-yond the sky, When the an-gels gent-ly car-ry me a-way To the Fa-ther's home on high.

CHORUS

In a house where glad ho-san-nas ev-er ring, I will make my home a-bove In im-mor-tal glo-ry, ev-er more to sing Of the Sav-ior's match-less love.

The Gates Swing Outward Never 241

Ab-4-SOL
C. H. G.

And the gates of it shall not be shut at all by day: for there shall be no night there.
Rev. 21:25

H-2

Chas. H. Gabriel

1. Just a few more days to be filled with praise, And to tell the
2. Just a few more years with their toil and tears, And the jour-ney
3. What a joy 'twill be when I wake to see Him for whom my

old, old sto-ry; Then, when twi-light falls, and my Sav-ior calls,
will be end-ed; Then I'll be with Him, where the tide of time
heart is burn-ing! Nev-er-more to sigh, nev-er-more to die—

CHORUS

I shall go to Him in glo-ry.
With e-ter-ni-ty is blend-ed. I'll ex-change my cross for a
For that day my heart is yearn-ing.

shin-ing crown, Where the gates swing out-ward nev-er; At His feet I'll

lay ev-'ry bur-den down, And with Je-sus live for-ev-er.

242 Only A Shadow Between

F-2-MI

Seek Him that . . . turneth the shadow of death into the morning . . . Amos 5:8

C-15, H-2

E. C. Baird   J. C. Blaker

1. I have a home in a fair sum-mer-land, Its beau-ties I
2. Je - sus has prom-ised a home to pre-pare, Thro' faith on this
3. When I have fin-ished my task here be - low, I pass thro' this

nev - er have seen (have seen), I have a place on an
prom - ise I lean (I lean), I have a man-sion that's
shad - ow - y screen (the screen), Be with the ran-somed for-

ev - er-green strand, There's on - ly a shad-ow be - tween.
won-drous-ly fair, There's on - ly a shad-ow be - tween.
ev - er I know,

CHORUS

On - ly a shad-ow, a shad-ow be - tween, On - ly a

shad-ow be - tween, (be - tween,) One step to go — O the

way's all a-glow, There's on-ly a shad-ow be-tween.

I Share The Perfect Love

243
F-2, L-5

F-4-SOL
Harold V. Trimble

*God is love; and he that dwelleth in love
dwelleth in God, and God in him.*
I John 4:16

Melody by Richard G. Ladd
Arranged by R. J. Stevens

1. I share the per-fect love, the love of God, The love God
2. I share the per-fect love be-cause He cares, We care and
3. There is no fear in love, the per-fect love. Love cast-eth
4. I hear His pre-cious words "Come un-to me"; We know His

has for all the sin-ful world; His love was man-i-fest, this
that's the rea-son why we share His love to friend and foe — All
out its fear and leads a-bove, For ev-'ry mem-ber of the
truth and love will set us free; So has-ten to o-bey; Don't

rit.

shame-ful world to bless, I share, I share the per-fect love.
see we love Him so, We share, we share the per-fect love.
house-hold of the Lord Doth care and share the love of God.
waste an-oth-er day, Come share, come share the per-fect love.

244 Over The Sunset Sea

*The time of my departure is at hand...I have finished my
course, I have kept the faith. II Tim. 4:6,7*

Eb-2-MI
Beulah Rowden

C-15, H-2
E. Sexton Daugherty
Arr. R. J. Stevens

1. Dark - ness is fall - ing, the night draw - eth nigh, Shad - ows fall
2. Our hearts are heav - y as they jour - ney on, Leav - ing a
3. When my long jour - ney on this earth is o'er, Dear Lord I'm

dark on the lea; Voic - es of saved ones are beck - on - ing come,
dear mem - o - ry; Je - sus is wait - ing to wel - come them home,
com - ing to Thee; Ev - er to rest in that heav - en - ly home,

CHORUS

O - ver the sun - set sea. Soon I shall jour - ney to

heav - en, my home, and from all sor - row be free; Har - bor lights

gleam - ing are light - ing the way, O - ver the sun - set sea.

Where The Soul Never Dies

245

F-4-DO
W. M. G.

H-2
Wm. M. Golden

*And there shall be no more death, neither sorrow,
nor crying . . . for the former things are passed away.* Rev. 21:4

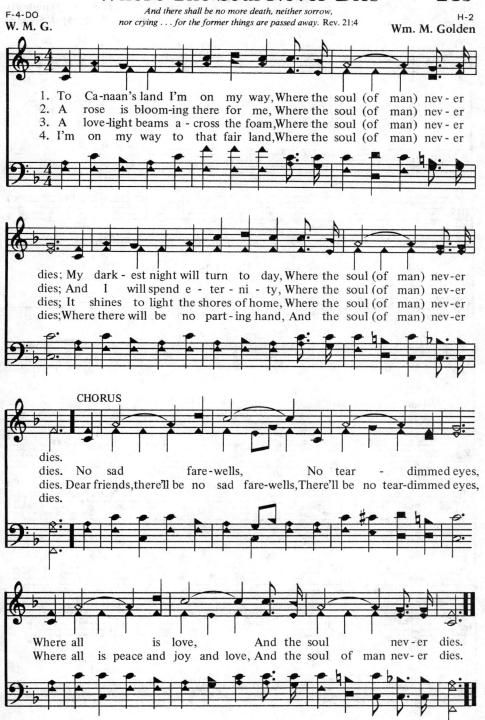

1. To Ca-naan's land I'm on my way, Where the soul (of man) nev-er
2. A rose is bloom-ing there for me, Where the soul (of man) nev-er
3. A love-light beams a-cross the foam, Where the soul (of man) nev-er
4. I'm on my way to that fair land, Where the soul (of man) nev-er

dies; My dark-est night will turn to day, Where the soul (of man) nev-er
dies; And I will spend e-ter-ni-ty, Where the soul (of man) nev-er
dies; It shines to light the shores of home, Where the soul (of man) nev-er
dies; Where there will be no part-ing hand, And the soul (of man) nev-er

CHORUS

dies.
dies. No sad fare-wells, No tear-dimmed eyes,
dies. Dear friends, there'll be no sad fare-wells, There'll be no tear-dimmed eyes,
dies.

Where all is love, And the soul nev-er dies.
Where all is peace and joy and love, And the soul of man nev-er dies.

246 Gathering Home

Eb-2-MI

Mariana B. Slade

H-2

R. M. McIntosh

He will dwell with them and they shall be His people . . .
And God shall wipe away all tears from their eyes. Rev. 21:3,4

1. Up to the boun-ti-ful Giv-er of life, Gath-er-ing home!
2. Up to the cit-y where fall-eth no night, Gath-er-ing home!
3. Up to the beau-ti-ful man-sions a-bove, Gath-er-ing home!

Gath-er-ing home! Up to the dwell-ing where com-eth no strife,
Gath-er-ing home! Up where the Sav-ior's own face is the light, The
Gath-er-ing home! Safe in the arms of His in-fi-nite love,

dear ones are gath-er-ing home.

CHORUS

Gath-er-ing home! Gath-er-ing home!

Gath-er-ing home! Gath-er-ing home! Nev-er to sor-row more,

nev-er to roam; Gath-er-ing home! Gath-er-ing
Gath-er-ing home!

home! God's chil-dren are gath-er-ing home.
Gath - er - ing home!

D-3-SOL

Wounded For Me

247

W. G. Ovens &
Gladys Watkin Roberts

But He was wounded for our transgressions, He was bruised for our iniquities. Isa. 53:5

E-1
W. G. Ovens

1. Wound-ed for me, wound-ed for me, There on the cross
2. Dy - ing for me, dy - ing for me, There on the cross
3. Ris - en for me, ris - en for me, Up from the grave
4. Liv - ing for me, liv - ing for me, Up in the skies
5. Com - ing for me, com - ing for me, One glor - ious day

He was wound-ed for me; Gone my trans - gres-sions, and
He was dy - ing for me; Now in His death my re -
He has ris - en for me; Now ev - er - more from death's
He is liv - ing for me; Dai - ly He's plead - ing and
He is com - ing for me; Then with what joy His dear

now I am free, All be-cause Je - sus was wound-ed for me.
demp-tion I see, All be-cause Je - sus was dy - ing for me.
sting I am free, All be-cause Je - sus has ris - en for me.
pray - ing for me All be-cause Je - sus is liv - ing for me.
face I shall see, Oh, how I praise Him, He's com - ing for me.

248 Home On The Banks Of The River

A-2-SOL
A. T.

In My Father's house are many mansions . . . I go to prepare a place for you.
John 14:2

H-2
Austin Taylor

1. There's a beau-ti-ful home be-yond the dark riv-er, There's a
2. 'Tis a beau-ti-ful home, and God is its Mak-er, In a
3. I have fol-lowed the way of life to the riv-er, I can

man-sion by faith I can see; And the Sav-ior is there His
land that no mor-tal has trod; Soon the an-gels will come and
see the glad por-tals a-bove; I am read-y to go and

faith-ful to wel-come, There's a beau-ti-ful home for me.
car-ry me o-ver, To that beau-ti-ful home of God.
live with my Sav-ior, In the beau-ti-ful home of love.

CHORUS

Home on the banks of the riv-er, Home
Home, yes, home, Home, sweet home,

where the ran-somed ones gath-er, Home with the
Home for me

Seek Ye First

But seek ye first the kingdom of God,
and His righteousness . . . Matt. 6:33

249
E-1

Eb-2-MI
Matt. 6:33, 7:7; 4:4

Karen Lafferty
Arr. by D. Shepard

Descant: Al - le - lu - ia! Al -

an - gels for - ev - er, On the beau - ti - ful banks of the riv - er.

1. Seek ye first the king - dom of God, And His
2. Ask and it shall be giv - en un - to you, Seek and
3. Man shall not live by bread a - lone, But by

le - lu - ia! Al - le -

righ - teous - ness. And all these things shall be
ye shall find; Knock and the door shall be
ev - 'ry word That pro - ceeds from the

lu - ia! Al - le - lu - ia!

add - ed un - to you.
o - pened un - to you. Al - le - lu, Al - le - lu - ia!
mouth of God.

250 Wonderful City

A city which hath foundations, whose builder and maker is God. Heb. 11:10

G-3-SOL
C. D. W.

H-2
C. D. Williams

1. O - ver the riv - er, shin - ing for - ev - er,
2. Home of the sag - es, saints of the a - ges,
3. Has - ten to - mor - row, end of all sor - row,

There is a cit - y, I know, Won - der - ful sto - ry!
Mar - tyrs and an - gels of light; Free of all sad - ness,
When this glad home I shall see; When with my Sav - ior,

man - sions of glo - ry Wait - ing for pil - grims be - low.
cit - y of glad - ness, Al - ways so peace - ful and bright!
hap - py for - ev - er, Rest - ing a - bove I shall be.

REFRAIN

Won - der - ful cit - y; beau - ti - ful cit - y,

Built with - out hands by our King; Mar - vel - ous cit - y,

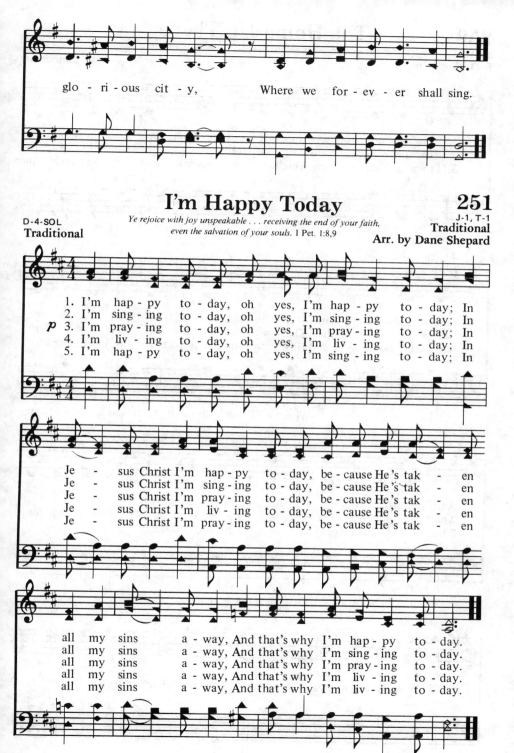

glo - ri - ous cit - y, Where we for - ev - er shall sing.

I'm Happy Today

251

Ye rejoice with joy unspeakable . . . receiving the end of your faith, even the salvation of your souls. I Pet. 1:8,9

D-4-SOL
Traditional

J-1, T-1
Traditional
Arr. by Dane Shepard

1. I'm hap - py to - day, oh yes, I'm hap - py to - day; In
2. I'm sing - ing to - day, oh yes, I'm sing - ing to - day; In
3. I'm pray - ing to - day, oh yes, I'm pray - ing to - day; In
4. I'm liv - ing to - day, oh yes, I'm liv - ing to - day; In
5. I'm hap - py to - day, oh yes, I'm sing - ing to - day; In

Je - sus Christ I'm hap - py to - day, be - cause He's tak - en
Je - sus Christ I'm sing - ing to - day, be - cause He's tak - en
Je - sus Christ I'm pray - ing to - day, be - cause He's tak - en
Je - sus Christ I'm liv - ing to - day, be - cause He's tak - en
Je - sus Christ I'm pray - ing to - day, be - cause He's tak - en

all my sins a - way, And that's why I'm hap - py to - day.
all my sins a - way, And that's why I'm sing - ing to - day.
all my sins a - way, And that's why I'm pray - ing to - day.
all my sins a - way, And that's why I'm liv - ing to - day.
all my sins a - way, And that's why I'm liv - ing to - day.

252
The Home Up There

G-4-SOL
T. O. Chisholm

H-2

L. O. Sanderson

Ye have in heaven a better and an enduring substance. Heb. 10:34

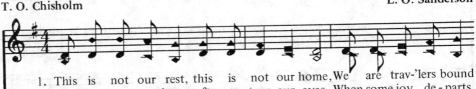

1. This is not our rest, this is not our home, We are trav-'lers bound
2. To the home up there oft we turn our eyes, When some joy de - parts,
3. Pre-cious home up there which the Lord pre-pares For the ones whose names

for a world to come; Comes full soon the end of life's lit - tle day,
when a dear one dies; Then we vi - sion here of a cit - y fair,
in His book ap-pears! How our fond hearts yearn for the Lord's re - turn,

D. S.–Where we'll sigh no more 'Neath the loads we bear,

Fine CHORUS

And our place found emp-ty, for we fly a - way.
Where will end the part-ings— in the home up there. O! it won't be long
When we'll meet to - geth - er in the home up there.

Be with Christ for - ev - er in the home up there.

D. S.

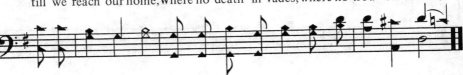

till we reach our home, Where no death in-vades, where no trou - ble comes;

Heaven Will Surely Be Worth It All 253

F-3-MI

The sufferings of this present time are not worthy to be compared with the glory which shall be revealed in us. Rom. 8:18

C-15, H-2

W. Oliver Cooper

Minzo C. Jones

1. Of - ten I'm hin-dered on my way, Bur-dened so heav-y I
2. Man - y the tri - als, toils and tears, Man - y a heart-ache may
3. Toil - ing and pain I will en - dure, Till I shall hear the death

al - most fall; Then I hear Je - sus sweet - ly say; "Heav - en will
here ap - pall; But the dear Lord so tru - ly says:"Heav - en will
an - gel call; Je - sus has prom-ised and I'm sure Heav - en will

CHORUS

sure - ly be worth it all."
sure - ly be worth it all." Heav - en will sure - ly be worth it
sure - ly be worth it all.

all. Worth all the sor - rows that here be - fall; Af - ter this

life with all its strife, Heav - en will sure - ly be worth it all.

254 On Jordan's Stormy Banks

And they sing the song of Moses . . . and the song of the Lamb . . . Rev. 15:3

G-4-DO

Samuel Stennett, 1787

H-2

T. C. O'Kane

1. On Jor - dan's storm-y banks I stand, And cast a wish-ful
2. O'er all those wide ex - tend - ed plains Shines one e - ter - nal
3. Filled with de - light, my rap - tured soul Would here no long - er

eye To Ca - naan's fair and hap - py land, Where my pos -
day; There God the Sun for - ev - er reigns, And scat - ters
stay; Tho' Jor - dan's waves a - round me roll, Fear - less I'd

CHORUS

ses - sions lie.
night a - way. We will rest in the fair and hap - py
launch a - way.

land, Just a - cross on the ev - er - green
by and by,

shore, Sing the song of Mo - ses and the
ev - er - green shore,

Lamb, by and by, And dwell with Je - sus ev - er - more.

O Love That Will Not Let Me Go 255

A♭-4-SOL
George Matheson, 1882

I have loved thee with an everlasting love . . .
with loving-kindness have I drawn thee.
Jer. 31:3

C-15, L-4
Albert L. Peace, 1884

1. O Love that will not let me go, I rest my wea - ry
2. O Light that fol-low'st all my way, I yield my flick - 'ring
3. O Joy that seek - est me thru pain, I can - not close my
4. O Cross that lift - est up my head, I dare not ask to

soul in Thee; I give Thee back the life I owe, That
torch to Thee; My heart re - stores its bor-rowed ray, That
heart to Thee; I trace the rain-bow thru the rain, And
hide from Thee; I lay in dust life's glo - ry dead, And

in Thine o - cean depths its flow May rich - er, ful - ler be.
in Thy sun-shine's glow its day May bright-er, fair - er be.
feel the prom-ise is not vain That morn shall tear - less be.
from the ground there blossoms red Life that shall end - less be.

256 Each Step Of The Way

Eb-4-MI
T. M. J.

The steps of a good man are ordered by the Lord: and He delights in his way.
Psa. 37:23

G-3, H-2
Thelma M. Jordan

1. I walk with the Sav-ior each step of the way,
2. With joy we shall en-ter the cit-y, up there,

I trust Him to guide me by night and by day;
Of won-der-ful beau-ty and man-sions all fair;

Not dread-ing to-mor-row nor what it may bring,
His own shall be changed and made like Him that day,

D. S.—Where we shall meet loved ones, a-wait-ing us there,

Fine

I'm safe in the keep-ing of Je-sus the King.
Be-cause we've walked with Him each step of the way.

Who walked here with Je-sus each step of the way.

CHORUS

Each step of the way, by night and by day,
Each step of the way, by night and by day;

Leads near-er the home e - ter - nal - ly fair,
Leads near- er the home e - ter-nal- ly fair,

How Sweet The Name
Of Jesus Sounds

257

Ab-2-SOL
John Newton, 1779

Unto you therefore which believe He is precious . . . I Pet. 2:7

N-1
Thomas Hastings

1. How sweet the name of Je - sus sounds In a be - liev - er's
2. It makes the wound - ed spir - it whole, And calms the trou - bled
3. Weak is the ef - fort of my heart, And cold my warm - est
4. Till then, I would Thy love pro - claim With ev - 'ry fleet - ing

ear! It soothes his sor - rows, heals his wounds, And
breast; 'Tis man - na to the hun - gry soul, And
tho't; But when I see Thee as Thou art, I'll
breath; And may the mu - sic of Thy name Re -

drives a - way his fear, And drives a - way his fear.
to the wea - ry, rest, And to the wea - ry, rest.
praise Thee as I ought, I'll praise Thee as I ought.
fresh my soul in death, Re - fresh my soul in death.

258 Home Of The Soul

There remaineth therefore a rest to the people of God. Heb. 4:9

G-2-MI
James Rowe

H-2, R-3
Samuel W. Beazley

1. If for the prize we have striv-en, Af-ter our la-bors are
2. Yes, a sweet rest is re-main-ing For the true chil-dren of
3. Soon, the bright homeland a-dorn-ing, We shall be-hold the glad

o'er, Rest to our souls will be giv-en, On the e-ter-nal
God, Where there will be no com-plain-ing, Nev-er a chast-'ning
dawn; Lean on the Lord till the morn-ing, Trust till the night is

CHORUS

shore. Home of the soul, beau-ti-ful home,
rod. Home of the soul, bless-ed
gone.

there we shall rest, nev-er to roam; Free from all care,
king - - - dom of light, Free

259 In Heaven They're Singing

And they sing the song of Moses the servant of God, and the song of the Lamb . . .
Rev. 15:3

F-2-MI
T. S. T.

H-2, S-4
Tillit S. Teddlie

1. In heav-en they're sing-ing a won-der-ful song, A theme that
2. We read of its beau-ty, but some-how we know, Its glo-ry
3. What mu-sic we'll hear when the ran-somed of earth, Shall en-ter

shall nev-er grow old; And glo-ri-fied mil-lions are
has nev-er been told, But think of the rap-tur-ous
that heav-en-ly fold, When all redeemed sing-ers shall

sing-ing it now,
sing-ing up there In that beau-ti-ful cit-y of gold.
join in that song

CHORUS

They're sing-ing the songs of sal-va-tion, A sto-ry that

nev-er grows old; And glo-ri-fied mil-lions are

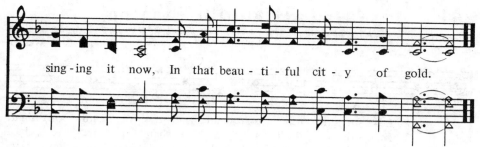

Hand In Hand With Jesus

260

I the Lord have called thee . . . and will hold thine hand, and will keep thee . . .

Johnson Oatman, Jr. Isa. 42:6 L. D. Huffstutler

Eb-2-MI F-2

1. Once from my poor sin-sick soul Christ did ev-'ry bur-den roll,
2. In my night of dark de-spair, Je-sus heard and answered pray'r,
3. When the stars are back-ward rolled And His home I shall be-hold,

Now I walk re-deemed and whole,
Now I'm walk-ing free as air, Hand in hand with Je - sus.
I will walk the street of gold,

Fine

D. S.—Walk-ing thus I will not stray,

CHORUS

Hand in hand we walk each day, Hand in hand a - long the way,

D. S.

Beautiful

261

Db-4-DO
B. E. W.

And have washed their robes and made them white in the blood of the Lamb.
Rev. 7:14

H-2, R-3
B. E. Warren

1. Beau - ti - ful robes so white, Beau - ti - ful land of light,
2. Beau - ti - ful tho't to me, We shall for - ev - er be
3. Beau - ti - ful things on high, O - ver in yon - der sky,

Beau - ti - ful home so bright, Where there shall come no night; Beau - ti - ful
Thine in e - ter - ni - ty, When from this world we're free; Free from its
Thus I shall leave this shore, Count - ing my treas - ures o'er; Where we shall

crown I'll wear, Shin - ing and bright o'er there, Yon - der in man - sions fair,
toil and care, Heav - en - ly joys to share, Let me cross o - ver there;
nev - er die, Car - ry me by and by, Nev - er to sor - row more,

CHORUS

Gath - er us there.
This is my pray'r.
Heav - en - ly store.

Beau - ti - ful robes, ...

Beau - ti - ful

Some Blessed Day

262

Eb-2-Mi
G. C. T.

H-2, S-2
Grant Colfax Tullar

*He shall come to be glorified in His saints, and to be admired in all
them that believe . . . in that day. 1 Thess. 1:10*

1. Some day in Je - sus' name, The sun will shine a - gain,
2. Some day we'll need no sun, 'Twill mean that heav'n's be - gun,
3. Per - haps it soon may be That shad-ows dark shall flee,

Hope on, nor hope in vain, 'Twill come some day! . . . .
With all earth's bat - tles won, When dawns that day! . . . .
And from earth's fet - ters free, We'll greet that day! . . . .

Grief then shall change to joy, God's will our pow'rs em - ploy,
With shad - ows past, and woe, All dark things clear - er grow,
Thro' grace from heav - en's throne, Not mer - it of our own,

And sin no more de - stroy, Some bless - ed day!
And we great joy shall know Some bless - ed day!
We'll find a bet - ter home Some bless - ed day!

Is Thy Heart Right With God
263

Bb-2-SOL
E. A. H.
H-1, I-1

Serve Him with a perfect heart . . . for the Lord searcheth all hearts. I Chr. 28:9

Elisha A. Hoffman

1. Have thine af - fec - tions been nailed to the cross? Is thy heart
2. Hast thou do - min - ion o'er self and o'er sin? Is thy heart
3. Are all thy pow'rs un - der Je - sus' con - trol? Is thy heart

right with God?   Dost thou count all things for Je - sus but loss?
right with God?   O - ver all e - vil with - out and with - in?
right with God?   Does He each mo - ment a - bide in thy soul?

REFRAIN

Is thy heart right with God?
Is thy heart right with God?   Is thy heart right with God,
Is thy heart right with God?

Washed in the crim - son flood,   Cleansed and made ho - ly,

hum - ble and low - ly,   Right in the sight of God? (of God)

264 "Whosoever Will"

D-4-SOL
P. P. B.

Philip P. Bliss
Arr. by R. E. Winsett

I-1

And the Spirit and the bride say, Come . . .
And whosoever will, let him take of the water of life freely.
Rev. 22:17

1. "Who - so - ev - er hear - eth," shout, shout the sound!
2. Who - so - ev - er com - eth, need not de - lay,
3. "Who - so - ev - er will!" the prom - ise is se - cure,

Spread the bless - ed ti - dings all the world a - round, Tell the joy - ful
Now the door is o - pen, en - ter while you may; Je - sus is the
"Who - so - ev - er will," for - ev - er must en - dure; "Who - so - ev - er

news wher - ev - er man is found,
true, the on - ly Liv - ing Way; "Who - so - ev - er will may come."
will!" 'tis life for - ev - er - more;

CHORUS

"Who - so - ev - er will, who - so - ev - er will!" Send the proc - la -

ma - tion o - ver vale and hill; 'Tis a lov - ing Fa - ther

Faith Of Our Fathers 265

Fight the good fight of faith.
I Tim. 6:12

A♭-3-MI
Frederick W. Faber, 1849
Adapted by J. G. Walton, 1874
L-6, W-4

calls the wan-d'rer home: "Who - so - ev - er will may come."

1. Faith of our fa - thers! liv - ing still, In spite of dun-geon,
2. Our fa - thers, chained in pris - ons dark, Were still in heart and
3. Faith of our fa - thers! we will love Both friend and foe in

fire, and sword; O how our hearts beat high with joy
con - science free; How sweet would be their chil - dren's fate,
all our strife; And preach thee, too, as love knows how,

When-e'er we hear that glo - rious word:
If they, like them, could die for thee! Faith of our fa - thers,
By kind-ly words and vir - tuous life:

ho - ly faith! We will be true to thee till death!

266 Have You Counted The Cost?

G-3-DO
A. J. H.

For what is a man profited, if he shall gain the whole world and lose his own soul?
Matt. 16:26

I-1
A. J. Hodge

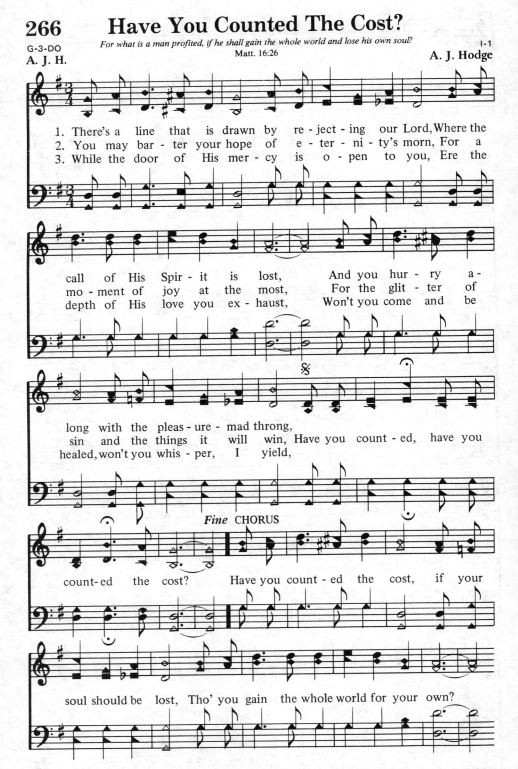

1. There's a line that is drawn by re-ject-ing our Lord, Where the
2. You may bar-ter your hope of e-ter-ni-ty's morn, For a
3. While the door of His mer-cy is o-pen to you, Ere the

call of His Spir-it is lost, And you hur-ry a-
mo-ment of joy at the most, For the glit-ter of
depth of His love you ex-haust, Won't you come and be

long with the pleas-ure-mad throng,
sin and the things it will win, Have you count-ed, have you
healed, won't you whis-per, I yield,

Fine CHORUS

count-ed the cost? Have you count-ed the cost, if your

soul should be lost, Tho' you gain the whole world for your own?

E - ven now it may be that the line you have crossed,

Jesus Loves Me
267

Eb-2-SOL   *He that loveth Me shall be loved of My Father, and I will love him . . . John 14:21*   L-4

Anna B. Warner   **Wm. B. Bradbury**

1. Je - sus loves me! this I know, For the Bi - ble tells me so;
2. Je - sus loves me! He who died, Heav - en's gate to o - pen wide;
3. Je - sus, take this heart of mine, Make it pure and whol - ly Thine;

Lit - tle ones to Him be - long; They are weak but He is strong.
He will wash a - way my sin, Let His lit - tle child come in.
Thou hast bled and died for me; I will hence-forth live for Thee.

CHORUS

Yes, Je - sus loves me; Yes, Je - sus loves me;

Yes, Je - sus loves me; The Bi - ble tells me so.

268 Hark, The Gentle Voice

D-4-MI

Come unto Me all ye that labor and are heavy laden, and I will give you rest.
Matt. 11:28

Mrs. M. B. C. Slade

I-1

A. B. Everett

1. Hark! the gen - tle voice of Je - sus fall - eth Ten - der - ly up -
2. Take His yoke, for He is meek and low - ly; Bear His bur - den,
3. Then, His lov - ing, ten - der voice o - bey - ing, Bear His yoke, His

on your ear; Sweet His cry of love and pit - y call - eth:
to Him turn; He who call - eth is the Mas - ter ho - ly:
bur - den take; Find the yoke His hand is on you lay - ing,

D.S.-Ye that la - bor and are heav - y la - den,

CHORUS

Fine

Turn and lis - ten, stay and hear.
He will teach if you will learn. Ye that la - bor
Light and eas - y for His sake.

Come, and I will give you rest.

D. S.

and are heav - y la - den, Lean up - on your dear Lord's breast;

Nothing But The Blood

269

G-4-DO
R. L.

We have redemption through His blood, even the forgiveness of sins. Col. 1:14

C-2

Robert Lowry

1. What can wash a - way my sins? Noth-ing but the blood of Je - sus;
2. For my par - don this I see, Noth-ing but the blood of Je - sus;
3. Noth-ing can for sin a - tone, Noth-ing but the blood of Je - sus;
4. This is all my hope and peace, Noth-ing but the blood of Je - sus;

What can make me whole a - gain? Noth-ing but the blood of Je - sus.
For my cleans-ing, this my plea, Noth-ing but the blood of Je - sus.
Naught of good that I have done, Noth-ing but the blood of Je - sus.
This is all my right-eous-ness, Noth-ing but the blood of Je - sus.

CHORUS

Oh! pre - cious is the flow That makes me white as snow;

No oth - er fount I know, Noth-ing but the blood of Je - sus.

270 Give Me Thy Heart

F-2-SOL
Eliza E. Hewitt, 1898

Thou shalt love the Lord thy God with all thy heart . . . soul, and . . . mind.
Matt. 22:37

H-1, I-1
William J. Kirkpatrick, 1898

1. "Give me thy heart," says the Fa - ther a - bove, No gift so
2. "Give me thy heart," says the Sav - ior of men, Call - ing in
3. "Give me thy heart," says the Spir - it di - vine, "All that thou

pre - cious to Him as our love, Soft - ly He whis - pers wher-
mer - cy a - gain and a - gain; "Turn now from sin, and from
hast to my keep - ing re - sign; Grace more a - bound - ing is

rit.

ev - er thou art, "Grate - ful - ly trust me, and
e - vil de - part, Have I not died for thee? Give me thy
mine to im - part, Make full sur - ren - der, and

CHORUS   *p*

heart." "Give me thy heart, Give me thy heart," Hear the soft whis - per, wher-

ev - er thou art; From this dark world He would draw thee a-

part, Speak - ing so ten - der - ly, "Give me thy heart."

Near To The Heart Of God 271

D-4-MI
C. B. McAfee

Keep silence before Me . . . and let the people renew their strength;
let them come near. Isa. 41:1

F-2
C. B. McAfee

1. There is a place of qui - et rest, Near to the heart of God,
2. There is a place of com - fort sweet, Near to the heart of God,
3. There is a place of full re - lease, Near to the heart of God,

A place where sin can - not mo - lest, Near to the heart of God.
A place where we our Sav - ior meet, Near to the heart of God.
A place where all is joy and peace, Near to the heart of God.

CHORUS

O Je - sus, blest Re - deem - er, Sent from the heart of God,

Hold us, who wait be - fore Thee, Near to the heart of God.

272 Jesus, The Loving Shepherd

F-2-DO

W. A. O.

C-11

W. A. Ogden

I am the good shepherd, and know My sheep . . . and they shall hear My voice.
John 10:14-16

1. Je - sus, the lov - ing Shep - herd, Call - eth thee now to come
2. Je - sus, the lov - ing Shep - herd, Gave His dear life for thee;
3. Lin - ger - ing is but fol - ly, Wolves are a - broad to - day,

In - to the fold of safe - ty, Where there is rest and room;
Ten - der - ly now He's call - ing, "Wan - der - er, come to Me;"
Seek - ing the sheep who're stray - ing, Seek - ing the lambs to slay;

Come in the strength of man - hood, Come in the morn of youth,
Haste! for with - out is dan - ger, "Come," cries the Shep - herd blest;
Je - sus, the lov - ing Shep - herd, Call - eth thee now to come;

En - ter the fold of safe - ty, En - ter the way of
En - ter the fold of safe - ty, En - ter the place of
En - ter the fold of safe - ty, Where there is rest and

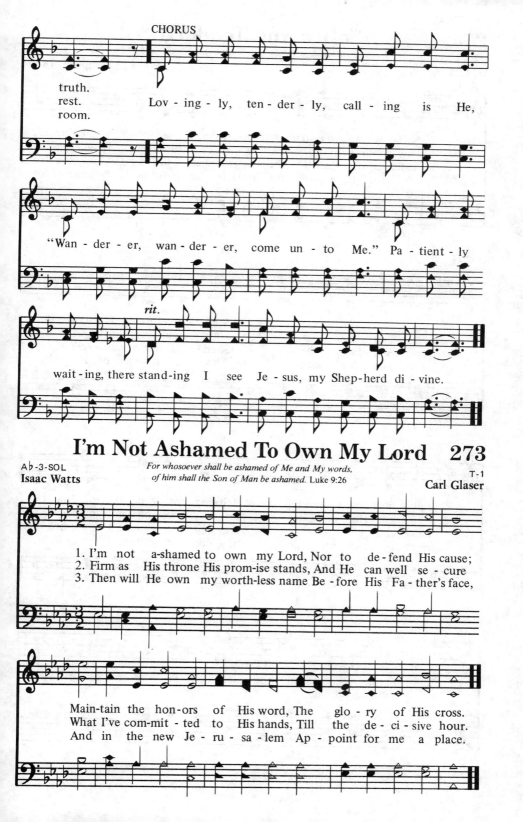

CHORUS

truth.
rest.
room.

Lov - ing - ly, ten - der - ly, call - ing is He,

"Wan - der - er, wan - der - er, come un - to Me." Pa - tient - ly

rit.

wait - ing, there stand - ing I see Je - sus, my Shep - herd di - vine.

I'm Not Ashamed To Own My Lord   273

Ab-3-SOL

Isaac Watts

For whosoever shall be ashamed of Me and My words,
of him shall the Son of Man be ashamed. Luke 9:26

T-1

Carl Glaser

1. I'm not a-shamed to own my Lord, Nor to de - fend His cause;
2. Firm as His throne His prom-ise stands, And He can well se - cure
3. Then will He own my worth-less name Be - fore His Fa - ther's face,

Main - tain the hon-ors of His word, The glo - ry of His cross.
What I've com-mit - ted to His hands, Till the de - ci - sive hour.
And in the new Je - ru - sa - lem Ap - point for me a place.

274 Softly And Tenderly

A♭-2-MI
W. L. T.

I came not to call the righteous, but sinners to repentance. Luke 5:32

I-1
Will L. Thompson, 1880

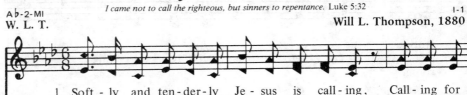
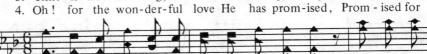

1. Soft - ly and ten-der-ly Je - sus is call - ing, Call - ing for
2. Why should we tar - ry when Je - sus is plead-ing, Plead - ing for
3. Time is now fleet-ing, the mo-ments are pass-ing, Pass - ing from
4. Oh! for the won-der-ful love He has prom-ised, Prom - ised for

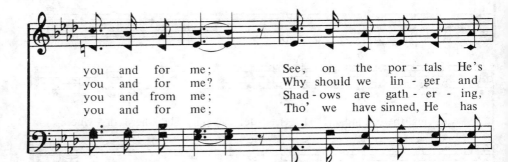

you and for me; See, on the por - tals He's
you and for me? Why should we lin - ger and
you and from me; Shad - ows are gath - er - ing,
you and for me; Tho' we have sinned, He has

wait - ing and watch-ing, Watch-ing for you and for me.
heed not His mer - cies, Mer - cies for you and for me?
life's end is com - ing, Com - ing for you and for me.
mer - cy and par - don, Par - don for you and for me.

CHORUS

Come home, come home, Ye who are wea - ry, come
Come home, Come home,

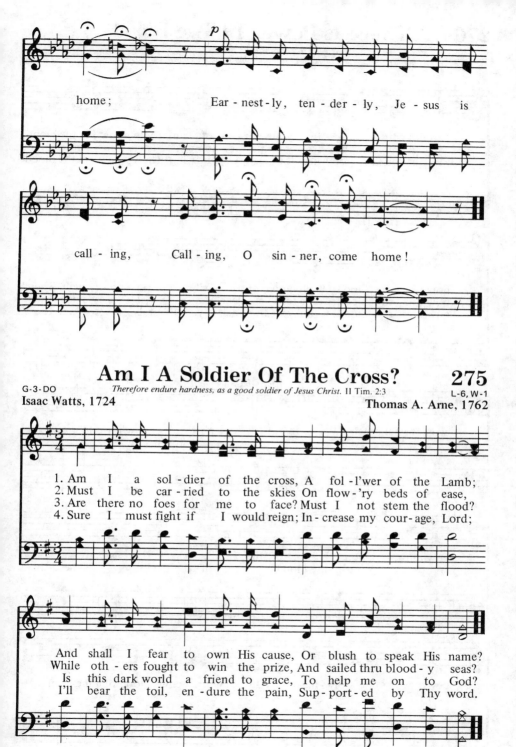

home; Ear - nest - ly, ten - der - ly, Je - sus is

call - ing, Call - ing, O sin - ner, come home!

Am I A Soldier Of The Cross? 275

G-3-DO *Therefore endure hardness, as a good soldier of Jesus Christ.* II Tim. 2:3 L-6, W-1

Isaac Watts, 1724 **Thomas A. Arne, 1762**

1. Am I a sol - dier of the cross, A fol - l'wer of the Lamb;
2. Must I be car - ried to the skies On flow-'ry beds of ease,
3. Are there no foes for me to face? Must I not stem the flood?
4. Sure I must fight if I would reign; In - crease my cour - age, Lord;

And shall I fear to own His cause, Or blush to speak His name?
While oth - ers fought to win the prize, And sailed thru blood - y seas?
Is this dark world a friend to grace, To help me on to God?
I'll bear the toil, en - dure the pain, Sup - port - ed by Thy word.

276 There Is Power In The Blood

Bb-4-SOL
L. E. J.

Ye were not redeemed with corruptible things . . .
but with the precious blood of Christ, as a lamb without blemish . . . 1 Pet. 1:18,19

C-2

L. E. Jones

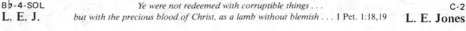

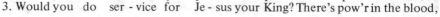

1. Would you be free from your bur-den of sin? There's pow'r in the blood,
2. Would you be free from your pas-sion and pride? There's pow'r in the blood,
3. Would you do ser-vice for Je-sus your King? There's pow'r in the blood,

pow'r in the blood; Would you o'er e-vil a vic-to-ry win? There's
pow'r in the blood; Come for a cleans-ing to Cal-va-ry's tide, There's
pow'r in the blood; Would you live dai-ly, His prais-es to sing? There's

CHORUS

won-der-ful pow'r in the blood. There is pow'r, pow'r, wonder working
                                                there is pow'r,

pow'r in the blood   of the Lamb;   There is pow'r,
    In the blood   of the Lamb;   there is

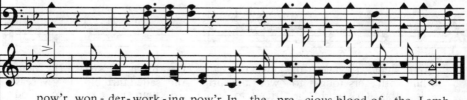

pow'r, won-der-work-ing pow'r In the pre-cious blood of the Lamb.
pow'r,

Precious Words

277

A-2-SOL

W-3

The words that I speak unto you, they are spirit, and they are life. John 6:63

Mrs. Loula K. Rodgers

R. M. McIntosh

1. Pre - cious for - ev - er! oh, won - der - ful words, Teach me the
2. Free - ly He of - fers their prom - ise to all, "Come un - to
3. Wouldst thou re - fuse the sweet sol - ace He gives, In the mid-

path - way of du - ty; Lead me be - side the still wa - ters of life,
me who - so - ev - er," Sin - ners op - pressed with a bur - den of woe,
night of Thy sor - row? Wouldst thou go on in the dark - ness of sin,

REFRAIN

Flow - ing thru val - leys of beau - ty.
Drink of the boun - ti - ful riv - er. Pre - cious for - ev - er to
Long - ing for no bright to - mor - row?

you and to me, Words that our Sav - ior has spok - en, Bear - ing sal -

va - tion far o - ver the sea, Heal - ing the hearts that are bro - ken!

278 God Is Calling The Prodigal

Bb-4-SOL
C. H. G.

For this my son was dead, and is alive again; he was lost, and is found. Luke 15:24

1-1

Chas. H. Gabriel

1. God is call-ing the prod-i-gal, come with-out de-lay,
2. Pa-tient, lov-ing and ten-der-ly still the Fa-ther pleads,
3. Come, there's bread in the house of thy Fa-ther, and to spare,

Hear, O hear Him call-ing, call-ing now for thee;
Hear, O hear Him call-ing, call-ing now for thee;
Hear, O hear Him call-ing, call-ing now for thee;

for thee;

Tho' you've wan-dered so far from His pres-ence, come to-day,
Oh! re-turn while the Spir-it in mer-cy in-ter-cedes,
Lo! the ta-ble is spread and the feast is wait-ing there,

Hear His lov-ing voice call-ing still.

call-ing still.

279 He Is Able To Deliver Thee

Bb-4-SOL
W. A. O.

Call upon Me in the day of trouble: I will deliver thee . . . Psa. 50:15

W. A. Ogden

1-1

1. 'Tis the grand-est theme, thru the a-ges rung; 'Tis the
2. 'Tis the grand-est theme, in the earth or main; 'Tis the
3. 'Tis the grand-est theme, let the ti-dings roll To the

grand-est theme, for a mor-tal tongue; 'Tis the grand-est theme
grand-est theme for a mor-tal strain; 'Tis the grand-est theme
guilt-y heart, to the sin-ful soul; Look to God in faith,

that the world e'er sung,
tell the world a-gain, "Our God is a-ble to de-
He will make thee whole,

Fine CHORUS

D. S.-rest, "Our God is a-ble to de-

liv-er thee." He is a - - - ble to de-
a-ble, He is a-ble

liv-er thee."

liv-er thee, He is a - - - ble to de-
a-ble, He is a-ble

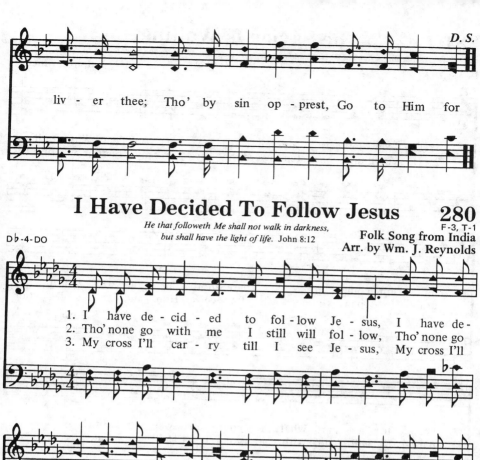

liv - er thee; Tho' by sin op - prest, Go to Him for

I Have Decided To Follow Jesus 280

F-3, T-1

He that followeth Me shall not walk in darkness,
but shall have the light of life. John 8:12

Db -4- DO

Folk Song from India
Arr. by Wm. J. Reynolds

1. I have de - cid - ed to fol - low Je - sus, I have de -
2. Tho' none go with me I still will fol - low, Tho' none go
3. My cross I'll car - ry till I see Je - sus, My cross I'll

cid - ed to fol - low Je - sus, I have de - cid - ed to fol - low
with me I still will fol - low, Tho' none go with me I still will
car - ry till I see Je - sus, My cross I'll car - ry till I see

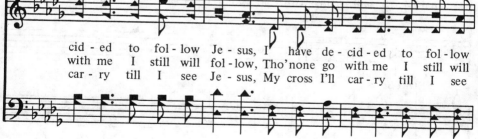

Je - sus, No turn - ing back, no turn - ing back.
fol - low, No turn - ing back, no turn - ing back.
Je - sus, No turn - ing back, I'll fol - low Him.

The Savior Is Waiting

Behold, I stand at the door, and knock: if any man hear My voice and open the door,
I will come in . . . Rev. 3:20

Ralph Carmichael

1-1

1. The Sav-ior is wait-ing to en-ter your heart Why don't you
2. If you'll take one step toward the Sav-ior, my friend, You'll find His

let Him come in? There's noth-ing in this world to
arms o-pen wide; Re-ceive Him and all of your

keep you a-part What is your an-swer to Him?
dark-ness will end, With-in your heart He'll a-bide.

CHORUS

Time af-ter time He has wait-ed be-fore, And now He is

wait-ing a-gain To see if you're will-ing to

o - pen the door — O how He wants to come in!

Love For All

For God so loved the world, that He gave His only begotten Son . . . John 3:16

282

A-3-SOL

S. Longfellow

L-5

Xavier Schnyder

1. Love for all — and can it be? Can I hope it is for me — I, who strayed so long a - go, Strayed so far, and fell so low?

2. I, the dis - o - be - dient child, Way - ward, pas - sion - ate, and wild — I, who left my Fa - ther's home, In for - bid - den ways to roam.

3. I, who spurned His lov - ing hold; I, who would not be con - trolled — I, who would not hear His call; I, the will - ful prod - i - gal.

4. To my Fa - ther can I go? At His feet my - self I'll throw; In His house there yet may be Place — a serv - ant's place — for me.

5. See! my Fa - ther wait - ing stands; See! He reach - es out His hands: God is love, I know, I see, Love for me — yes, e - ven me.

283 There's A Great Day Coming

For we must all appear before the judgment seat of Christ . . . II Cor. 5:10

G-4-SOL
W. L. T.

1-1, J-2

Will L. Thompson

1. There's a great day com - ing,   A great day com - ing,
2. There's a bright day com - ing,   A bright day com - ing,
3. There's a sad day com - ing,   A sad day com - ing,

There's a great day com - ing by and by; When the saints and the
There's a bright day com - ing by and by; But its bright - ness shall
There's a sad day com - ing by and by; When the sin - ner shall

sin - ners shall be part - ed right and left,
on - ly come to them that love the Lord, Are you read - y for that
hear his doom, "De - part, I know ye not,"

CHORUS *pp*

day to come?   Are you read - y?   Are you read - y?

1 mf Are you read - y for the judg - ment day? *2 mf* for the judg - ment day?

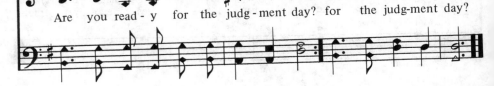

What Will Your Answer Be?

284

Bb-2-SOL
T. S. T.

1-1, J-2

So then every one of us shall give account of himself to God. Rom. 14:12

Tillit S. Teddlie

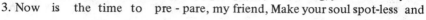

1. Some-day you'll stand at the bar on high, Some-day your re - cord you'll
2. Sad - ly you'll stand, if you're un - pre-pared, Trembling, you'll fall on your
3. Now is the time to pre - pare, my friend, Make your soul spot-less and

see; Some-day you'll an - swer the quest-ion of life, What will your
knee; Fac - ing the sen - tence of life or of death, What will that
free; Washed in the blood of the Cru - ci - fied One, He will your

CHORUS

an - swer be?
sen - tence be? What will it be? What will it be?
an - swer be.

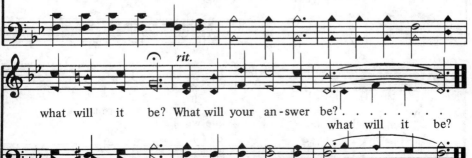

Where will you spend your e - ter - ni - ty? What will it be, O

rit.

what will it be? What will your an - swer be?. . . . . . .
what will it be?

285 Zion's Call

For out of Zion shall go forth the law, and the word of the Lord . . . Isa. 2:3

F-4-DO

J. R. B., Jr.

J. R. Baxter, Jr.

1-1

1. Zi-on's call sweet-ly rings o-ver land and sea, Bid-ding
2. On the road to the goal bur-dens we must bear, But we
3. While we tar-ry be-low there is work to do And our

us look to realms a-bove; While the light from the throne shines for
have help from realms a-bove; We re-ceive cour-age new when we
strength com-eth from a-bove; As we la-bor and wait we must

CHORUS

you and me, Let us list to the call of love. Zi-on's call . . .
kneel in pray'r, Let us list to the call of love. Zi-on's
all be true, Let us list to the call of love.

. . . is ring-ing, Com-ing from the throne a-
call clear-ly ring-ing,

bove, While we hear it ring-ing, . . .
in heav'n a-bove, While we hear clear-ly

ring - ing, Let us heed the call of love.
of per - fect love.

Must Jesus Bear The Cross Alone 286

A-2-MI *If any man come after Me, let him deny himself, and take up his cross, and follow Me.* C-16, C-17

Thos. Shepherd Matt. 16:24 **Geo. N. Allen**

1. Must Je - sus bear the cross a - lone And
2. The con - se - crat - ed cross I'll bear, Till
3. O pre - cious cross! O glo - rious crown! O

all the world go free? No, there's a
death shall set me free, And then go
res - ur - rec - tion day! Ye an - gels,

cross for ev - 'ry one, And there's a cross for me.
home my crown to wear, For there's a crown for me.
from the stars come down, And bear my soul a - way.

287 There's A Fountain Free

G-4-DO

Mrs. M. B. C. Slade

For the Lamb which is in the midst of the throne . . .
shall lead them unto living fountains of waters. Rev. 7:17

A. B. Everett

I-1

1. There's a foun-tain free, 'tis for you and me: Let us haste, O haste
2. There's a liv - ing stream, with a crys - tal gleam: From the throne of life
3. There's a rock that's cleft and no soul is left, That may not its pure

to its brink; 'Tis the fount of love from the Source a - bove, And He
now it flows; While the wa - ters roll let the wea - ry soul Hear the
wa - ters share; 'Tis for you and me, and its stream I see: Let us

bids us all free - ly drink.
call that forth free - ly goes. Will you come   to the foun-tain
has - ten joy - ful - ly there.
                                                        Will you come,

free? Will you come?   'tis for you and me; Thirst-y soul, . . .
free?   Will you come,

. . . .   hear the wel - come call: 'Tis a foun - tain o - pened for all.
      Thirst-y soul,

Lord, I'm Coming Home

288

Ab-2-SOL
W. J. K.
C-16

Wm. J. Kirkpatrick
Arr. by R. J. Stevens

I will arise and go to my father, and will say unto him,
Father, I have sinned . . . Luke 15:18

1. I've wan-dered far a - way from God, Now I'm com-ing home;
2. I'm tired of sin and stray - ing Lord, Now I'm com-ing home;
3. I need His cleans-ing blood, I know, Now I'm com-ing home;

The paths of sin too long I've trod, Lord, I'm com-ing home.
I'll trust Thy love, be - lieve Thy word, Lord, I'm com-ing home.
O wash me whit - er than the snow, Lord, I'm com-ing home.

CHORUS

Com - ing home, com - ing home, Nev - er more to roam;

O - pen wide Thine arms of love, Lord, I'm com-ing home.

289

When I See The Blood

And when I see the blood, I will pass over you,
and the plague shall not be upon you . . . Ex. 12:13

C-4-SOL
J. G. F.

C-2
John G. Foote

1. Christ, our Re-deem-er, died on the cross, Died for the sin-ner,
2. Chief-est of sin-ners Je-sus can save, As He has prom-ised,
3. Judg-ment is com-ing, all will be there, Who have re-ject-ed,
4. O what com-pas-sion, O bound-less love, Je-sus hath pow-er,

paid all his due; All who re-ceive Him need nev-er fear, Yes, He will
so will He do; O sin-ner, hear Him, trust in His word, Then He will
who have re-fused; O sin-ner, hast-en, let Je-sus in, Then God will
Je-sus is true; All who o-bey are safe from the storm. O He will

CHORUS

pass, will pass o-ver you. When I see the blood,
pass, will pass o-ver you.
pass, will pass o-ver you. When I see the blood,
pass, will pass o-ver you.

When I see the blood, When I see the
When I see the blood, When I

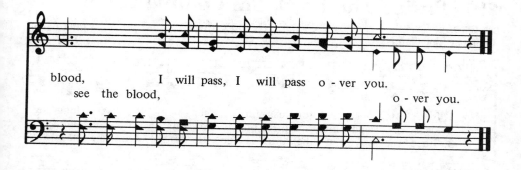

blood, I will pass, I will pass o-ver you.
see the blood, o - ver you.

In The Cross Of Christ I Glory 290

God forbid that I should glory, save in the cross of our Lord . . . Gal. 6:14

C-3-SOL

John Bowring, 1825

C-15, C-17

Ithamar Conkey, 1849

1. In the cross of Christ I glo-ry, Tow-'ring o'er
2. When the woes of life o'er-take me, Hopes de-ceive,
3. When the sun of bliss is beam-ing Light and love
4. Bane and bless-ing, pain and pleas-ure, By the cross

the wrecks of time; All the light of sa - - -
and fears an-noy, Nev-er shall the cross
up-on my way, From the cross the ra - - -
are sanc-ti-fied; Peace is there that knows

cred sto - ry Gath-ers round its head sub-lime.
for-sake me: Lo! it glows with peace and joy.
diance stream-ing Adds new lus-ter to the day.
no meas-ure, Joys that thro' all time a-bide.

291 Praise The Lord, I'm Coming Home

H-2

But now they desire a better country,
that is, an heavenly: Heb. 11:16

Bb-2-SOL

Gilbert & Joe Gann

Jay Conner

Arr. by R. J. Stevens

1. I am look-ing for treas-ure e - ter-nal; I am long-ing
2. Dear-est friend-ships are the on - ly treas-ures I can claim on
3. Since the way of the world is en - tic-ing, Oft the path-way

to dwell in that land Where my Sav - ior has prom-ised to
this earth as my own; But in heav - en I'm blest be - yond
of sin I did roam; But o - be - dience to His word has

build me A mansion with His own hand.
mea - sure; Praise the Lord, I'm com - ing home!
saved me; Praise the Lord, I'm com - ing home!

CHORUS

God has prom-ised His saints thru the a - ges He'll pro - vide

in that land o'er the foam; With each day I get

clos-er to heav-en — Praise the Lord, I'm com-ing home.

The Lord's My Shepherd 292

F-3-SOL

I am the good shepherd . . . I lay down My life for the sheep. John 10:14,15

C-11

F. Rous

Jessie Seymour Irvine

1. The Lord's my Shep - herd, I'll not want; He
2. My soul He doth re - store a - gain, And
3. Yea, tho' I walk in death's dark vale, Yet
4. My ta - ble Thou hast fur - nish - ed In
5. Good-ness and mer - cy all my life Shall

makes me down to lie In pas - tures green;
me to walk doth make With - in the paths
will I fear none ill; For Thou art with
pres - ence of my foes; My head Thou dost
sure - ly fol - low me, And in God's house

He lead - eth me The qui - et wa - ters by.
of right - eous - ness, E'en for His own name's sake.
me, and Thy rod And staff me com - fort still.
with oil a - noint, And my cup o - ver flows.
for ev - er - more My dwell - ing place shall be.

293 Come To Jesus Today

Behold, now is the accepted time; behold, now is the day of salvation. II Cor. 6:12

D-4-MI

E. R. Latta

I-1

J. H. Tenney

1. Come to Je - sus! He will save you, Tho' your sins as crim-son glow;
2. Come to Je - sus! do not tar - ry, En - ter in at mer - cy's gate;
3. Come to Je - sus, dy - ing sin - ner! Oth - er Sav - ior there is none;

If you give your hearts to Je - sus, He will make them white as snow.
O de - lay not till the mor-row, Lest thy com - ing be too late.
He will share with you His glo - ry, When your pil - grim - age is done.

CHORUS

Come to Je - - sus! Come to Je - - sus! Come to
Come, come to - day! Come, come to - day!

Je - sus! come to - day, Come to Je - - sus!
yes, come, come to - day! Come, come to - day!

Come to Je - - sus! Come to Je - sus! come, come to - day!
Come, come to - day!

Jesus Is Calling

294

Come unto Me . . . and learn of Me; for I am meek and lowly in heart . . .

C-2-SOL

Fanny J. Crosby, 1883

Matt. 11:28,29

George C. Stebbins, 1883

I-1

1. Je - sus is ten - der - ly call - ing thee home— Call - ing to - day,
2. Je - sus is call - ing the wea - ry to rest— Call - ing to - day,
3. Je - sus is wait - ing, O come to Him now— Wait - ing to - day,
4. Je - sus is plead - ing, O list to His voice— Hear Him to - day,

call - ing to - day; Why from the sun - shine of love wilt thou roam
call - ing to - day; Bring Him thy bur - den, and thou shalt be blest;
wait - ing to - day; Come with thy sins, at His feet low - ly bow;
hear Him to - day; They who be - lieve on His name shall re - joice;

CHORUS

Far - ther and far - ther a - way?
He will not turn you a - way.
Come, and no lon - ger de - lay.
Quick - ly a - rise and o - bey.

Call - ing to - day!
Call - ing, call - ing to - day, to - day!

Call - ing to - day! . . . Je - - - sus is
Call - ing, call - ing to - day, to - day! Je - sus is ten - der - ly

call - - - ing, Is ten - der - ly call - ing to - day.
call - ing to - day,

295 Christ Receiveth Sinful Men

Christ Jesus came into the world to save sinners. 1 Tim. 1:15

D-3-MI

Erdmann Neumaster, 1718

E-1, I-1

James McGranahan, 1883

1. Sin - ners Je - sus will re - ceive: Sound this word of grace to all
2. Come, and He will give you rest; Trust Him, for His word is plain;
3. Christ re - ceiv - eth sin - ful men, E - ven me with all my sin;

Who the heav'n - ly path - way leave, All who lin - ger, all who fall.
He will take the sin - ful - est; Christ re - ceiv - eth sin - ful men.
Purged from ev - 'ry spot and stain, Heav'n with Him I en - ter in.

CHORUS

Sing it o'er . . . . and o'er a - gain; . .
Sing it o'er a - gain, Sing it

Christ re - ceiv - - - - eth sin - ful
o'er a - gain; Christ re - ceiv - eth sin - ful men, Christ re -

men; . . . . . . Make the mes - - - - - - sage
ceiv - eth sin - ful men; Make the mes - sage plain,

clear and plain: Christ re - ceiv - eth sin - ful   men.
     Make the mes - sage plain:

How Firm A Foundation

296

A-2-SOL
George Keith

The foundation of God standeth sure, having this seal,
the Lord knoweth them that are His. II Tim. 2:19

A-1, P-4

1. How firm a foun - da - tion, ye saints of the Lord, Is laid
2. "Fear not, I am with thee, O be not dis - mayed;For I
3. "The soul that on Je - sus hath leaned for re - pose, I will

for your faith in His ex - cel - lent word! What more can He say than to
am thy God, and will still give thee aid; I'll strength-en thee, help thee, and
not, I will not de - sert to his foes; That soul, tho' all hell should en-

you He has said, You who un - to Je - sus for ref - uge have fled?
cause thee to stand, Up - held by My gra - cious, om - nip - o - tent hand."
deav - or to shake, I'll nev - er, no nev - er, no nev - er for - sake."

297 Prepare To Meet Thy God

It is appointed unto men once to die, but after this the judgment. Heb. 9:27

B♭-3-MI
J. H. S.

I-1, J-2

J. H. Stanley

1. Care-less soul, why will you lin - ger, Wand'ring from the fold of God?
2. Why so tho't-less are you stand-ing While the fleet - ing years go by,
3. If you spurn the in - vi - ta - tion Till the Spir - it shall de - part,

Hear you not the in - vi - ta - tion? O pre - pare to meet thy God.
And your life is spent in fol - ly? O pre - pare to meet thy God.
Then you'll see your sad con - di - tion, Un - pre - pared to meet thy God.

CHORUS

Care - less soul, ... O heed the warn-ing, ...
O care-less soul, heed the warn - ing,

For your life . . . . will soon be gone; . . . .
will soon be gone, O yes, your life will soon be gone;

O how sad . . . . to face the judg-ment, ...
to face the judg-ment, O how sad to face the judg-ment,

Un - pre - pared . . . . . to meet thy God.
Un - pre - pared to meet thy God.

O Perfect Love

298

*For this cause shall a man leave his father and mother,
and shall be joined unto his wife, and the two shall be one flesh. Eph. 5:31*

Eb-4-DO
Dorothy B. Gurney

H-5, W-2
John Barnby

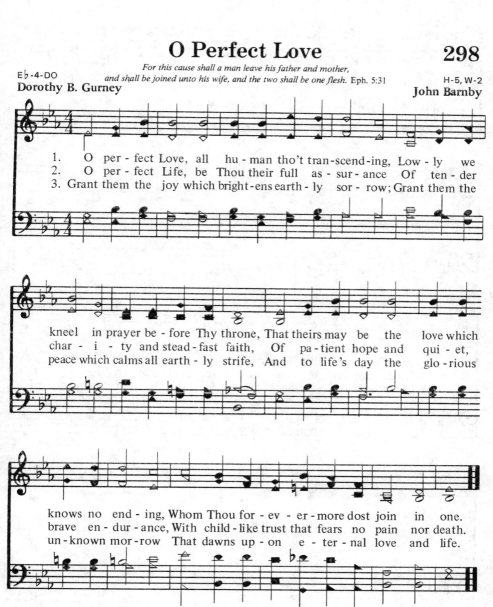

1. O per - fect Love, all hu - man tho't tran-scend-ing, Low - ly we
2. O per - fect Life, be Thou their full as - sur - ance Of ten - der
3. Grant them the joy which bright-ens earth - ly sor - row; Grant them the

kneel in prayer be - fore Thy throne, That theirs may be the love which
char - i - ty and stead-fast faith, Of pa - tient hope and qui - et,
peace which calms all earth - ly strife, And to life's day the glo - rious

knows no end - ing, Whom Thou for - ev - er-more dost join in one.
brave en - dur - ance, With child - like trust that fears no pain nor death.
un - known mor - row That dawns up - on e - ter - nal love and life.

Glory To God

299
E-4-MI

Sammy Stirling
Arr. by Dane K. Shepard

Steve Kearney

To Him be glory and dominion
forever and ever. Amen. 1 Pet. 5:11

P-2

CHORUS

Glo-ry to God, Yes, glo-ry to You, Splen-dor and maj-es-ty, Right-eous-ness too; E-ter-nal do-min-ion, the prais-es of men Are Yours for-ev-er and ev-er a-gain.

Fine

1. For Yours is the King-dom, the pow'r and the glo-ry, Yours is cre-a-tion, re-demp-tion's sto-ry; Yours is the love
2. Lord, give me com-pas-sion for souls that are lost, Give me a mind that's coun-ted the cost; Give me the cour-age
3. O how can I thank You for all You have done: For Christ who died, my heav-en-ly home, Love of the faith-ful,

D.C.

in Christ we see, Yours is the beau-ty of Je-sus in me.
to mas-ter my sin, Give me the Spir-it of Je-sus with-in.
Your Word so true, The hope of glo-ry for-ev-er with You.

E♭-3-DO
L. H.

I Am Coming, Lord

300
C-16, I-1

Unto Him that loved us, and washed us from our sins in His own blood . . . be glory . . . **L. Hartsough**
Rev. 1:5,6

1. I   hear Thy wel-come voice, That calls   me, Lord, to
2. Tho'   com-ing weak and vile, Thou dost   my strength as-
3. 'Tis   Je-sus calls me on   To per-fect faith and

Thee, For cleans-ing   in Thy pre-cious blood That flowed on Cal-va-
sure; Thou dost my   vile-ness ful-ly cleanse,Till spot-less all and
love, To per-fect   hope,and peace and trust, For earth and heav'n a-

CHORUS

ry.
sure; I   am com-ing, Lord! Com-ing   now to Thee!
bove.

Wash me, cleanse me in the blood That flowed on Cal-va-ry!

301 Soul, A Savior Thou Art Needing

F-3-SOL

For all have sinned, and come short of the glory of God. Rom 3:23

1-1

Jessie Brown Pounds

J. H. Fillmore

1. Soul, a Sav - ior thou art need-ing! Soul, a Sav -
2. He has died for thy trans - gres - sion, If thou wilt,
3. Do not lin - ger till the mor-row, Let thy lov -

ior waits for thee! Hear His words of ten - der plead - ing,
thou canst be free; Soul, He waits for thy con - fes - sion,
ing an - swer be, "Sav - ior, in my joy or sor - row,

CHORUS

Hear His gra - cious "Come to Me." He is call - ing,
"Sav - ior, I will go to Thee." He is call - ing,
I will ev - er go to Thee."

soft - ly call - ing, On thine ear His
soft - ly call - ing, On thine ear His

voice is fall - ing; He is call - ing, soft - ly
voice is fall - ing; He is call - ing,

call - ing, "Come to Me and be at rest."
soft - ly call - ing, "Come to Me and be at rest."

Blest Be The Tie

302
C-14, L-2

Truly our fellowship is with the Father, and with His Son

F-3-MI

John Fawcett, 1782

Jesus Christ. I John 1:3

Johann Georg Nageli
Arr. Lowell Mason, 1845

1. Blest be the tie that binds Our hearts in
2. Be - fore our Fa - ther's throne We pour our
3. We share our mu - tual woes, Our mu - tual
4. When we a - sun - der part, It gives us

Christ - ian love; The fel - low - ship of
ar - dent pray'rs; Our fears, our hopes, our
bur - dens bear; And oft - en for each
in - ward pain; But we shall still be

kin - dred minds Is like to that a - bove.
aims are one, Our com - forts and our cares.
oth - er flows The sym - pa - thiz - ing tear.
joined in heart, And hope to meet a - gain.

303 Whiter Than Snow

Wash me, and I shall be whiter than snow. Psa. 51:7

A♭-3-SOL

James Nicholson, 1872

C-16, I-1

Wm. G. Fischer, 1872

1. Lord Je-sus, I long to be per-fect-ly whole; I want Thee for-
2. Lord Je-sus, look down from Thy throne in the skies, And help me to
3. Lord Je-sus, Thou see-est I pa-tient-ly wait; Come now, and with-

ev - er to live in my soul; Break down ev-'ry i - dol, cast
make a com-plete sac - ri - fice; I give up my-self and what-
in me a new heart cre-ate; To those who have sought Thee, Thou

out ev -'ry foe:
ev - er I know: Now wash me, and I shall be whit-er than snow.
nev - er saidst No:

CHORUS

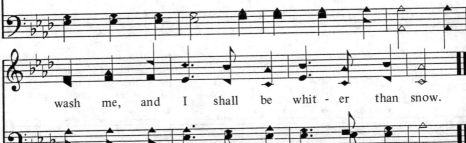

Whit - er than snow, yes, whit - er than snow; Now

wash me, and I shall be whit - er than snow.

Why Do You Wait?

304

I made haste, and delayed not to keep Thy commandments. Psa. 119:60

G. F. R.

I-1

Geo. F. Root

1. Why do you wait, dear broth-er, O why do you tar-ry so long? Your Sav-ior is wait-ing to give you A place in His sanc-ti-fied throng.

2. What do you hope, dear broth-er, To gain by a fur-ther de-lay? There's no one to save you but Je-sus, There's no oth-er way but His way.

3. Why do you wait, dear broth-er, The har-vest is pass-ing a-way; Your Sav-ior is long-ing to bless you: There's dan-ger and death in de-lay.

CHORUS

Why not? why not? Why not come to Him now? now?

305 Let Him In

Db-4-MI

J. B. Atchinson

If any man hear My voice, and open the door, I will come in . . . Rev. 3:20

1-1

E. O. Excell

1. There's a stran-ger at the door, Let Him
2. O - pen now to Him your heart, Let Him
3. Hear you now His lov-ing voice? Let the Sav-ior in,

in; He has been there oft be - fore,
let the Sav-ior in; If you wait He will de - part,
let the Sav-ior in; Now, O now make Him your choice,

Let Him in;
Let the Sav-ior in, let the Sav-ior in; Let Him in, ere
Let Him in, He
He is stand-ing

He is gone, Let him in, the Ho - ly One, Je - sus Christ, the
is your Friend, He your soul will sure de - fend, He will keep you
at your door, Joy to you He will re - store, And His name you

Fa - ther's Son,   Let   Him   in.
to the end,
will a - dore,   Let the Sav - ior in,   let the Sav - ior in.

Lord, Dismiss Us   306

F-4-DO   *The Lord will give strength unto His people; the Lord will bless His people with peace.*   C-14

John Fawcett   Psa. 29:11   **J. G. Bitthauer**

1. Lord, dis - miss us with Thy bless - ing,   Fill   our
2. Thanks we give, and ad - o - ra - tion,   For   the

hearts with joy and peace;   Let   us each, Thy love pos -
Gos - pel's joy - ful sound;   May   the fruits of Thy sal -

sess - ing,   Tri - umph in re - deem - ing grace.
va - tion   In our hearts and lives a - bound.   A - men.

307 Are You Washed In The Blood?

And washed us from our sins in His blood . . . Rev. 1:5

Ab -4- MI
E. A. H.

H-3, 1-1
E. A. Hoffman

1. Have you been to Je - sus for the cleans - ing pow'r? Are you
2. Are you walk - ing dai - ly by the Sav - ior's side? Are you
3. Lay a - side the gar - ments that are stained with sin, And be

washed in the blood of the Lamb? Are you ful - ly trust - ing
washed in the blood of the Lamb? Do you rest each mo - ment
washed in the blood of the Lamb; There's a foun - tain flow - ing

in His grace this hour? Are you washed in the blood of the Lamb?
in the Cru - ci - fied? Are you washed in the blood of the Lamb?
for the soul un - clean, O be washed in the blood of the Lamb!

CHORUS

Are you washed in the blood,
Are you washed in the blood,

In the
soul-cleans-ing blood of the Lamb? Are your gar - ments spot - less,
of the Lamb?

are they white as snow? Are you washed in the blood of the Lamb?

Where Love Is In The Home 308

F-3-SOL
J. E. P.

Let everyone of you . . . so love his wife even as himself;
and the wife see that she reverance her husband. Eph. 5:33

H-5, L-2
Joe E. Parks

1. Where love is in the home there's hap - pi - ness, Where love is
2. Where love is in the home there's har - mo - ny, Where love is
3. Where love is in the home con - tent-ment reigns, Where love is

in the home there's joy; Tho' the fare may sim - ple be, Still it's
in the home there's bliss; If ad-vanced in age you be, You may
in the home there's peace; Gold and sil - ver can - not buy What it

ver - y plain to see—Where love is in the home, there's joy.
call to mem - o - ry—Where love is in the home, there's bliss.
takes to sat - is - fy—Where love is in the home, there's peace.

309 I Am Praying For You

G-4-SOL
S. O'Maley Cluff

He is able to save them . . . that come unto God by Him,
seeing He ever liveth to make intercession for them. Heb. 7:25

I-1
Ira D. Sankey

1. I have a Savior, He's plead - ing in glo - ry, A dear,
2. I have a Fa - ther: to me He has giv - en A hope
3. I have a peace: it is calm as a riv - er, A peace

lov - ing Sav - ior, tho' earth-friends be few; And now He is watch-
for e - ter - ni - ty, bless - ed and true; And soon He will call
that the friends of this world nev - er knew; My Sav - ior a - lone

ing in ten - der-ness o'er me, But O, that my Sav - ior were
me to meet Him in heav - en, But O, that He'd let me bring
is its Au - thor and Giv - er, And O, could I know it was

f CHORUS   *p*

your Sav - ior too!
you with me too! For you I am pray - ing, For you I am
giv - en to you!

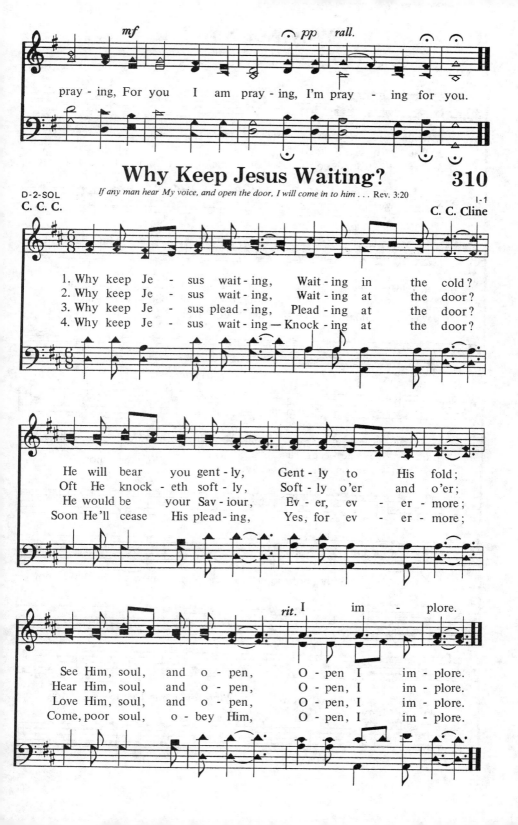

pray - ing, For you I am pray - ing, I'm pray - ing for you.

Why Keep Jesus Waiting? 310

If any man hear My voice, and open the door, I will come in to him . . . Rev. 3:20

D-2-SOL
C. C. C.

I-1
C. C. Cline

1. Why keep Je - sus wait - ing, Wait - ing in the cold?
2. Why keep Je - sus wait - ing, Wait - ing at the door?
3. Why keep Je - sus plead - ing, Plead - ing at the door?
4. Why keep Je - sus wait - ing — Knock - ing at the door?

He will bear you gent - ly, Gent - ly to His fold;
Oft He knock - eth soft - ly, Soft - ly o'er and o'er;
He would be your Sav - iour, Ev - er, ev - er - more;
Soon He'll cease His plead - ing, Yes, for ev - er - more;

See Him, soul, and o - pen, O - pen I im - plore.
Hear Him, soul, and o - pen, O - pen, I im - plore.
Love Him, soul, and o - pen, O - pen, I im - plore.
Come, poor soul, o - bey Him, O - pen, I im - plore.

311

Why Not Now?

Call ye upon Him while He is near . . . return unto the Lord,
and He will have mercy . . . Isa. 55:6,7

D-3-SOL
El Nathan

I-1
C. C. Case

1. While we pray, and while we plead, While you see your
2. You have wan-dered far a-way; Do not risk an-
3. Come to Christ, con-fes-sion make; Come to Christ, and

soul's deep need, While your Fa-ther calls you home,
oth-er day, Do not turn from God your face,
par-don take; Trust in Him from day to day,

CHORUS

Will you not, dear sin-ner, come? Why not now? . . . why not
But to-day ac-cept His grace. Why not now?
He will keep you all the way.

now? . . . .Why not come to Je-sus now? Why not
why not now?

now? . . why not now? . .Why not come to Je-sus now?
Why not now? why not now?

Are You Coming To Jesus Tonight? 312

The Spirit and the bride say, Come. Rev. 22:17

E-4-SOL

I-1

Jessie H. Brown

J. E. Hawes

1. The voice of the Sav-ior says "Come," The cross where He died is in sight, E'en now at the cross there is room, Are you com-ing to Je-sus to-night?

2. The voice of the Fa-ther im-plores, From mer-cy's most won-der-ful height, His love in that call He out-pours, Are you com-ing to Je-sus to-night? Are you com-ing to Je-sus to-night?

3. O who to him-self will be true, Of all whom these voic-es in-vite? Who an-swers, my broth-er, do you? I am com-ing to Je-sus to-night?

CHORUS

Are you com-ing to Je-sus to-night? The Bride and the Spir-it in-vite, Are you com-ing to Je-sus to-night?

313 Though Your Sins Be As Scarlet

A♭-3-SOL

Though your sins be as scarlet, they shall be as white as snow. Isa. 1:18

E-1, I-1

Fanny J. Crosby

Wm. H. Doane

1. "Tho' your sins be as scar-let, They shall be as white
2. Hear the voice that en-treats you: Oh, re-turn ye un-
3. He'll for-give your trans-gres-sions, And re-mem-ber them

as snow; as snow; Tho' they be red . . . . like
to God! to God! He is of great . . . . com-
no more; no more; "Look un-to Me . . . . ye
Tho' they be red,

crim-son, They shall be as wool;" "Tho' your sins be as
pas-sion, And of won-drous love; Hear the voice that en-
peo-ple," Saith the Lord your God; He'll for-give your trans-

scar-let, Tho' your sins be as scar-let, They shall
treats you, Hear the voice that en-treats you, Oh, re-
gres-sions, He'll for-give your trans-gres-sions, And re-

p   rit.

be   as   white   as   snow, They   shall   be   as   white   as   snow."
turn   ye   un - to   God! Oh,   re - turn   ye   un - to   God!
mem - ber   them   no   more, And   re - mem - ber   them   no   more.

There Is A Fountain 314

In that day there shall be a fountain opened . . . for sin and for uncleanness. Zech. 13:1

C-4-DO

Wm. Cowper, 1771

C-2

Lowell Mason

1. There   is   a foun - tain   filled with blood, Drawn from Im - man - uel's   veins;
2. Dear   dy - ing Lamb, Thy   pre - cious blood Shall nev - er lose   its   pow'r,
3. E'er   since by faith I   saw the stream Thy flow - ing wounds sup - ply,

Fine

And   sin - ners, plunged be - neath that flood, Lose   all   their guilt - y   stains.
Till   all   the ran - somed Church of God Be   saved   to sin no   more.
Re - deem - ing love has   been my theme, And   shall   be till I   die.

D.S.

Lose   all   their guilt - y   stains, ... Lose all   their guilt - y   stains;
Be   saved   to   sin   no   more, ... Be saved to   sin   no   more;
And   shall   be   till   I   die, ... And shall   be   till   I   die;

315

O Why Not Tonight?

Eb-4-DO
Elizabeth Reed

J. Calvin Bushey

I-1

If ye will hear His voice, harden not your heart . . . Psa. 95:7,8

1. O do not let the word depart, And close thine eyes against the light; Poor sinner, harden not thy heart, Be saved, O tonight.
2. Tomorrow's sun may never rise To bless thy long-deluded sight; This is the time, O then be wise, Be saved, O tonight.
3. Our blessed Lord refuses none Who would to Him their souls unite; Believe, obey, the work is done, Be saved, O tonight.

CHORUS

O why not tonight? O why not tonight? why not tonight? why not tonight? Wilt thou . . . be saved? Then why not tonight?

O why not tonight? Why not tonight? why not tonight? Wilt thou be saved, wilt thou be saved? Then why not, O why not tonight?

I Heard The Voice Of Jesus Say

316

Db-2-SOL

I am the light of the world; he that followeth Me shall not walk in darkness . . .
John 8:12

Horatius Bonar

I-1, T-1

Louis Spohr, 1859

1. I heard the voice of Je - sus say, "Come un - to me and rest;
2. I heard the voice of Je - sus say, "Be - hold, I free - ly give
3. I heard the voice of Je - sus say, "I am this dark world's light;

Lay down, thou wea - ry one, lay down Thy head up - on my breast."
The liv - ing wa - ter: thirst - y one, Stoop down, and drink, and live."
Look un - to me, thy morn shall rise, And all thy day be bright!

I came to Je - sus as I was, Wea - ry and worn and sad;
I came to Je - sus and I drank Of that life - giv - ing stream:
I looked to Je - sus and I found In Him my Star, my Sun;

I found in Him a rest - ing place, And He has made me glad.
My thirst was quench'd, my soul re - vived, And now I live in Him.
And in that light of life I'll walk Till trav' - ling days are done.

317 All Things Are Ready

Tell them . . . I have prepared my dinner . . . all things are ready. Matt. 22:4

B♭-4-SOL

Charlotte G. Homer

I-1

W. A. Ogden

1. "All things are read-y," come to the feast! Come, for the ta-ble now is spread; Ye fam-ish-ing, ye wea-ry, come, And thou shalt be rich-ly fed.

2. "All things are read-y," come to the feast! Come, for the door is o-pen wide; A place of hon-or is re-served For you at the Mas-ter's side.

3. "All things are read-y," come to the feast! Come, while He waits to wel-come thee; De-lay not while this day is thine, To-mor-row may nev-er be.

4. "All things are read-y," come to the feast! Leave ev'-ry care and world-ly strife, Come, feast up-on the love of God, And drink ev-er-last-ing life.

CHORUS

Hear . . . . . . the in-vi-ta - - - tion. Come, "who - - - - -so-ev-er will;" . . . . . . Praise God . . . . . .

Hear the in-vi-ta - - tion, "Who-so-ev-er will," Hear the in-vi-ta - tion, "Who-so-ev-er will;" Praise God for full sal-

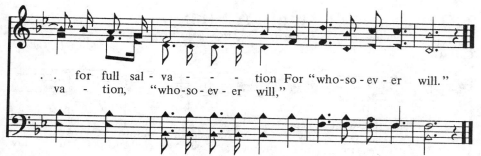

.. for full sal - va - - - - tion For "who-so-ev - er will."
va - tion, "who-so-ev - er will,"

Where Livest Thou? 318

So then everyone of us shall give account of himself to God. Rom. 14:12

F-4-SOL
Vana R. Raye

I-1
L. O. Sanderson

1. Where liv - est thou?   In pleas-ures of the world?   Or   in that
2. Where liv - est thou?   In mal - ice and in strife?   Where dark-ness
3. Where liv - est thou?   There is   a   place to stay—   'Tis   in the

realm whence Sa-tan's darts are hurled? Choose now to   fol - low with the
veils   and mars the right-eous   life?   Choose now to   make a   liv - ing
Christ, the true and liv - ing way!   With - in His king-dom la - bor

sons of God;   Far bet - ter this than where the great have trod.
sac - ri - fice —   'Tis bet - ter thus; for we   be - long to Christ.
while you may;   Hear what He says, in   loy - al trust o - bey.

319 Only A Step

Eb-3-MI
C. H. G.

He became the author of eternal salvation unto all them that obey Him. Heb. 5:9

Chas. H. Gabriel

1-1

1. Hear the sweet voice of Je-sus say, "Come un-to me, I am the way;" Heark-en, the lov - ing call o - bey; Come, for He loves you so.

2. Cast-ing your heav - y bur-den down, Come to the cross, the world may frown; Yet you shall wear a glo - rious crown, When He makes up His own.

3. O - pen, for you, the pearl-y gate; Saved ones for you now watch and wait; Ter - ri - ble tho't, to cry "too late"—"Je - sus, I come to Thee."

CHORUS

On - ly a step, on - ly a step: Come, for He bled for you and died; He's the same lov - ing Sav - ior yet, Je - sus the Cru - ci - fied.

Will Jesus Find Us Watching?　320

Bb-4-SOL

Blessed are those . . . whom the Lord when He cometh shall find watching . . .

Luke 12:37

E-1, S-2

Fanny J. Crosby

W. H. Doane

1. When Je - sus comes to re - ward His serv - ants, Wheth - er it be
2. If at the dawn of the ear - ly morn - ing, He shall call us
3. Bless - ed are those whom the Lord finds watch - ing, In His Glo - ry

noon or night, Faith - ful to Him will He find us watch - ing,
one by one, When to the Lord we re - store our tal - ents,
they shall share; If He shall come at the dawn or mid - night,

CHORUS

With our lamps all trimmed and bright?
Will He an - swer thee, "Well done?" O can we say, we are read - y,
Will He find us watch - ing there?

broth - er? Read - y for the soul's bright home? Say will He find you and

me still watch - ing, Wait - ing, wait - ing when the Lord shall come?

321

Jesus I Come

If the Son therefore shall make you free, ye shall be free indeed. John 8:36

A-2-SOL
William T. Sleeper, 1887

Geo. C. Stebbins, 1887

1-1

1. Out of my bond-age, sor-row and night, Je - sus, I come,
2. Out of my shame-ful fail - ure and loss, Je - sus, I come,
3. Out of the fear and dread of the tomb, Je - sus, I come,

Je - sus, I come; In - to Thy free-dom, glad-ness and light, Je - sus, I
Je - sus, I come; In - to the glo - rious gain of Thy cross, Je - sus, I
Je - sus, I come; In - to the joy and light of Thy home, Je - sus, I

come to Thee; Out of my sick - ness in - to Thy health, Out of my
come to Thee; Out of earth's sor - rows in - to Thy balm, Out of life's
come to Thee; Out of the depths of ru - in un - told, In - to the

want and in - to Thy wealth, Out of my sin and
storms and in - to Thy calm, Out of dis - tress to
peace of Thy shel - ter - ing fold, Ev - er Thy glo - rious

into Thy - self, Je - sus, I come to Thee.
ju - bi - lant psalm, Je - sus, I come to Thee.
face to be - hold, Je - sus, I come to Thee. A - men.

Bring Christ Your Broken Life — 322

I am feeble and sore broken . . . Lord, all my desire is before Thee. Psa. 38:8,9

F-3-SOL

T. O. Chisholm

1-1

L. O. Sanderson

1. Bring Christ your bro - ken life, So marred by sin, He will cre-
2. Bring Him your ev - 'ry care If great or small— What-ev - er
3. Blest Sav - ior of us all! Al - might - y Friend! His pres - ence

ate a - new, Make whole a - gain; Your emp - ty, wast - ed years
trou - bles you— O bring it all! Bring Him the haunt - ing fears,
shall be ours Un - to the end; With - out Him life would be

He will re - store, And your in - i - qui - ties Re - mem - ber no more.
The name - less dread, Thy heart He will re - lieve, And lift up thy head.
How dark, how drear! But with Him morn - ing breaks And heav - en is near!

323 Where Will You Spend Eternity?

All that are in the graves shall hear His voice, and shall come forth . . . unto the
resurrection of life and . . . of damnation. John 5:28, 29

F-4-MI

E. A. Hoffman

I-1

J. H. Tenney

1. Where will you spend e - ter - ni - ty? This ques - tion comes to
2. Man - y are choos-ing Christ to - day, Turn-ing from all their
3. Leav - ing the strait and nar - row way, Go - ing the down-ward
4. Re - pent, o - bey, this ver - y hour, Trust in the Sav - ior's

you and me! Tell me, what shall your an - swer be?
sins a - way; Heav'n shall their hap - py por - tion be;
road to - day, Sad will their fi - nal end - ing be,
grace and pow'r, Then will your joy - ous an - swer be,

Where will you spend e - ter - ni - ty? E - ter - ni -
Where will you spend e - ter - ni - ty? E - ter - ni -
Lost thro' a long e - ter - ni - ty! E - ter - ni -
Saved thro' a long e - ter - ni - ty! E - ter - ni -

ty! e - ter - ni - ty! Where will you spend e - ter - ni - ty?
ty! e - ter - ni - ty! Where will you spend e - ter - ni - ty?
ty! e - ter - ni - ty! Lost thro' a long e - ter - ni - ty!
ty! e - ter - ni - ty! Saved thro' a long e - ter - ni - ty!

Come, Sinner, Come

324

Whereunto He called you by our gospel . . . II Thess. 2:14

F-2-MI

W. E. Witter

I-1

H. R. Palmer

1. While thru His Word He calls you, Come, sin - ner, come!
2. Are you too heav - y - la - den? Come, sin - ner, come!
3. O hear His ten - der plead-ing, Come, sin - ner, come!

While we are pray-ing for you, Come, sin - ner, come!
Je - sus will bear your bur - den, Come, sin - ner, come!
Come and re - ceive the bless-ing, Come, sin - ner, come!

Now is the time to own Him, Come, sin - ner, come!
Je - sus will not de-ceive you, Come, sin - ner, come!
While Je - sus now in -vites you, Come, sin - ner, come!

Now is the time to know Him, Come, sin - ner, come!
Je - sus can now re - deem you, Come, sin - ner, come!
While we are pray - ing for you, Come, sin - ner, come!

325 I Am Resolved

Bb-4-SOL
Palmer Hartsough

Lord, to whom shall we go? Thou hast the words of eternal life. John 6:68

T-1
J. H. Fillmore

1. I am re-solved no long-er to lin-ger, Charmed by the world's de-light; Things that are high-er, things that are no-bler, These have al-lured my sight.
2. I am re-solved to go to the Sav-ior, Leav-ing my sin and strife; He is the true One, He is the just One, He hath the words of life.
3. I am re-solved to fol-low the Sav-ior, Faith-ful and true each day, Heed what He say-eth, do what He will-eth, He is the liv-ing way.
4. I am re-solved to en-ter the king-dom, Leav-ing the paths of sin; Friends may op-pose me, foes may be-set me, Still will I en-ter in.

CHORUS

I will has-ten to Him, has-ten so glad and free, I will has-ten, has-ten to Him, Je-sus, great-est, high-est, I will come to Thee. Je-sus, Je-sus, has-ten glad and free,

Trust And Obey

Blessed are all they that put their trust in Him. Psa. 2:12

326

F-3-DO

John H. Sammis, 1887

F-2

Daniel B. Towner, 1887

1. When we walk with the Lord In the light of His word,
2. Not a bur-den we bear, Not a sor-row we share,
3. But we nev-er can prove The de-lights of His love,
4. Then in fel-low-ship sweet We will sit at His feet,

What a glo-ry He sheds on our way! While we do His good will,
But our toil He doth rich-ly re-pay; Not a grief or a loss,
Un-til all on the al-tar we lay; For the fa-vor He shows,
Or we'll walk by His side in the way; What He says, we will do;

He a-bides with us still, And with all who will trust and o-bey.
Not a frown or a cross, But is blest if we trust and o-bey.
And the joy He be-stows, Are for those who will trust and o-bey.
Where He sends, we will go; Nev-er fear, on-ly trust and o-bey.

CHORUS

Trust and o-bey, for there's no oth-er way To be

hap-py in Je-sus, but to trust and o-bey.

327

What Shall It Be?

What shall I do then with Jesus which is called Christ? Matt. 27:22

Db-2-SOL
James Robinson

B. D. Ackley

1-1

1. What will you do with Je-sus? The ques-tion comes to you! And you must give an an-swer, For some-thing you must do.

2. "What will you do with Je-sus?" It comes by night and day; With pierc-ed hands up-lift-ed, He waits—what will you say?

3. What will you do with Je-sus? He's knock-ing at the door! Re-fuse Him, soul, no lon-ger, Lest He should plead no more.

CHORUS

What shall it be? what shall it be? What shall your an-swer be? . . . . What will you do with Je-sus? O what shall your an-swer be?

What shall your an-swer be?

rit.

His Sheep Am I

328

He maketh me to lie down in green pastures:
He leadeth me beside the still waters. Psa. 23:2

Eb-4-DO
Orien Johnson
St. 2, Dane K. Shepard

C-11
Orien Johnson
Arr. by R. J. Stevens

1. In God's green pas-tures feed-ing, by His cool wa-ters lie,
2. In God's way gent-ly lead-ing, o'er the path low or high,

Soft— in the eve-ning walk my Lord and I. All the sheep of His
Ear-ly in the morn-ing walk my Lord and I.

pas-ture fare so won-drous-ly fine. His sheep am I.

CHORUS

Wa-ters cool, pas-tures green, In the
Dark the night, rough the way, Step by

In the val-ley, on the moun-tain,
In the val-ley, on the moun-tain,

eve - ning walk my Lord and I;
step my Lord and

1
2
I.

In the eve-ning walk my
Step by step, my Lord and

God Calling Yet

Today if ye will hear His voice, harden not your hearts . . . Heb. 3:7,8

Bb-4-SOL

J. Borthwick, *trans.*

1-1

1. God call-ing yet! shall I not hear? Earth's pleasures shall I
2. God call-ing yet! shall I not rise? Can I His lov-ing
3. God call-ing yet! I can-not stay; My heart I yield with-

still hold dear? Shall life's swift pass-ing years all fly, And still my
voice de-spise, And base-ly His kind care re-pay? He calls me
out de-lay; Vain world, fare-well! from thee I part; The voice of

CHORUS

soul in slum-ber lie? God is
still; can I de-lay? God is call-ing yet,
God has reach'd my heart: God is call-ing yet,

call - - - ing, call - - - ing
God is call-ing yet, Heed His plead-ing voice,

yet, God is
God is call-ing yet, God is call-ing yet,

rit.

call - - - ing,
God is call - ing yet, Sin - ner, heed His plead - ing voice.

Just As I Am

Ho, every one that thirsteth come . . . without money and without price. Isa. 55:1

E♭-2-DO

Charlotte Elliott

C-16, I-1

Wm. B. Bradbury

1. Just as I am, with - out one plea, But that Thy
2. Just as I am, and wait - ing not To rid my
3. Just as I am, tho tossed a - bout With man - y a
4. Just as I am — Thou wilt re - ceive, Wilt wel - come,

blood was shed for me, And that Thou bidd'st me
soul of one dark blot, To Thee whose blood can
con - flict, man - y a doubt, Fight - ings and fears with -
par - don, cleanse, re - lieve; Be - cause Thy prom - ise

p

come to Thee, O Lamb of God, I come! I come!
cleanse each spot, O Lamb of God, I come! I come!
in with - out, O Lamb of God, I come! I come!
I be - lieve, O Lamb of God, I come! I come!

331 Kneel At The Cross

Wherefore He is able also to save them . . .seeing He ever liveth to make intercession for them. Heb. 7:25

B♭-4-SOL
C. E. M.

D-1
Chas. E. Moody

1. Kneel at the cross, Christ will meet you there, He in-ter-cedes for
2. Kneel at the cross, There is room for all Who would His glo-ry
3. Kneel at the cross, Give your i-dols up, Look un-to realms a-

you; Lift up your voice, Leave with Him your care And be-gin life a-
share; Bliss there a-waits, Harm can ne'er be-fall Those who are an-chored
bove; Turn not a-gain To life's spar-kling cup; Trust al-ways in His

CHORUS

new. Kneel at the cross, Leave . . . . .
there. Kneel at the cross, Kneel at the cross, Leave ev-'ry
love.

. . . ev-'ry care; Kneel at the
care, Leave ev-'ry care; Kneel at the cross,

cross, Je-sus will meet you there.
Kneel at the cross, meet you there.

I Surrender All

D-4-MI

Whosoever he be of you that forsaketh not all that he hath, he cannot be My disciple.

J. W. Van De Venter

Luke 14:33

B-1

W. S. Weeden

1. All to Je-sus I sur-ren-der, All to Him I free-ly give;
2. All to Je-sus I sur-ren-der, Hum-bly at His feet I bow;
3. All to Je-sus I sur-ren-der, Lord, I give my-self to Thee;

I will ev-er love and trust Him, In His pres-ence dai-ly live.
World-ly pleas-ures all for-sak-en, Take me, Je-sus, take me now.
Fill me with Thy love and pow-er, Let Thy bless-ings fall on me.

CHORUS

I sur-ren-der all I sur-ren-der all; . . .
I sur-ren-der all, I sur-

. . . . All to Thee, my bless-ed Sav-ior, I sur-ren-der all!
ren-der all;

333 Jesus Will Give You Rest

Come unto Me . . . and I will give you rest. Matt. 11:28

G-4-SOL
Fanny Crosby

J. R. Sweney

I-1

1. Will you come, will you come, With your poor brok-en heart,
2. Will you come, will you come? There is mer-cy for you,
3. Will you come, will you come? How He pleads with you now;

Bur-dened and sin o-press'd? Lay it down at the
Balm for your ach-ing breast; O-bey Je-sus your
Fly to His lov-ing breast; And what-ev-er your

feet of your Sav-ior and Lord,
Lord, heed His ev-'ry com-mand, Je-sus will give you rest.
sin or your sor-row may be,

CHORUS

O hap-py rest, sweet hap-py rest, Je-sus will give you

rest. (hap-py rest.) O why won't you come in

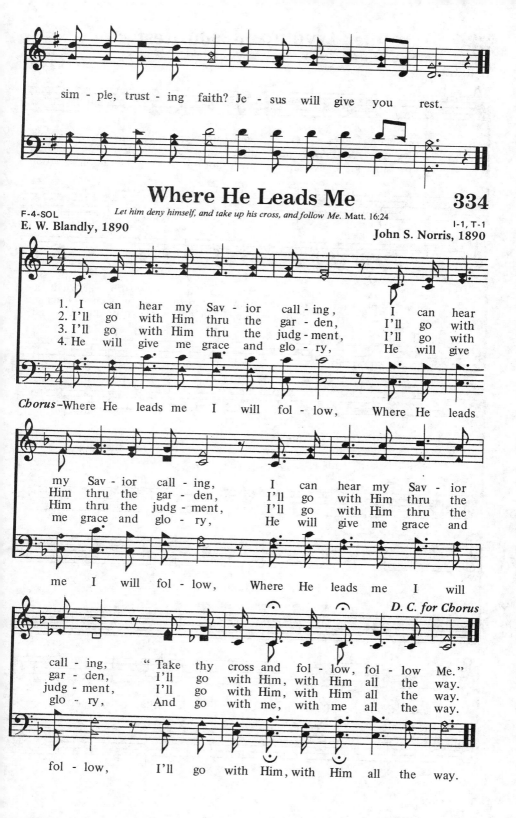

sim - ple, trust - ing faith? Je - sus will give you rest.

Where He Leads Me
334

Let him deny himself, and take up his cross, and follow Me. Matt. 16:24

F-4-SOL
E. W. Blandly, 1890

I-1, T-1
John S. Norris, 1890

1. I can hear my Sav - ior call - ing,   I can hear
2. I'll go with Him thru the gar - den,   I'll go with
3. I'll go with Him thru the judg - ment,   I'll go with
4. He will give me grace and glo - ry,   He will give

Chorus - Where He leads me I will fol - low,   Where He leads

my Sav - ior call - ing,   I can hear my Sav - ior
Him thru the gar - den,   I'll go with Him thru the
Him thru the judg - ment,   I'll go with Him thru the
me grace and glo - ry,   He will give me grace and

me I will fol - low,   Where He leads me I will

D. C. for Chorus

call - ing,   "Take thy cross and fol - low, fol - low Me."
gar - den,   I'll go with Him, with Him all the way.
judg - ment,   I'll go with Him, with Him all the way.
glo - ry,   And go with me, with me all the way.

fol - low,   I'll go with Him, with Him all the way.

335 Live For Jesus

E-3-MI
E. R. Latta

C-12, L-6
Frank M. Davis

Yet not I, but Christ liveth in me; and the life which I now live . . .
I live by the faith of the Son of God . . . Gal. 2:20

1. Live for Je-sus, O my broth-er, His dis-ci- ple
2. Live for Je-sus, wand-'ring sin-ner, Un-der Sa- tan
3. Live for Je-sus in life's morn-ing; At the noon- tide

ev- er be; Ren-der not to a- ny oth-er, What a-
serve no more; Of the prom-ised prize a win-ner Thou may'st
hour be His, And at eve, when day is turn-ing, And in-

CHORUS

lone the Lord's should be.
be, when life is o'er. Live for Je-sus, live for
her- it end-less bliss.

Je-sus; Give Him all thou hast to give; On the

cross the world's Re-deem-er, Gave His life that thou mightst live.

The Only Way

336

A♭-2-SOL

I am the way, the truth, and the life: no man cometh unto the Father, but by Me.

John 14:6

T. O. Chisholm

Samuel W. Beazley

1-1

1. Would you be freed from your bur-den of sin? Hear the sweet
2. Would you have light that no clouds can ob-scure? Would you have
3. Would you find rest in a bless-ed re-treat, Rest un-dis-

whis-per of par-don with-in? Would you this mo-ment a
joys that are fade-less and pure? Would you have help that is
turbed by the temp-ests that beat? Would you be read-y the

new life be-gin? This is the on-ly way:
might-y and sure? This is the on-ly way:
judg-ment to meet? This is the on-ly way:

CHORUS

Come to the

cross of the Son of God, Trust in the pow'r of His sav-ing blood,

Walk in the path where His feet once trod—This is the on-ly way.

337 Once For All

Eb-3-DO
P. P. B.

We are sanctified through the offering of the body of Jesus Christ once for all.
Heb. 10:10

Philip P. Bliss

1. Free from the law, O hap-py con-di-tion, Je-sus hath
2. Now are we free—there's no con-dem-na-tion, Je-sus pro-
3. "Chil-dren of God," O glo-ri-ous call-ing, Tru-ly His

bled, and there is re-mis-sion, Cursed by the law and bruised by the
vides a per-fect sal-va-tion; "Come un-to Me," O hear His sweet
grace will help us from fall-ing; Pass-ing from death to life at His

CHORUS

fall, Grace hath re-deemed us once for all.
call, Come, un-to Je-sus once for all. Once for
call, Bless-ed sal-va-tion once for all.

all, O sin-ner, re-ceive it; Once for all, O

won't you be-lieve it; Cling to the Sav-ior, o-bey His

The Great Physician **338**

They that be whole need not a physician, but they that are sick . . . Matt. 9:2

Wm. Hunter, 1859

John H. Stockton, 1869

call, Christ hath re-deemed us once for all.

1. The great Phy-si-cian now is near, The sym-pa-thiz-ing Je-sus;
2. All glo-ry to the dy-ing Lamb! I now be-lieve in Je-sus;
3. His name dis-pels my guilt and fear, No oth-er name but Je-sus;
4. And when to that bright world a-bove, We rise to see our Je-sus,

D. S.–Sweet-est car-ol ev-er sung, Je-sus, bless-ed Je-sus.

He speaks the droop-ing heart to cheer: O hear the voice of Je-sus.
I love the bless-ed Sav-ior's name, I love the name of Je-sus.
O how my soul de-lights to hear The charm-ing name of Je-sus.
We'll sing a-round the throne of love His name, the name of Je-sus.

CHORUS

Sweet-est note in ser-aph song, Sweet-est name on mor-tal tongue,

339 Ye Must Be Born Again

Except a man be born again he cannot see the kingdom of God. John 3:3

Eb-2-DO

B-1

William T. Sleeper, 1877

Geo. C. Stebbins, 1877

1. A rul-er once came to Je-sus by night, To ask Him the way of sal-va-tion and light; The Mas-ter made an-swer in words true and plain: "Ye must be born a-gain."

2. Ye chil-dren of men at-tend to the word So sol-emn-ly ut-tered by Je-sus, the Lord, And let not this mes-sage to you be in vain: "Ye must be born a-gain."

3. O ye who would en-ter that glo-ri-ous rest, And sing with the ran-somed the song of the blest! The life ev-er-last-ing if ye would ob-tain, "Ye must be born a-gain."

CHORUS

"Ye must be born a-gain, a-gain, "Ye must be born a-gain, a-gain, Ye must be born a-gain, a-gain, I ver-i-ly, a-gain,

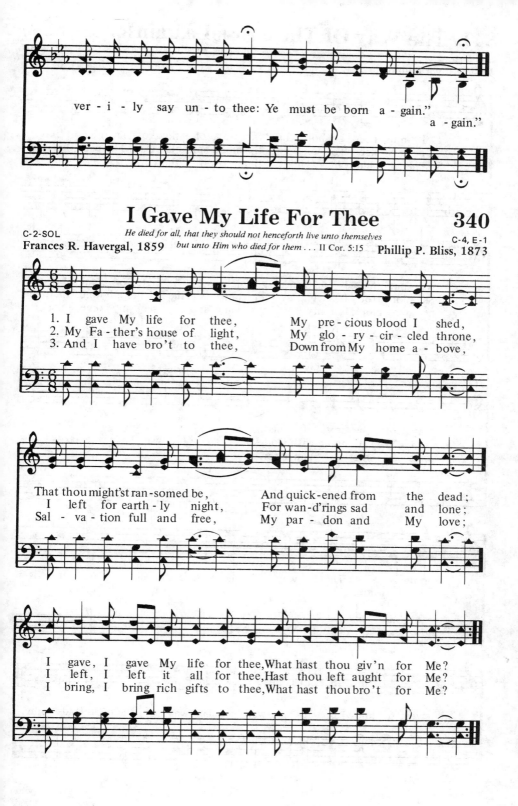

ver - i - ly say un - to thee: Ye must be born a - gain."

a - gain."

I Gave My Life For Thee

340

He died for all, that they should not henceforth live unto themselves
but unto Him who died for them . . . II Cor. 5:15

C-2-SOL
Frances R. Havergal, 1859

C-4, E-1
Phillip P. Bliss, 1873

1. I gave My life for thee, My pre - cious blood I shed,
2. My Fa - ther's house of light, My glo - ry - cir - cled throne,
3. And I have bro't to thee, Down from My home a - bove,

That thou might'st ran - somed be, And quick-ened from the dead;
I left for earth - ly night, For wan - d'rings sad and lone;
Sal - va - tion full and free, My par - don and My love;

I gave, I gave My life for thee, What hast thou giv'n for Me?
I left, I left it all for thee, Hast thou left aught for Me?
I bring, I bring rich gifts to thee, What hast thou bro't for Me?

341 The Way Of The Cross Leads Home

Ab-4-SOL

Jessie Brown Pounds

Come, take up the cross, and follow Me. Mark 10:21

C-17

Chas. H. Gabriel

1. I must needs go home by the way of the cross, There's no oth-er
2. I must needs go on in the blood-sprinkled way, The path that the
3. Then I bid fare-well to the way of the world, To walk in it

way but this; I shall ne'er get sight of the Gates of Light If the
Sav-ior trod, If I ev-er climb to the heights sub-lime, Where the
nev-er-more; For my Lord says"Come" and I seek my home, Where He

CHORUS

way of the cross I miss.
soul is at home with God.   The way of the cross leads
waits at the o-pen door.

home, The way of the cross leads home; It is
leads home,   leads home;

sweet to know, as I on-ward go, The way of the cross leads home.

I Come To Thee

Behold, we come unto Thee; for Thou art the Lord our God. Jer. 3:22

C-2-MI

E. M. Z.

D-1

E. M. Zerr

1. Oh Lord, I come to Thee, Thy blood is all my plea,
2. Oh Lord of truth and love, All earth-ly things a-bove,
3. Thy Word I would o-bey, And keep from day to day,

My-self I give for Thee to live, De-vot-ed thus to be;
Thy life be-stow and make me know, Thy right-eous will to prove;
Thy pre-cepts pure and thus se-cure, My heart from er-ror's way.

Oh let Thy love be mine, And fill with joy di-vine,
Oh keep me in the light, And lead me by Thy might,
Then let the world de-ride, With-in Thy love I'll hide,

Thy ten-der care now let me share, My life, my all, are Thine.
Till life shall end and I as-cend, To Heav'n where all is bright.
No foes can harm nor fears a-larm, While keep-ing near Thy side.

343 Let Him Have His Way With Thee

Humble yourselves therefore under the mighty hand of God, that He may exalt you . . .
1 Pet. 5:6

G-4-SOL
C. S. N.

Cyrus S. Nusbaum

I-1

1. Would you live for Je-sus, and be al-ways pure and good? Would you
2. Would you have Him make you free, and fol-low at His call? Would you
3. Would you in His king-dom find a place of con-stant rest? Would you

walk with Him with-in the nar-row road? Would you have Him bear your
know the peace that comes by giv-ing all? Would you have Him save you,
prove Him true each prov-i-den-tial test? Would you in His ser-vice

bur-den, car-ry all your load? Let Him have His way with thee.
so that you need nev-er fall? Let Him have His way with thee.
la-bor al-ways at your best? Let Him have His way with thee.

CHORUS

His pow'r can make you what you ought to be; His blood can

cleanse your heart and make you free; His love can fill your soul, and

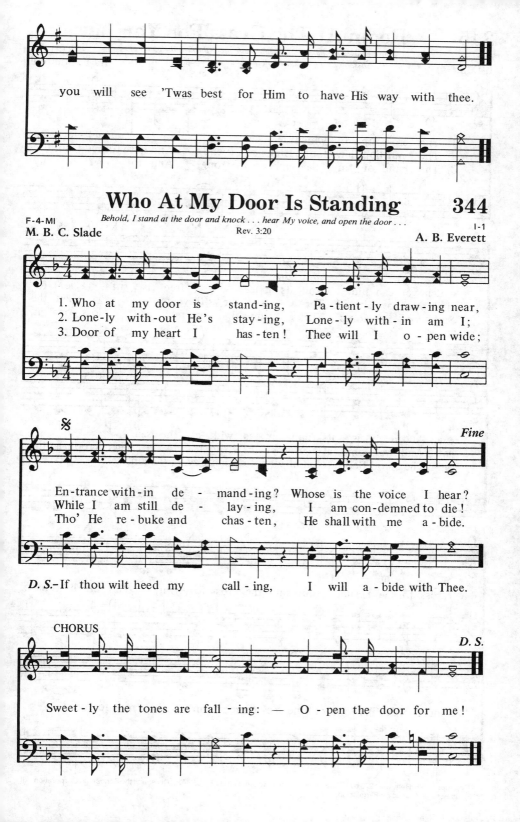

you will see 'Twas best for Him to have His way with thee.

Who At My Door Is Standing   344

Behold, I stand at the door and knock . . . hear My voice, and open the door . . .
Rev. 3:20

F-4-MI

M. B. C. Slade

I-1

A. B. Everett

1. Who at my door is stand-ing, Pa-tient-ly draw-ing near,
2. Lone-ly with-out He's stay-ing, Lone-ly with-in am I;
3. Door of my heart I has-ten! Thee will I o-pen wide;

Fine

En-trance with-in de - mand-ing? Whose is the voice I hear?
While I am still de - lay-ing, I am con-demned to die!
Tho' He re - buke and chas-ten, He shall with me a-bide.

D. S.–If thou wilt heed my call-ing, I will a-bide with Thee.

CHORUS

D. S.

Sweet-ly the tones are fall-ing: — O-pen the door for me!

345 Room At The Cross For You

G-2-SOL
I. F. S.

For it pleased the Father . . . having made peace through the blood of His cross, by Him to reconcile all things unto Himself. Col. 1:19,20

C-17, I-1

Ira F. Stanphill

1. The cross up-on which Je-sus died Is a shel-ter in
2. Tho' mil-lions have found Him a friend And have turned from the
3. The hand of my Sav-ior is strong, And the love of my

which we can hide; And its grace so free is suf-fi-cient for
sins they have sinned, The Sav-ior still waits to o-pen the
Sav-ior is long; Thru sun-shine or rain, thru loss or in

me, And deep is its foun-tain—as wide as the sea.
gates And wel-come a sin-ner be-fore it's too late. There's room at the
gain, The blood flows from Cal-v'ry to cleanse ev-'ry stain.

CHORUS

cross for you, There's room at the cross for you; Tho' mil-lions have

come, There's still room for one—Yes, there's room at the cross for you.

Shall I Crucify My Savior?

346

Eb-4-SOL

If they shall fall away... they crucify to themselves the
Son of God afresh, and put Him to an open shame. Heb. 6:6

C-3

Mrs. Frank A. Breck

Grant Colfax Tullar
Arr. by R. J. Stevens

1. Shall I cru - ci - fy my Sav - ior, When for
2. Are temp - ta - tions so al - lur - ing? Do earth's
3. 'Twas my sins that cru - ci - fied Him— Shall they
4. Oh! The kind - ly hands of Je - sus, Pour - ing

me He bore such loss? Shall I put to shame my Sav - ior?
plea - sures so en - thrall, That I can - not love my Sav - ior
cru - ci - fy Him yet? Black - est day of name - less an - guish,
bless - ings on all men! Bleed - ing, nail - scarred hands of Je - sus!

D.S. Once! Oh once I cru - ci - fied Him!

Fine CHORUS

Can I nail Him to the cross?
Well e - nough to leave them all?
Can my thank - less soul for - get? Shall I cru - ci - fy
Can I nail them once a - gain?

Shall I cru - ci - fy a - gain?

D.S.

my Sav - ior? Cru - ci - fy my Lord a - gain?

347 Who Will Follow Jesus?

He that is not with Me is against Me. Matt. 12:30

D-4-SOL
F-3, W-1

E. E. Hewitt

Wm. J. Kirkpatrick

1. Who will fol-low Je - sus, Stand-ing for the right, Hold-ing up His
2. Who will fol-low Je - sus In life's bus - y ways, Work-ing for the
3. Who will fol-low Je - sus In His work of love, Lead-ing oth - ers

ban - ner In the thick-est fight? Lis-t'ning for His or-ders, Read-y
Mas-ter, Giv-ing Him the praise; Ear-nest in His vine-yard, Hon-or-
to Him, Lift- ing prayers a - bove? Cour-age, faith-ful serv-ant! In His

to o - bey, Who will fol - low Je - sus, Serv-ing Him to - day?
ing His laws, Faith-ful to His coun - sel, Watch-ful for His cause?
word we see, On our side for - ev - er Will this Sav-ior be.

Fine

CHORUS

D. S.-Mas - ter, here am I"?

Who will fol - low Je - sus? Who will make re - ply, "I am

on the Lord's side; Mas - ter, here am I"? Who will fol - low

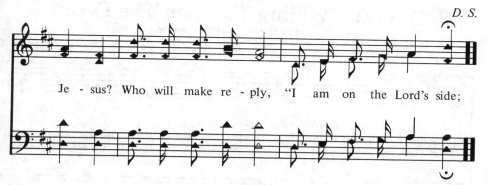

Je - sus? Who will make re - ply, "I am on the Lord's side;

Almost Persuaded

348

Almost thou persuadest me to be a Christian. Acts 26:28

G-2-MI
P. P. B.

I-1
Phillip P. Bliss

1. "Al - most per - suad - ed " now to be - lieve; "Al - most per - suad - ed "
2. "Al - most per - suad - ed " come, come to - day; "Al - most per - suad - ed,"
3. "Al - most per - suad - ed " har - vest is past ! "Al - most per - suad - ed,"

Christ to re - ceive; Seems now some soul to say, "Go, Spir - it,
turn not a - way; Je - sus in - vites you here, An - gels are
doom comes at last ! "Al - most " can - not a - vail; "Al - most " is

go Thy way; Some more con - ven - ient day On Thee I'll call."
lin - g'ring near, Prayers rise from hearts so dear, O wan - d'rer, come.
but to fail; Sad, sad, that bit - ter wail— "Al - most— but lost !"

349 Are You Willing To Open The Door?

Behold, I stand at the door, and knock; if any man hear My voice,
and open the door, I will come in . . . Rev. 3:20

I-1

F-2-SOL
J. E. P.

Joe E. Parks

1. Are you will - ing to o - pen the door and let the Sav - ior
2. Are you will - ing to o - pen the door where com - fort waits and
3. Are you will - ing to o - pen the door in an - swer to His

in? Are you will - ing to walk in His way and leave the
rest? Are you will - ing to trust Him just now? He tru - ly
call? Are you will - ing to bid Him come in and give to

CHORUS

paths of sin?
knows what's best. He can take your guilt a - way, Give you life a-
Him your all?

new; Lost in sin, why long - er stray? Je - sus cares for you.

I Know Whom I Have Believed 350

D-4-DO
Daniel W. Whittle, 1883

I know whom I have believed, and am persuaded that He is able
to keep that which I have committed unto Him . . .
II Tim. 1:12

F-1, T-1
J. McGranahan, 1883

1. I know not why God's won-drous grace To me He
2. I know not what of good or ill May be re-
3. I know not when my Lord may come, At night or

hath made known, Nor why, un-wor - thy, Christ in
served for me, Of wea - ry ways or gold - en
noon - day fair, Nor if I'll walk the vale with

CHORUS

love Re - deemed me for His own.
days, Be - fore His face I see. But "I know whom I
Him, Or "meet Him in the air."

have be - liev - ed, And am per - suad - ed that He is a - ble

To keep that which I've com - mit - ted Un - to Him a - gainst that day."

351 Will You Not Tell It Today

Eb-2-DO

Go . . . tell them how great things the Lord hath done for thee . . . Mark 5:19

S-5

Jessie Brown Pounds

J. H. Fillmore

1. If the name of the Sav-ior is pre-cious to you, If His
2. If your faith in the Sav-ior has bro't its re-ward, If a
3. If the souls all a-round you are liv-ing in sin, If the

care has been con-stant and ten-der and true, If the light of His
strength you have found in the strength of your Lord, If the hope of a
Mas-ter has told you to bid them come in, If the sweet in-vi-

pres-ence has bright-ened your way, O will you not tell of your
rest in His pal-ace is sweet, O will you not, broth-er, the
ta-tion they nev-er have heard, O will you not tell them the

glad-ness to-day?
sto-ry re-peat?
cheer-bring-ing word?

CHORUS

O will you not tell it to-day?
will you not tell it to-day?

Will you not tell it to-day?
will you not tell it to-day?

If the light of His

pres-ence has bright-ened your way, O will you not tell it to-day?

More Holiness Give Me

352

E♭-4-MI
P. P. B.

Put on the new man, which after God is created in righteousness and true holiness.
Eph. 4:24

D-1, H-3

Philip P. Bliss, 1873

1. More ho-li-ness give me, More striv-ings with-in, More pa-tience in
2. More grat-i-tude give me, More trust in the Lord, More pride in His
3. More pu-ri-ty give me, More strength to o'ercome, More free-dom from

suf-f'ring, More sor-row for sin, More faith in my Sav-ior,
glo-ry, More hope in His word, More tears for His sor-rows,
earth-stains, More long-ings for home; More fit for the king-dom,

More sense of His care, More joy in His serv-ice, More pur-pose in prayer.
More pain at His grief, More meekness in tri-al, More praise for re-lief.
More use-ful I'd be, More bless-ed and ho-ly, More, Sav-ior, like Thee.

353 He Lives

B♭-2-SOL
A. H. A.

Be strengthened by His Spirit in the inner man;
that Christ may dwell in your hearts by faith. Eph. 3:16,17

F-2
A. H. Ackley

1. I serve a ris - en Sav - ior, He's in the world to - day;
2. In all the world a-round me I see His lov - ing care,
3. Re-joice, re-joice, O Chris-tian, lift up your voice and sing

I know that He is liv-ing, what-ev-er men may say; I
And tho' my heart grows wea-ry I nev-er will de-spair; I
E - ter-nal hal-le-lu-jahs to Je-sus Christ the King! The

see His hand of mer - cy, I hear His voice of cheer, And
know that He is lead - ing, thru all the storm - y blast, The
hope of all who seek Him, the help of all who find, None

CHORUS *Spirited*

just the time I need Him He's al - ways near.
day of His ap-pear - ing will come at last. He lives, . . .
oth - er is so lov - ing, so good and kind.
He

354 O How Love I Thy Law

The law of the Lord is perfect, converting the soul. Psa. 19:7

F-2-SOL
Ps. 19: 7-11, Arr.

W-3
James McGranahan

1. Un-spot-ted is the fear of God, And ev-er doth en-
2. They more than gold, yea, much fine gold, To be de-sir-ed
3. More-o-ver they, Thy serv-ant warn, How he his life should

dure; The judg-ments of the Lord are truth, And right-eous-
are, Than hon-ey from the hon-ey-comb That drop-peth
frame. A great re-ward pro-vid-ed is For them that

ness most pure.
sweet-er far.   CHORUS
keep the same.

Faster

"O how love I Thy law, O how love I Thy law; It is my med-i-ta-tion all the day; O how love I Thy law, O how love I Thy law;

It is my med-i-ta-tion all the day. (all the day.)"

Break Thou The Bread Of Life   355

E♭-2-MI

Mary A. Lathbury, 1877

For the bread of God is He which cometh down from Heaven,
and giveth life unto the world. John 6:33

S-3, W-3

Wm. F. Sherwin, 1877

1. Break Thou the bread of life, Dear Lord, to me, As Thou didst
2. Bless Thou the truth, dear Lord, To me, to me, As Thou didst
3. Thou art the bread of life, O Lord, to me, Thy ho - ly

break the loaves Be - side the sea; With - in the sa - cred page
bless the bread By Gal - i - lee; Then shall all bond-age cease,
Word the truth That sav - eth me; Give me to eat and live

I seek Thee, Lord; My spir - it pants for Thee, O liv - ing Word.
All fet - ters fall; And I shall find my peace, My All in all.
With Thee a - bove; Teach me to love Thy truth, For Thou art love.

356 If Jesus Goes With Me

C-2-MI
C. A. M.

F-2, F-3
C. Austin Miles

Go ye therefore, and teach all nations . . . and lo, I am with you always . . .
Matt. 28:19,20

1. It may be in the val-ley, where count-less dan-gers hide; It may be in the sun-shine that I, in peace, a-bide; But this one thing I know — if it be dark or fair, If

2. It may be I must car-ry the bless-ed word of life A-cross the burn-ing des-erts to those in sin-ful strife; And tho' it be my lot to bear my col-ors there, If

3. It is not mine to ques-tion the judg-ments of my Lord, It is but mine to fol-low the lead-ings of His word; But if to go or stay, or wheth-er here or there, I'll

CHORUS

Je-sus is with me, I'll go an-y-where!
Je-sus goes with me, I'll go an-y-where! If
be, with my Sav-ior, con-tent an-y-where!

357 The Hollow Of God's Hand

C-4-DO
E. S. L.

For Thou art my strength. Into Thine hand I commit my spirit;
Thou hast redeemed me . . . Psa. 31:4,5

C-15, P-5
E. S. Lorenz

1. I am safe, what-ev-er may be-tide me; I am safe who-
2. What tho' fierce the storm blast roar a-round me; What tho' sore life's
3. Ev-er-last-ing arms of love en-fold me; Words of peace the

ev-er may de-ride me; I am safe, as long as I con-
tri-als oft con-found me; I am safe, for naught of ill can
voice di-vine has told me; I am safe, while God Him-self doth

CHORUS

fide me In the hol-low of God's hand. In the bless-ed
harm me In the hol-low of God's hand. In the
hold me In the hol-low of God's hand.

hol-low of His hand, In the bless-ed
hol-low, in the hol-low of His hand, In the

hol-low of His hand; I am safe while
hol-low, in the hol-low of His hand

God Him - self doth hold me In the hol - low of His hand.

Asleep In Jesus

358

D-3-SOL

Even so them also which sleep in Jesus will God bring with Him. I Thess. 4:14

Margaret MacKay

C-15, R-2

Wm. B. Bradbury

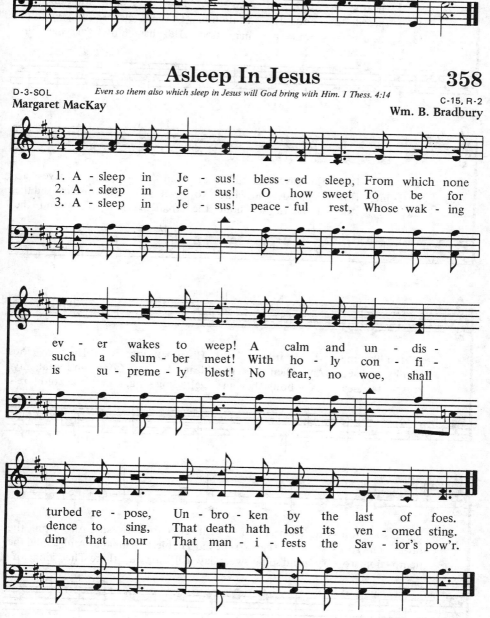

1. A - sleep in Je - sus! bless - ed sleep, From which none ev - er wakes to weep! A calm and un - dis - turbed re - pose, Un - bro - ken by the last of foes.

2. A - sleep in Je - sus! O how sweet To be for such a slum - ber meet! With ho - ly con - fi - dence to sing, That death hath lost its ven - omed sting.

3. A - sleep in Je - sus! peace - ful rest, Whose wak - ing is su - preme - ly blest! No fear, no woe, shall dim that hour That man - i - fests the Sav - ior's pow'r.

359

Victory In Jesus

Thanks be to God which giveth us the victory through our Lord Jesus Christ.
I Cor. 15:57

S-1, V-1
E. M. Bartlett

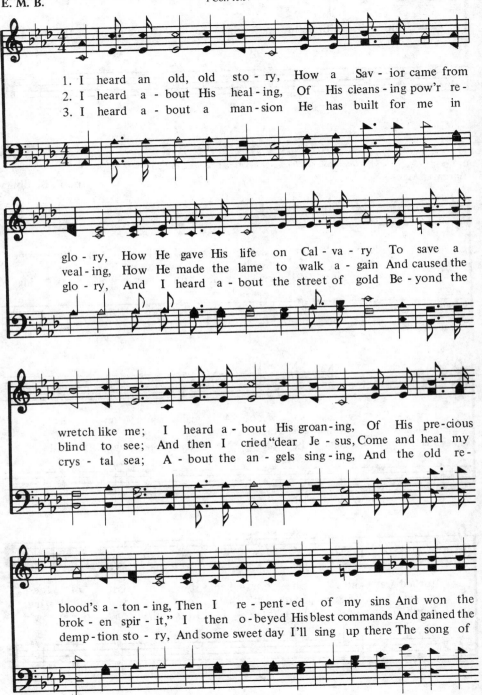

1. I heard an old, old sto-ry, How a Sav-ior came from glo-ry, How He gave His life on Cal-va-ry To save a wretch like me; I heard a-bout His groan-ing, Of His pre-cious blood's a-ton-ing, Then I re-pent-ed of my sins And won the

2. I heard a-bout His heal-ing, Of His cleans-ing pow'r re-veal-ing, How He made the lame to walk a-gain And caused the blind to see; And then I cried "dear Je-sus, Come and heal my brok-en spir-it," I then o-beyed His blest commands And gained the

3. I heard a-bout a man-sion He has built for me in glo-ry, And I heard a-bout the street of gold Be-yond the crys-tal sea; A-bout the an-gels sing-ing, And the old re-demp-tion sto-ry, And some sweet day I'll sing up there The song of

CHORUS

vic - to - ry. O vic - to - ry in Je - sus, My Sav - ior, for-

ev - er, He sought me and bo't me with His re - deem - ing

blood; He loved me ere I knew Him, and all my love is

due Him, He plunged me to vic - to - ry, be-neath the cleans - ing flood.

360 Standing On The Promises

Bb-4-SOL
R. K. C.

P-4, W-3

Whereby are given unto us exceeding great and precious promises. II Pet. 1:4

R. Kelso Carter, 1886

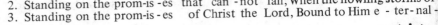

1. Standing on the prom-is-es of Christ my King, Thru e-ter-nal a-ges
2. Standing on the prom-is-es that can-not fail, When the howling storms of
3. Standing on the prom-is-es of Christ the Lord, Bound to Him e-ter-nal-

let His prais-es ring; Glo-ry in the high-est, I will shout and sing,
doubt and fear as-sail, By the liv-ing word of God I shall pre-vail,
ly by love's strong cord, O-ver-com-ing dai-ly with the Spir-it's sword,

CHORUS

Stand-ing on the prom-is-es of God. Stand - ing,
Stand-ing on the prom-is-es,

stand - ing, Stand-ing on the prom-is-es of
stand-ing on the prom-is-es,

God my Sav-ior; Stand - ing, stand -
Stand-ing on the prom-is-es, stand-ing on the

ing,   I'm stand-ing on the prom-is-es of God.
prom-is-es,

Eb-2-DO
D. B.

In His Time

I wait for the Lord, my soul doth wait, and in His word do I hope.
Psa. 130:5

361
H-6, P-5
Dianne Ball, 1978
Arr. D. Shepard, 1985

1. In His time,   in His time,   He makes all things beau-ti-
2. In Your time,   in Your time,   You make all things beau-ti-

ful, in His time.   Lord, please show me ev-'ry day, As You're
ful, in Your time.   Lord   my   life to You I   bring, May each

teach-ing me Your way, That You do   just what You say, in Your time.
song I have to sing, Be   to You   a love-ly thing, in Your time.

362 I Have Been Redeemed

Bb-4-SOL
James Rowe

Blessed be the Lord God of Israel; for He hath visited and redeemed His people . . .
Luke 1:68

R-1, T-1
S. A. Ganus

1. Sweet is the song . . . . I am sing-ing to-day; . . . . I'm re-deemed! . . . .
2. Great is my joy . . . . now as on-ward I go; . . . . I'm re-deemed! . . . .
3. Pre-cious in-deed . . . . is my Sav-ior to me; . . . . I'm re-deemed! . . . .

I'm re-deemed! . . . . Trou-ble and sor-row . . . . have van-ished a-way; . . . .
I'm re-deemed! . . . . All the way home-ward . . . . my prais-es shall flow; . . . .
I'm re-deemed! . . . . Hap-py in glo-ry . . . . some day I shall be; . . . .

I

I have been. . .

CHORUS

have been re-deemed! I'm re-deemed by love di-
re-deemed! I'm re-deemed

vine, Glo - ry, glo - ry, Christ is mine, Christ is
by love di - vine,

mine, All to him I now re-
Christ is mine, All to him

sign, I have been re-deemed.
I now re-sign, I have been re-deemed.

363   He Hideth My Soul

D-2-SOL

Fanny J. Crosby, 1890

I will put thee in a cleft of the rock, and will cover thee with My hand . . . Ex. 33:22

C-10

Wm. J. Kirkpatrick, 1890

1. A won-der-ful Sav-ior is Je-sus my Lord, A won-der-ful
2. A won-der-ful Sav-ior is Je-sus my Lord, He tak-eth my
3. When clothed in His bright-ness, trans-port-ed I rise To meet Him in

Sav-ior to me; He hid-eth my soul in the cleft of the
bur-den a-way; He hold-eth me up, and I shall not be
clouds of the sky; His per-fect sal-va-tion, His won-der-ful

CHORUS

Rock, Where riv-ers of pleas-ure I see.
moved, He giv-eth me strength as my day. He hid-eth my soul
love, I'll shout with the mil-lions on high.

in the cleft of the Rock That shad-ows a dry, thirs-ty land;

He hid-eth my life in the depth of His love, And cov-ers me

there with His hand, And cov-ers me there with His hand.

The Lord My Shepherd Is

364

The Lord is my shepherd; I shall not want. Psa. 23:1

E♭-3-SOL
Isaac Watts
C-11
Arr. by Ralph Harrison

1. The Lord my Shep-herd is: I shall be
2. He leads me to the place Where heav'n-ly
3. If e'er I go a-stray, He doth my
1. The Lord my Shep-herd is: I shall be well

well sup-plied; Since He is mine, and I am His, What
pas-ture grows, Where liv-ing wa-ters gent-ly pass, And
soul re-claim, And guides me in His own right way, For
sup-plied;

p

can I want be-side? What can I want be-side?
full sal-va-tion flows, And full sal-va-tion flows.
His most ho-ly name, For His most ho-ly name.
1. What can I want be-side?

365 The Haven Of Rest

Come unto Me, all ye that labor and are heavy laden, and I will give you rest.
Matt. 11:28

A♭-2-SOL
H. L. Gilmour

A-1, T-1
George D. Moore

1. My soul in sad ex-ile was out on life's sea, So
2. I yield-ed my-self to His ten-der em-brace, And
3. The song of my soul, since the Lord made me whole, Has

bur-dened with sin and dis-tress: I heard a sweet
faith tak-ing hold of the word, My fet-ters fell
been the old sto-ry so blest, Of Je-sus who'll

D. S.-The tem-pest may

voice say-ing, "Make me your choice;" I en-tered the Ha-
off, and I an-chored my soul: The Ha-ven of Rest
save who-so-ev-er will have A home in the Ha-

sweep o'er the wild storm-y deep: In Je-sus I'm safe

Fine CHORUS

ven of Rest.
is my Lord.   I've an-chored my soul in the
ven of Rest.

ev-er-more.

D. S.

Ha-ven of Rest; I'll sail the wide seas no more;

Rescue The Perishing

366

Bb-4-SOL

The Lord is . . . not willing that any should perish, but . . .
come to repentance. II Pet. 3:9

Fanny J. Crosby, 1869

S-5

Wm. H. Doane, 1870

1. Res - cue the per - ish - ing, Care for the dy - ing, Snatch them in
2. Down in the hu - man heart, Crushed by the temp - ter, Feel - ings lie
3. Res - cue the per - ish - ing, Du - ty de - mands it; Strength for thy

pit - y from sin and the grave; Weep o'er the
bur - ied that grace can re - store: Touched by a
la - bor the Lord will pro - vide: Back to the

err - ing one, Lift up the fall - en, Tell them of Je - sus the
lov - ing heart, Wak-ened by kind-ness, Chords that were bro - ken will
nar - row way Pa - tient - ly win them; Tell the poor wan - d'rer a

REFRAIN

might - y to save.
vi - brate once more. Res - cue the per - ish - ing, Care for the
Sav - ior has died.

dy - ing; Je - sus is mer - ci - ful, Je - sus will save.

367 The Rock That Is Higher Than I

Lead me to the Rock that is higher than I. Psa. 61:2

A♭-4-SOL
Wm. G. F.

C-9
Wm. G. **Fischer**

1. O, some - times the shad - ows are deep, And rough seems the
2. O, some - times how long seems the day, And some - times how
3. O, near to the Rock let me keep, If bless - ings or

path to the goal; And sor - rows, sometimes how they sweep Like
wea - ry my feet; But toil - ing in life's dus - ty way, The
sor - rows pre - vail; Or climb - ing the moun - tain way steep, Or

CHORUS

tem - pests down o - ver the soul.
Rock's bless - ed shad - ow, how sweet! O, then, to the Rock let me
walk - ing the shad - ow - y vale.

fly,
let me fly, To the Rock that is high - er than
is

I;
high - er than I; O, then, to the Rock let me

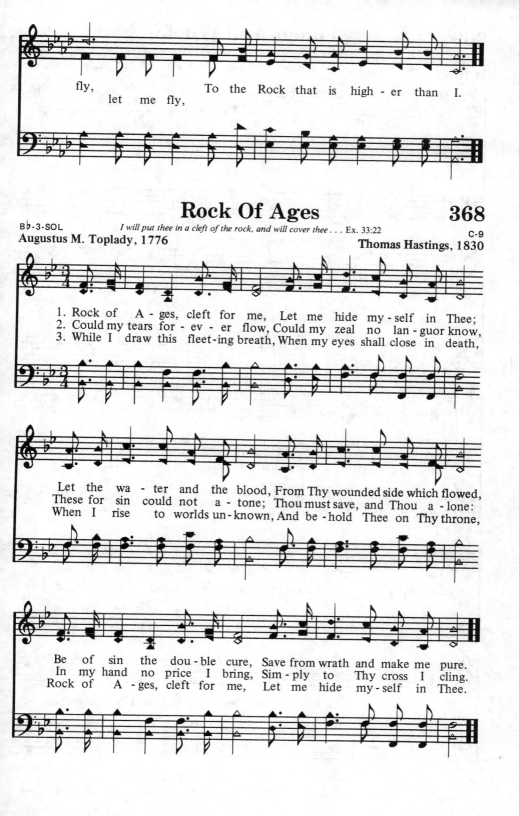

fly,   let   me   fly,   To the Rock that is high - er than I.

Rock Of Ages

368

Bb-3-SOL   *I will put thee in a cleft of the rock, and will cover thee . . .* Ex. 33:22   C-9

Augustus M. Toplady, 1776   **Thomas Hastings, 1830**

1. Rock of A - ges, cleft for me, Let me hide my - self in Thee;
2. Could my tears for - ev - er flow, Could my zeal no lan - guor know,
3. While I draw this fleet-ing breath, When my eyes shall close in death,

Let the wa - ter and the blood, From Thy wounded side which flowed,
These for sin could not a - tone; Thou must save, and Thou a - lone:
When I rise to worlds un - known, And be - hold Thee on Thy throne,

Be of sin the dou - ble cure, Save from wrath and make me pure.
In my hand no price I bring, Sim - ply to Thy cross I cling.
Rock of A - ges, cleft for me, Let me hide my - self in Thee.

369 Mended And Whole

Who His own self bare our sins in His own body on the tree . . .
by whose stripes ye were healed. 1 Pet. 2:24

C-17, T-1
Donald M. Alexander
Arr. by R. J. Stevens

F-2-SOL
D. M. A.

1. Oh how great the sal-va-tion in Je-sus, that the pro-phets of old tes-ti-fied! E-ven an-gels de-sire its re-veal-ing.
2. As a lamb that was led to the slaught-er, not a threat, not a word did You say. Help me, Lord when my heart fills with an-ger.
3. I've been saved by Your Word that is liv-ing, to a love that is fer-vent-ly pure. Pre-cious blood from Your cross brings re-demp-tion

CHORUS

Praise and glo-ry to Christ cru-ci-fied! You were
Your ex-am-ple I will not be-tray. You were
with a hope that is liv-ing and sure.

threat-ened for me, You were slan-dered for me. Ev-'ry thorn, ev-'ry nail, ev-'ry tear was for me. Sweet the tho't that my soul may be

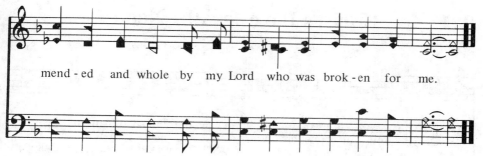

mend-ed and whole by my Lord who was brok-en for me.

Father, Take This Heart Of Mine 370

Eb-4-DO
A. A. J.

*Our Father which art in heaven . . . Thy will
be done in earth, as it is in heaven . . . Matt. 6:9,10*

D-1, H-1

**Annette A. Jenkins
Arr. by Dane K. Shepard**

1. Fa - ther, take this heart of mine, Make my
2. Give me wis - dom so I may, Teach some -
3. When this life on earth is o'er, Take me

will to be as Thine; Help me in the
one Thy sav - ing way; Let me love as
to that peace - ful shore; Then I'll spend e -

things I do, Ev - er to my Lord be true.
You com - mand, And in truth for - ev - er stand.
ter - ni - ty, With Thy chil - dren prais - ing Thee. A - men.

371 Christ's Love Is All I Need

E♭-2-SOL
G. W. S.

Know the love of Christ, which passeth knowledge,
that ye might be filled with all the fulness of God. Eph. 3:19

L-4

Geo. W. Sides

1. Tho' dark and drear-y be life's way And bur-dens hard to bear;
2. Tho' tri - als press on ev - 'ry side And man - y snares there be;
3. And when I hear the boatman's call, Come cross the chill - y tide;

There's One whose love will nev - er fail, My heart shall ne'er de - spair.
I look in sim - ple faith to Him Who calmed the storm-y sea.
I shall not fear to launch my barque, For Christ is at my side.

My hope is staid in Him to - day And He will safe - ly lead,
He is the Shep-herd kind and true, His sheep He'll ev - er feed;
He bore the sting of death for me, Has met my ev - 'ry need;

To that sweet home be - yond the sea, Christ's love is all I need.
This cheers me on and makes me strong, Christ's love is all I need.
And so I sing the sweet re-frain, Christ's love is all I need.

CHORUS

Christ's love is all I need, each day,
O, His love pre-cious love's all I need, need each day,

I know, I know, Christ's pre-cious love is all I need,
Yes, I know, pre-cious love is all,

He'll lead me safe - ly on life's way,
O, He'll lead, yes, He'll lead safe - ly on, on life's way,

I know, I know Christ's pre-cious, pre-cious love is all I need.
O, I know His love I need.

372 We Thank Thee, O Father

Db-2-DO

Matthias Claudius, 1782
Trans. Jane M. Campbell, 1861

Now therefore, our God, we thank Thee,
and praise Thy glorious name. I Chr. 29:13

T-2

R. J. Stevens

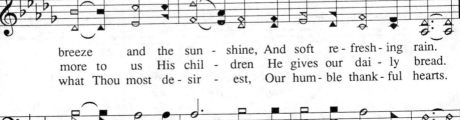

1. We plow the fields for sow-ing The good seed on the land.
2. He on-ly is the Mak-er Of all things near and far.
3. We thank Thee, then, O Fa-ther, For all things bright and good:

But it is fed and wa-tered By God's al-might-y hand. He
He paints the way-side flow-ers, He lights the eve-ning star. The
The seed time and the har-vest, Our life, our health, our food. Ac-

sends the snow in win-ter, The warmth to swell the grains, The
wind and waves o-bey Him. By Him the birds are fed; Much
cept the gifts we of-fer, For all Thy love im-parts, And,

breeze and the sun-shine, And soft re-fresh-ing rain.
more to us His chil-dren He gives our dai-ly bread.
what Thou most de-sir-est, Our hum-ble thank-ful hearts.

Hold Thou My Hand

Hold Thou me up, and I shall be safe . . . Psa. 119:117

Ab-2-SOL
Fanny J. Crosby

D-1, G-3
Hubert P. Main

1. Hold Thou my hand, so weak I am, and help - less,
2. Hold Thou my hand, and clos - er, clos - er draw me
3. Hold Thou my hand, that when I reach the mar - gin

I dare not take one step with - out Thine aid;
To Thy dear self, my hope, my joy my all;
Of that lone riv - er Thou didst cross for me;

Hold Thou my hand, for then, O lov - ing Sav - ior,
Hold Thou my hand, lest hap - ly I should wan - der;
A heav'n - ly light may flash a - long its wa - ters

No dread of ill shall make my soul a - fraid.
And miss - ing Thee, my trem - bling feet shall fall.
And ev - 'ry wave like crys - tal bright shall be.   A - men.

374 Ring Out The Message

Eb-4-DO
James Rowe

Behold, I bring you good tidings of great joy,
which shall be to all people . . . a Savior, which is Christ . . .
Luke 2:10,11

S-5

Samuel W. Beazley

1. There's a mes-sage true and glad For the sin-ful and the sad,
2. Tell the world of sav-ing grace, Make it known in ev-'ry place,
3. Sin and doubt to sweep a-way, Till shall dawn the bet-ter day,

Ring it out, ring it out; It will give them
Help the need-y
Ring it out, ring it out; Till the sin-ful

cour-age new, It will help them to be true; Ring it out, ...
ones to know Him from whom all bless-ings flow;
world be won For Je-ho-vah's might-y Son; Ring it

CHORUS

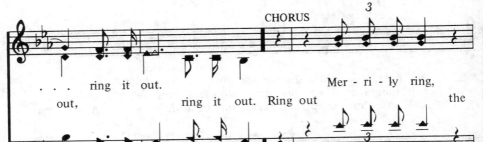

. . . ring it out.
out, ring it out. Ring out

Mer-ri-ly ring,
the

375

The Lord's My Shepherd, I'll Not Want

Bb-3-SOL

Scottish Psalter, 1650

He shall feed His flock like a shepherd. Isa. 40:11

C-11

John Campbell

1. The Lord's my Shep - herd, I'll not want: He makes me
2. My soul He doth re - store a - gain, And me to
3. Yea, tho' I walk in death's dark vale, Yet will I
4. My ta - ble Thou hast fur - nish - ed In pres - ence
5. Good - ness and mer - cy all my life Shall sure - ly

down to lie In pas - tures green; He
walk doth make With - in the paths of
fear none ill; For Thou art with me,
of my foes; My head Thou dost with
fol - low me; And in God's house for -

lead - eth me In pas - tures green, He
right - eous - ness, With - in the paths of
and Thy rod, For Thou art with me,
oil a - noint, My head Thou dost with
ev - er - more, And in God's house for -

lead - eth me The qui - et wa - ters by.
right - eous - ness, E'en for His own name's sake.
and Thy rod And staff me com - fort still.
oil a - noint, And my cup o - ver - flows.
ev - er - more My dwell - ing place shall be.

Onward, Christian Soldiers

E-4-SOL
Sabine Baring-Gould, 1864

*Therefore endure hardness, as a good
soldier of Jesus Christ.* II Tim. 2:3

U-1, W-1
Arthur Sullivan, 1871

1. On - ward, Chris-tian sol - diers! Marching as to war, With the
2. Crowns and thrones may per - ish, King-doms rise and wane, But the
3. On - ward, then, ye peo - ple, Join our hap - py throng; Blend with

cross of Je - sus Go - ing on be - fore; Christ, the roy - al Mas - ter,
Church of Je - sus Con-stant will re - main; Gates of hell can nev - er
ours your voic - es In the tri - umph-song; Glo - ry, laud and hon - or

Leads a - gainst the foe; For-ward in - to bat - tle, See His ban-ners go!
'Gainst that Church prevail; We have Christ's own promise, And that cannot fail.
Un - to Christ the King, This thru countless a - ges Men and an - gels sing.

REFRAIN

On-ward, Chris-tian sol - diers! March-ing as to war,

With the cross of Je - sus Go - ing on be - fore.

377 Lord, I Believe

And we have known and believed the love that God hath to us. I John 4:16

Bb-4-MI
A. W. D.

F-1, T-1
A. W. Dicus

Moderately

1. When we be-hold the won-ders of cre - a - tion, The
2. No fi - nite mind, by mor - tal cal-cu-la - tion Could
3. When we per - ceive the state of al-ien-a - tion In
4. Some days are filled with joy and ex-pec-ta - tion, Some

flow'rs that bloom, the rain-drops as they fall; The spa-cious
frame the Truths re-vealed with-in His Word; In ev-'ry
which the soul, from Thee, O God, was lost; We must be-
days are dark, with cares we are be-set; In hours of

skies and life's per-pet - u - a - tion, We can not doubt that
trace of na-ture's op - er - a - tion, Thy voice, O God, in
lieve, by heav-en's or - di - na-tion, Our Lord re-deemed and
joy or hours of trib - u - la-tion, Be with us Lord, lest

CHORUS

God con-trolled it all.
mys-t'ry can be heard.
paid the bit - ter cost.
we, lest we for - get.

Lord, I be - lieve, Lord, I be - lieve, yes,

yes, I be-lieve, I be-lieve, I can not doubt

I be-lieve, I can not doubt

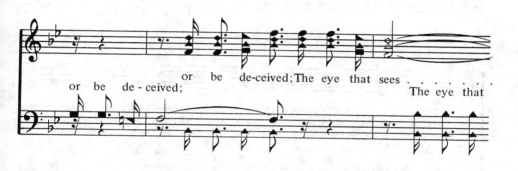

or be de-ceived; The eye that sees . . . . . .

or be de-ceived; The eye that

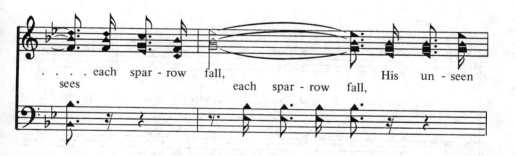

. . . . each spar-row fall, His un-seen

sees each spar-row fall,

hand is in it all.

His un-seen hand is in it all.

378   The Solid Rock

G-3-SOL   *For they drank of that spiritual Rock . . . and that Rock was Christ.* 1 Cor. 10:4   H-6

Edward Mote, 1834   **William B. Bradbury, 1863**

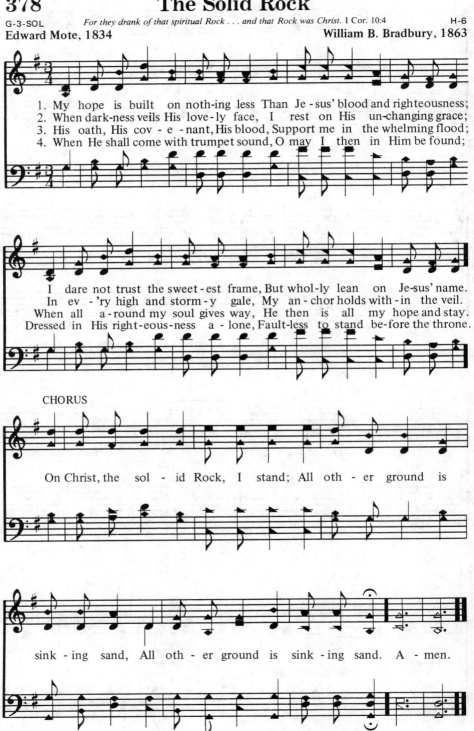

1. My hope is built on noth-ing less Than Je-sus' blood and righteousness;
2. When dark-ness veils His love-ly face, I rest on His un-changing grace;
3. His oath, His cov-e-nant, His blood, Support me in the whelming flood;
4. When He shall come with trumpet sound, O may I then in Him be found;

I dare not trust the sweet-est frame, But whol-ly lean on Je-sus' name.
In ev-'ry high and storm-y gale, My an-chor holds with-in the veil.
When all a-round my soul gives way, He then is all my hope and stay.
Dressed in His right-eous-ness a-lone, Fault-less to stand be-fore the throne.

CHORUS

On Christ, the sol-id Rock, I stand; All oth-er ground is

sink-ing sand, All oth-er ground is sink-ing sand. A-men.

Hiding In Thee

379

My God is the rock of my refuge. Psa. 93:22

F-4-SOL

William O. Cushing, 1876

C-9

Ira D. Sankey, 1877

1. O safe to the Rock that is high - er than I, My
2. In calm of the noon - tide, in sor - row's lone hour, In
3. How oft in the con - flict, when pressed by the foe, I've

soul in its con - flicts and sor - rows would fly; So sin - ful, so
times when temp - ta - tions cast o'er me its pow'r; In tem - pest of
fled to my Ref - uge and breathed out my woe; How oft - en, when

wea - ry, Thine, Thine would I be; Thou blest Rock of A - ges, I'm
life, on its wide heav - ing sea, Thou blest Rock of A - ges, I'm
tri - als like sea - bil - lows roll, I've hid - den in Thee, O Thou

CHORUS

hid - ing in Thee.
hid - ing in Thee. Hid - ing in Thee, Hid - ing in
Rock of my soul.

Thee, Thou blest Rock of A - ges, I'm hid - ing in Thee.

380 It Won't Be Very Long

Watch therefore: for ye know not what hour your Lord doth come . . .
Therefore be ye also ready. Matt. 24:42,44

Bb-4-SOL
Morgan Williams

E. M. Bartlett

S-2

1. It won't be ver-y long till this short life shall end, It
2. It won't be ver-y long till here we cease to roam, It
3. It won't be ver-y long till earth shall pass a-way, It

won't be ver-y long till Je-sus shall de-scend; And then the
won't be ver-y long till all the saints get home; And then with
won't be ver-y long till works of men de-cay; But Je-sus

dead in Christ from beds of clay shall rise To meet the Lord and King
smil-ing face we'll walk the streets of gold, And sing the Sav-ior's praise
has pre-pared a hap-py dwell-ing place, For all who look a-bove

up yon-der in the skies. It won't be ver-y long, It
where saints are nev-er old.
and trust His matchless grace. It won't be ver-y long, It

REFRAIN

381 Work, For The Night Is Coming

F-4-SOL

The night cometh, when no man can work. John 9:4

E-1, W-4

Annie L. Walker

Lowell Mason

1. Work, for the night is com - ing, Work thru the morn-ing hours;
2. Work, for the night is com - ing, Work thru the sun - ny noon;
3. Work, for the night is com - ing, Un - der the sun - set skies;

Work while the dew is spark - ling, Work 'mid spring-ing flow'rs.
Fill bright-est hours with la - bor, Rest comes sure and soon.
While their bright tints are glow - ing, Work, for day - light flies.

Work when the day grows bright - er, Work in the glow-ing sun;
Give ev - 'ry fly - ing min - ute, Some-thing to keep in store;
Work till the last beam fad - eth, Fad - eth to shine no more;

Work, for the night is com - ing, When man's work is done.
Work, for the night is com - ing, When man works no more.
Work while the night is dark - 'ning, When man's work is o'er.

In Heavenly Love Abiding

382

If ye keep My commandments, ye shall abide in My love. John 15:10

E♭-4-SOL

Anna L. Waring, 1850

G-3, L-5

F. Mendelssohn

1. In heav'n-ly love a - bid - ing, No change my heart shall fear; And
2. Wher - ev - er He may guide me, No want shall turn me back; My
3. Green pas-tures are be - fore me, Which yet I have not seen; Bright

safe is such con - fid - ing, For noth - ing chang - es here. The
Shep-herd is be - side me, And noth - ing can I lack. His
skies will soon be o'er me, Where the dark clouds have been. My

storm may roar with - out me, My heart may low be laid, But God is
wis - dom ev - er wak-eth, His sight is nev - er dim; He knows the
hope I can - not meas-ure, My path to life is free; My Sav - ior

round a - bout me, And can I be dis - mayed?
way He tak - eth, And I will walk with Him.
has my treas - ure, And He will walk with me.

(1.) And can . . . . I be dis - mayed?

383 Whispering Hope

Db-2-SOL
A. H.

We . . . have a strong consolation, who have fled for refuge to lay hold upon the hope set before us. Heb. 6:18

C-15, H-6

Alice Hawthorne
Arr. by L. O. Sanderson

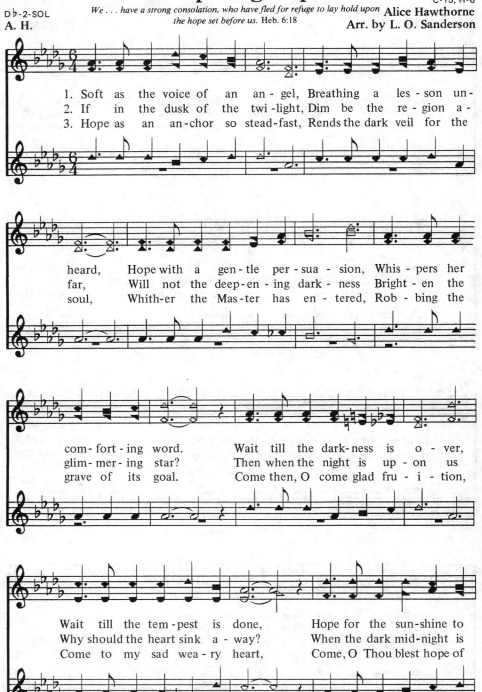

1. Soft as the voice of an an-gel, Breathing a les-son un-
2. If in the dusk of the twi-light, Dim be the re-gion a-
3. Hope as an an-chor so stead-fast, Rends the dark veil for the

heard, Hope with a gen-tle per-sua-sion, Whis-pers her
far, Will not the deep-en-ing dark-ness Bright-en the
soul, Whith-er the Mas-ter has en-tered, Rob-bing the

com-fort-ing word. Wait till the dark-ness is o-ver,
glim-mer-ing star? Then when the night is up-on us
grave of its goal. Come then, O come glad fru-i-tion,

Wait till the tem-pest is done, Hope for the sun-shine to
Why should the heart sink a-way? When the dark mid-night is
Come to my sad wea-ry heart, Come, O Thou blest hope of

384 A Shelter In The Time Of Storm

For Thou hast been a shelter for me. Psa. 61:3

F-4-SOL

C-9

V. J. Charlesworth

Ira D. Sankey, 1885

1. The Lord's our Rock, in Him we hide, A shel-ter in the
2. A shade by day, de-fence by night, A shel-ter in the
3. O Rock di-vine, O Ref-uge dear, A shel-ter in the

time of storm; Se-cure what-ev-er ill be-tide, A
time of storm; No fears a-larm, no foes af-fright, A
time of storm; Be Thou our help-er ev-er near, A

Fine CHORUS *Omit fermata on repeat*

shel-ter in the time of storm.
shel-ter in the time of storm. O Je-sus is a
shel-ter in the time of storm.

D. S.

Rock in a wea-ry land, A wea-ry land, a wea-ry land;

What Did He Do?

385

Db-2-DO
W. O.

C-4, C-10
W. Owen

It is Christ who died . . . that is risen again, who is even at the right hand of God, who also maketh intercession for us. Rom. 8:34

1. O lis-ten to our won-drous sto - ry, Count-ed once a-
2. No an - gel could His place have tak - en, High-est of the
3. Will you sur - ren - der to this Sav - ior? To His scep-ter

mong the   lost: Yet, One came down from heav-en's glo - ry,
high though   He;   The   loved One on the cross for - sak - en
hum - bly   bow?   You, too, shall come to know His fa - vor,

CHORUS

Sav - ing us   at   aw - ful   cost!
Was one of the God - head three!   Who saved us from e -
He will save you, save you   now.

ter-nal loss?   What   did He do?
       Who but God's Son up - on the cross!   He died for

Where   is He now?   In   heav-en in - ter - ced - ing!
you!   Be - lieve it thou, In heav-en in - ter - ced - ing!

386 Jesus Is Coming Soon

Eb-4-DO
R. E. W.

*For the Lord Himself shall descend from heaven . . . with the trump of God; and the
dead in Christ shall rise first . . . 1 Thess. 4:16*

S-2

R. E. Winsett

1. Trou-ble-some times are here, fill-ing men's hearts with fear, Free-dom we all hold dear now is at stake; (is at stake) Hum-b'ling your heart to God, saves from the chast - 'ning rod. Seek the way pil - grims trod, Chris-tians, a-wake.

2. Trou-bles will soon be o'er, hap-py for-ev - er - more; When we meet on that shore free from all care; (from all care) Ris - ing up in the sky; tell-ing this world good - by. Homeward we then will fly, glo - ry to share.

Fine CHORUS
Je - sus is

D. S.–Heav-en-ward bound.

387 Far And Near

A♭-3-MI

J. O. Thompson

Pray ye therefore for the Lord of the harvest, that He would send forth laborers into His harvest.
Luke 10:2

S-5

J. B. O. Clemm

1. Far and near the fields are teem - ing With the waves of
2. Send them forth with morn's first beam - ing, Send them in the
3. O thou, whom thy Lord is send - ing, Gath - er now the

rip - ened grain; Far and near their gold is gleam - ing
noon - tide's glare; When the sun's last rays are gleam - ing,
sheaves of gold; Heaven-ward then at eve - ning wend - ing,

D.S.- Send them now the sheaves to gath - er,

Fine **CHORUS**

O'er the sun - ny slope and plain.
Bid them gath - er ev - 'ry - where. Lord of har - vest,
Thou shalt come with joy un - told.

Ere the har - vest - time pass by.

D. S.

send forth reap - ers! Hear us, Lord, to Thee we cry;

Give Of Your Best To The Master 388

Eb-3-MI

Howard B. Grose

Present your bodies a living sacrifice, holy, acceptable
unto God which is your reasonable service. Rom. 12:1

E-1, W-4

Charlotte Barnard

1. Give of your best to the Mas-ter; Give of the strength of your youth;
2. Give of your best to the Mas-ter; Give Him first place in your heart;
3. Give of your best to the Mas-ter; Naught else is wor-thy His love;

D. C.–Give of your best to the Mas-ter; Give of the strength of your youth;

Fine

Throw your soul's fresh, glowing ar - dor In - to the bat - tle for truth.
Give Him first place in your serv - ice, Con - se - crate ev - 'ry part.
He gave Him-self for your ran-som, Gave up His glo - ry a - bove;

Clad in sal - va-tion's full ar - mor, Join in the bat - tle for truth.

Je - sus has set the ex - am-ple; Daunt-less was He, young and brave;
Give, and to you shall be giv - en; God His be - lov - ed Son gave;
Laid down His life with-out mur-mur, You from sin's ru - in to save;

rall.   **D. C.**

Give Him your loy - al de - vo-tion, Give Him the best that you have.....
Grate-ful - ly seek-ing to serve Him, Give Him the best that you have.....
Give Him your heart's ad - o - ra-tion, Give Him the best that you have.....

389 Sing On, Ye Joyful Pilgrims

My servants shall sing for joy . . . Isa. 65:14

F-4-SOL

Carrie M. Wilson, 1886

J-1, S-4

John R. Sweney, 1886

1. Sing on, ye joy-ful pil-grims, Nor think the mo-ments long; My
2. Sing on, ye joy-ful pil-grims, While here on earth we stay; Let
3. Sing on, ye joy-ful pil-grims, The time will not be long, Till

faith is heav'n-ward ris - ing With ev-'ry tune-ful song; Lo!
songs of home and Je - sus Be-guile each fleet-ing day; Sing
in our Fa-ther's king - dom We swell a no-bler song, Where

on the mount of bless - ing, The glo-rious mount, I stand; And
on the grand old sto - ry Of His re-deem-ing love, The
those we love are wait - ing To greet us on the shore, We'll

look-ing o - ver Jor - dan, I see the prom-ised land.
ev - er-last-ing cho - rus That fills the realms a-bove.
meet be-yond the riv - er, Where sur-ges roll no more.

CHORUS

Sing on, O bliss-ful mu-sic! With ev-'ry note you raise My heart is filled with rap - ture, My soul is lost in praise; Sing Sing on on, O bliss-ful mu - sic! bliss-ful, bliss-ful mu - sic! With ev-'ry note you raise My heart is filled with rap - ture, My soul is lost in praise.

390 Anywhere With Jesus

D-2-SOL

Lo, I am with you always, even unto the end of the world. Matt. 28:20

F-3, G-3

Jessie Brown Pounds, 1887
D. B. Towner, 1887
Adapt by Helen C. Dixon

1. An-y-where with Je-sus I can safe-ly go, An-y-where He
2. An-y-where with Je-sus I am not a-lone; Oth-er friends may
3. An-y-where with Je-sus, o-ver land and sea, Tell-ing souls in

leads me in this world be-low; An-y-where with-out Him dear-est
fail me, He is still my own; Tho' His hand may lead me o-ver
dark-ness of sal-va-tion free; Read-y as He sum-mons me to

joys would fade; An-y-where with Je-sus I am not a-fraid.
drear-est ways, An-y-where with Je-sus is a house of praise.
go or stay, An-y-where with Je-sus when He points the way.

CHORUS

An-y-where, an-y-where! Fear I can-not know;

An-y-where with Je-sus I can safe-ly go.

Savior, Like A Shepherd Lead Us

391

Eb-4-MI

And when he putteth his own sheep, he goeth before them,

Attr. to Dorothy A. Thrupp *and the sheep follow him . . . John 10:4*

C-11, G-3

William B. Bradbury, 1859

1. Sav - ior, like a shep-herd lead us, Much we need Thy ten - der care;
2. We are Thine; do Thou be - friend us, Be the Guard-ian of our way;
3. Thou hast promised to re - ceive us, Poor and sin - ful tho' we be;
4. Ear - ly let us seek Thy fa - vor; Ear - ly let us do Thy will;

In Thy pleas-ant pas-tures feed us, For our use Thy folds pre - pare:
Keep Thy flock, from sin de-fend us, Seek us when we go a - stray:
Thou hast mer-cy to re - lieve us, Grace to cleanse, and pow'r to free:
Bless-ed Lord and on - ly Sav - ior, With Thy love our bos - oms fill:

Bless-ed Je - sus, bless-ed Je - sus, Thou hast bought us, Thine we are.
Bless-ed Je - sus, bless-ed Je - sus, Hear Thy chil - dren when they pray;
Bless-ed Je - sus, bless-ed Je - sus, Ear - ly let us turn to Thee;
Bless-ed Je - sus, bless-ed Je - sus, Thou hast loved us, love us still;

Bless-ed Je - sus, bless-ed Je - sus, Thou hast bought us, Thine we are.
Bless-ed Je - sus, bless-ed Je - sus, Hear Thy chil - dren when they pray.
Bless-ed Je - sus, bless-ed Je - sus, Ear - ly let us turn to Thee.
Bless-ed Je - sus, bless-ed Je - sus, Thou hast loved us, love us still.

392 Count Your Blessings

Many, O Lord my God, are Thy wonderful works . . .
they are more than can be numbered. Psa. 40:5

Eb -2-MI
Johnson Oatman

P-5, T-2
E. O. Excell

1. When up - on life's bil - lows you are tem - pest - tossed,
2. Are you ev - er bur - dened with a load of care?
3. So, a - mid the con - flict, wheth-er great or small,

1. you are tem - pest tossed,

When you are dis - cour-aged, think-ing all is lost,
Does the cross seem heav - y you are called to bear?
Do not be dis - cour-aged, God is o - ver all;

think - ing all is lost,

Count your man - y bless - ings, name them one by one,
Count your man - y bless - ings, ev - 'ry doubt will fly,
Count your man - y bless - ings, an - gels will at - tend,

name them one by one,

And it will sur - prise you what the Lord hath done.
And you will be sing - ing as the days go by.
Help and com - fort give you to your jour - ney's end.

what the Lord hath done.

CHORUS

Count your bless-ings, name them one by one;
Count your man - y bless-ings, name them one by one;

Count your bless-ings, see what God hath done;
Count your man - y bless-ings, see what God hath done;

rit.

Count your bless - ings, Name them one by one;
Count your man - y bless-ings,

a tempo

Count your man - y bless - ings, see what God hath done.

393 Love Divine

Bb-4-SOL

Above all these things put on love, which is the bond of perfectness. Col. 3:14

H-4, L-4

Charles Wesley, 1747

John Zundel, 1870

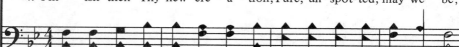

1. Love   di-vine, all loves ex-cel-ling, Joy of heav'n, to earth come down!
2. Breathe, O breathe Thy lov-ing Spir-it In-to ev-'ry trou-bled breast;
3. Come, Al-might-y to de-liv-er, May we all Thy life re-ceive;
4. Fin-ish then Thy new cre-a-tion, Pure, un-spot-ted, may we be;

Fix in us Thy hum-ble dwell-ing, All Thy faith-ful mer-cies crown;
May we all in Thee in-her-it; May we find the prom-ised rest;
Sud-den-ly re-turn, and nev-er, Nev-er-more Thy tem-ples leave;
May we see our whole sal-va-tion Per-fect-ly se-cured by Thee;

Je-sus, Thou art all com-pas-sion, Pure, unbounded love Thou art;
Take a-way the love of sin-ning, Take our load of guilt a-way;
Thee we would be al-ways bless-ing, Serve Thee as Thy hosts a-bove;
Changed from glo-ry, in-to glo-ry, Till in heav'n we take our place,

Vis-it us with Thy sal-va-tion, En-ter ev-'ry trem-bling heart!
End the work of Thy be-gin-ning, Bring us to e-ter-nal day.
Pray, and praise Thee, with-out ceas-ing, Glo-ry in Thy per-fect love.
Till we cast our crowns be-fore Thee, Lost in won-der, love and praise.

Love One Another

394

Eb-3-SOL
D. K. P.

L-2, U-1
H. R. Palmer
Arr. by Will W. Slater

A new commandment I give unto you, that ye love one another;
as I have loved you . . . John 13:34

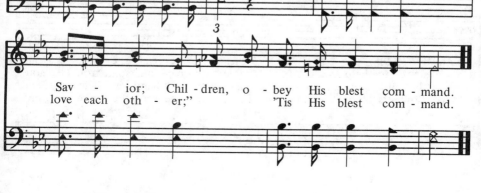

1. An-gry words! O let them nev-er From the tongue un-bri-dled slip;
2. Love is much too pure and ho-ly, Friendship is too sa-cred far,
3. An-gry words are light-ly spok-en, Bit-t'rest tho'ts are rash-ly stirred,

May the heart's best im-pulse ev - er Check them ere they soil the lip.
For a mo-ment's reckless fol - ly Thus to des - o - late and mar.
Bright-est links of life are bro - ken, By a sin - gle an - gry word.

CHORUS

"Love one an - oth - er," thus saith the Sav - ior; Chil-dren, o-
"Love each oth - er, love each oth - er;"

bey the Fa-ther's blest com-mand; "Love one anoth - er," thus saith the
'Tis the Fa-ther's blest com-mand; "Love each oth - er,

Sav - ior; Chil - dren, o - bey His blest com - mand.
love each oth - er;" 'Tis His blest com - mand.

395   A Beautiful Life

C-4-DO

Wm. M. G.

Let us do good unto all men, especially unto them who are of the household of faith.
Gal. 6:10

C-12, W-4

Wm. M. Golden

1. Each day I'll do............ a gold - en deed,............
2. To be a child............ of God each day,............
3. The on - ly life............ that will en - dure,............
4. While go - ing down............ life's wea - ry road,............

By help - ing those............who are in need;............
My light must shine............a - long the way;............
Is one that's kind............and good and pure;............
I'll try to lift............some trav - 'ler's load;............

My life on earth............ is but a span,............
I'll sing His praise............while a - ges roll............
And so for God............ I'll take my stand,............
I'll try to turn............ the night to day,............

And so I'll do............ the best I can, the best I can.
And strive to help............some trou - bled soul, some trou-bled soul.
Each day I'll lend............a help - ing hand, a help -ing hand.
Make flow - ers bloom............a - long the way, the lone - ly way.

CHORUS

Life's eve-ning sun
Life's eve-ning sun   is sink-ing low,
is sink-ing low,

A few more days
A few more days   and I must go
and I must go

To meet the deeds
To meet the deeds   that I have done,
that I have done,

Where there will be
Where there will be   no set-ting sun.
no set-ting sun.

396 We'll Work Till Jesus Comes

F-4-DO

Let us labor therefore to enter into that rest . . . Heb. 4:11

S-2, W-4

Mrs. Elizabeth Mills

Wm. Miller

1. O land of rest, for thee I sigh; When will the mo-ment
2. No tran-quil joys on earth I know, No peace-ful, shel-t'ring
3. To Je-sus Christ I fled for rest; He bade me cease to

come, When I shall lay my ar-mor by, And
dome, This world's a wil-der-ness of woe, This
roam, And lean for suc-cor on His breast, Till

CHORUS

dwell in peace at home? We'll work till Je-sus
world is not my home. We'll work,
He con-duct me home.

comes, We'll work till Je-sus comes, We'll
We'll work

work till Je-sus comes, And we'll be gath-ered home.
We'll work

Stand Up, Stand Up For Jesus!   397

Watch ye, stand fast in the faith . . . be strong. 1 Cor. 16:13

Bb-4-SOL
George Duffield, 1858

E-1, W-1
George J. Webb, 1837

1. Stand up, stand up for Je - sus! Ye sol - diers of the cross;
2. Stand up, stand up for Je - sus! The trum - pet call o - bey;
3. Stand up, stand up for Je - sus! Stand in His strength a - lone;
4. Stand up, stand up for Je - sus! The strife will not be long;

Lift high His roy - al ban - ner, It must not suf - fer loss:
Forth to the might - y con - flict, In this His glo - rious day:
The arm of flesh will fail you; Ye dare not trust your own;
This day the noise of bat - tle, The next the vic - tor's song:

From vic - t'ry un - to vic - t'ry His ar - my shall He lead,
Ye that are men, now serve Him, A - gainst un - num-bered foes;
Put on the gos - pel ar - mor, Each piece put on with pray'r;
To him that o - ver - com - eth, A crown of life shall be;

Till ev - 'ry foe is van - quished And Christ is Lord in - deed.
Your cour - age rise with dan - ger, And strength to strength op-pose.
Where du - ty calls, or dan - ger, Be nev - er want - ing there.
He with the King of glo - ry Shall live e - ter - nal - ly.

398 My Redeemer

A♭-3-SOL

Philip P. Bliss, 1876

C-7, S-4

James McGranahan

Our Savior Jesus Christ; who gave Himself for us, that He might redeem us . . .
Tit. 2:14

1. I will sing of my Re - deem - er, And His won - drous
2. I will tell the won - drous sto - ry, How my lost es -
3. I will sing of my Re - deem - er, And His heav'n - ly

love to me; On the cru - el cross He suf - fered,
tate to save, In His bound-less love and mer - cy,
love to me; He from death to life hath bro't me,

From the curse to set me free.
He the ran - som free - ly gave.
Son of God with Him to be.

CHORUS

Sing, oh,
Sing, oh,

sing . . . . of my Re - deem - er,
sing of my Re - deem-er, Sing, oh, sing of my Re - deem - er,

399 Face To Face

Now we see through a glass, darkly; but then face to face . . . I Cor. 13:12

Bb-4-SOL
Carrie E. Breck, 1898

S-2, T-1
Grant Colfax Tullar, 1898

1. Face to face with Christ my Sav - ior, Face to face, what
2. On - ly faint-ly now I see Him, With the dark-ling
3. Face to face! O bliss-ful mo - ment! Face to face— to

will it be, When with rap-ture I be-hold Him, Je - sus
veil be-tween, But a bless-ed day is com-ing, When His
see and know; Face to face with my Re-deem-er, Je - sus

CHORUS

Christ, who died for me?
glo - ry shall be seen.
Christ, who loves me so.

Face to face shall I be-hold Him,

Far be-yond the star-ry sky; Face to

face in all His glo-ry, I shall see Him by and by!

When I Get To The End Of The Way 400

Db-2-SOL
C. D. T.

C-12, F-3

For our light affliction . . . worketh for us a
far more exceeding and eternal weight of glory. II Cor. 4:17

Charlie D. Tillman

1. The   sands have been washed in the foot-prints Of the Stran-ger   on
2. There are so man-y hills to climb up-ward, I   of-ten   am
3. When the last fee-ble step has been ta-ken, And the gates of   that

Gal-i-lee's shore— And the voice that sub-dued the rough bil-lows
long-ing for rest; But   He who ap-points me my path-way,
cit-y ap-pear, And the beau-ti-ful songs of the an-gels

D. S.-And the toils of the road will seem noth-ing,
last verse-Then the toils *(etc.)*

Will be heard in Ju-de-a no more. But the path of that
Knows   just what is need-ful and best.   I   know in His
Float   out on my lis-ten-ing ear; When   all   that now

When I get to the end of the way.

lone Gal-i-le-an With   joy I will fol-low to-day;
word He hath prom-ised That my strength "it shall be as my day;"
seems so mys-te-rious Will be bright and as clear as the day;

401 I Know That My Redeemer Liveth

For I know that my Redeemer liveth . . . Job 19:25

Db-4-SOL

C-7, T-1

Jessie Brown Pounds, 1893

James H. Fillmore, 1893

1. I know that my Re-deem-er liv - eth, And that His throne shall ev - er stand; I know e - ter - nal life He giv - eth, That grace and pow'r are in His hand.

2. I know His prom-ise nev-er fail - eth, The word He speaks, it can-not die; Tho' cru - el death my flesh as - sail - eth, Yet I shall see Him by and by.

3. I know my man-sion He pre-par - eth, That where He is, there I may be; O won - drous tho't, for me He car - eth, And He at last will come for me.

1. And that His throne shall ev - er stand;

That grace and pow'r are in His hand.

CHORUS

I know I

know   that Je - sus liv - eth,
I know, I know

And that His throne   shall ev - er stand;
And that His throne

I know, I know   that life He giv - eth,
I know, I know

That grace and pow'r   are in His hand.
That grace and pow'r

402 Leaning On The Everlasting Arms

A-4-MI

God is thy refuge, and underneath are the everlasting arms. Deut. 33:27

C-15, F-2

E. A. Hoffman

A. J. Showalter

1. What a fel-low-ship, what a joy di-vine, Lean-ing on the ev-er-
2. O how sweet to walk in this pil-grim way, Lean-ing on the ev-er-
3. What have I to dread, what have I to fear, Lean-ing on the ev-er-

last-ing arms; What a bless-ed-ness, what a peace is mine,
last-ing arms; O how bright the path grows from day to day,
last-ing arms? I have bless-ed peace with my Lord so near,

REFRAIN

Lean-ing on the ev-er-last-ing arms. Lean - ing,
Lean-ing on the ev-er-last-ing arms. Lean-ing on Je - sus,
Lean-ing on the ev-er-last-ing arms.

lean - ing, Safe and se-cure from all a-larms; Lean -
lean-ing on Je - sus, Lean-ing on

ing, lean - ing, Lean-ing on the ev-er-last-ing arms.
Je - sus, lean-ing on Je - sus,

I've Found A Friend

A-3-SOL
James G. Small, 1863

*Greater love hath no man that this, that a man lay
down his life for his friends.* John 15:13

C-5, T-1
Geo. C. Stebbins, 1878

1. I've found a Friend, oh, such a Friend! He loved me ere I knew Him;
2. I've found a Friend, oh, such a Friend! He bled, He died to save me;
3. I've found a Friend, oh, such a Friend! So kind, and true, and ten-der,

He drew me with the cords of love, And thus He bound me to Him.
And not a-lone the gift of life, But His own self He gave me.
So wise a Coun-sel-or and Guide, So might-y a De-fend-er!

And round my heart still close-ly twine Those ties which naught can sev-er,
Naught that I have my own I call, I hold it for the Giv-er:
From Him who loves me now so well, What pow'r my soul can sev-er?

For I am His, and He is mine, For-ev-er and for-ev-er.
My heart, my strength, my life, my all, Are His, and His for-ev-er.
Shall life or death, or earth or hell? No; I am His for-ev-er.

404

Harvest Time

G-2-SOL

Lift up your eyes, and look on the fields; for they are white already to harvest.
John 4:35

S-5, W-4

Mary Brown

Chas. H. Gabriel

1. A - rise! the Mas - ter calls for thee, The har - vest days are
2. Go seek the lost and err - ing ones, Who nev - er knew the
3. The mes - sage bear to dis - tant lands Be - yond the roll - ing

here! No long - er sit with fold - ed hands, But gath - er,
Lord; Go, lead them from the ways of sin, And thou shalt
sea; Go tell them of a Sav - ior's love— The Lamb of

far and near. The no - ble ranks of vol - un - teers Are
have re - ward. Go out in - to the hedg - es, where The
Cal - va - ry. A - rise! the Mas - ter calls for thee! Sal -

A - rise!
A - rise!
A -
A -

dai - ly grow - ing ev - 'ry - where, But still there's work for
care - less drift up - on the tide, And from the high - ways
va - tion full and free pro - claim, Till ev - 'ry kin - dred,

rise, a - rise!

405 Wonderful Words Of Life

G-2-MI
P. P. B.

Lord, to whom shall we go? Thou hast the words of eternal life. John 6:68

S-4

Philip P. Bliss, 1874

1. Sing them o - ver a - gain to me, Won-der-ful words of Life;
2. Christ, the bless - ed One, gives to all, Won-der-ful words of Life;
3. Sweet-ly ech - o the gos - pel call, Won-der-ful words of Life;

Let me more of their beau - ty see, Won-der-ful words of Life.
Sin - ner list to the lov - ing call, Won-der-ful words of Life.
Of - fer par - don and peace to all, Won-der-ful words of Life.

Words of Life and beau - ty, Teach me faith and du - ty:
All so free - ly giv - en, Woo - ing us to heav - en:
Je - sus, on - ly Sav - ior, Sanc - ti - fy for - ev - er:

REFRAIN

Beau - ti - ful words, won-der-ful words, Wonder-ful words of Life;

Beau - ti - ful words, won-der - ful words, Won-der-ful words of Life.

More About Jesus

406

Ab-2-SOL

But grow in grace and . . . knowledge of our Lord Jesus Christ. II Pet. 3:18

W-3

Eliza E. Hewitt, 1887

John R. Sweney, 1887

1. More a-bout Je-sus would I know, More of His grace to others show;
2. More a-bout Je-sus let me learn, More of His ho-ly will dis-cern;
3. More a-bout Je-sus in His word, Hold-ing commun-ion with my Lord;
4. More a-bout Je-sus on His throne, Rich-es in glo-ry all His own;

More of His sav-ing full-ness see, More of His love who died for me.
Spir-it of God my teach-er be, Show-ing the things of Christ to me.
Hear-ing His voice in ev-'ry line, Mak-ing each faith-ful say-ing mine.
More of His king-dom's sure in-crease; More of His com-ing, Prince of Peace.

CHORUS

More, more a-bout Je-sus, More, more a-bout Je-sus; More of His

sav-ing full-ness see, More of His love who died for me.

407 He Leadeth Me

D-4-SOL

I am the Lord thy God . . . which leadeth thee by the way that thou shouldest go.
Isa. 48:17

G-3

Joseph H. Gilmore, 1862

Wm. B. Bradbury, 1864

1. He lead - eth me! O bless - ed tho't! O words with heav'n-ly
2. Sometimes 'mid scenes of deep - est gloom, Sometimes where E - den's
3. And when my task on earth is done, When, by Thy grace, the

com-fort fraught! Whate'er I do, where-e'er I be, Still 'tis God's
bow - ers bloom, By wa - ters still, o'er trou - bled sea, Still 'tis His
vic - t'ry's won, E'en death's cold wave I will not flee, Since God thru

CHORUS

hand that lead - eth me.
hand that lead - eth me! He lead - eth me, He lead - eth me, By
Jor - dan lead - eth me.

His own hand He lead - eth me: His faith - ful fol - low'r

I would be, For by His hand He lead - eth me.

Cleanse Me

408

G-2-MI

Edwin Orr, 1936

*Wash me thoroughly from mine iniquity,
and cleanse me from my sin. Psa. 51:2*

C-16, H-3

Maori Folk Melody
Arr. by R. J. Stevens

1. Search me, O God, and know my heart to-day,
2. I praise Thee Lord, for cleans-ing me from sin,
3. Lord, take my life, and make it whol-ly Thine,
4. O Lord a-bove, re-vi-val comes from Thee,

Try me, O Sav-ior, know my thoughts, I pray;
Ful-fill Thy Word, and make me pure with-in;
Fill my poor heart with Thy great love di-vine;
Send a re-vi-val — start the work in me;

See if there be some wick-ed way in me;
fill me with fire, where once I burned with shame,
Take all my will, my pas-sion, self and pride,
Thy Word de-clares Thou wilt sup-ply our need,

Cleanse me from ev-'ry sin, and set me free.
Grant me de-sire to mag-ni-fy Thy name.
I now sur-ren-der, Lord, in me a-bide.
For bless-ing now, O Lord, I hum-bly plead.

409 The Church's One Foundation

Bb-4-SOL

S. J. Stone

For other foundation can no man lay than that is laid, which is Jesus Christ.
I Cor. 3:11

K-1, U-1

G. J. Webb

1. The Church-'s one foun-da-tion Is Je-sus Christ her Lord; She
2. E - lect from ev-'ry na-tion, Yet one o'er all the earth; Her
3. Tho' with a scorn-ful won-der We see her sore op-pressed, Her

is His new cre-a-tion By wa-ter and the word; From
char-ter of sal-va-tion: One Lord, one faith, one birth; One
doc-trine rent a-sun-der, By names and creeds dis-tressed. Yet

heav'n He came and sought her To be His ho-ly bride;
ho-ly name she bless-es, Par-takes one ho-ly food,
saints their watch are keep-ing, They cry:"How long, how long?"

With his own blood He bought her, And for her life He died.
And to one hope she press-es With ev-'ry grace en-dued.
And soon the night of weep-ing Shall be the morn of song.

The Church's One Foundation

410

Other foundation can no man lay than . . . Jesus Christ. 1 Cor. 3:11

Eb-4-MI

Samuel J. Stone, 1868

K-1, U-1

Samuel S. Wesley, 1864

1. The church-'s one foun-da-tion Is Je-sus Christ her Lord;
2. E-lect from ev-'ry na-tion, Yet one o'er all the earth,
3. 'Mid toil and trib-u-la-tion, And tu-mult of her war,

She is His new cre-a-tion By wa-ter and the word:
Her char-ter of Sal-va-tion, One Lord, one faith, one birth;
She waits the con-sum-ma-tion Of peace for-ev-er-more;

From heav'n He came and sought her To be His ho-ly bride;
One ho-ly name she bless-es, Par-takes one ho-ly food,
Till, with the vi-sion glo-rious, Her long-ing eyes are blest,

With His own blood He bought her, And for her life He died.
And to one hope she press-es, With ev-'ry grace en-dued.
And the great church vic-to-rious Shall be the church at rest. A-men.

411 Redeemed

A♭-2-SOL

R-1, S-1

In whom we have redemption through His blood, the forgiveness of sins . . . Eph. 1:7

Fanny J. Crosby, 1882

Wm. J. Kirkpatrick

1. Re-deemed, how I love to pro-claim it! Re-deemed by the
2. Re-deemed and so hap-py in Je - sus, No lan-guage my
3. I know I shall see in His beau-ty, The King in whose

blood of the Lamb; Redeemed thru His in - fi - nite mer - cy,
rap-ture can tell; I know that the light of His pres - ence
law I de-light; Who lov-ing-ly guard-eth my foot-steps,

His child, and for - ev - er, I am. Re - deemed, Re-
With me doth con - tin - ual - ly dwell. Re - deemed,
And giv - eth me songs in the night.

CHORUS

deemed, Re-deemed by the blood of the Lamb; Re -
Re-deemed,

deemed, Re-deemed, His child, and for-ev-er, I am.
Re-deemed, Re-deemed,

God Is Love

412

D-4-DO

Anon.

God is love; and he that dwelleth in love dwelleth in God . . . I John 4:16

L-5, S-4

E. S. Lorenz

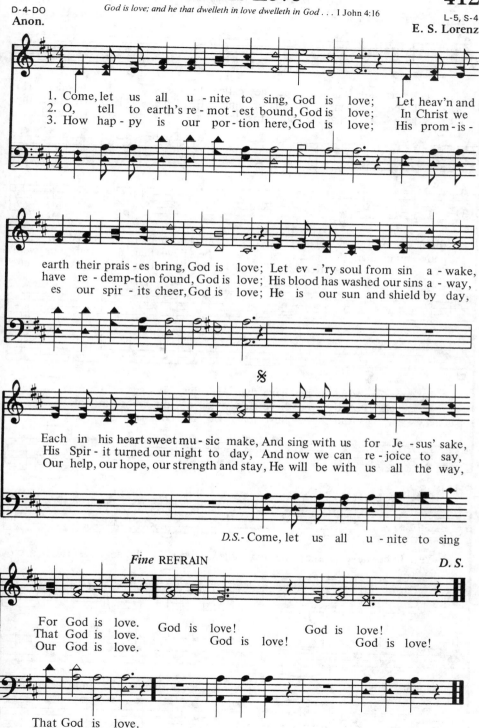

1. Come, let us all u-nite to sing, God is love; Let heav'n and
2. O, tell to earth's re-mot-est bound, God is love; In Christ we
3. How hap-py is our por-tion here, God is love; His prom-is-

earth their prais-es bring, God is love; Let ev-'ry soul from sin a-wake,
have re-demp-tion found, God is love; His blood has washed our sins a-way,
es our spir-its cheer, God is love; He is our sun and shield by day,

Each in his heart sweet mu-sic make, And sing with us for Je-sus' sake,
His Spir-it turned our night to day, And now we can re-joice to say,
Our help, our hope, our strength and stay, He will be with us all the way,

D.S.-Come, let us all u-nite to sing

Fine REFRAIN

D. S.

For God is love. God is love! God is love!
That God is love. God is love! God is love!
Our God is love. God is love! God is love!

That God is love.

413 I Believe In Jesus

Though now you see Him not,
yet believing, you rejoice . . . 1 Pet. 1:8

F-3-DO
A. H. H.

F-1, C-17
Alton H. Howard

1. I believe in the One they called Jesus, I believe He
2. I believe in the words of the Bible, How He made the
3. I believe that He spoke to dead Lazarus, And He said

stilled storm Galilee; I believe that He walked on the
poor blind man to see; I believe that the deaf ears were
"unbind and set free;" I believe that He reigns up in

water, And I believe that He's the answer for me.
opened, And I believe He's made a diff'rence in me.
heaven, And I believe that He is coming again.

CHORUS

Yes, I believe in the One they called Jesus, I believe He died on

Mount Calvary; And I believe that the tomb was found

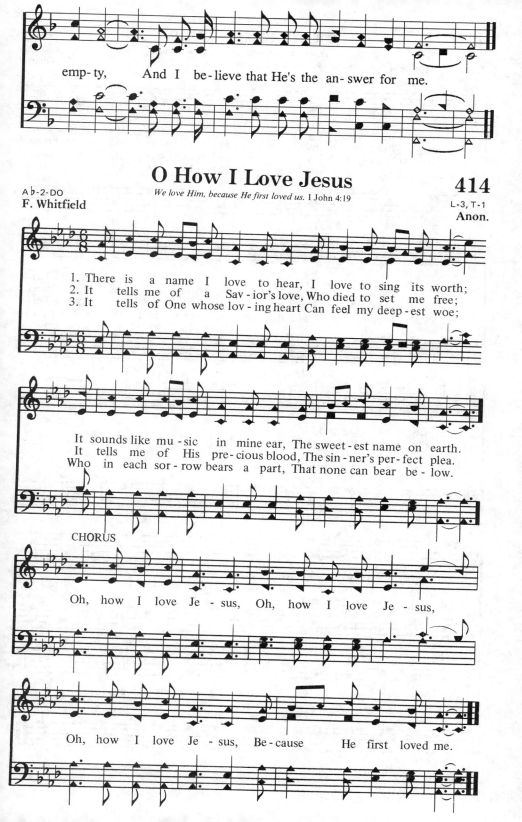

emp-ty, And I be-lieve that He's the an-swer for me.

O How I Love Jesus

414

We love Him, because He first loved us. I John 4:19

A♭-2-DO
F. Whitfield

L-3, T-1
Anon.

1. There is a name I love to hear, I love to sing its worth;
2. It tells me of a Sav-ior's love, Who died to set me free;
3. It tells of One whose lov-ing heart Can feel my deep-est woe;

It sounds like mu-sic in mine ear, The sweet-est name on earth.
It tells me of His pre-cious blood, The sin-ner's per-fect plea.
Who in each sor-row bears a part, That none can bear be-low.

CHORUS

Oh, how I love Je-sus, Oh, how I love Je-sus,

Oh, how I love Je-sus, Be-cause He first loved me.

415

To Christ Be True

C-4-MI

The Lord preserveth the faithful . . . Be of good courage, and He shall strengthen your heart . . . Psa. 31:23,24

C-16, L-6

Elisha A. Hoffman

D. M. Wilson

1. To Christ be loy - al and be true; His ban - ner be un - furled, And borne a - loft till is se - cured The con - quest of the world.
2. To Christ be loy - al and be true; He needs brave vol - un - teers To stand a - gainst the pow'rs of sin, Moved not by frowns or fears.
3. To Christ be loy - al and be true; In no - ble serv - ice prove Your faith and your fi - del - i - ty, The fer - vor of your love.
4. To Christ be loy - al and be true, And He will be your friend, De - fend - ing and pro - tect - ing you To life's tri - umph - ant end.

REFRAIN

To Christ, the Lord, be true, ... ev - er . . . true, For He will ev - er go with you, And help you all your con - flicts thru; To Christ, the Lord, be true. For He will go with you, ev - er true.

Do All In The Name Of The Lord 416

G-2-DO
A. T.

E-1, N-1

And whatsoever ye do in word or deed, do all in the name of the Lord Jesus . . .
Col. 3:17

Austin Taylor

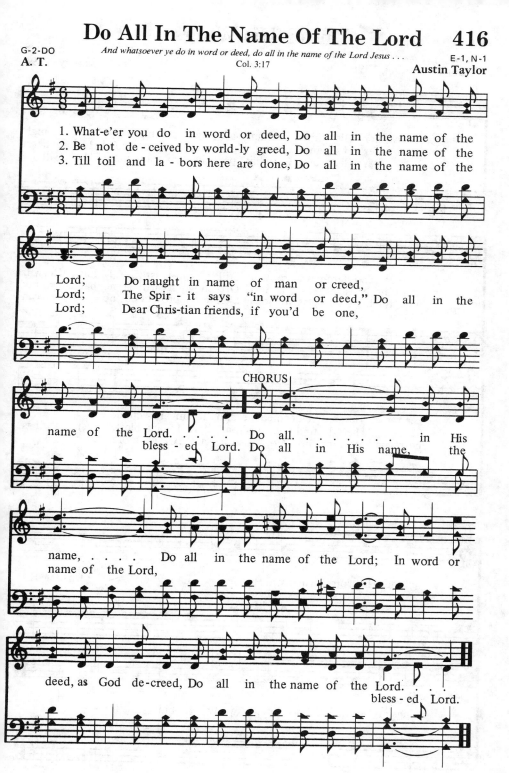

1. What-e'er you do in word or deed, Do all in the name of the
2. Be not de-ceived by world-ly greed, Do all in the name of the
3. Till toil and la-bors here are done, Do all in the name of the

Lord; Do naught in name of man or creed,
Lord; The Spir-it says "in word or deed," Do all in the
Lord; Dear Chris-tian friends, if you'd be one,

CHORUS

name of the Lord. . . . Do all. . . . . . . in His
bless-ed Lord. Do all in His name, the

name, ... Do all in the name of the Lord; In word or
name of the Lord,

deed, as God de-creed, Do all in the name of the Lord. . . .
bless-ed Lord.

417 Under His Wings

He shall cover thee with His feathers, and under His wings shalt thou trust. Psa. 91:4

Db-2-MI

C-15, P-5

William O. Cushing, 1896

Ira D. Sankey, 1896

1. Un - der His wings I am safe - ly a - bid - ing; Tho' the night
2. Un - der His wings, what a ref - uge in sor - row! How the heart
3. Un - der His wings, O what pre - cious en - joy - ment! There will I

deep-ens and tem-pests are wild, Still I can trust Him; I know He will
yearn-ing-ly turns to His rest! Oft-en when earth has no balm for my
hide till life's tri - als are o'er; Shel-tered, pro-tect-ed, no e - vil can

CHORUS

keep me; He has re-deemed me, and I am His child.
heal - ing, There I find com-fort, and there I am blest. Under His wings,
harm me; Rest-ing in Je - sus I'm safe ev - er-more.

un - der His wings, Who from His love can sev - er? Un-der His

wings my soul shall a - bide, Safe - ly a - bide for - ev - er.

Sweet Peace, The Gift Of God's Love 418

And the peace of God, which passeth all understanding,
shall keep your heart and minds . . . Phil 4:7

A-2-SOL
P. P. B.

L-5, P-1
Peter P. Bilhorn

1. There comes to my heart one sweet strain, (sweet strain,) A glad and a joy-ous re-frain, (re-frain,) I sing it a-gain and a-gain, Sweet peace, the gift of God's love.

2. Thru Christ on the cross peace was made, (was made,) My debt by His death was all paid, (all paid,) No oth-er foun-da-tion is laid, For peace, the gift of God's love.

3. In Je-sus for peace I a-bide, (a-bide,) And as I keep close to His side, (His side,) There's noth-ing but peace doth be-tide, Sweet peace, the gift of God's love.

CHORUS

Peace, peace, sweet peace, Won-der-ful peace from a-bove, (a-bove,) Oh,

rit.

won-der-ful, won-der-ful peace, Sweet peace, the gift of God's love.

419 Thou Thinkest, Lord, Of Me

G-3-SOL

E. S. L.

But I am poor and needy: yet the Lord thinketh upon me : Thou art my help . . .
Psa. 40:17

C-15

E. S. Lorenz

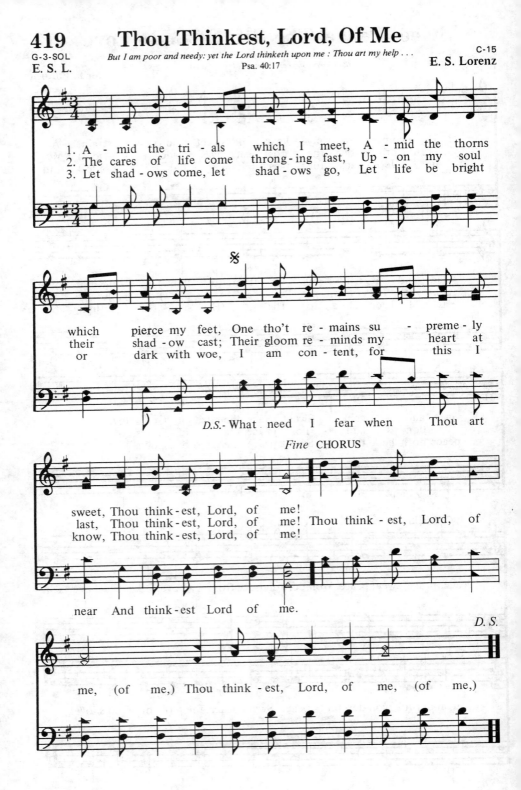

1. A - mid the tri - als which I meet, A - mid the thorns
2. The cares of life come throng - ing fast, Up - on my soul
3. Let shad - ows come, let shad - ows go, Let life be bright

which pierce my feet, One tho't re - mains su - preme - ly
their shad - ow cast; Their gloom re - minds my heart at
or dark with woe, I am con - tent, for this I

D.S.- What need I fear when Thou art

Fine CHORUS

sweet, Thou think - est, Lord, of me! Thou think - est, Lord, of
last, Thou think - est, Lord, of me!
know, Thou think - est, Lord, of me!

near And think - est Lord of me.

D. S.

me, (of me,) Thou think - est, Lord, of me, (of me,)

O Thou Fount Of Every Blessing 420

E♭-3-MI
Robert Robinson

Samuel took a stone, and set it . . . and called the name of it Ebenezer, saying,
Hitherto hath the Lord helped us. I Sam. 7:12

C-16, G-2
A. Nettleton

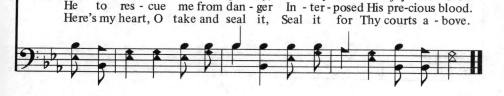

1. O Thou Fount of ev-'ry bless-ing, Tune my heart to sing Thy grace;
2. Here I raise my Eb-en-e-zer; Hith-er by Thy help I've come;
3. O to grace how great a debt-or Dai-ly I'm con-strained to be!

Streams of mer-cy, nev-er ceas-ing, Call for songs of loud-est praise.
And I hope by Thy good pleas-ure Safe-ly to ar-rive at home.
Let Thy good-ness like a fet-ter Bind my wand'ring heart to Thee.

Teach me ev-er to a-dore Thee: May I still Thy good-ness prove;
Je-sus sought me when a strang-er, Wand'ring from the fold of God;
Nev-er let me wan-der from Thee, Nev-er leave the God I love;

While the hope of end-less glo-ry, Fills my heart with joy and love.
He to res-cue me from dan-ger In-ter-posed His pre-cious blood.
Here's my heart, O take and seal it, Seal it for Thy courts a-bove.

421 Sweeter Than All

Unto you therefore which believe He is precious. I Pet. 2:7

E-2-DO
A-1

Johnson Oatman, Jr.
J. Howard Entwisle

1. Christ will me His aid af - ford, When - e'er I call,
2. I can fol - low all the way, Hear - ing Him call,
3. When I reach the crys - tal sea, Voic - es will call,

when - e'er I call; While I find my pre - cious Lord
hear - ing Him call; Find - ing Him from day to day,
voic - es will call; But my Sav - ior's voice will be

CHORUS

Sweet - er than all, sweet - er than all. Je - sus is now and

ev - er will be, Sweet - er than all the world to me, Since I

heard His lov - ing call, Sweet - er than all, sweet - er than all.

Jesus Saves

G-3-SOL

For the Son of man is come to seek and to save that which was lost. Luke 19:10

Priscilla J. Owens, 1882

S-1, S-5

Wm. J. Kirkpatrick, 1882

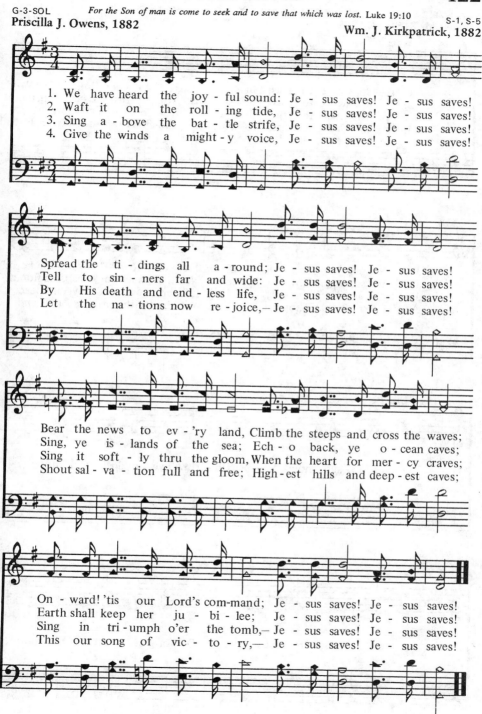

1. We have heard the joy-ful sound: Je-sus saves! Je-sus saves!
2. Waft it on the roll-ing tide, Je-sus saves! Je-sus saves!
3. Sing a-bove the bat-tle strife, Je-sus saves! Je-sus saves!
4. Give the winds a might-y voice, Je-sus saves! Je-sus saves!

Spread the ti-dings all a-round; Je-sus saves! Je-sus saves!
Tell to sin-ners far and wide: Je-sus saves! Je-sus saves!
By His death and end-less life, Je-sus saves! Je-sus saves!
Let the na-tions now re-joice,— Je-sus saves! Je-sus saves!

Bear the news to ev-'ry land, Climb the steeps and cross the waves;
Sing, ye is-lands of the sea; Ech-o back, ye o-cean caves;
Sing it soft-ly thru the gloom, When the heart for mer-cy craves;
Shout sal-va-tion full and free; High-est hills and deep-est caves;

On-ward! 'tis our Lord's com-mand; Je-sus saves! Je-sus saves!
Earth shall keep her ju-bi-lee; Je-sus saves! Je-sus saves!
Sing in tri-umph o'er the tomb,— Je-sus saves! Je-sus saves!
This our song of vic-to-ry,— Je-sus saves! Je-sus saves!

423   'Tis So Sweet To Trust In Jesus

Ab-4-MI   *We trust in the living God, who is the Savior of all men . . . I Tim. 4:10*   E-1, T-1

Louisa M. R. Stead, 1882   Wm. J. Kirkpatrick, 1882

1. 'Tis so sweet to trust in Je-sus, Just to take Him at His Word;
2. O, how sweet to trust in Je-sus, Just to trust His cleansing blood,
3. Yes, 'tis sweet to trust in Je-sus, Just from sin and self to cease;
4. I'm so glad I learned to trust Thee, Pre-cious Je-sus, Savior, Friend;

Just to rest up-on His prom-ise; Just to know, "Thus saith the Lord."
Just in sim-ple faith to plunge me 'Neath the heal-ing, cleansing flood.
Just from Je-sus sim-ply tak-ing Life, and rest, and joy, and peace.
And I know that Thou art with me, Wilt be with me to the end.

CHORUS

Je-sus, Je-sus, how I trust Him; How I've prov'd Him o'er and o'er;

Je-sus, Je-sus, Pre-cious Je-sus! O for grace to trust Him more.

The Gospel Is For All

424

Go ye therefore and teach all nations . . . Matt. 28:19

A♭-2-SOL
J. M. McCaleb

W-3
Arr. R. M. McIntosh

1. Of one the Lord has made the race, Thro' one has
2. Say not the hea - then are at home, Be - yond we
3. Re - ceived ye free - ly, free - ly give, From ev - 'ry

come the fall; Where sin has gone must go His
have no call; For why should we be blest a -
land they call; Un - less they hear they can - not

D. S.–Where sin has gone must go His

Fine CHORUS

grace: The Gos - pel is for all.
lone? The Gos - pel is for all. The bless - ed
live: The Gos - pel is for all.

grace: The Gos - pel is for all.

D. S.

Gos - pel is for all, The Gos - pel is for all.

425 Sunshine In My Soul

Ab-4-DO

Eliza Hewitt, 1887

For God, who commanded the light to shine . . . hath shined in our hearts . . .

II Cor. 4:6

F-2, J-1

Jno. R. Sweney, 1887

1. There's sun-shine in my soul to - day, More glo - ri - ous and bright
2. There's mu - sic in my soul to - day, A car - ol to the King,
3. There's glad - ness in my soul to - day, And hope, and praise, and love,

Than glows in an - y earth - ly skies, For Je - sus is my light.
And Je - sus, lis - ten - ing, can hear The songs I can - not sing.
For bless - ings which He gives me now, For joys "laid up" a - bove.

CHORUS

O there's sun - - shine, bless - ed sun - - shine,
O there's bless - shine in the soul, bless - ed sun - shine in the soul,

When the peace-ful hap - py mo - ments roll; When
hap - py mo - ments roll;

Je - sus shows His smil - ing face There is sun - shine in the soul.

At Calvary

426

C-4-SOL

And when they were come to . . . Calvary, there they crucified Him . . . Luke 23:33

T-1

Wm. R. Newall

D. B. Towner

1. Years I spent in van - i - ty and pride, Car - ing not my Lord was
2. By God's word at last my sin I learned; Then I trem - bled at the
3. Now I've giv'n to Je - sus ev - 'ry-thing, Now I glad - ly own Him
4. Oh, the love that drew sal - va - tion's plan! Oh, the grace that bro't it

cru - ci - fied, Know-ing not it was for me He died on Cal - va - ry!
law I'd spurned, Till my guilt- y soul im - plor - ing turned to Cal - va - ry!
as my King, Now my rap-tured soul can on - ly sing of Cal - va - ry!
down to man! Oh, the might - y gulf that God did span at Cal - va - ry!

CHORUS

Mer - cy there was great, and grace was free; Par - don there was mul - ti -

plied to me; There my bur-dened soul found lib - er - ty, at Cal - va - ry.

427 Sweet Will Of God

As the servants of Christ, doing the will of God from the heart. Eph. 6:6

Bb-4-SOL
Mrs. C. H. M.

C-16, D-1
Mrs. C. H. Morris

Duet

1. My stub-born will at last hath yield-ed; I would be Thine and
2. I'm tired of sin, foot-sore and wea-ry; The dark-some path hath
3. Thy pre-cious will, O con-qu'ring Sav-ior, Doth now em-brace and
4. Shut in with Thee, O Lord, for - ev - er, My way-ward feet no

Thine a - lone; And this the prayer my lips are
drear - y grown; But now a light has ris'n to
com - pass me; All dis - cords hushed my peace a
more to roam; What pow'r from Thee my soul can

CHORUS

bring - ing, "Lord, let in me Thy will be done."
cheer me: I find in Thee my Star, my Sun.
riv - er, My soul a pris-oned bird set free. Sweet
sev - er? The cen - ter of God's will my home.

will of God, still fold me clos - er, Till I am

whol - ly lost in Thee; Sweet will of God still

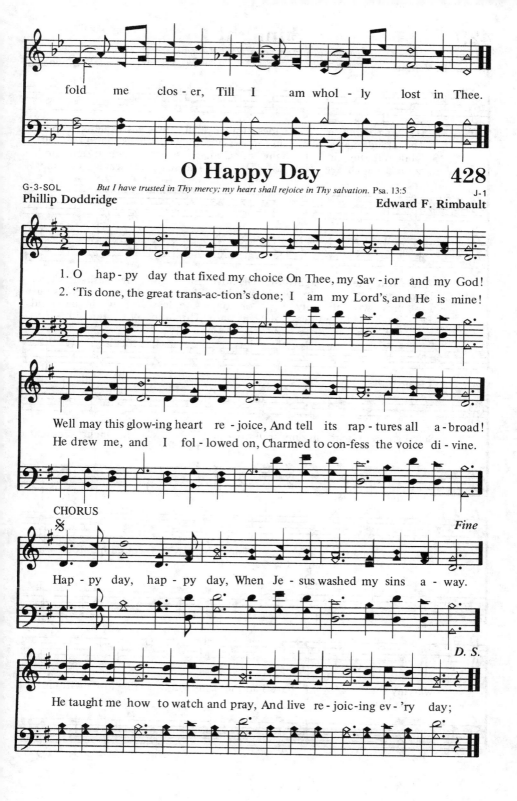

fold me clos - er, Till I am whol - ly lost in Thee.

O Happy Day

428

G-3-SOL   *But I have trusted in Thy mercy; my heart shall rejoice in Thy salvation. Psa. 13:5*   J-1

Phillip Doddridge   **Edward F. Rimbault**

1. O hap - py day that fixed my choice On Thee, my Sav - ior and my God!
2. 'Tis done, the great trans-ac-tion's done; I am my Lord's, and He is mine!

Well may this glow-ing heart re - joice, And tell its rap - tures all a - broad!
He drew me, and I fol - lowed on, Charmed to con-fess the voice di - vine.

CHORUS

Fine

Hap - py day, hap - py day, When Je - sus washed my sins a - way.

D. S.

He taught me how to watch and pray, And live re - joic-ing ev - 'ry day;

429 Sunlight

E-4-SOL
W. Van DeVenter

Who hath delivered us from the power of darkness, and hath translated us into the kingdom of His dear Son. Col. 1:13

T-1
W. S. Weeden

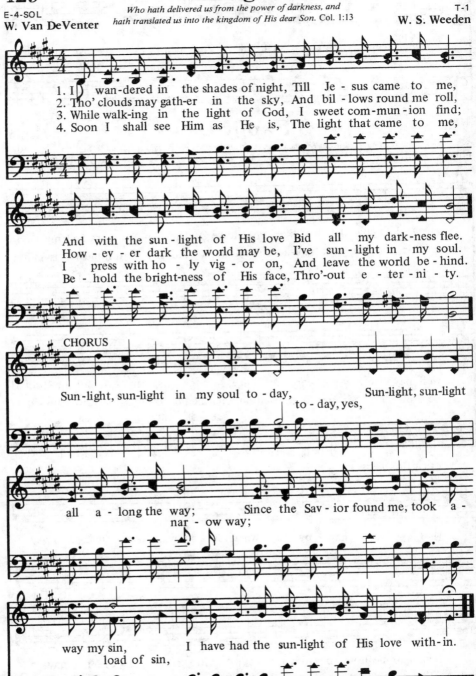

1. I wan-dered in the shades of night, Till Je-sus came to me,
2. Tho' clouds may gath-er in the sky, And bil-lows round me roll,
3. While walk-ing in the light of God, I sweet com-mun-ion find;
4. Soon I shall see Him as He is, The light that came to me,

And with the sun-light of His love Bid all my dark-ness flee.
How-ev-er dark the world may be, I've sun-light in my soul.
I press with ho-ly vig-or on, And leave the world be-hind.
Be-hold the bright-ness of His face, Thro'-out e-ter-ni-ty.

CHORUS

Sun-light, sun-light in my soul to-day,
to-day, yes,
Sun-light, sun-light

all a-long the way;
nar-ow way;
Since the Sav-ior found me, took a-

way my sin,
load of sin,
I have had the sun-light of His love with-in.

Take The Name Of Jesus With You 430

Ab-4-SOL
Lydia Baxter, 1870

For there is none other name under heaven given among men whereby we must be saved. Acts 4:12

E-1, N-1
Wm. H. Doane, 1871

1. Take the name of Je - sus with you, Child of sor - row and of
2. Take the name of Je - sus ev - er As a shield from ev - 'ry
3. O the pre-cious name of Je - sus! How it thrills our souls with

woe; It will joy and com-fort give you, Take it then, wher-
snare; If temp - ta - tions round you gath - er, Breathe that ho - ly
joy, When His lov - ing arms re - ceive us, And His songs our

CHORUS

e'er you go.
name in pray'r. Pre - cious name, O how sweet!
tongues em - ploy! Pre - cious name, O how sweet!

Hope of earth and joy of heav'n; Pre - cious name, Pre - cious name,

O how sweet! Hope of earth and joy of heav'n.
O how sweet, how sweet,

431 None Of Self And All Of Thee

C-3-MI

Whosoever will come after Me, let him deny himself,
and take up his cross, and follow Me. Mark 8:34

C-16

Theo. Monod, Arr.

James McGranahan, Arr.

Not too fast

1. O, the bit-ter pain and sor-row That a time could ev-er be,
2. Yet He found me; I be-held Him Bleed-ing on th'ac-curs-ed tree,
3. Day by day His ten-der mer-cy Heal-ing, help-ing, full and free,
4. High-er than the high-est heav-ens, Deep-er than the deep-est sea,

When I proud-ly said to Je-sus "All of self, and none of Thee,"
And my wist-ful heart said faint-ly, "Some of self, and some of Thee,"
Bro't me low-er while I whis-pered "Less of self, and more of Thee,"
Lord, Thy love at last has con-quered "None of self, and all of Thee,"

All of self and none of Thee, All of self and none of Thee,
Some of self and some of Thee, Some of self and some of Thee,
Less of self and more of Thee, Less of self and more of Thee,
None of self and all of Thee, None of self and all of Thee,

When I proud-ly said to Je-sus "All of self and none of Thee."
And my wist-ful heart said faint-ly "Some of self and some of Thee."
Bro't me low-er while I whis-pered "Less of self and more of Thee."
Lord, Thy love at last has con-quered "None of self and all of Thee."

I Know God's Promise Is True

432

Bb-2-SOL
C. H. M.
P-4, T-1

And this is the promise that He hath promised us, even eternal life. 1 John 2:25

Mrs. C. H. Morris

1. For God so loved this sin - ful world, His Son He free - ly
2. The "who - so - ev - er" of the Lord, I trust - ed was for
3. E - ter - nal life, the prom - ise be - low, Now fills my heart and

gave, That who - so - ev - er would o - bey, E - ter - nal
me; I took Him at His gra - cious word, From sin He
soul; I'll sing His praise for - ev - er - more, Who has re -

CHORUS

life should have.
set me free. 'Tis true, O yes, 'tis true, God's
deemed my soul. the prom - ise is true,

won - der - ful prom - ise is true, 'tis true, For I've trust - ed, and

test - ed, and tried it, And I know God's prom - ise is true. 'tis true.

433 I Love Thy Kingdom, Lord

A-4-SOL

Lord, I have loved the habitation of Thy house. Psa. 26:8

K-1, T-1

Timothy Dwight, 1800

A. B. Everett

1. I love Thy king-dom, Lord, The house of Thine a - bode; The
2. For her my tears shall fall, For her my pray'rs as - cend; To
3. Je - sus, Thou Friend di - vine, Our Sav - ior and our King! Thy

church our blest Re - deem - er saved With His own pre - cious blood.
her my cries and toils be giv'n, Till toils and cares shall end.
hand from ev - 'ry snare and foe Shall great de - liv - 'rance bring.

I love Thy church, O God! Her walls be - fore Thee stand, Dear,
Be - yond my high-est joy I prize her heav'n-ly ways, Her
Sure as Thy truth shall last, To Zi - on shall be giv'n The

as the ap - ple of Thine eye, And grav - en on Thy hand.
sweet com - mun-ion, sol - emn vows, Her hymns of love and praise.
bright-est glo - ries earth can yield, And bright-est bliss of heav'n.

All Hail The Power Of Jesus' Name 434

G-4-SOL

But we see Jesus . . . crowned with glory and honor . . . Heb. 2:9

Edward Perronet, et al.

P-2

Oliver Holden

1. All hail the pow'r of Je - sus' name! Let an - gels pros - trate
2. Ye cho - sen seed of Is - rael's race, Ye ran - somed from the
3. Let ev - 'ry kin - dred, ev - 'ry tribe, On this ter - res - trial
4. O that with yon - der sa - cred throng We at His feet may

fall! Bring forth the roy - al di - a - dem, And
fall, Hail Him who saves you by His grace, And
ball, To Him all maj - es - ty as - cribe, And
fall! We'll join the ev - er - last - ing song, And

crown Him Lord of all; Bring forth the roy - al
crown Him Lord of all; Hail Him who saves you
crown Him Lord of all; To Him all maj - es -
praise Him Lord of all; We'll join the ev - er -

di - a - dem, And crown Him Lord of all.
by His grace, And crown Him Lord of all.
ty as - cribe, And crown Him Lord of all.
last - ing song, And praise Him Lord of all.

435 How Shall The Young Secure

E-4-SOL

Isaac Watts. (Ps. 119)

Wherewithal shall a young man cleanse his way?
By taking heed thereto according to Thy word. Psa. 119:9

E-1, W-3

Beethoven

1. How shall the young se - cure their hearts, And
2. 'Tis like the sun, a heav'n - ly light, That
3. Thy word is ev - er - last - ing truth; How

guard their lives from sin? Thy word the choic - est
guides us all the day; And, thro' the dan - gers
pure is ev - 'ry page! That ho - ly book shall

rules im - parts To keep the con-science clean, ...
of the night, A lamp to lead our way, ...
guide our youth, And well sup - port our age, ...
To keep the

. . . . . To keep the con - science clean.
. . . . . A lamp to lead our way.
. . . . . And well sup - port our age.
con - science clean, To keep the con-science clean!

con - science clean, To keep the con - science clean!

I'll Fly Away

436

Bb-4-MI

Oh that I had wings like a dove!
For then would I fly away, and be at rest. Psa. 55:6

Albert E. Brumley

H-2

Albert E. Brumley

1. Some glad morn-ing when this life is o'er, I'll fly a-way;
2. When the shad-ows of this life have grown, fly a-way;
3. Just a few more wea-ry days and then, fly a-way

To a home on God's ce-les-tial shore, I'll fly a-way.
Like a bird from pris-on bars has flown, fly a-way, fly a-way.
To a land where joys shall nev-er end, fly a-way,

REFRAIN

I'll fly a-way, O glo-ry, I'll fly a-way;
fly a-way, fly a-way, in the morn-ing,

When I die, Hal-le-lu-jah, by and by, I'll fly a-way.
fly a-way, fly a-way, fly a-way.

437 Thy Will Be Done

I delight to do Thy will, O my God . . . Psa. 40:8

E♭-4-MI

Larry L. Dickens

W-5

R. J. Stevens

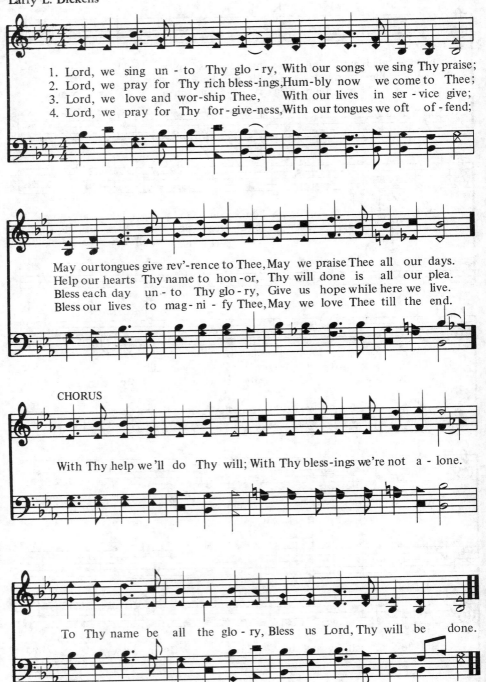

1. Lord, we sing un-to Thy glo-ry, With our songs we sing Thy praise;
2. Lord, we pray for Thy rich bless-ings, Hum-bly now we come to Thee;
3. Lord, we love and wor-ship Thee, With our lives in ser-vice give;
4. Lord, we pray for Thy for-give-ness, With our tongues we oft of-fend;

May our tongues give rev'-rence to Thee, May we praise Thee all our days.
Help our hearts Thy name to hon-or, Thy will done is all our plea.
Bless each day un-to Thy glo-ry, Give us hope while here we live.
Bless our lives to mag-ni-fy Thee, May we love Thee till the end.

CHORUS

With Thy help we'll do Thy will; With Thy bless-ings we're not a-lone.

To Thy name be all the glo-ry, Bless us Lord, Thy will be done.

We Walk By Faith

438

For we walk by faith, not by sight . . . II Cor. 5:7

B ♭-2-MI
R. J. S.

F-1, S-2
R. J. Stevens

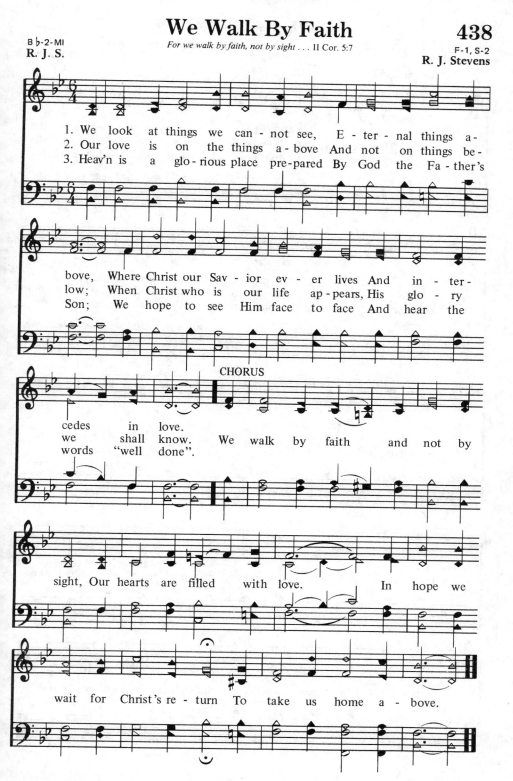

1. We look at things we can-not see, E - ter - nal things a-
2. Our love is on the things a - bove And not on things be-
3. Heav'n is a glo - rious place pre-pared By God the Fa - ther's

bove, Where Christ our Sav - ior ev - er lives And in - ter-
low; When Christ who is our life ap - pears, His glo - ry
Son; We hope to see Him face to face And hear the

CHORUS

cedes in love.
we shall know. We walk by faith and not by
words "well done".

sight, Our hearts are filled with love. In hope we

wait for Christ's re - turn To take us home a - bove.

439

Psalm 19

E♭-4-DO
Psalm 19:7-10

Moreover by them is Thy servant warned: and in keeping them is great reward.
Psa. 19:11

W-3
Traditional

Not too fast

1. The law of the Lord is per-fect, con-vert-ing the
2. The stat-utes of the Lord are right, re-joic-ing the
3. The fear of the Lord is clean, en-dur-ing for-

soul, The tes-ti-mo-ny of the Lord is sure, mak-ing
heart, The com-mand-ment of the Lord is pure, en-
ev-er, The judg-ments of the Lord are true, and

wise the sim-ple,
light-'ning the eyes,
right-eous al-to-geth-er,

CHORUS

More to be de-sired are

they than gold, yea, than much fine gold, sweet-er

al-so than hon-ey and the hon-ey comb.

Silent Night, Holy Night

440

C-2-SOL
Joseph Mohr, 1818

For unto you is born this day in the city of David a Savior, which is Christ the Lord.
Luke 2:11

C-1
Franz Gruber

1. Si - lent night, ho - ly night! All is calm, all is
2. Si - lent night, ho - ly night! Shep-herds quake at the
3. Si - lent night, ho - ly night! Son of God lend Thy

bright; Round yon vir - gin moth - er and child. Ho - ly
sight, Wise - men pon - der heav - en's bright star, An - gels
light; With the host we joy - ful - ly sing: "Glo - ry,

in - fant so ten - der and mild; Sleep in heav - en - ly
sing - ing their "Hal - le - lu - jah! Christ the Sav - ior is
hon - or, to Je - sus our King! Christ the Sav - ior was

peace, Sleep in heav - en - ly peace!
born, Christ the Sav - ior is born."
born, Christ the Sav - ior was born."

441 Christ Liveth In Me

Nevertheless I live; yet not I, but Christ liveth in me. Gal. 2:20

G-2-SOL

T-1

Daniel W. Whittle

James McGranahan

1. Once far from God and dead in sin, No light my heart could see; But in God's Word the light I found, Now Christ liveth in me.
2. As rays of light from yon - der sun, The flow'rs of earth set free, So life and light and love came forth From Christ living in me. Christ liv - eth in me,...
3. With long - ing all my heart is filled, That like Him I may be, As on the won - drous tho't I dwell That Christ liveth in me. Christ

CHORUS

Christ liv - eth in me, Oh! liv - eth in me, Christ liv - eth in me, Oh!

what a sal - va - tion this, That Christ liv - eth in me.

Yield Not To Temptation

442

A♭-2-MI
H. R. P.

E-1
H. R. Palmer

Watch and pray, that ye enter not into temptation. Matt. 26:41

1. Yield not to temp-ta - tion, For yield-ing is sin; Each vic-t'ry will
2. Shun e - vil com-pan-ions, Bad lan-guage dis - dain, God's name hold in
3. To him that o'er-com-eth, God giv - eth a crown; Thro' faith we shall

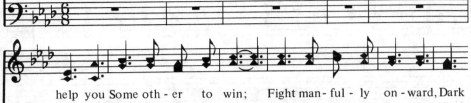

help you Some oth - er to win; Fight man-ful - ly on - ward, Dark
rev-'rence, Nor take it in vain; Be thought-ful and ear - nest, Kind
con-quer, Tho' of - ten cast down; He who is our Sav - ior, Our

pas - sions sub - due,
heart-ed and true, Look ev - er to Je - sus: He'll car - ry you
strength will re - new;

CHORUS

thro'. Ask the Sav - ior to help you, Com-fort, strength-en and

keep you; He is will-ing to aid you, He will car - ry you thro'.

443

G-4-MI

Henry Alford

Come, Ye Thankful People, Come

He that soweth the good seed is the Son of man; the field is the world;
the good seed are the children of the kingdom. Matt. 13:37,38

E-1, T-2

George J. Elvey

1. Come, ye thank-ful peo-ple, come, Raise the song of har-vest-home:
2. All the world is God's own field, Fruit un-to His praise to yield;
3. For the Lord our God shall come, And shall take His har-vest-home;
4. E-ven so, Lord, quick-ly come To Thy fi-nal har-vest-home;

All is safe-ly gath-ered in, Ere the win-ter storms be-gin;
Wheat and tares to-geth-er sown, Un-to joy or sor-row grown;
From His field shall in that day All of-fens-es purge a-way;
Gath-er Thou Thy peo-ple in, Free from sor-row, free from sin;

God, our Mak-er, doth pro-vide For our wants to be sup-plied;
First the blade, and then the ear, Then the full corn shall ap-pear:
Give His an-gels charge at last In the fire the tares to cast;
There, for-ev-er pu-ri-fied, In Thy pres-ence to a-bide:

Come to God's own tem-ple, come, Raise the song of har-vest-home.
Lord of har-vest, grant that we Whole-some grain and pure may be.
But the fruit-ful ears to store In His gar-ner ev-er-more.
Come, with all Thine an-gels, come, Raise the glo-rious har-vest-home.

Set Your Mind

444

Seek those things which are above . . . set your affections on things above,
not on things on the earth. Col. 3:1,2

Eb-4-MI
D. O.

E-1
Dusty Owens
Arr. by Margie Garrett & R. J. S.

1. {Where on earth may joy be found? In the midst of sin-ful-ness?
   If you have been raised with Christ, Seek the things in heav-en's realm,

2. {This old world has naught for you, With its sor-row, pain and sin,
   Christ shall come to claim His own, In the midst of toil and strife,

{In God's word the truth a-bounds; He pro-vides the rest;
On-ly fol-low God's ad-vice; He will lead you home.

{You have died to sin, be true: You are hid in Him.
Crowned with glo-ry we'll be home; He will give us life.

CHORUS

Set your mind on things a-bove, Not on all that's here be-low;

Keep your heart in Spir-it's love And the bless-ings He'll be-stow.

445 Jesus, Rose Of Sharon

E-3-MI

Ida A. Guirey

That Christ may dwell in your hearts by faith . . .
being rooted and grounded in love . . . Eph. 3:17

D-1

Chas. H. Gabriel

1. Je-sus, Rose of Shar-on, bloom with-in my heart; Beau-ties of Thy
2. Je-sus, Rose of Shar-on, sweet-er far to see Than the fair-est
3. Je-sus, Rose of Shar-on, bloom for-ev-er-more; Be Thy glo-ry

truth and ho-li-ness im-part, That wher-e'er I go my life may
flow'rs of earth could ev-er be, Fill my life com-plete-ly, add-ing
seen on earth from shore to shore, Till the na-tions own Thy sov-'reign-

shed a-broad Fra-grance of the knowl-edge of the love of God.
more each day Of Thy grace di-vine and pu-ri-ty, I pray.
ty com-plete, Lay their hon-ors down and wor-ship at Thy feet.

CHORUS

Je-sus, Rose of Shar-on,
Bless-ed Je-sus, Rose of Shar-

on, Bloom in ra-diance and in love with-in my heart.

Jesus, My Precious Savior

446
C-10

Bb-2-SOL
Russell G. Elliott

Ye were not redeemed with corruptible things . . .
but with the precious blood of Christ . . . I Pet. 1:18, 19

D. Joyce Elliott
Arr. R. J. Stevens

1. Je - sus, my pre - cious Sav - ior, Je - sus, the Lamb of Light,
2. Je - sus, my great Re - deem - er, Thou who hast shown the way,

Je - sus, who came to save me, Je - sus, the Au - thor of right.
Je - sus, my hope and ref - uge, Guid - ing me day af - ter day.

Je - sus, whose love is great - er, Je - sus of Gal - i - lee,
Je - sus, who stands be - side me, Je - sus of Cal - va - ry,

Let me be wor - thy, Oh Mas - ter, of all that You've done for me.
Let me be wor - thy, Oh Sav - ior, of heav - en's e - ter - ni - ty.

447 Ivory Palaces

All Thy garments smell of myrrh, and aloes . . . out of the ivory palaces . . . Psa. 45:8

E-2-SOL

H. B.

L-4

Henry Barraclough

1. My Lord has gar-ments so won-drous fine, And myrrh their tex-ture
2. His life had al - so its sor-rows sore, For al - oes had a
3. In gar-ments glo - ri - ous He will come, To o - pen wide the

fills; Its fra-grance reached to this heart of mine, With
part; And when I think of the cross He bore, My
door; And I shall en - ter my heav'n - ly home, To

CHORUS

joy my be - ing thrills.
eyes with tear-drops start.   Out of the i - vo - ry
dwell for - ev - er - more.

pal - ac - es, In - to a world of woe;   On - ly His

rit.

great e - ter - nal love,   Made   my Sav - ior go.

To Love The Lord

448

Thou shalt love the Lord thy God with all thy heart... soul... strength... and with all thy mind; and thy neighbor as thyself. Luke 10:27

A♭-4-SOL

Robert Fudge & R. J. S.

L-2, L-3

R. J. Stevens

1. To love the Lord with heart and soul, To love Him with the mind,
2. To love my neigh-bor as my-self, To love Him fer-vent-ly,
3. To love my neigh-bor and my Lord With all my heart and soul,

Ful - fills the first and great com-mand, In Him true peace I find.
Ful - fills the roy - al law of love, And sets my spir-it free.
Ful - fils the pro-phets and the law And makes my spir-it whole.

CHORUS

I love the Lord with heart and soul, I love Him with my mind. In

Him I'll live while a - ges roll; In Him true peace I find.

449 Now I Believe In Jesus

Blessed are they that have not seen, and yet have believed. . . John 20:29

Eb-2-MI

R. J. S.

F-1

R. J. Stevens

1. Je - sus came down from heav-en, Do -ing His Fa -ther's will;
2. Je - sus a - rose tri - um-phant O - ver the grave for me;
3. Je - sus went back to heav-en To in - ter - cede a - bove;
4. Je - sus will come from heav-en And ev - 'ry eye shall see;

He gave His life a ran - som There up - on Cal - v'ry's Hill.
He took a - way the death sting, Christ won the vic - to - ry.
Oh what a great Re - deem - er, Shar - ing with me His love.
Saved ones He'll bless for - ev - er, In heav'n e - ter - nal - ly.

CHORUS

Now I be - lieve in Je - sus, E'en tho' I did not see

rit.

His nail-scarred hands, His wounded side; Je - sus is dear to me.

Yes, For Me He Careth

450

B♭-3-SOL

Casting all your care upon Him; for He careth for you. 1 Pet. 5:7

L-4, P-5

Horatius Bonar, arr.

L. O. Sanderson

1. Yes, for me, for me He car - eth, With lov - ing, ten - der care;
2. Yes, for me, He stand-eth plead-ing At mer - cy's seat a - bove,
3. Yes, in me, in me He dwell-eth! In me and I in Him,

Yes, with me, with me He shar - eth Each bur - den and each fear.
Ev - er for me in - ter - ced - ing In love, un - tir - ing love.
And my soul with hope He fill - eth, Tho' fu - ture plans are dim.

Yes, o'er me, o'er me He watch-eth, Cease-less watch-eth night and
Yes, in me a - broad He shed-deth Joys un - earth - ly, love and
Thus I wait for His re - turn - ing, Sing - ing all the way to

day; Yes, e'en me, e'en me He snatch-eth From per - ils of the way.
light; And to cov - er me He spread-eth His lov - ing wings of might.
heav'n; Such the joy - ful song of morn - ing, Such tran-quil song of ev'n.

451 Jesus Is All The World To Me

I can do all things through Christ which strengtheneth me. Phil 4:13

Ab-2-MI
W. L. T.

C-5, F-2
Will L. Thompson

1. Je - sus is all the world to me, My life, my joy, my all;
2. Je - sus is all the world to me, My friend in tri - als sore;
3. Je - sus is all the world to me, And true to Him I'll be;
4. Je - sus is all the world to me, I want no bet - ter friend;

He is my strength from day to day, With-out Him I would fall;
I go to Him for bless-ings, and He gives them o'er and o'er;
Oh, how could I this friend de - ny, When He's so true to me?
I trust Him now, I'll trust Him when Life's fleet-ing days shall end;

When I am sad, to Him I go, No oth - er one can cheer me
He sends the sun-shine and the rain, He sends the har-vest's gold-en
Fol - low-ing Him I know I'm right, He watch - es o'er me day and
Beau - ti - ful life with such a friend; Beau - ti - ful life that has no

so; When I am sad, He makes me glad, He's my friend.
grain; Sun-shine and rain, har - vest of grain, He's my friend.
night; Fol-low-ing Him, by day and night, He's my friend.
end; E - ter - nal life, e - ter - nal joy, He's my friend.

He Keeps Me Singing

452

A♭-4-MI
L. B. B.

N-1, S-4
L. B. Bridgers

Let the word of Christ dwell in you richly . . .
singing with grace in your hearts to the Lord. Col. 3:16

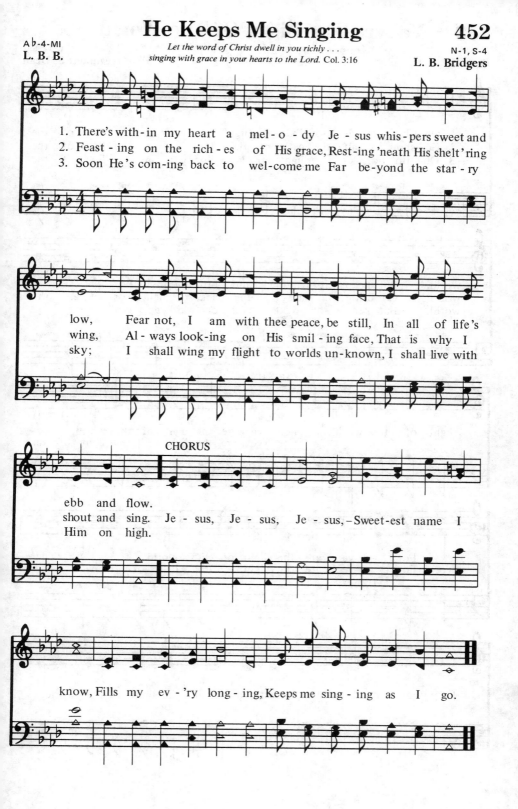

1. There's with-in my heart a mel-o-dy Je-sus whis-pers sweet and low, Fear not, I am with thee peace, be still, In all of life's ebb and flow.

2. Feast-ing on the rich-es of His grace, Rest-ing 'neath His shelt'ring wing, Al-ways look-ing on His smil-ing face, That is why I shout and sing.

3. Soon He's com-ing back to wel-come me Far be-yond the star-ry sky; I shall wing my flight to worlds un-known, I shall live with Him on high.

CHORUS

Je-sus, Je-sus, Je-sus,—Sweet-est name I know, Fills my ev-'ry long-ing, Keeps me sing-ing as I go.

453 Ye Are The Light Of The World

F-2-DO

Pearl Hatchett

C-12, E-1

Emmett S. Dean

Ye are the light of the world . . . Let your light so shine
before men, that they may see your good works . . . Matt. 5:14,16

1. Oh, Chris-tian, do not hide your light! For ye are the light of the world, But keep it trimmed and burn-ing bright, For light of the world.

2. Go show to all the path of right, For ye are the light of the world, Go bring the stray-ing back to light, For ye are the

3. Oh, do not let your light burn low, For ye are the light of the world, But keep it bright and on-ward go, For

CHORUS

For ye are the light of the world, ... For ye are the light, the light of the

. . . For ye are the light of the world; Then world, For ye are the light, the light of the world;

keep your lamps all burn-ing bright, For ye are the light of the world.

Let The Beauty Of Jesus Be Seen 454

Eb-2-MI

George L. Johnson

Christ also suffered for us, leaving us an example,
that ye should follow His steps. I Pet. 2:21

C-12, C-13

Arr. Cleavant Derricks

1. Let the beau - ty of Je - sus be seen in me,
2. When some-bo - dy has been so un - kind to you,
3. From the dawn of the morn-ing to close of day,

All His won - der - ful pas - sion and pur - i - ty,
Some word spo - ken that pierc - es you thru, and thru,
In ex - am - ple in deeds and in all you say;

May His spir - it di - vine all my be - ing re - fine,
Think how He was be - guiled, spat up - on and re - viled,
Lay your gifts at His feet, ev - er strive to keep sweet,

Let the beau - ty of Je - sus be seen in me.
Let the beau - ty of Je - sus be seen in you.
Let the beau - ty of Je - sus be seen in you.

455 Take My Hand And Lead Me

Bb-3-MI
J. W. G.

F-2, H-4
J. W. Galner

Show me Thy ways, O Lord; teach me Thy paths.
Lead me in Thy truth, and teach me. Psa. 25:4,5

1. I want to live, dear Lord, for Thee, Oh! keep me ev-'ry
2. When Sa-tan would my hopes a-larm, Oh! shel-ter Thou, my
3. Let me each day, Thy spir-it feel; In-crease my cour-age,

day; A faith-ful ser-vant let me be A-long life's
soul; Pro-tect me with Thy might-y arm, Thy strength will
Lord, To walk by faith, en-dowed with zeal, Di-rect-ed

CHORUS

rug-ged way. Take my hand and lead me,
keep me whole. Take my hand and lead me, lead me ev-'ry day,
by Thy word.

An-y-where you need me; With Thy
An-y-where you need me on life's rug-ged way; With Thy Ho-ly

Spir-it feed me, Till I'm safe at home.
Spir-it feed me, Lord, I pray, Till I'm safe with Thee at home.

Hold His Nail-Scarred Hand

456

Db-4-SOL
Geneva T. McDonald
3rd Verse — R. J. S.

I live by faith of the Son of God, who loved me, and gave Himself for me . . . Gal. 2:20

E-1
R. J. Stevens

1. I was not on the jour-ney up to Gol- go-tha's hill, Nor
2. I did not see the light-ning as it flashed on that sad day; Nor
3. I know my Sav-ior loves me, He gave His life so free; Up-

was I in the gar-den that night when time stood still. I
help the wom-an, Ma- ry, place spi- ces where He lay. I
on the cross of Cal- v'ry He died for you and me. Let's

did not sell the Sav- ior un- to the an- gry crowd, Nor
live my life much la- ter and in a dif-f'rent land, But
live our lives for Je- sus, Don't cru-ci- fy a - gain, Give

Rit.

hear the words as Si - mon de - nied the Lord a - loud.
as I sin, I drive a - gain a nail in - to His hand.
praise and hon - or to the Lord, and hold His nail- scarred hand.

457 The Last Mile Of The Way

F-2-DO

I have finished my course, I have kept the faith: henceforth there is laid up for me a
crown of righteousness . . . II Tim. 4:7,8

A-1, W-4

Johnson Oatman, Jr.

Wm. Edie Marks

1. If I walk in the path-way of du-ty, If I work till the
2. If for Christ I pro-claim the glad sto-ry, If I seek for His
3. And if here I have earn-est-ly striv-en And have tried all His

close of the day, I shall see the great King in His beau-ty
sheep gone a-stray, I am sure He will show me His glo-ry
will to o-bey, 'Twill en-hance all the rap-ture of heav-en

Fine CHORUS

When I've gone the last mile of the way. When I've gone the last

mile of the way, I will rest at the close of the
the last mile of the way, at the

D. S.

day, And I know there are joys that a-wait me
close of the day,

In The Garden

458

Ab-2-SOL
C. A. M.

F-2
C. Austin Miles

*But if we walk in the light, as He is in the light,
we have fellowship one with another . . . I John 1:7*

1. I come to the gar-den a-lone, While the dew is still
2. He speaks, and the sound of His voice Is so sweet the birds
3. I'd stay in the gar-den with Him Though the night a-round

on the ros-es; And the voice I hear, fall-ing on my ear; The
hush their sing-ing, And the mel-o-dy that He gave to me, With
me be fall-ing, But He bids me go; thru the voice of woe, His

CHORUS

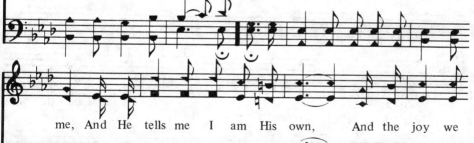

Son of God dis-clos-es.
in my heart is ring-ing. And He walks with me, and He talks with
voice to me is call-ing.

me, And He tells me I am His own, And the joy we

share as we tar-ry there, None oth-er has ev-er known.

459 The Precious Book Divine

Thy word is a lamp unto my feet, and a light unto my path. Psa. 119:105

E♭-2-DO
L. O. S.

W-3, W-4
L. O. Sanderson

1. How pre-cious is the Book di-vine, By in-spi-ra-tion
2. It sweet-ly cheers my droop-ing heart, In this dark vale of
3. This lamp, thro' all the te-dious night Of life, shall guide my

giv'n! Bright as a lamp its pre-cepts shine, To
tears; Light to my life it still im-parts, And
way, Till I be-hold the clear-er light Of

guide my soul to heav'n.
quells my ris - ing fears.
an e -ter - nal day.

CHORUS

Ho - ly Book di-
Ho - ly Bi - ble,

vine! Pre-cious treas-ure mine! Lamp to my
Book di vine! Pre-cious treas-ure, thou art mine!

feet and a light to my way To guide me safe-ly home.

The World's Bible

460

A b-4-SOL

Annie J. Flint

Ye are manifestly declared to be the epistle of Christ . . .
written not with ink, but with the Spirit . . . II Cor. 3:3

C-12

J. E. Hamilton

1. Christ has no hands but our hands To do His work to-day,
2. We are the on-ly Bi-ble The care-less world will read,
3. What if our hands are bus-y With oth-er things than His?

He has no feet but our feet To lead men in His way;
We are the sin-ner's gos-pel, We are the scoff-ers' creed;
What if our feet are walk-ing Where sin's al-lure-ment is?

He has no tongue but our tongues To tell men how He died,
We are the Lord's last mes-sage Giv-en in deed and word,
What if our tongues are speak-ing Of things His life would spurn,

He has no help but our help To bring them to His side.
What if the type is crook-ed? What if the print is blurred?
How can we hope to help Him And wel-come His re-turn?

461

He Changes Not

G-3-SOL
T. O. Chisholm

Jesus Christ the same yesterday and today, and for ever. Heb. 13:8

C-5, C-6
Bertha Mae Lillenas

1. A - mid the chang - ing scenes be - low, Where man - y come and
2. The years pass on, a shift - ing train, Of things fa - mil - iar,
3. As it has been, so will it be Till comes life's fi - nal

man - y go, My wist - ful soul will oft cry out For
few re - main, How sweet, how com - fort - ing the tho't, That
hour for me, Mine sure - ly is a fa - vored lot— I

CHORUS

one who stays, who chang - es not.
one re - mains who chang - es not. He chang - es not, Christ chang - es not!
have a Friend who chang - es not.

Though I should be by all for - got, He still re - mains and

rit.

will re - main! My pre - cious Lord who chang - es not.
My

God Will Take Care Of You

462

Bb-2-MI

Fear thou not; for I am with thee: be not dismayed; for I am thy God. Isa. 41:10

C-14, C-15

Civilla D. Martin, 1904

W. S. Martin, 1904

1. Be not dis-mayed what-e'er be - tide, God will take care of you;
2. Thro' days of toil when heart doth fail, God will take care of you;
3. All you may need He will pro-vide, God will take care of you;
4. No mat-ter what may be the test, God will take care of you;

Be - neath His wings of love a - bide, God will take care of you.
When dan-gers fierce your path as - sail, God will take care of you.
Noth-ing you ask will be de - nied, God will take care of you.
Lean, wea - ry one, up - on His breast, God will take care of you.

CHORUS

God will take care of you, Thro' ev - 'ry day, O'er all the way;

He will take care of you, God will take care of you.
take care of you.

463 Hold To God's Unchanging Hand

Ab-4-DO

Jennie Wilson

Every good gift . . . cometh down from the Father . . .
with whom is no variableness, neither shadow of turning. Jas. 1:17

L-6

F. L. Eiland

1. Time is filled with swift tran - si - tion—Naught of earth unmoved can
2. Trust in Him who will not leave you, What - so - ev - er years may
3. When your jour - ney is com - plet - ed, If to God you have been

stand— Build your hopes on things e - ter - nal, Hold to
bring, If by earth - ly friends for - sak - en, Still more
true, Fair and bright the home in glo - ry Your en-

God's un - chang - ing hand. Hold to God's un - chang - ing
close - ly to Him cling.
rap - tured soul will view. Hold to His hand

hand! Hold to God's un - chang - ing hand! Build your
Hold to His hand

hopes on things e - ter - nal, Hold to God's un - chang - ing hand.

Precious Memories

464

Ab-4-SOL

J. B. F. W.

C-12

J. B. F. Wright

They shall abundantly utter the memory of
Thy great goodness and shall sing of Thy righteousness. Psa. 145:7

1. Pre - cious mem -'ries, un - seen an - gels, Sent from some-where
2. In the still - ness of the mid - night, Ech - oes from the
3. As I trav - el on life's path - way, Know not what the

to my soul; How they lin - ger, ev - er near me,
past I hear; Old time sing - ing, glad -ness bring - ing,
years may hold; As I pon - der, hope grows fon - der,

D. S. - In the still - ness of the mid - night,

Fine CHORUS

And the sa - cred past un - fold.
From that love - ly land some-where. Pre - cious mem -'ries,
Pre - cious mem -'ries flood my soul.

Pre - cious, sa - cred scenes un - fold.

D. S.

how they lin - ger, How they ev - er flood my soul,

465 Jesus Knows And Cares

Db-4-MI
P. H. E.

In all things it behoved Him to be made like unto His brethren, that He might be a merciful and faithful high priest . . . Heb. 2:17

C-15, L-4
Paul H. Epps

1. When the road is rough and the way is dim, Je-sus
2. When the heart is sad o-ver one un-true, Je-sus
3. When you say good-by to your dear-est friend, Je-sus

knows, Je-sus cares; When the dark-ness comes we can go to
knows, Je-sus cares; Go to Him in prayer, He will strengthen
knows, Je-sus cares; He will com-fort you un-til life shall

Fine

Him, Je-sus knows, Je-sus cares. He knows from His
you, Je-sus knows, Je-sus cares.
end, Je-sus knows, Je-sus cares. He sees it all

throne a-bove; He cares with a per-fect love!
O yes He cares

D. S.

Go to Je-sus for peace, go to Him for rest;

Does Jesus Care?

466

Casting all your care upon Him; for He careth for you. I Pet. 5:7

Db-2-SOL
Frank E. Graeff, 1901

C-15, L-4
J. Lincoln Hall, 1901

1. Does Je - sus care when my heart is pained Too deep - ly for
2. Does Je - sus care when my way is dark With a name - less
3. Does Je - sus care when I've said "good- by" To the dear - est on

mirth or song, As the bur- dens press, And the cares dis - tress,
dread and fear? As the day-light fades In - to deep night shades,
earth to me, And my sad heart aches Till it near - ly breaks,

CHORUS

And the way grows wea - ry and long?
Does He care e -nough to be near? O yes, He cares, I know He
Is it aught to Him? does He see?

cares, His heart is touched with my grief; When the days are wea-

ry, The long night drear -y, I know my Sav - ior cares.

He cares.

467 Turn Your Eyes Upon Jesus

F-3-MI
H. H. L.

*But we see Jesus, who was made a little lower than angels for
the suffering of death, crowned with glory . . . Heb. 2:9*

C-15
Helen H. Lemmel

1. O soul, are you wea-ry and trou - bled? No light in the
2. Thru death in - to life ev - er - last - ing He passed, and we
3. His word shall not fail you— He prom - ised; Be - lieve Him, and

dark-ness you see? There's light for a look at the Sav - ior, And
fol - low Him there; O - ver us sin no more hath do - min - ion— For
all will be well: Then go to a world that is dy - ing, His

life more a - bun-dant and free!
more than con-q'rors we are!
per - fect sal - va - tion to tell!

CHORUS

Turn your eyes up - on Je - sus,

Look full in His won - der - ful face,
won - der - ful face,

And the things of

earth will grow strange-ly dim In the light of His glo - ry and grace.

Happiness Is The Lord

468

Rejoice in the Lord always: and again I say, Rejoice. Phil 4:4

Eb-4-MI
I. F. S.

C-12, J-1
Ira F. Stanphill

1. Hap - pi - ness is to know the Sav - ior, Liv - ing a life with -
2. Hap - pi - ness is a new cre - a - tion, "Je - sus and me" in
3. Hap - pi - ness is to be for - giv - en, Liv - ing a life that's

in His fa - vor, Hav - ing a change in my be - hav - ior—Hap - pi -
close re - la - tion, Hav - ing a part in His sal - va - tion—Hap - pi -
worth the liv - in', Tak - ing a trip that leads to heav - en—Hap - pi -

ness is the Lord;
ness is the   Lord. Real joy is mine, no mat - ter if
ness is the

tear-drops start, I've found the se - cret—it's Je - sus in my heart!

Lord,   Hap - pi - ness is the Lord,   Hap - pi - ness is the Lord!

469 Why Do I Sing About Jesus?

Ab-2-MI
A. A. K.

Who His own self bare our sins in His own body on the tree . . .
by whose stripes ye were healed. 1 Pet. 2:24

C-10, S-4
Albert A. Ketchum

1. Deep in my heart there's a glad-ness, Je - sus has saved me from
2. On - ly a glimpse of His good-ness, That was suf - fi - cient for
3. He is the fair - est of fair ones, He is the Lil - y, the

sin! Praise to His name, what a Sav - ior! Cleans-ing with-
me; On - ly one look at the Sav - ior, Then was my
Rose; Riv - ers of mer - cy sur - round Him, Grace, love and

CHORUS

out and with - in.
spir - it set free. Why do I sing a - bout Je - sus?
pit - y He shows.

Why is He pre - cious to me? He is my Lord and my

Sav - ior, Dy - ing, He set me free!
(set me free!)

Do You Know My Jesus?

470

Know the grace of our Lord Jesus, that, though He was rich,
yet for your sakes He became poor . . . II Cor. 8:9

C-3-SOL
W. F. L. & V. B. E

C-5, C-15
W. F. Lakey & V. B. Ellis

1. Have you a heart that's wea-ry, Tend-ing a load of care;
2. Where is your heart, O, pil-grim, What does your light re-veal;
3. Who knows your dis-ap-point-ment, Who hears each time you cry;

Are you a soul that's seek-ing Rest from the bur-den you
Who hears your call for com-fort When naught but sor-row you
Who un-der-stands your heart-aches, Who dries the tears from your

CHORUS

bear? Do you know my Je-sus, Do you
feel? Do you know
eyes?

know (Do you know) my friend, Have you heard (Have you heard) He

loves you, And that He will a-bide till the end? (till the end?)

471 Why Can't We See?

471

Eb-4-DO
L. S.

He hath said, I will never leave thee . . . we may boldly say, the Lord is my helper . . .
Heb. 13:5, 6

E-1

Lanier Stevens

1. This life's too short and filled with pain, To waste our time for
2. If I could live my life a - gain, I'd keep it free from
3. When strife is stirred by an - gry words, Help me to think of

earth - ly gain. It has to be much sweet - er there, Why
so much sin. I would not hurt the ones I love, I
Thee, O Lord. Help me to know that Thou art there, Help

CHORUS

can't we see? Lord hear our prayer.
want to please my Lord a - bove. Why can't we see? Why
me to see, Lord hear my prayer.

rit.

do we sin? We must not let the temp - ter in. O

Je-sus make our hearts Thy throne, So we can see we're not a - lone.

God Give Us Christian Homes

472

Eb-2-MI
B. B. McK.

H-5
B. B. McKinney

Fathers, provoke not your children . . .
but bring them up in the nurture and admonition of the Lord . . . Eph. 6:4

1. God, give us Chris - tian homes! Homes where the Bi - ble is
2. God, give us Chris - tian homes! Homes where the fa - ther is
3. God, give us Chris - tian homes! Homes where the moth-er, in
4. God, give us Chris - tian homes! Homes where the chil - dren are

loved and taught, Homes where the Mas - ter's will is sought,
true and strong, Homes that are free from the blight of wrong,
queen - ly quest, Strives to show oth - ers Thy way is best,
led to know Christ in His beau - ty Who loves them so,

Homes crowned with beau- ty Thy love hath wrought; God, give us
Homes that are joy - ous with love and song; God, give us
Homes where the Lord is an hon - ored guest; God, give us
Homes where the al - tar fires burn and glow; God, give us

Chris - tian homes; God, give us Chris - tian homes!
Chris - tian homes; God, give us Chris - tian homes!
Chris - tian homes; God, give us Chris - tian homes!
Chris - tian homes; God, give us Chris - tian homes! A - men.

473 When He Comes In Glory By And By

For the Lord Himself shall descend from heaven with a shout . . .
then we . . . shall be caught up . . . I Thess. 4:16,17

Bb-4-SOL
A. A. W.

A. A. Westbrook

S-2

1. O how sweet 'twill be to meet the Lord, When He
2. We will have our robes all white as snow, When He
3. I am long-ing for that hap-py day, When He

comes in glo-ry, by and by; What a song of praise will
comes in glo-ry, by and by; O be read-y, with the
comes in glo-ry, by and by; For with Him I hope to

be out-poured,
Lord to go, When He comes in glo-ry, by and by.
soar a-way,

CHORUS

How sweet! how sweet! When He comes. . . .
'twill be! 'twill be! When He comes a-

. . . in the sky! What joy! what joy!
gain in the love-lit sky! 'twill be! 'twill be!

Grace Greater Than Our Sin

474

G-3-DO

G-2

That as sin hath reigned unto death, even so might grace reign through righteousness
unto eternal life by Jesus Christ . . . Rom. 5:21

Julia H. Johnston

D. B. Towner

1. Mar - vel - ous grace of our lov - ing Lord, Grace that ex - ceeds our
2. Dark is the stain that we can - not hide, What can a - vail to
3. Mar - vel - ous, in - fi - nite, match-less grace, Free - ly be-stowed on

sin and our guilt, Yon - der on Cal - va - ry's mount out - poured,
wash it a - way? Look! there is flow - ing a crim - son tide;
all who be - lieve; You that are long - ing to see His face,

CHORUS

There where the blood of the Lamb was shed. Grace, grace,
Whit - er than snow you may be to - day. Mar - vel - ous grace,
Will you this mo - ment His grace re - ceive?

God's grace, Grace that will par - don and cleanse with - in; Grace,
In - fi - nite grace, Mar-vel - ous

grace, God's grace, Grace that is great - er than all our sin.
grace, In - fi - nite grace,

475

One Holy Church

G-4-DO

Samuel Longfellow
2-3 stanzas and chorus by T. S. T.

*Christ also loved the church, and gave Himself for it;
that He might sanctify and cleanse it . . .*
Eph. 5:25, 26

E-1, U-1

Tillit S. Teddlie

1. One ho-ly church of God ap-pears, Through ev-'ry age and
2. One book to guide the pil-grim's feet, Un-err-ing coun-sel
3. One name by which each one is known From Heav'n di-vine-ly

race, Un-wast-ed by the lapse of years, Un-changed by chang-ing
give; In-struc-tions so di-vine, com-plete, How God would have us
giv'n; One way that leads the saints of God To joys and bliss in

CHORUS

place.
live. "There shall be one fold; one shep-herd." "One Lord, one hope, one
Heav'n. (Jno. 10:17)   (Eph. 4:1-4)

faith." There shall be one fold, one shepherd, one plan of sav-ing grace!

Lead Me To Some Soul Today

476

G-4-DO

Will H. Houghton
vs. 2-4 by Ellis J. Crum

He which converteth the sinner from the error of his way shall save a soul from death . . . Jas. 5:20

S-5

Wendell P. Loveless

1. Lead me to some soul to - day; O teach me, Lord, just what to say; Friends of mine are lost in sin, And can - not find their way.
2. Lead me to some way-ward soul, To one who's wan-dered from the fold; Help me turn him un - to Thee, Thy bless-ings to be - hold.
3. Lead me from self - right-eous- ness, may Christ al - ways be seen in me; How can I do an - y less than lead more souls to Thee?
4. O - pen hearts of those I love, to hear and heed the gos - pel call; May they start to heav'n a - bove, And may they nev - er fall.

CHORUS

Few there are who seem to care, And few there are who pray; who pray;

Melt my heart and fill my life; Give me one soul to - day.

477
My Task

Eb-4-MI

L-2

Maude Louise Ray, vs. 1,2
F. H. Pickup, v. 3

*Press toward the mark for the prize of the
high calling of God in Christ Jesus . . . Phil 3:14*

E. L. Ashford

Slowly

1. To love some-one more dear - ly ev - 'ry day, To
2. To fol - low truth as blind men long for light, To
3. And then my Sav - ior by and by to meet, When

help a wan - d'ring child to find his way, To
do my best from dawn of day till night, To
faith hath made her task on earth com - plete, And

pon - der o'er a no - ble tho't and pray, And smile when
keep my heart fit for His ho - ly sight, And an - swer
lay my hom - age at the Mas - ter's feet, With - in the

eve - ning falls, And smile when eve - ning falls: This is my task.
when He calls, And an - swer when He calls: This is my task.
jas - per walls, With-in the jas - per walls: This crowns my task.

The Lord Has Been Mindful Of Me 478

Bb-2-SOL
L. O. S.

Blessed be the Lord, who daily loadeth us with benefits, even the God of our salvation.
Psa. 68:19

G-3, P-5
L. O. Sanderson

1. Though I, thro' the val-ley of shad-ow, O'er moun-tain or trou-
2. Much more than my grief and my sor-row, Much more than ad-ver-
3. I'm rich! I am saved! I am hap-py! I've health and pros-per-

bled sea, And oft in the dark-ness, have trav-elled, The
si - ty, Much more than the all I have giv-en, The
i - ty! I've friends! I have doors ev - er o - pen! The

CHORUS

Lord has been mind-ful of me!
Lord has been mind-ful of me! The Lord has been mind-ful of
Lord has been mind-ful of me!

me! He bless-es and bless-es a - gain! My God is the

God of the liv-ing! How ex - cel - lent is His name!

479 I Know That My Redeemer Lives

Bb-4-SOL
F. A. F.

It is Christ that died, yea rather, that is risen again . . .
who also maketh intercession for us. Rom. 8:34

C-7, T-1
Fred A. Fillmore

1. I know (I know) that my Re-deem-er lives, And ev-er
2. He wills (He wills) that I should ho-ly be, In word, in
3. I know (I know) that un-to sin-ful men His sav-ing
4. I know (I know) that o-ver yon-der stands A place pre-

prays (and ev-er prays) for me; I know (I know) e-ter-nal
tho't, (in word, in tho't,) in deed; Then I (then I) His ho-ly
grace (His sav-ing grace) is nigh; I know (I know) that He will
pared (a place pre-pared) for me; A home, (a home,) a house not

life He gives, From sin and sor-row free.
face may see, When from this earth life freed.
come a-gain To take me home on high.
made with hands, Most won-der-ful to see.

CHORUS

I know, I know that my Re-deem-er lives, I know, I know e-ter-nal life He gives;

I know, I know that my Re-deem-er lives.
I know that my Re- deem-er lives, that

Dare To Stand Like Joshua

480

B♭-4-DO
C. M. Robinson

W–4

Choose you this day whom ye will serve . . .
but as for me and my house, we will serve the Lord.
Josh. 24:15

P. P. Bilhorn
Arr. by Dane Shepard

1. We are bound for Ca - naan land, Tent-ing by the way.
2. When the dark Red Sea of doubt Bil - lowed in our way,
3. Just be - fore us Jor - dan rolls, Just a - cross the way.

Who shall lead us on the road? Choose your King to-day.
Then He part - ed ev - 'ry wave— So He will to-day.
We can safe - ly trust the Lord; He shall lead to-day.

CHORUS

Dare to stand like Josh - u - a; Dare to say the word.

As for me and for my house, We will serve the Lord.

481 Give Me A Love Like Thine

Ab-2-SOL
Oswald J. Smith

*Herein is love, not that we loved God, but that He loved us,
and sent His Son . . . for our sins. I John 4:10*

L-3, S-5
Merrill Dunlop

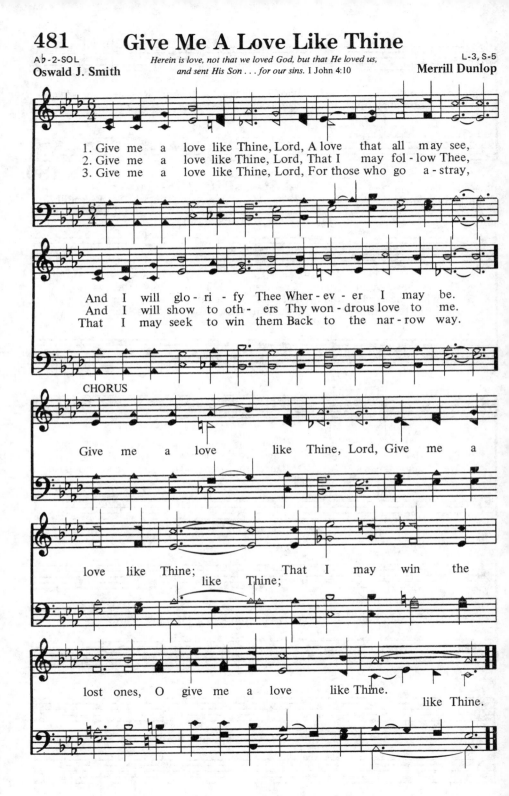

1. Give me a love like Thine, Lord, A love that all may see,
2. Give me a love like Thine, Lord, That I may fol-low Thee,
3. Give me a love like Thine, Lord, For those who go a-stray,

And I will glo-ri-fy Thee Wher-ev-er I may be.
And I will show to oth-ers Thy won-drous love to me.
That I may seek to win them Back to the nar-row way.

CHORUS

Give me a love like Thine, Lord, Give me a

love like Thine; That I may win the
like Thine;

lost ones, O give me a love like Thine.
like Thine.

Just A Closer Walk With Thee

482

C-4-SOL
Anon.

F-2, G-3
Spiritual
Arr. by Mosie Lister

And the Lord shall deliver me from every evil work and
will preserve me unto His heavenly kingdom. II Tim. 4:18

1. I am weak but Thou art strong; Je - sus, keep me from all
2. Thro' this world of toil and snares, If I fal - ter, Lord, who
3. When my fee - ble life is o'er, Time for me will be no

wrong. I'll be sat - is - fied as long As I
cares? Who with me my bur - den shares? None but
more, Guide me gent - ly, safe - ly o'er To Thy

CHORUS

walk, dear Lord, close to Thee.
Thee, dear Lord, none but Thee. Just a clos - er walk with Thee,
king - dom shore, to Thy shore.

Grant it, Je - sus, is my plea. Dai - ly walk-

ing close to Thee, Let it be, dear Lord, let it be.

Now I Belong To Jesus

483

A♭-4-DO
N. J. C.

Ye are not your own. For ye are bought with a price: therefore glorify God . . .
I Cor. 6:19,20

A-1, F-2
Norman J. Clayton

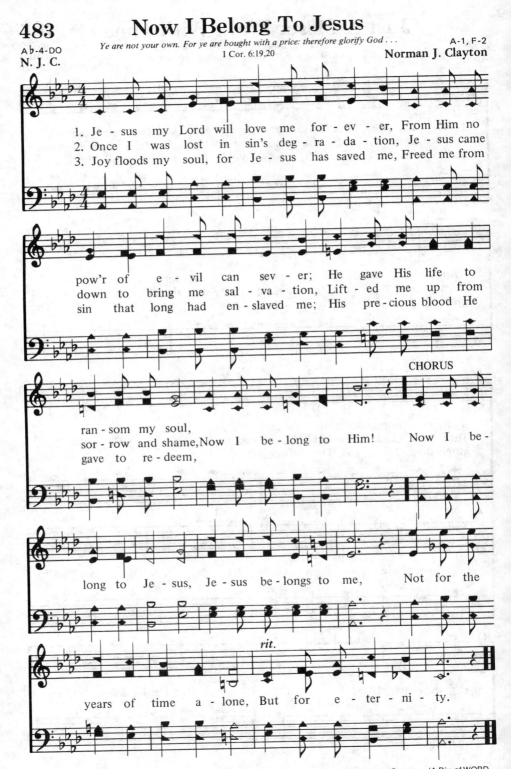

1. Je - sus my Lord will love me for - ev - er, From Him no
2. Once I was lost in sin's deg - ra - da - tion, Je - sus came
3. Joy floods my soul, for Je - sus has saved me, Freed me from

pow'r of e - vil can sev - er; He gave His life to
down to bring me sal - va - tion, Lift - ed me up from
sin that long had en - slaved me; His pre - cious blood He

CHORUS

ran - som my soul,
sor - row and shame, Now I be - long to Him! Now I be -
gave to re - deem,

long to Je - sus, Je - sus be - longs to me, Not for the

rit.

years of time a - lone, But for e - ter - ni - ty.

D♭-2-DO

I'll Never Forsake My Lord

484

L-6, T-1

Mrs. Damon Canter Snoddy
Arr. by L. O. S.

*For He hath said, I will never leave thee,
nor forsake thee. Heb. 13:5*

L. O. Sanderson

1. Though my cross may be hard to bear, Though my life may be filled
2. Though the tempt-er in ef-forts bold, Or in sub-tle-ty as
3. Though so help-less I can-not see What the fu-ture may hold

with care; Though mis-for-tune be mine to share—I'll nev-er for-
of old, Should es-say to al-lure my soul—I'll nev-er for-
for me; Je-sus knows and my guide will be —I'll nev-er for-

CHORUS

sake my Lord.
sake my Lord.   I'll nev-er for-sake the Sav-ior, He has
sake my Lord.

nev-er for-sak-en me! 'Neath His shel-ter-ing arm I am

safe from all harm—I'll nev-er for-sake my Lord.

485 I Know The Lord Will Make A Way

F-3-SOL
Arr. M. Lynwood Smith

Yea, the Lord shall give that which is good . . . and shall set us in the way of His steps.
Psa. 85:12,13

A-1, T-1
Arr. V. O. Fossett

I know the Lord will make a way for me,

I know the Lord will make a way for me;

1. When my way I can-not see, seems there is no hope for
2. When the host of sin as-sail and I try and al-most
3. If I trust, be-lieve, o-bey, let His ho-ly word hold

me,
fail, I know the Lord will make a way for me.
sway,

What Shall It Profit?

486

What shall a man give in exchange for his soul? Mark 8:37

B♭-2-SOL

Johnson Oatman

E-1

J. B. Herbert

1. Not all earth's gold and sil - ver Can make a sin - ner whole;
2. The heap - ing up of rich - es To man - y seems life's goal;
3. This sol - emn ques - tion an - swer; Is world - ly gain thy goal?

What shall it prof - it thee, O man, If thou should'st lose thy soul?
But in the ea - ger rush for wealth, For - got - ten is the soul.
Can fleet - ing rich - es be com-pared To an im - mor - tal soul?

CHORUS

What shall it prof - it a man, What shall it prof - it a man,

If He gain the whole world, And lose His own soul?

487 A New Creature

I am crucified with Christ: nevertheless I live; yet not I, but Christ liveth in me.
Gal. 2:20

A♭-3-MI

B-1

T. O. Chisholm

L. O. Sanderson

1. Bur - ied with Christ, my bless - ed Re - deem - er, Dead to the
2. Dead un - to sin, a - live thru the Spir - it, Ris - en with
3. Sin hath no more its cru - el do - min - ion, Walk - ing "in

old life of fol - ly and sin; Sa - tan may call, the
Him from the gloom of the grave, All things are new, and
new - ness of life," I am free— Glo - ri - ous life of

world may en - treat me, There is no voice that an - swers with - in.
I am re - joic - ing, In His great love, His pow - er to save.
Christ, my Re - deem - er, Which He so rich - ly shar - eth with me.

CHORUS

Dead to the world, to voic - es that call me, Liv - ing a -

new, o - be - dient but free; Dead to the joys that once did en -

thrall me — Yet 'tis not I, Christ liv - eth in me.

Jesus Paid It All

488

E♭-3-DO

1-1, T-1

Purge me . . . and I shall be clean: wash me, and I shall be whiter than snow. Psa. 51:7

Mrs. H. M. Hall

John T. Grape

1. I   hear   the   Sav - ior   say, "Thy   strength in - deed   is   small,
2. Lord, now   in - deed   I   find   Thy   pow'r, and Thine a - lone,
3. And   when, be - fore   the   throne,   I   stand   in   Him com - plete,

Child of   weak - ness, watch and pray, Find in   Me   thine   all   in   all."
Can   change the   lep - er's   spots, And   melt   the   heart   of stone.
"Je - sus   died   my   soul   to   save,"   My   lips   shall still   re - peat.

CHORUS

Je - sus   paid   it   all,   All   to   Him   I   owe;

Sin   had   left   a   crim - son stain,   He washed it   white   as   snow.

489 Blessed Are They

A♭-4-MI

E-1

H. R. Trickett

Blessed are they that do His commandments, that they may have the right to the tree of life and may enter . . . into the city. Rev. 22:14

J. H. Fillmore

1. Bless - ed are they who do His commandments, They shall
2. Bless - ed are they who do His commandments, They shall
3. Bless - ed are they who do His commandments, They shall

claim the tree of life; In - to the cit - y they shall
wear the robes of white; Un - der the por - tals God shall
stand be - fore the throne; In - to the life of joy e -

CHORUS

en - ter, They are vic - tors in the strife. Bless - - -
lead them, They shall serve Him day and night.
ter - nal, God shall claim them for His own. Bless - ed are

ed, bless - - - ed, bless - - - ed are
they who do His com - mand - ments, Bless - ed are they,

they,
bless - ed are they,

In - to the cit - y they shall

en - ter, Bless - ed, bless - ed, bless - ed are they.

Give Me A Burning Heart

490

I will praise Thee, O Lord, with my whole heart;
I will show forth all Thy marvelous works. Psa. 9:1

Eb-2-MI

Avis B. Christianson

C-16, H-1

Homer Hammontree

1. Give me, O Lord, a burn - ing heart With heav'n-ly love a - flame,
2. Touch Thou my lips, dear Lord, to - day With liv - ing coals of fire,
3. Make me an in - stru - ment of praise, Thy name to glo - ri - fy

An ea - ger long - ing to im - part The won - ders of Thy name.
And cleanse my wayward heart, I pray, From ev - 'ry vain de - sire.
Now thru-out all my earth-ly days, And ev - er - more on high.

CHORUS

Re - kin - dle dai - ly in my soul The flame of love di - vine,

That Thy blest name I may ex - tol And in Thy like - ness shine.

491 Remember Me, O Mighty One

According to Thy mercy remember Thou me for Thy goodness' sake, O Lord.
Psa. 25:7

Joanna Kinkel. Arr.

1. When storms a - round are sweep - ing,   When lone my watch I'm
2. When walk - ing on life's o - cean,   Con - trol its rag - ing
3. When weight of sin op - press - es,   When dark de - spair dis -

keep - ing,   'Mid fires of e - vil fall - ing,   'Mid
mo - tion;   When from its dan - gers shrink - ing,   When
tress - es;   All through the life that's mor - tal,   And

CHORUS

tempt - ers' voic - es call - ing,   Re - mem - ber me, O
in its dread deeps sink - ing,   Re - mem - ber me, O
when I pass death's por - tal,   Re - mem - ber me, O

might - y One! Re - mem - ber me, O might - y One!

Something Worth Living For

492

F-3-MI

He hath sent Me to bind up the brokenhearted, to proclaim liberty to the captives . . .
to comfort all that mourn. Isa. 61:1, 2

C-12

Dale Oldham

William J. Gaither

1. Life was shat-tered and hope was gone—Crush-ing the load that I
2. O the joy of sins for-giv'n—Noth-ing's the same as be-

bore; Then out of the depths I cried, "O God,
fore; My life o-ver-flows since Je-sus came

Please give me some-thing worth liv-ing for."
And gave me some-thing worth liv-ing for.

CHORUS

Some-thing more than my yes-ter-days, More than I had be-fore, Something more than wealth or fame—He gave me some-thing worth liv-ing for.

493 Heaven Came Down

Know the love of Christ, which passeth knowledge,
that ye might be filled with all the fulness of God. Eph. 3:19

F-2-MI
J. W. P.

S-1, T-1
John W. Peterson

1. Oh, what a won-der-ful, won-der-ful day— Day I will
2. Now I've a hope that will sure-ly en-dure Af-ter the

nev-er for-get! Af-ter I'd wan-dered in dark-ness a-
pass-ing of time; I have a fu-ture in heav-en for

way, Je-sus, my Sav-ior, I met. Oh, what a ten-der com-
sure, There in those man-sions sub-lime. And it's be-cause of that

pas-sion-ate Friend! He met the need of my heart, Shad-ows dis-
won-der-ful day When at the Cross I be-lieved; Rich-es e-

pel-ling, With joy I am tell-ing, He made all the dark-ness de-
ter-nal And bless-ings su-per-nal From His pre-cious hand I re-

494 Lead On, O King Eternal

D-4-SOL

Ernest W. Shurtleff

Who is the King of Glory? The Lord strong and mighty, the Lord mighty in battle.
Psa. 24:8

F-3, W-1

Henry Smart

1. Lead on, O King E-ter-nal, The day of march has come;
2. Lead on, O King E-ter-nal, Till sin's fierce war shall cease,
3. Lead on, O King E-ter-nal, We fol-low, not with fears;

Hence-forth in fields of con-quest Thy tents shall be our home;
And ho-li-ness shall whis-per The sweet A-men of peace;
For glad-ness breaks like morn-ing Wher-e'er Thy face ap-pears;

Thro' days of prep-a-ra-tion Thy grace has made us
For not with swords loud clash-ing, Nor roll of stir-ring
Thy cross is lift-ed o'er us: We jour-ney in its

strong, And now, O King E-ter-nal, We lift our bat-tle song.
drums: With deeds of love and mer-cy, The heav'n-ly king-dom comes.
light; The crown a-waits the con-quest: Lead on, O God of might!

Joy To The World

495

Make a joyful noise unto the Lord, all the earth . . . Psa. 98:4

D-2-DO
Issac Watts

C-1, C-6
Arr. from George F. Handel

1. Joy to the world! the Lord is come; Let earth re - ceive
2. Joy to the earth! the Sav - ior reigns; Let men their songs
3. No more let sins and sor - rows grow, Nor thorns in - fest
4. He rules the world with truth and grace, And makes the na-

her King; Let ev - ery heart pre - pare Him room,
em - ploy; While fields and floods, rocks, hills and plains
the ground; He comes to make His bless - ings flow
tions prove The glo - ries of His right - eous - ness,

And heav'n and na - ture sing, And heav'n and na - ture
Re - peat the sound - ing joy, Re - peat the sound - ing
Far as the curse is found, Far as the curse is
And won - ders of His love, And won - ders of His

1. And heav'n and na - ture sing, And

sing, And heav'n and heav'n and na - ture sing.
joy, Re - peat, re - peat the sound - ing joy.
found, Far as, far as the curse is found.
love, And won - ders and won - ders of His love.
heav'n and na - ture sing,

496 We Have An Anchor

Which hope we have as an anchor of the soul both sure and steadfast . . . Heb. 6:19

F-4-DO

A-1, E-1

Priscilla J. Owens

Wm. J. Kirkpatrick

1. Will your an-chor hold in the storms of life, When the clouds un-se-
2. It is safe-ly moored, 'twill the storm withstand, For 'tis well se-
3. When our eyes be-hold thru the gath-'ring night The cit-y of

fold their wings of strife? When the strong tides lift, and the
cured by the Sav-ior's hand; And the ca-bles, passed from His
gold, our har-bor bright, We shall an-chor fast by the

ca-bles strain, Will your an-chor drift, or firm re-main?
heart to mine, Can de-fy the blast, thru strength di-vine.
heav'n-ly shore, With the storms all past for-ev-er-more.

REFRAIN

We have an an-chor that keeps the soul Stead-fast and

sure while the bil-lows roll, Fas-tened to the Rock which

can - not move, Ground-ed firm and deep in the Sav - ior's love.

Psalm 24

497

Tune: How Firm A Foundation

A-2-SOL
Psalm 24

C 6
Traditional

1. The earth and the rich - es with which it is stored, The world
2. O who shall the mount of Je - ho - vah as - cend? Or who
3. O gates, lift your heads! Age - less doors, lift them high! The great

and its dwell-ers, be-long to the Lord; For He on the seas its foun-
in the place of His ho - li - ness stand? The man of pure heart and of
King of glo - ry to en - ter draws nigh! This great King of glo - ry, O

da - tion has laid, And firm on the wa - ters its pil - lars has stayed.
hands with-out stain, Who has not sworn false - ly nor loved what is vain.
who can He be? Je - ho - vah of hosts, King of glo - ry is He!

498 Where He Leads I'll Follow

E-4-DO
W. A. O.

Christ also suffered for us leaving us an example, that ye should follow His steps.
1 Pet. 2:21

C-13, F-3
W. A. Ogden

1. Sweet are the prom-is-es, Kind is the word; Dear-er far than
2. Sweet is the ten-der love Je-sus has shown; Sweet-er far than
3. List to His lov-ing words, "Come un-to Me;" Wea-ry, heav-y-

an-y mes-sage man ev-er heard, Pure was the mind of Christ,
an-y love that mor-tals have known, Kind to the err-ing one,
lad-en, there is sweet rest for thee, Trust in His prom-is-es,

Sin-less I see; He the great ex-am-ple is, and pat-tern for me.
Faith-ful is He; He the great ex-am-ple is, and pat-tern for me.
Faith-ful and sure; Lean up-on the Sav-ior, and thy soul is se-cure.

CHORUS

Where He leads I'll fol - low,
Where He leads I'll fol-low, where He leads I'll fol-low,

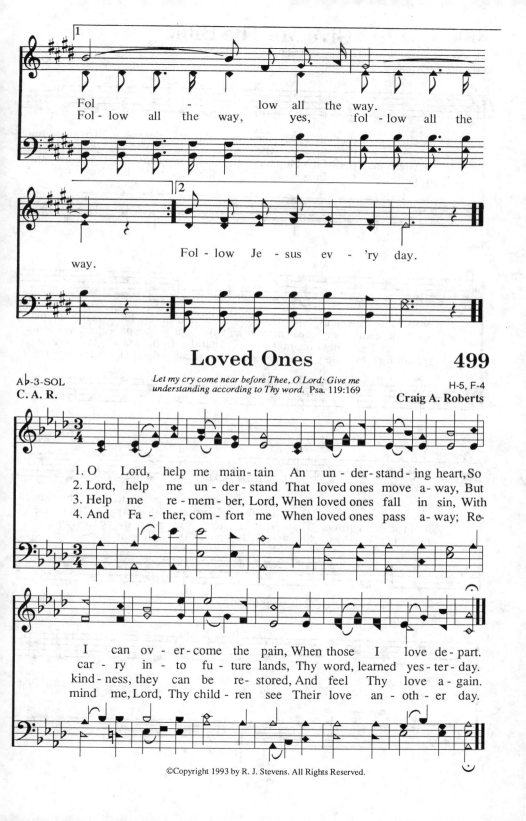

Fol - low all the way.
Fol - low all the way, yes, fol - low all the way.

Fol - low Je - sus ev - 'ry day.

Loved Ones

499

A♭-3-SOL
C. A. R.

*Let my cry come near before Thee, O Lord: Give me
understanding according to Thy word. Psa. 119:169*

H-5, F-4
Craig A. Roberts

1. O Lord, help me main - tain An un - der - stand - ing heart, So
2. Lord, help me un - der - stand That loved ones move a - way, But
3. Help me re - mem - ber, Lord, When loved ones fall in sin, With
4. And Fa - ther, com - fort me When loved ones pass a - way; Re -

I can ov - er - come the pain, When those I love de - part.
car - ry in - to fu - ture lands, Thy word, learned yes - ter - day.
kind - ness, they can be re - stored, And feel Thy love a - gain.
mind me, Lord, Thy chil - dren see Their love an - oth - er day.

500 Give Me The Bible

Thy word is a lamp unto my feet, and a light unto my path. Psa. 119:105

A♭-4-MI

Priscilla J. Owens

E. S. Lorenz

1. Give me the Bi - ble, star of glad-ness gleam-ing, To cheer the
2. Give me the Bi - ble when my heart is bro - ken, When sin and
3. Give me the Bi - ble, all my steps en - light - en, Teach me the
4. Give me the Bi - ble, lamp of life im - mor - tal, Hold up that

wan -d'rer lone and tem-pest-tossed; No storm can hide that ra - diance
grief have filled my soul with fear; Give me the pre - cious words by
dan - ger of these realms be - low; That lamp of safe - ty o'er the
splen - dor by the o - pen grave; Show me the light from heav - en's

Fine

peace - ful beam-ing, Since Je - sus came to seek and save the lost.
Je - sus spo - ken, Hold up faith's lamp to show my Sav - ior near.
gloom shall bright-en, That light a - lone the path of peace can show.
shin - ing por - tal, Show me the glo - ry gild - ing Jor - dan's wave.

D. S.-love com - bin - ing, Till night shall van - ish in e - ter - nal day.

CHORUS

Give me the Bi - ble, Ho - ly mes-sage shin - ing; Thy light shall

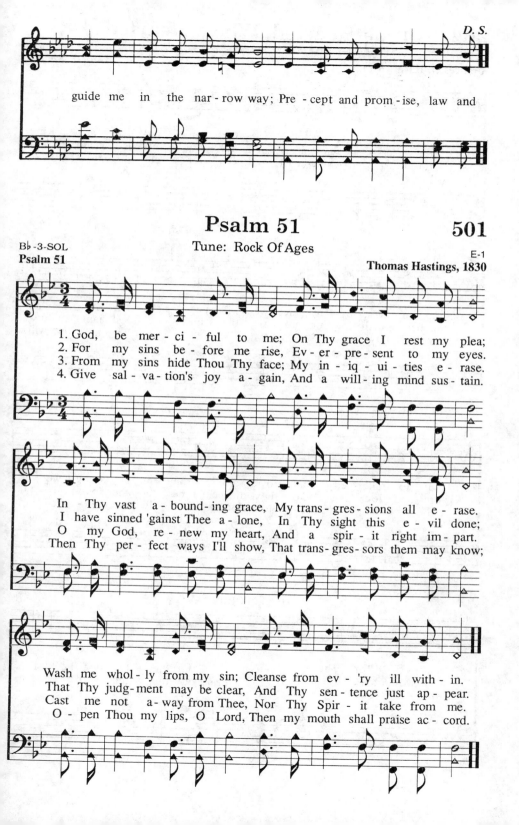

guide me in the nar - row way; Pre - cept and prom - ise, law and

Psalm 51

Tune: Rock Of Ages

501

Bb -3-SOL
Psalm 51

E-1
Thomas Hastings, 1830

1. God, be mer - ci - ful to me; On Thy grace I rest my plea;
2. For my sins be - fore me rise, Ev - er - pre - sent to my eyes.
3. From my sins hide Thou Thy face; My in - iq - ui - ties e - rase.
4. Give sal - va - tion's joy a - gain, And a will - ing mind sus - tain.

In Thy vast a - bound - ing grace, My trans - gres - sions all e - rase.
I have sinned 'gainst Thee a - lone, In Thy sight this e - vil done;
O my God, re - new my heart, And a spir - it right im - part.
Then Thy per - fect ways I'll show, That trans - gres - sors them may know;

Wash me whol - ly from my sin; Cleanse from ev - 'ry ill with - in.
That Thy judg - ment may be clear, And Thy sen - tence just ap - pear.
Cast me not a - way from Thee, Nor Thy Spir - it take from me.
O - pen Thou my lips, O Lord, Then my mouth shall praise ac - cord.

502 True-Hearted, Whole-Hearted

Let us draw near with a true heart in full assurance of faith . . . Heb. 10:22

F-2-DO

C-16, L-6

Frances R. Havergal

Geo. C. Stebbins

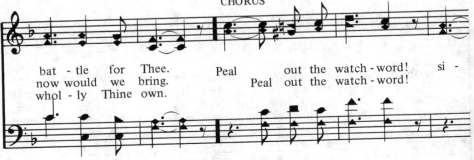

1. True-heart-ed, whole-heart-ed, faith-ful and loy-al, King
2. True-heart-ed, whole-heart-ed, full-est al-le-giance Yield-
3. True-heart-ed, whole-heart-ed, Sav-ior all-glo-rious! Take

of our lives, by Thy grace we will be; Un-der the stand-
ing hence-forth to our glo-ri-ous King; Val-iant en-deav-
Thy great pow-er and reign there a-lone, O-ver our wills

ard ex-alt-ed and roy-al, Strong in Thy strength we will
or and lov-ing o-be-dience, Free-ly and joy-ous-ly
and af-fec-tions vic-to-rious, Free-ly sur-ren-dered and

CHORUS

bat-tle for Thee. Peal out the watch-word! si-
now would we bring. Peal out the watch-word!
whol-ly Thine own.

Enter Into His Gates 503

E♭-4-SOL
Psalm 100:4,5

Enter into His gates with thanksgiving. Psa. 100:4

T-2, P-2
Nettie D. Ellsworth, 1907

504 I Want To Be A Worker

I will show thee my faith by my works. Jas. 2:18

Ab-4-SOL
L. B.

W-4
L. Baltzell

1. I want to be a work-er for the Lord, I want to love and trust His ho-ly word; I want to sing and pray, and be bus-y ev-'ry day

2. I want to be a work-er ev-'ry day, I want to lead the err-ing in the way That leads to heav'n a-bove, where all is peace and love, In the king-dom of the Lord.

3. I want to be a work-er strong and brave, I want to trust in Je-sus' pow'r to save; All who will tru-ly come, shall find a hap-py home

CHORUS

I will work, I will pray In the vine-yard, in the vine-yard of the Lord; of the Lord; I will work, I will pray,

and pray, work and pray

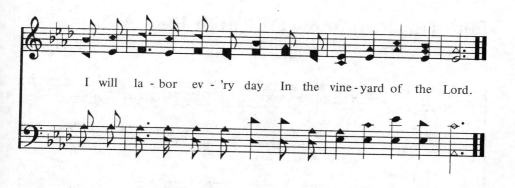

I will la-bor ev-'ry day In the vine-yard of the Lord.

Glorify Thy Name

505

Father, glorify Thy name. John 12:28

C-2-MI
Donna Adkins

W-5, P-2
Donna Adkins

1. Fa - ther, we love You, we wor - ship and a - dore You;
2. Je - sus, we love You, we wor - ship and a - dore You;
3. Spir - it, we love You, we wor - ship and a - dore You;

CHORUS

Glo - ri - fy Thy name in all the earth. Glo - ri - fy Thy name,

glo - ri - fy Thy name, Glo - ri - fy Thy name in all the earth.

506 The Kingdoms Of Earth Pass Away

A-4-SOL

H. R. Trickett

And in the days of these kings shall the God of heaven set up a kingdom . . .
and it shall stand forever. Dan. 2:44

H-2, K-1

J. H. Fillmore

1. The king-doms of earth pass a - way one by one, But the king-dom of heav - en re - mains; It is built on a rock and the Lord is its King, And for - ev - er and ev - er He reigns.

2. The tem - pest may rage and its an - ger ac - claim, Yea, the wind and the tor - rents may roar, And the strong gates of hell may as - sail it in vain, Still the king - dom shall stand ev - er - more.

3. The king - dom of God is now o - pen to all, E'en the vil - est may now en - ter in; There's a wel - come for all who will turn to the Lord, Full sal - va - tion and par - don for sin.

CHORUS

It shall stand, It shall stand, It shall stand, It shall stand,

For - ev - er and ev - er and ev - er, It shall stand,

It shall stand, It shall stand, It shall stand, It shall stand, For - ev - er and ev - er. A - men and A - men.

Psalm 136

C-3-MI

Tune: When My Love To Christ Grows Weak

P -2

Psalm 136

Phoebe Palmer Knapp

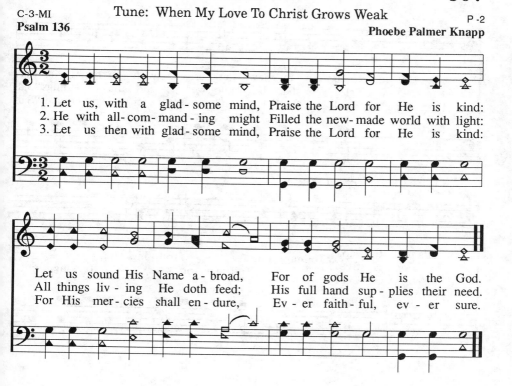

1. Let us, with a glad - some mind, Praise the Lord for He is kind:
2. He with all - com - mand - ing might Filled the new - made world with light:
3. Let us then with glad - some mind, Praise the Lord for He is kind:

Let us sound His Name a - broad, For of gods He is the God.
All things liv - ing He doth feed; His full hand sup - plies their need.
For His mer - cies shall en - dure, Ev - er faith - ful, ev - er sure.

508 To The Work

F-4-MI

Wm. H. D.

Be ye steadfast, unmoveable, always abounding in the work of the Lord . . .
1 Cor. 15:58

W-4

Wm. H. Doane

1. To the work! to the work! we are ser-vants of God, Let us
2. To the work! to the work! let the hun-gry be fed; To the
3. To the work! to the work! in the strength of the Lord, And a

fol-low the path that our Mas-ter has trod; With the balm of His
foun-tain of Life let the wea-ry be led; In the cross and its
robe and a crown shall our la-bor re-ward; When the home of the

coun-sel our strength to re-new, Let us do with our might what our
ban-ner our glo-ry shall be, While we her-ald the ti-dings,"Sal-
faith-ful our dwell-ing shall be, And we shout with the ran-somed,"Sal-

CHORUS

hands find to do!" Toil-ing on, toil-ing on,
va-tion is free!" Toil-ing on, toil-ing on,
va-tion is free!"

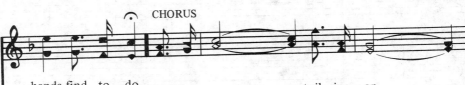

Toil-ing on, toil-ing on, Let us hope,
Toil-ing on, toil-ing on, and trust,

let us watch, And la-bor till the Mas-ter comes.
and pray,

We Shall Stand Before The Throne 509

D minor-4-LA

And I saw the dead, small and great, stand before God;
and the books were opened. Rev. 20:12

I -1, J -2

Craig A. Roberts

R. J. Stevens

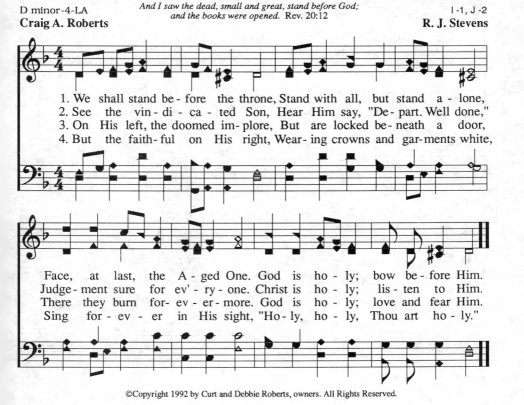

1. We shall stand be - fore the throne, Stand with all, but stand a - lone,
2. See the vin - di - ca - ted Son, Hear Him say, "De - part. Well done,"
3. On His left, the doomed im - plore, But are locked be - neath a door,
4. But the faith-ful on His right, Wear- ing crowns and gar-ments white,

Face, at last, the A - ged One. God is ho - ly; bow be - fore Him.
Judge- ment sure for ev' - ry - one. Christ is ho - ly; lis - ten to Him.
There they burn for- ev - er - more. God is ho - ly; love and fear Him.
Sing for - ev - er in His sight, "Ho - ly, ho - ly, Thou art ho - ly."

510 I Will Not Forget Thee

A♭-4-SOL
C. H. G.

*Can a woman forget her suckling child, that she should not have compassion . .
yet will I not forget thee. Isa. 49:15*

C-15, P-4
Chas. H. Gabriel

1. Sweet is the prom-ise, "I will not for-get thee;" Noth-ing can mo-
2. Trust-ing the prom-ise, "I will not for-get thee," On-ward will I
3. When at the gold-en por-tals I am stand-ing, All my trib-u-

lest or turn my soul a-way; E'en tho' the night be dark with-
go with songs of joy and love; Tho' earth des-pise me, tho' my
la-tions, all my sor-rows past, How sweet to hear the bless-ed

in the val-ley, Just be-yond is shin-ing an e-ter-nal day.
friends for-sake me, I shall be re-mem-bered in my home a-bove.
proc-la-ma-tion, "En-ter, faith-ful ser-vant, wel-come home at last."

CHORUS

I will not for-get thee or leave thee;
I will not for-get thee; I will nev-er leave thee;

In my hands I'll hold thee, In my arms I'll fold thee;

I will not for-get thee or
I will not for-get thee, for-get

leave thee; I am thy Re-deem-er, I will care for thee.

Visions Of Calvary

511

A♭-2-MI

O. E. Landrum

Worthy is the Lamb, who was slain,
to receive power ... honor and glory
and praise! Rev. 5:12

C -4, L -1

O. E. (Sam) Landrum
Arr. by R. J. Stevens

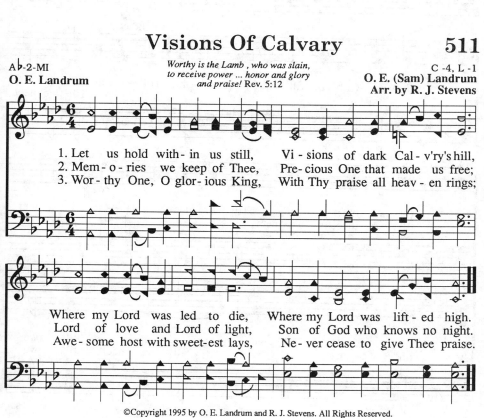

1. Let us hold with-in us still,   Vi - sions of dark Cal - v'ry's hill,
2. Mem - o - ries we keep of Thee,   Pre - cious One that made us free;
3. Wor - thy One, O glor-ious King,   With Thy praise all heav - en rings;

Where my Lord was led to die,   Where my Lord was lift-ed high.
Lord of love and Lord of light,   Son of God who knows no night.
Awe - some host with sweet-est lays,   Ne - ver cease to give Thee praise.

512 God Be With You

The Lord watch between me and thee, when we are absent one from another.
Gen. 31:49

Db-4-MI
Jeremiah E. Rankin, 1880

C-14, C-15
Wm. G. Tomer, 1883

1. God be with you till we meet a-gain; By His coun-sels
2. God be with you till we meet a-gain; 'Neath His wings pro-
3. God be with you till we meet a-gain; Keep love's ban-ner

guide, up-hold you, With His sheep se-cure-ly fold you;
tect-ing hide you, Dai-ly man-na still pro-vide you;
float-ing o'er you, Smite death's threat'ning wave be-fore you;

CHORUS

God be with you till we meet a-gain. Till we meet, ...
Till we meet,

.. till we meet, Till we meet at Je-sus' feet;
till we meet, till we meet,

.... Till we meet, ... till we
till we meet; Till we meet, till we

meet, God be with you till we meet a - gain.
meet a - gain,

Psalm 104:31-35

Tune: O Worship The King

513

A-3-SOL
Psalm 104:31-35

P -2

Arr. from J. Michael Haydn

1. For - ev - er O may the Lord's glo - ry stand! The Lord shall en-
2. I'll sing to the Lord as long as I live, Sing praise to my
3. Con - sumed from the earth let sin - ners then be; The wick - ed in

joy each work of His hand. He looks on the earth and it
God while life He will give. My thoughts a - bout Him will sweet
life no more let us see. And now, O my soul, bless - ing

trem - bles in fear; When He touch - es moun - tains, the smoke will ap - pear.
plea - sure af - ford. For I am re - joic - ing each day in the Lord.
give to the Lord. Let glad hal - le - lu - jahs ring; O praise the Lord.

514 Singing Redemption's Song

By His own blood . . . obtained eternal redemption for us. Heb. 9:12

Bb-2-SOL
T. S. T.

R-1, S-4

Tillit S. Teddlie

1. An - gels are sing - ing re-demp-tion's sweet song, Won-der-ful theme,
2. O - ver and o - ver the mel - o - dies ring, Won-der-ful theme,
3. Joy be - yond meas-ure a - waits us up there, Won-der-ful theme,

glo - ri - ous theme! Shout the glad mes-sage and join in the throng,
glo - ri - ous theme! Heav-en re - sounds with the trib - ute they bring,
glo - ri - ous theme! Soon we shall join with the an - gels up there,

CHORUS

Sing-ing re - demp-tion's song! Sing the sweet sto -
Sing it a - gain, sing the sweet

ry — re - demp - tion's sweet song; O - -
song, sing the sweet sto - ry, re-demp-tion's sweet song; Sing it a-

- ver and o - ver the cho - rus pro-
gain, sing it a - gain, O - ver and o - ver the

long;
cho - rus pro - long; Shout it a - gain,
Shout the glad mes -
sing the sweet

sage and join with the throng, Ev - er we'll
song, Shout the glad mes-sage and join with the throng,

sing praise to the King, Sing - ing re - demp-tion's song.
won - der - ful song.

With One Accord

515

Eb-4-DO

D -1, P -3

D. D. H.

They lifted up their voice
to God with one accord. Acts 4:24

D. Douglas Hoffman
Arr. by R. J. Stevens

1. With one ac - cord we pray; "Lord, help us learn this day That ev - 'ry
2. "Lord, help us now to know Our Christ who loves us so." May we with
3. "Lord, when we fail to see, All bless - ings come from Thee, Re - move from

step we dare to take, Must be with - in 'The Way'!"
fer - vent ef - fort make, Our love for Him to grow!
us our love of self, And turn our eyes to Thee!" A - men.

516   I Love To Tell The Story

And they sang a new song, saying, Thou art worthy . . .
for Thou wast slain, and hast redeemed us . . .
Rev. 5:9

Ab-4-SOL

Catherine Hankey, 1866

L-3, T-1

Wm. G. Fischer, 1869

1. I love to tell the sto - ry Of un - seen things a -
2. I love to tell the sto - ry: 'Tis pleas - ant to re -
3. I love to tell the sto - ry, For those who know it

bove, Of Je - sus and His glo - ry, Of Je - sus and His
peat What seems, each time I tell it, More won - der - ful - ly
best Seem hun - ger - ing and thirst - ing To hear it like the

love; I love to tell the sto - ry Be - cause I know 'tis true; It
sweet; I love to tell the sto - ry, For some have nev - er heard The
rest; And when, in scenes of glo - ry, I sing the new, new song, 'Twill

CHORUS

sat - is - fies my long - ings As noth - ing else can do.
mes - sage of sal - va - tion From God's own ho - ly word. I
be the old, old sto - ry That I have loved so long.

love to tell the sto-ry! 'Twill be my theme in glo-ry

To tell the old, old sto-ry Of Je-sus and His love.

Quiet Joy

517

E♭-3-DO
G. B. S.

J-1

*You rejoice with joy unspeakable
and full of glory.* 1 Pet. 1:8

Glenda Barnhart Schales
Arr. by G. B. S. & R. J. Stevens

1. Oh joy that soars a-bove my ways, In ev-'ry song of praise.
2. My joy springs from hu-mi-li-ty, It's held se-cure in trust.
3. Oh, qui-et joy from know-ing God; A pre-cious in-ner peace,

Borne high with rev-'rent awe,— To touch the hem of God.
My joy grows strong in suf-fring, It's kept in thank-ful-ness.
Re-veals e-ter-nal glo-ry, Where joy will ne-ver cease.

518 Stepping In The Light

Db-4-SOL
Eliza E. Hewitt

But if we walk in the light, as He is in the light,
we have fellowship one with another . . . 1 John 1:7

C-12, F-3
William J. Kirkpatrick

1. Try-ing to walk in the steps of the Sav-ior, Try-ing to
2. Press-ing more close-ly to Him who is lead-ing, When we are
3. Try-ing to walk in the steps of the Sav-ior, Up-ward, still

fol-low our Sav-ior and King; Shap-ing our lives by His
tempt-ed to turn from the way; Trust-ing the arm that is
up-ward we'll fol-low our Guide; When we shall see Him, "the

bless-ed ex-am-ple, Hap-py, how hap-py, the songs that we bring.
strong to de-fend us, Hap-py, how hap-py, our prais-es each day.
King in His beau-ty," Hap-py, how hap-py, our place at His side!

CHORUS

How beau-ti-ful to walk in the steps of the Sav-ior,

Step-ping in the light, step-ping in the light, How beau-ti-ful to

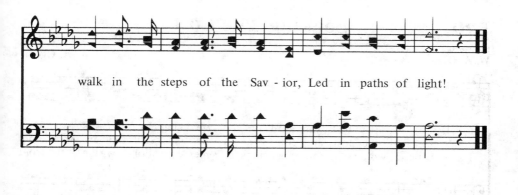

walk in the steps of the Sav-ior, Led in paths of light!

As We Partake

519

F-4-DO
Charles Willis

*But let a man examine himself, and so let him
eat of that bread, and drink of that cup.* 1 Cor. 11:28

L-1
Charles Willis

Solemnly

1. As we par-take of the sup-per of Je-sus, May we be-lieve
2. The Son of God came to earth to bring free-dom. He saw us chained

that He died on that tree. He gave His life that we might
in the bon-dage of sin. We had no hope un-less____

Rit.

have for-give-ness. He paid the price up-on Mount Cal-va-ry.
He would save us. He is our King, Re-deem-er and our Friend.

520 Seeking The Lost

Go ye into all the world, and preach the gospel to every creature. Mark 16:15

Bb-3-SOL
W. A. O.

S-5

W. A. Ogden

1. Seek-ing the lost, yes, kind-ly en-treat-ing Wan-der-ers on the
2. Seek-ing the lost, and point-ing to Je-sus, Souls that are weak, and
3. Thus I would go on mis-sions of mer-cy, Fol-low-ing Christ from

moun-tain a-stray; "Come un-to Me," His mes-sage re-peat-ing,
hearts that are sore; Lead-ing them forth in ways of sal-va-tion,
day un-to day; Cheer-ing the faint, and rais-ing the fall-en;

CHORUS

Words of the Mas-ter speak-ing to-day.
Show-ing the path to life ev-er-more.
Point-ing the lost to Je-sus the way.

{ Go - ing a-
{ In - to the

{ Go-ing a - far
{ In - to the fold

up - on the
of my Re -

far . . . . up - on the moun - tain, ...
fold . . . . of my Re-deem - er, ...

moun - tain, Bring - ing the wan - d'rer
deem - er, Je - sus the Lamb for

.... Bring - ing the wan - - - d'rer
.... Je - sus the Lamb .... for

|1 back a - gain, back a - gain,
|2 slain, for sin - ners slain.

back a - gain, ...
sin - ners slain. ....

Jesus My Savior, Look On Me   521

D-4-SOL   *When He saw the multitudes, He was*   D -1
Charlotte Elliott, 1869   *moved with compassion on them.. Matt. 9:36*   **Arthur S. Sullivan, 1874**

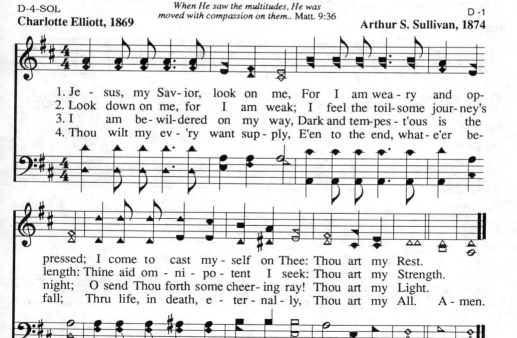

1. Je - sus, my Sav - ior, look on me, For I am wea - ry and op-
2. Look down on me, for I am weak; I feel the toil - some jour - ney's
3. I am be - wil - dered on my way, Dark and tem - pes - t'ous is the
4. Thou wilt my ev - 'ry want sup - ply, E'en to the end, what - e'er be-

pressed; I come to cast my - self on Thee: Thou art my Rest.
length: Thine aid om - ni - po - tent I seek: Thou art my Strength.
night; O send Thou forth some cheer - ing ray! Thou art my Light.
fall; Thru life, in death, e - ter - nal - ly, Thou art my All. A - men.

522 When The Roll Is Called Up Yonder

A♭-4-DO

J. M. B.

J-2, S-2

James M. Black

For the trumpet shall sound, and the dead shall be raised incorruptible and we shall be changed. 1 Cor. 15:52

1. When the trum-pet of the Lord shall sound, and time shall be no more,
2. On that bright and glo-rious morn-ing when the dead in Christ shall rise,
3. Let us la-bor for the Mas-ter from the dawn till set-ting sun,

And the morn-ing breaks, e-ter-nal, bright and fair; When the
And the glo-ry of His res-ur-rec-tion share; When His
Let us talk of all His won-drous love and care; Then when

saved of earth shall gath-er o-ver on the oth-er shore,
chos-en ones shall gath-er to their home be-yond the skies,
all of life is o-ver and our work on earth is done,

CHORUS

And the roll is called up yon-der, I'll be there. When the

roll is called up yon - der, When the
When the roll is called up yon-der, I'll be there,

roll   is called up yon - der, When the roll   is
When the roll is called up yon-der, I'll be there,   When the roll is

called up yon-der, When the roll is called up yon-der, I'll be there.

Take Up Your Cross

523

E♭ -3-MI

If any man will come after Me . . .
Take up His cross, and follow Me. Matt. 16:24

C -12, E -1

Charles W. Everest, 1833

Henry Baker, 1854

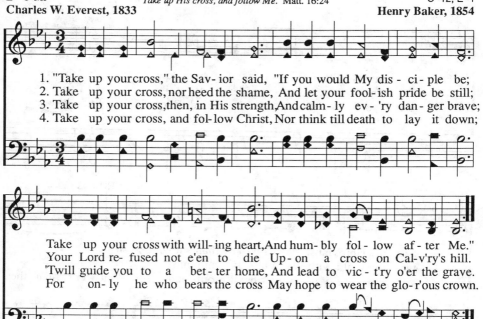

1. "Take up your cross," the Sav-ior said, "If you would My dis - ci - ple be;
2. Take   up your cross, nor heed the shame, And let your fool-ish pride be still;
3. Take   up your cross, then, in His strength, And calm-ly ev - 'ry dan - ger brave;
4. Take   up your cross, and fol-low Christ, Nor think till death to lay it down;

Take   up your cross with will-ing heart, And hum-bly fol - low af - ter Me."
Your Lord re-fused not e'en to die Up-on a cross on Cal-v'ry's hill.
'Twill guide you to a   bet - ter home, And lead to vic - t'ry o'er the grave.
For   on-ly   he who bears the cross May hope to wear the glo-r'ous crown.

524 Fear Not, Little Flock

A♭-2-SOL

Mrs. M. A. Kidder

Fear not, little flock; for it is your Father's good pleasure to give you the kingdom.
Luke 12:32

E-1, I-1

J. G. Dailey

1. Fear not, lit - tle flock, says the Sav - ior di - vine, The
2. Far whit - er than snow, and as fair as the day, For
3. Ride o - ver temp - ta - tion and cease your a - larms, Your

Fa - ther has willed that the king-dom be thine; O soil not your
Christ is the foun-tain to wash guilt a - way; O give Him, poor
Shep-herd is Je - sus, your ref - uge His arms; He'll nev - er for -

gar - ments with sin here be - low, My sheep
sin - ner, that bur - den of thine, And en -
sake you— a Broth - er and Friend, But love

and my lambs must be whit - er than snow. Whit - - -
ter the fold with the nine - ty - and -nine.
you and save you in worlds with-out end. Whit - er than the

CHORUS

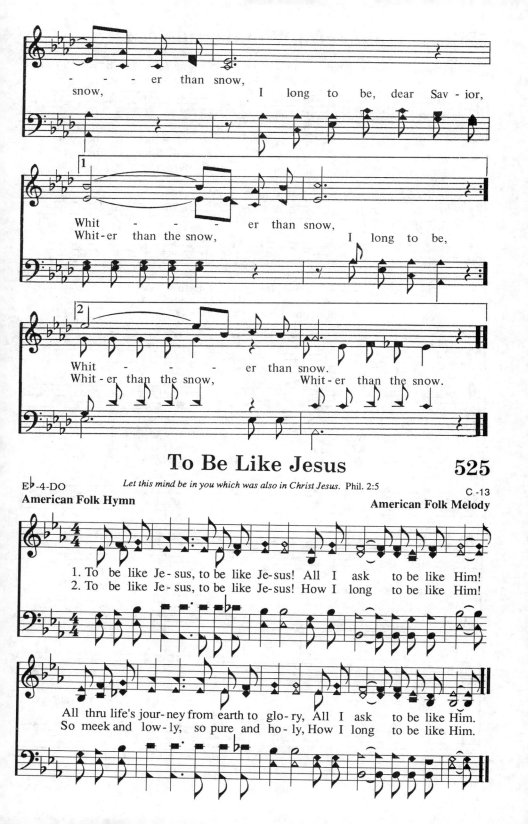

snow,
— — er than snow,
I long to be, dear Sav - ior,

Whit - — — er than snow,
Whit - er than the snow,
I long to be,

Whit - — — er than snow.
Whit - er than the snow,
Whit - er than the snow.

To Be Like Jesus
525

Eᵇ-4-DO
Let this mind be in you which was also in Christ Jesus. Phil. 2:5
C.-13

American Folk Hymn
American Folk Melody

1. To be like Je - sus, to be like Je - sus! All I ask to be like Him!
2. To be like Je - sus, to be like Je - sus! How I long to be like Him!

All thru life's jour-ney from earth to glo-ry, All I ask to be like Him.
So meek and low-ly, so pure and ho-ly, How I long to be like Him.

526 Wonderful, Wonderful Jesus

Bb-2-SOL

Anna B. Russell

My heart trusted in Him, and I am helped:
therefore my heart greatly rejoiceth; and with my song will I praise Him.

Psa. 28:7

P-2

Ernest O. Sellers

1. There is nev-er a day so drear-y, There is nev-er a
2. There is nev-er a care or bur-den, There is nev-er a
3. There is nev-er a guilt-y sin-ner, There is nev-er a

night so long (so long), But the soul that is trust - ing
grief or loss (or loss), But that Je - sus in love will
wan - d'ring one (not one), But that God can in mer - cy

Je - sus Will some - where find a song (a song).
light - en When car - ried to the cross (the cross).
par - don Thru Je - sus Christ, His Son (His Son).

CHORUS

Won - der - ful, won - der - ful Je - sus, In the heart He im-

plant-eth a song;

A song of de - liv-erance, of

He plant - eth a song,

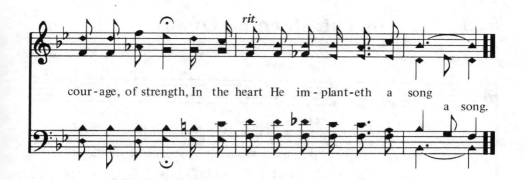

cour-age, of strength, In the heart He im-plant-eth a song   a song.

By Faith I See

527

D-3-DO
Vesta McDaniel

Looking unto Jesus the author and finisher of our faith; Who... endured the cross, despising the shame. Heb. 12:2

L -1, F -1

Mel. by Vesta McDaniel
Arr. by Dane K. Shepard

1. By faith I see Mount Cal - va - ry, By faith I
2. In awe I see His flesh so torn, In awe I
3. Thru tears I see that per - fect blood; Thru tears I

see that cru - el tree; I see His pain, I see His
see the peo - ples' scorn; God turns a - way, I hear His
see that bless - ed flood; He cries, "'Tis done!"; the bat - tle's

strife, By faith I see my ran - somed life.
plea, In awe I see His love for me.
o'er, Thru tears He sees my sins no more.

528 In The Morning Of Joy

For the Lord Himself shall descend from Heaven . . .
with a trump of God: and the dead in Christ shall rise first.
I Thess. 4:16

E-3-DO
Mrs. R. A. Evilsizer

R-2, S-2
A. J. Showalter

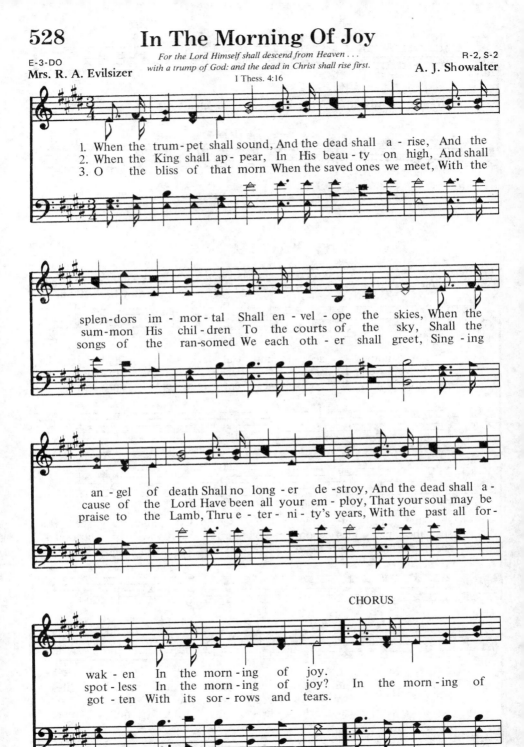

1. When the trum-pet shall sound, And the dead shall a-rise, And the
2. When the King shall ap-pear, In His beau-ty on high, And shall
3. O the bliss of that morn When the saved ones we meet, With the

splen-dors im-mor-tal Shall en-vel-ope the skies, When the
sum-mon His chil-dren To the courts of the sky, Shall the
songs of the ran-somed We each oth-er shall greet, Sing-ing

an-gel of death Shall no long-er de-stroy, And the dead shall a-
cause of the Lord Have been all your em-ploy, That your soul may be
praise to the Lamb, Thru e-ter-ni-ty's years, With the past all for-

CHORUS

wak-en In the morn-ing of joy.
spot-less In the morn-ing of joy? In the morn-ing of
got-ten With its sor-rows and tears.

joy, In the morn-ing of joy, We'll be gath-ered to glo-ry

1 In the morn-ing of joy; *2* In the morn-ing of joy.

Prayer Is The Soul's Sincere Desire 529

F-3-DO
James Montgomery, 1818

Praying always with all prayer and supplication in the Spirit. Eph. 6:18

P-3
Traditional American Melody
Arr. by Robert G. McCutchan, 1935

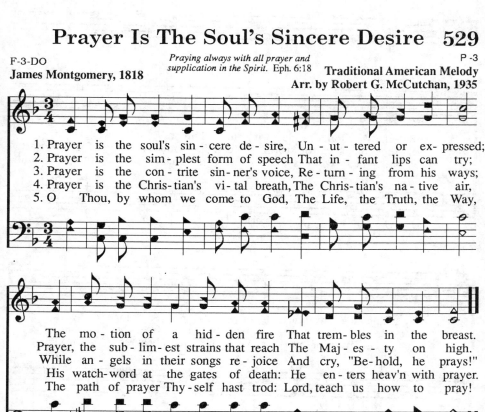

1. Prayer is the soul's sin-cere de-sire, Un-ut-tered or ex-pressed;
2. Prayer is the sim-plest form of speech That in-fant lips can try;
3. Prayer is the con-trite sin-ner's voice, Re-turn-ing from his ways;
4. Prayer is the Chris-tian's vi-tal breath, The Chris-tian's na-tive air,
5. O Thou, by whom we come to God, The Life, the Truth, the Way,

The mo-tion of a hid-den fire That trem-bles in the breast.
Prayer, the sub-lim-est strains that reach The Maj-es-ty on high.
While an-gels in their songs re-joice And cry, "Be-hold, he prays!"
His watch-word at the gates of death: He en-ters heav'n with prayer.
The path of prayer Thy-self hast trod: Lord, teach us how to pray!

530 Looking To Thee

A-4-SOL
James Rowe

Looking unto Jesus the author and finisher of our faith . . . Heb. 12:2

D-1
H. M. Eagle

1. Look-ing to Thee from day to day, Trust-ing Thy grace a-
2. Look-ing to Thee for all I need, Find-ing in Thee a
3. Af - ter a while in heav - en bright, Where there is nei - ther

long the way, Know-ing that Thou wilt safe - ly keep all that is Thine;
friend in-deed, All of the bur - dens of the day meek-ly I bear;
sin nor night, I shall be - hold Thee, face to face, Je - sus my own;

Sure of Thy soul re-deem-ing love, Sure of a crown of life a-
Nei - ther the foe nor storm I fear, Sav - ior di - vine, for Thou art
Then with the saved ones gone be - fore, I shall with rap - ture, more and

bove, Sing - ing Thy praise I press a - long, Sav - ior di - vine.
near, Read-y my cares and trou - bles all free - ly to share.
more, Praise Thee for - ev - er, near the bright, beau - ti - ful throne.

CHORUS

Look-ing to Thee, Trust-ing Thy grace. . . .
Con-stant-ly look-ing to Thee, Trust-ing Thy
Near-ing my own heav-en-ly place,
Near-ing, dear Sav-ior, my own beau-ti-ful,

. . . . I am as hap-py as a true sol-dier can
won-der-ful grace, Trust-ing Thy love I press a-long,
heav-en-ly place,

be; look-ing to Thee
ev-er can be; yes, look-ing to Thee.

Love, Love

531

E minor-4-LA
American Folk Hymn

*But the fruit of the Spirit
is love, joy, peace...Gal. 5:22*

L-2, L-3
English Folk Melody

Round

1. Love, love, love, love, the gos-pel in a word is love,
2. Peace, peace, peace, peace, the gos-pel in a word is peace,
3. Joy, joy, joy, joy, the gos-pel in a word is joy,
4. Christ, Christ, Christ, Christ, the gos-pel in a word is Christ,

Love thy neigh-bor as thy broth-er, love, love, love.
Peace that pass-es un-der-stand-ing, peace, peace, peace.
Joy that fills to ev-er-flow-ing, joy, joy, joy.
Love Him, serve Him, and a-dore Him, Christ, Christ, Christ.

532 We Shall See The King Some Day

D♭-4-SOL
L. E. J.

C-6, S-2
L. E. Jones

Then we . . . shall be caught up together . . . to meet the Lord in the air: and so shall
we ever be with the Lord. I Thess. 4:17

1. Tho' the way we jour-ney may be of-ten drear,
2. Af-ter pain and an-guish, af-ter toil and care,
3. Af-ter foes are con-quered, af-ter bat-tles won,

We shall see the King some day;
some day;

On that bless-ed
Thru the end-less
Af-ter strife is

morning clouds will dis-ap-pear;
a-ges joy and bless-ing share, We shall see the King some day.
o-ver, af-ter set of sun,

CHORUS

We shall see the King some day, (some day,) We shall shout and

sing some day (some day) Gath-ered 'round the throne when

He shall call His own, We shall see the King some day.

Fight The Good Fight

533

G-3-DO

John S. B. Monsell, 1863

Fight the good fight of faith. 1 Tim. 6:12

W -1, E -1

William Boyd, 1864

1. Fight the good fight with all thy might! Christ is thy
2. Run the straight race thro' God's good grace, Lift up thine
3. Cast care a - side, lean on thy Guide, His bound - less
4. Faint not nor fear, His arms are near, He chang - eth

strength, and Christ thy right; Lay hold on life, and it shall
eyes, and seek His face; Life with its way be - fore us
mer - cy will pro - vide; Trust, and thy trust - ing soul shall
not, and thou art dear; On - ly be - lieve, and thou shalt

be Thy joy and crown e - ter - nal - ly.
lies, Christ is the path, and Christ the prize.
prove Christ is its life, and Christ its love.
see That Christ is all in all to thee. A - men.

534 Tell Me The Old, Old Story

C-4-MI
Kate Hankey

Christ died for our sins . . . He was buried . . .
He rose again the third day according to the scriptures. 1 Cor. 15:3,4

D-1
W. H. Doane

1. Tell me the old, old Sto - ry, Of un - seen things a - bove, Of
2. Tell me the sto - ry slow - ly, That I may take it in— That
3. Tell me the sto - ry soft - ly, With ear - nest tones and grave; Re -

Je - sus and His glo - ry, Of Je - sus and His love;
won - der - ful re - demp - tion, God's rem - e - dy for sin;
mem - ber I'm the sin - ner Whom Je - sus came to save;

Tell me the sto - ry sim - ply, As to a lit - tle
Tell me the sto - ry of - ten, For I for - get so
Tell me the sto - ry al - ways, If you would real - ly

child, For I am weak and wea - ry, And help - less and de -
soon: The "ear - ly dew" of morn - ing Has passed a - way at
be, In an - y time of trou - ble, A com - fort - er to

CHORUS

filed.
noon. Tell me the old, old Sto - ry, Tell me the old, old
me.

Sto - ry, Tell me the old, old Sto - ry Of Je - sus and His love.

Savior, Mine, I Remember Thee 535

D-4-MI
Remember how He spake . . . saying the Son of Man must be delivered into the
hands of sinful men, and be crucified. Luke 24:6-7
L-1

Vesta A. McDaniel
St. 4 by Dane K. Shepard

Dane K. Shepard

1. Sav - ior, mine, I re - mem - ber Thee Suff - 'ring on that cru - el tree;
2. Glor - ious Sav - ior, Lamb of God, On this earth Thy feet once trod;
3. Blood and wa - ter flow - ing down, Grant - ing me a price - less crown;
4. Sav - ior, mine, re - mem - ber me As I serve and fol - low Thee;

Now I seek to do Thy will And in love Thy word ful - fill.
God as man— per - fect sac - ri - fice; On the cross You paid sin's price.
Hands and feet were nailed by me; From my guilt You set me free!
Dead to self, my cross I bear; Life in - deed! with Thee I share.

536 Oh, The Things We May Do

Ab-4-SOL

We then that are strong ought to bear the infirmities of the weak . . . Rom. 15:1

L-2, W-4

Lizzie DeArmond

J. M. Hagan

1. Have you lift - ed a stone from your broth - er's way, As He
2. Have you spok - en a word full of hope and cheer? Have you
3. Have you held up your light thro' the shad - ows dark, So that

strug - gled a - long life's road? Have you lov - ing - ly touched some frail,
walked with a slow - er pace, Till the wea - ry of heart who were
some - bod - y else might see? Have you lived with the Christ thro' the

CHORUS

toil-worn hand, Shared with some - one his heav - y load?
stum - bling on, Took new cour - age to run the race? Oh, the things
long, long day, Gain - ing man - y a vic - to - ry?

we may do, you and I, you and I; Oh, the love we can

give if we try; (if we try;) Just a word or a song as we're

Open Our Eyes

537

Blessed are the pure in heart; for they shall see God. Matt. 5:8

Eb-3-MI

Robert Cull, St. 2 Don Mullins

D-1

Robert Cull

538 Majesty

*Thine, O Lord, is the greatness, and the power,
and the glory, and the victory, and the majesty . . . 1 Chron. 29:11*

Bb-2-DO

Jack Hayford

C-6, W-5

Jack Hayford

Maj-es-ty, wor-ship His maj-es-ty, Un-to Je-sus be all glo-ry, pow-er and praise. Maj-es-ty, King-dom au-thor-i-ty, flow from His throne un-to His own, His an-them raise. So ex-alt, lift up-on high the name of Je-sus. Mag-ni-fy, come glo-ri-fy Christ Je-sus the

King. Maj-es-ty, wor-ship His maj-es-ty. Je-sus, who

died, now glo-ri-fied, King of All Kings. Kings.

Share My Burdens, Lord

539

A♭-4-SOL
Floyd D. Chappelear

And He said unto me, My grace is sufficient for thee.
2 Cor. 12:9

P-3

R. J. Stevens

1. Dear Lord, I pray that Thou wilt help me bear my hea-vy load; Please
2. For in this world I know I need a thorn with-in my side. On
3. If in this life I had no care to bur-den me each day, I
4. So, my dear God, I do not ask that I be bur-den free; Just

share it with me, pre-cious Lord, 'till I walk hea-ven's road.
Thee, my God, I will de-pend, and in Thy grace a-bide. A-men
may not long for heav-en's home as I pass by this way.
hold my hand in Thine, dear Lord, and lead me home to Thee.

540 Come Unto Me

Come unto Me, all ye that labor and are heavy laden and I will give you rest.
Matt. 11:28

C-3-SOL
F. E. B.

E-1, I-1
Franklin E. Belden

1. O heart bowed down with sor - row! O eyes that long for sight!
2. Di - vin - est con - so - la - tion Doth Christ the Heal - er give;
3. His peace is like a riv - er, His love is like a song;

There's glad - ness in be - liev - ing; In Je - sus there is light.
Art thou in con-dem - na - tion? Be - lieve, re - pent and live.
His yoke's a bur - den nev - er; 'Tis eas - y all day long.

CHORUS

"Come . . . . . un - to me . . . . . all ye . . . .
"Come, O come, come un - to me, Come, O

. . . . that la - - bor and . . . . are heav - y
come, all ye that la - bor; Come, O come,

la - den, and I . . . . . . will give you rest . . . .
la - den souls, I . . . . will give you rest.

I will give you rest.

Take . . . . . my yoke up - on you, and learn . . .
Come, O come, Come, take my yoke, Come, O

come, ... 'of me;.... .... for I .... am meek and
come, come learn of me; I am meek and

low - ly in heart: and ye shall find rest un - to your souls."
low - ly in heart:

Draw Thou My Soul, O Christ 541

A♭-4-SOL
Lucy Larcom, 1892

*Master, I will follow Thee
whithersoever Thou goest.* Matt. 8:19

D -1
William H. Doane, 1870

1. Draw Thou my soul, O Christ, clos - er to Thine; Breathe in - to
2. Lead forth my soul, O Christ, one with Thine own, Joy - ful to
3. Not for my - self a - lone may my prayer be; Lift Thou Thy

ev - 'ry wish Thy will di - vine; Raise my low self a - bove,
fol - low Thee thro' paths un - known; In Thee my strength re - new;
world, O Christ, clos - er to Thee; Cleanse it from guilt and wrong;

won by Thy death - less love; O Christ, thro' mine let Thy life shine.
Give me Thy work to do; Thy truth be shown, Thy love made known.
Teach it sal - va - tion's song, Till earth ful - fill God's ho - ly will.

He Lifted Me

542

G-3-SOL

I will extol Thee, O Lord; for Thou hast lifted me up . . . Psa. 30:1

S-1

Charlotte G. Homer

Chas. H. Gabriel

1. In lov-ing-kind-ness Je-sus came My soul in mer - cy
2. He called me long be-fore I heard, Be-fore my sin - ful
3. His brow was pierced with many a thorn, His hands by cru - el
4. Now on a high-er plane I dwell, And with my soul I

to re - claim, And from the depths of sin and shame Thro' grace He
heart was stirred, But when I took Him at His word, For-giv'n He
nails were torn, When from my guilt and grief, for - lorn, In love He
know 'tis well; Yet how or why, I can-not tell, He should have

CHORUS

lift - ed me.
lift - ed me.
lift - ed me.
lift - ed me.

He lift - ed me.

From sink-ing sand He lift - ed me,

With ten - der hand He lift - ed me, From shades of night to

plains of light, O praise His name, He lift - ed me!

Great God Of Nations 543

O praise the Lord, all ye nations, praise Him, all ye people. Psa. 117:1

Eb-3-DO

Alford A. Woodhull, 1872

T -2

William B. Bradbury, 1849

1. Great God of na - tions, now to Thee Our hymn of
2. Here free - dom spreads her ban - ner wide And casts her
3. We pray Thee let the gos - pel light Through all our
4. Great God, pre - serve us in Thy fear; In dan - ger

grat - i - tude we raise; With hum - ble heart and bend - ing
soft and hal - lowed ray; Here Thou our fa - thers' steps didst
land its ra - d'ance shed; Dis - pel the shades of er - ror's
still our Guar - dian be; O spread Thy truth's bright pre - cepts

knee We of - fer Thee our song of praise.
guide In safe - ty through their dan - g'rous way.
night, And heav - 'nly bless - ings round us spread.
here; Let all the peo - ple wor - ship Thee.

544 Send The Light

Ab-4-SOL
C. H. G.

For God . . . commanded the light to shine out of darkness . . . to give the light of the knowledge of the glory of God . . . II Cor. 4:6

Chas. H. Gabriel

S-5

1. There's a call comes ring-ing o'er the rest - less wave, "Send the
2. We have heard the Mac - e - do - nian call to - day, "Send the
3. Let us pray that grace may ev - 'ry-where a - bound; "Send the
4. Let us not grow wea - ry in the work of love, "Send the

light!   Send the light!"   There are souls to
light!   Send the light!"   And a gold - en
light!   Send the light!"   And a Christ-like
light!   Send the light!"   Let us gath - er

Send the light!   Send the light!

res - cue, there are souls to save,
of - f'ring at the cross we lay,
spir - it ev - 'ry - where be found,
jew - els for a crown a - bove,

Send the light!   Send the

Send the light!

CHORUS

light!   Send the light!   the bless - ed gos -
Send the light!   Send the light!   the bless - ed

pel light; Let it shine . . . . . from shore to shore! . . .

gos - pel light;   Let it shine   from

shine . . . . for - ev - er - more.

shore to shore!   Let it shine   for - ev - er - more.

Rise Up, O Child Of God!   545

A-4-SOL
William P. Merrill, 1911

Yet a little while, and . . . He will come, and will not tarry. Heb. 10:37

W -4, E -1
William H. Walter, 1894

1. Rise up, O child of God! Have done with less - er things; Give
2. Rise up, O child of God! His King - dom tar - ries long; Bring
3. Rise up, O child of God! The Church for you doth wait, Her
4. Lift high the cross of Christ! Tread where His feet have trod; As

heart and soul and mind and strength To serve the King of kings.
in the day of broth - er - hood And end the night of wrong.
strength un - e - qual to her task; Rise up, and make her great!
chil - dren of the Son of Man, Rise up, O child of God!

546 I Walk With The King

G-2-SOL
As ye have therefore received Christ Jesus the Lord, so walk ye in Him. Col. 2:6
F-2, J-1

James Rowe
B. D. Ackley

1. In sor-row I wan-dered, my spir-it op-prest, But now I am
2. For years in the fet-ters of sin I was bound, The world could not
3. O soul near de-spair in the low-lands of strife, Look up and let

hap-py—se-cure-ly I rest; From morn-ing till eve-ning glad
help me—no com-fort I found; But now like the birds and the
Je-sus come in-to your life; The joy of sal-va-tion to

car-ols I sing, and this is the rea-son; I walk with the King.
sun-beams of Spring, I'm free and re-joic-ing—I walk with the King.
you He would bring, Come in-to the sun-light and walk with the King.

CHORUS

I walk with the King, hal-le-lu-jah! I walk with the

King, praise His name! No long-er I roam, my

soul fac - es home, I walk and I talk with the King.

Give To Our God Immortal Praise 547

F-3-DO
Psalm 136

Tune: Sun Of My Soul

P -2
Arr. by William H. Monk, 1861

1. Give to our God im - mor - tal praise; Mer - cy and
2. He built the earth, He spread the sky, And fixed the
3. He sent His Son with pow'r to save From guilt and
4. Through this vast world He guides our feet, And leads us

truth are all His ways: Won - ders of grace to
star - ry lights on high: Won - ders of grace to
dark - ness and the grave: Won - ders of grace to
to His heav - 'nly seat: His mer - cies ev - er

God be - long; Re - peat His mer - cies in your song.
God be - long; Re - peat His mer - cies in your song.
God be - long; Re - peat His mer - cies in your song.
shall en - dure, When this our world shall be no more.

548   Since I Have Been Redeemed

G-4-SOL
E. O. E.

O give thanks unto the Lord, for He is good: for His mercy endureth for ever.
Let the redeemed of the Lord say so . . . Psa. 107:1,2

T-1

Edwin O. Excell

1. I have a song I love to sing, Since I have
2. I have a Christ who sat-is-fies, Since I have
3. I have a home pre-pared for me, Since I have

been re-deemed,   Of my Re-deem-er,
been re-deemed,   To do His will my
been re-deemed,   Where I shall dwell e-

Sav-ior, King, Since I have been re-deemed. Since
high-est prize, Since I have been re-deemed. Since
ter-nal-ly, Since I have been re-deemed.

CHORUS

I . . . . have been re-deemed, ...
I have been re-deemed, Since I have been re-

... Since I have been re-deemed, I will glo-ry in His
deemed,

name; Since I . . . . have been re-
Since I have been re-deemed, Since

deemed, I will glo-ry in my Sav-ior's name.
I have been re-deemed,

May The Grace Of Christ Our Savior 549

F-3-DO
John Newton, 1779

The grace of our Lord Jesus
Christ be with you all. Rev. 22:21

G -2, C -14
Corner's *Gesangbuch,* **1631**

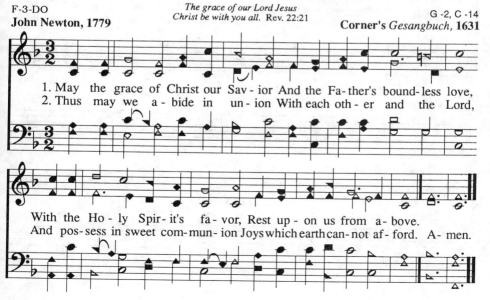

1. May the grace of Christ our Sav-ior And the Fa-ther's bound-less love,
2. Thus may we a-bide in un-ion With each oth-er and the Lord,

With the Ho-ly Spir-it's fa-vor, Rest up-on us from a-bove.
And pos-sess in sweet com-mun-ion Joys which earth can-not af-ford. A-men.

550 For Christ And The Church

Christ also loved the church, and gave Himself for it. Eph. 5:25

D-4-SOL
E. E. Hewitt

E-1, W-4
Wm. J. Kirkpatrick

1. "For Christ and the church" let our voic - es ring, Let us hon -
2. "For Christ and the church" be our ear - nest prayer, Let us fol -
3. "For Christ and the church" let us cast a - side, By His con -

or the name of our own bless - ed King; Let us work with a
low His ban - ner, the cross dai - ly bear; Let us yield, whol - ly
quer-ing grace, chains of self, fear, and pride; May our lives be en -

will in the strength of youth, And loy - al - ly stand for the
yield, to the gos - pel's pow'r, And serve faith - ful - ly ev - 'ry
riched by an aim so grand; Then hap - py the call to the

CHORUS

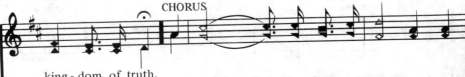

king - dom of truth.
day, ev - 'ry hour. For Christ, our dear Re - deem - er, For
Sav - ior's right hand. For Christ,

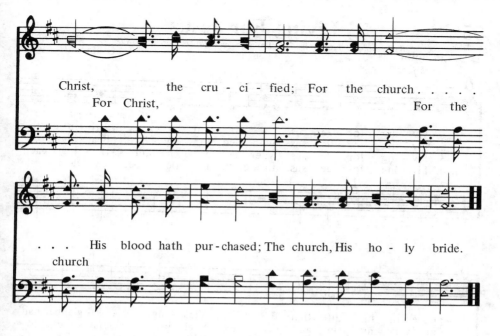

Christ, the cru - ci - fied; For the church . . . . .
For Christ, For the

. . . His blood hath pur - chased; The church, His ho - ly bride.
church

Walk In The Light   551

G-3-DO

Bernard Barton, 1826

*If we walk in the light
as He is in the light, . . .* 1 John 1:7

F -2

Henry W. Greatorex's *Collection,* 1851

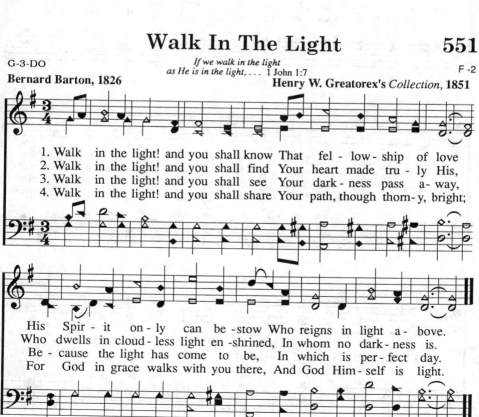

1. Walk in the light! and you shall know That fel - low - ship of love
2. Walk in the light! and you shall find Your heart made tru - ly His,
3. Walk in the light! and you shall see Your dark - ness pass a - way,
4. Walk in the light! and you shall share Your path, though thorn - y, bright;

His Spir - it on - ly can be - stow Who reigns in light a - bove.
Who dwells in cloud - less light en - shrined, In whom no dark - ness is.
Be - cause the light has come to be, In which is per - fect day.
For God in grace walks with you there, And God Him - self is light.

552 Living For Jesus

F-4-MI

C-12, D-1

T. O. Chisholm

Walk worthy of the Lord unto all pleasing, being fruitful in every good work . . .
Col. 1:10

C. Harold Lowden

Not fast

1. Liv - ing for Je - sus a life that is true, Striv - ing to
2. Liv - ing for Je - sus who died in my place, Bear - ing on
3. Liv - ing for Je - sus wher - ev - er I am, Do - ing each
4. Liv - ing for Je - sus thru earth's lit - tle while, My dear - est

please Him in all that I do; Yield - ing al - le - giance, glad -
Cal - v'ry my sin and dis - grace; Such love con - strains me to
du - ty in His ho - ly name; Will - ing to suf - fer af -
treas - ure, the light of His smile; Seek - ing the lost ones He

heart - ed and free, This is the path - way of bless - ing for me.
an - swer His call, Fol - low His lead - ing and give Him my all.
flic - tion and loss, Deem - ing each tri - al a part of my cross.
died to re - deem, Bring - ing the wea - ry to find rest in Him.

CHORUS

O Je - sus, Lord and Sav - ior, I give my - self to Thee, For

Thou in Thy a-tone-ment, Didst give Thy-self for me; I

own no oth-er Mas-ter, My heart shall be Thy throne; My

life I give, hence-forth to live, O Christ, for Thee a-lone.

Hear Our Prayer, O Lord 553

The Lord . . . heareth the prayer of the righteous. Prov. 15:29

Eb-4-MI
Psalm 143:1

P-3

George Whelpton, 1897

Hear our prayer, O Lord, Hear our prayer, O Lord;

In-cline Thine ear to us, And grant us Thy peace. A-men.

554

The King's Business

E-4-SOL
E. T. Cassel

We pray you . . . be ye reconciled to God. II Cor. 5:20

C-6, S-5
Flora H. Cassel

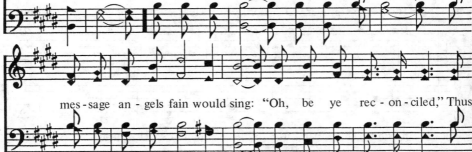

1. I am a stran-ger here, with-in a for-eign land; My
2. This is the King's com-mand: that all men, ev-'ry-where, Re-
3. My home is bright-er far than Shar-on's ro-sy plain, E-

home is far a-way up-on a gold-en strand; A mes-sen-
pent and turn a-way from sin's se-duc-tive snare; That all who
ter-nal life and joy thro'-out its vast do-main; My Sov-'reign

ger to be of realms be-yond the sea, I'm here on busi-ness for
will o-bey, with Him shall live for aye, And that's my busi-ness for
bids me tell how mor-tals there may dwell, And that's my busi-ness for

CHORUS

my King. This is the mes-sage that I bring, A

mes-sage an-gels fain would sing: "Oh, be ye rec-on-ciled," Thus

saith my Lord and King, "Oh, be ye rec-on-ciled to God." A-men.

Psalm 119

555

F-3-DO
W -3
Psalm 119:9-16
R. J. Stevens

1. How shall a young man cleanse his way? Let him with
2. Thy word I've treas-ured in my heart, That I give
3. I with my lips have oft de-clared The judg-ments
4. I'll on Thy pre-cepts med-i-tate, And have re-

care Thy word ob-serve. With all my heart I have
no of-fence to Thee. Thou, O Je-ho-vah, bless-
which Thy mouth hath shown. More joy Thy test-i-mo-
spect to all Thy ways. I in Thy stat-utes will

Thee sought; From Thy com-mands let me not swerve.
ed art; Thy stat-utes teach Thou un-to me.
nies gave Than all the rich-es I have known.
de-light, Thy word re-mem-ber all my days.

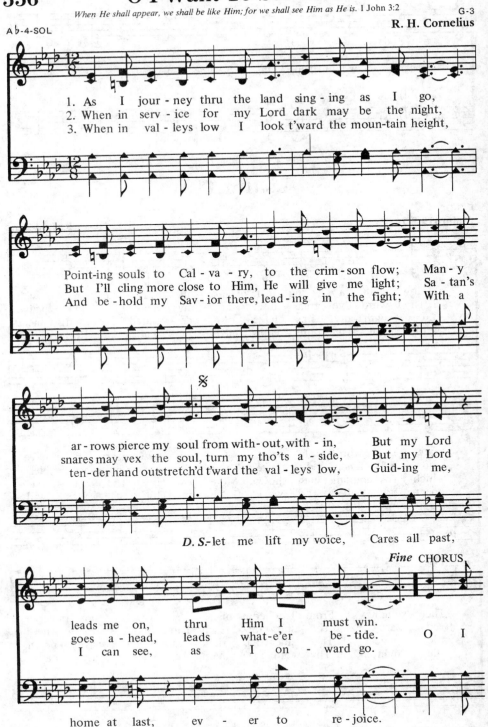

556 O I Want To See Him

When He shall appear, we shall be like Him; for we shall see Him as He is. I John 3:2

G-3

R. H. Cornelius

A♭-4-SOL

1. As I jour-ney thru the land sing-ing as I go,
2. When in serv-ice for my Lord dark may be the night,
3. When in val-leys low I look t'ward the moun-tain height,

Point-ing souls to Cal-va-ry, to the crim-son flow; Man-y
But I'll cling more close to Him, He will give me light; Sa-tan's
And be-hold my Sav-ior there, lead-ing in the fight; With a

ar-rows pierce my soul from with-out, with-in, But my Lord
snares may vex the soul, turn my tho'ts a-side, But my Lord
ten-der hand outstretch'd t'ward the val-leys low, Guid-ing me,

D. S.-let me lift my voice, Cares all past,

Fine CHORUS

leads me on, thru Him I must win.
goes a-head, leads what-e'er be-tide. O I
I can see, as I on-ward go.

home at last, ev-er to re-joice.

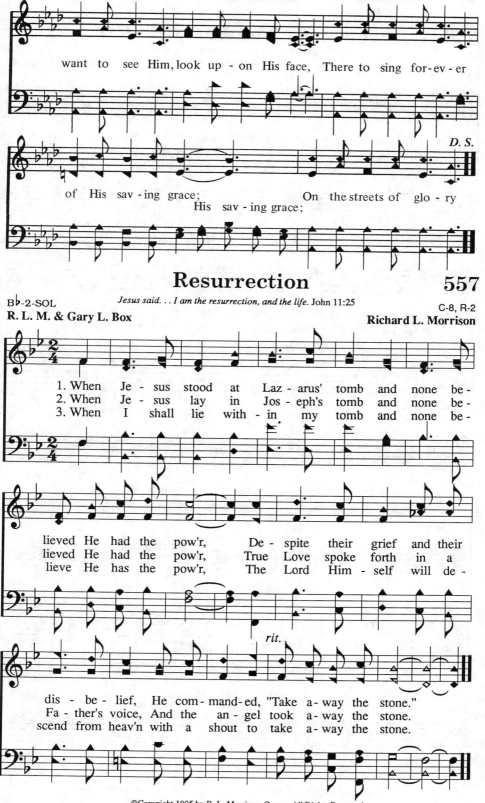

want to see Him, look up - on His face, There to sing for - ev - er

of His sav - ing grace; On the streets of glo - ry
His sav - ing grace;

D. S.

Resurrection

557

Jesus said. . . I am the resurrection, and the life. John 11:25

Bb-2-SOL
R. L. M. & Gary L. Box

C-8, R-2

Richard L. Morrison

1. When Je - sus stood at Laz - arus' tomb and none be -
2. When Je - sus lay in Jos - eph's tomb and none be -
3. When I shall lie with - in my tomb and none be -

lieved He had the pow'r, De - spite their grief and their
lieved He had the pow'r, True Love spoke forth in a
lieve He has the pow'r, The Lord Him - self will de -

rit.

dis - be - lief, He com - mand - ed, "Take a - way the stone."
Fa - ther's voice, And the an - gel took a - way the stone.
scend from heav'n with a shout to take a - way the stone.

558 Sweeter As The Years Go By

Unto Him that loved us, and washed us from our sins . . .
be glory and dominion for ever and ever. Rev. 1:5

Bb-3-SOL
Mrs. C. H. M.

L-4
Mrs. C. H. Morris

1. Of Je - sus' love that sought me, When I was lost in sin; Of
2. He trod in old Ju - de - a Life's path - way long a - go; The
3. 'Twas won - drous love which led Him For us to suf - fer loss— To

won - drous grace that brought me Back to His fold a - gain; Of
peo - ple throng'd a - bout Him, His sav - ing grace to know; He
bear with - out a mur - mur The an - guish of the cross; With

heights and depths of mer - cy, Far deep - er than the sea; And
healed the bro - ken heart - ed, And caused the blind to see; And
saints re - deemed in glo - ry Let us our voic - es raise, Till

high - er than the heav - ens, My theme shall ev - er be.
still His great heart yearn - eth In love for e - ven me.
heav'n and earth re - ech - o With our Re - deem - er's praise.

CHORUS

Sweet-er as the years go by, Sweet-er as the
Sweet - er as the years go by, 'Tis sweet - er

years go by; Rich -er, full - er, deep - er,
as the years go by;

rit.

Je - sus' love is sweet - er, Sweet-er as the years go by.

Psalm 106

559

A♭-3-SOL
Psalm 106:1-4

Tune: I'm Not Ashamed To Own My Lord

P -2
Arr. from Carl Glaser, 1828

1. O praise the Lord! O thank the Lord! For boun - ti - ful is He;
2. Who can ex - press Je - ho - vah's praise Or tell His deeds of might?
3. Re - gard me with the fa - vor Lord, Which Thou dost bear to Thine.

Be - cause His lov - ing kind - ness lasts To all e - ter - ni - ty.
O blest are they who jus - tice keep And ev - er do the right.
O vis - it Thou my soul in love; Make Thy sal - va - tion mine.

560 More Like The Master

Db-2-SOL
C. H. G.

Let this mind be in you, which was also in Christ Jesus. Phil. 2:5

C-13, C-16
Chas. H. Gabriel, 1906

1. More like the Mas-ter I would ev-er be, More of His meekness,
2. More like the Mas-ter is my dai-ly prayer; More strength to car-ry
3. More like the Mas-ter I would live and grow; More of His love to

more hu-mil-i-ty; More zeal to la-bor, more cour-age to be
cross-es I must bear; More ear-nest ef-fort His king-dom to in-
oth-ers I would show; More self-de-ni-al, like His in Gal-i-

rit.

true, More con-se-cra-tion for work He bids me do.
crease, More of His Spir-it, the wan-der-er to win.
lee, More like the Mas-ter I long to ev-er be.

CHORUS

Take Thou my heart, I would be Thine a-lone,
Take my heart, O take my heart, I would be Thine a-lone;

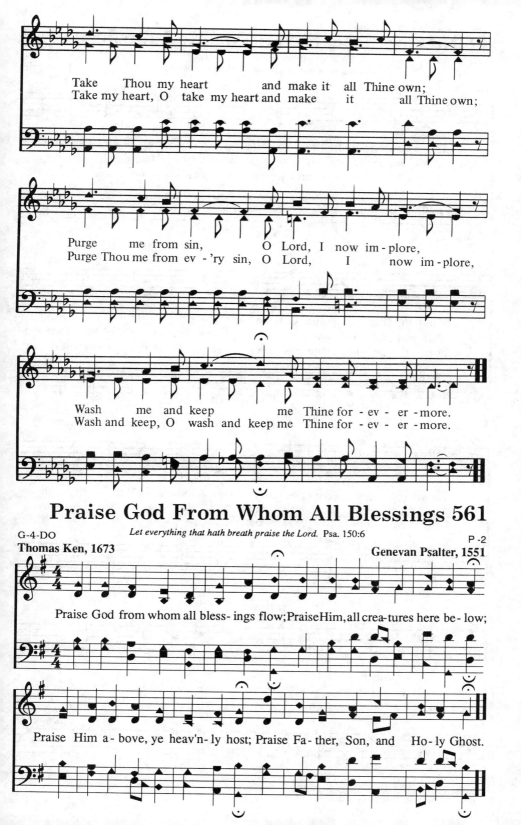

Take   Thou my heart   and make it   all Thine own;
Take my heart, O   take my heart and make   it   all Thine own;

Purge   me from sin,   O Lord, I now im-plore,
Purge Thou me from ev-'ry sin, O Lord,   I   now im-plore,

Wash   me and keep   me Thine for-ev-er-more.
Wash and keep, O   wash and keep me Thine for-ev-er-more.

Praise God From Whom All Blessings 561

Let everything that hath breath praise the Lord. Psa. 150:6

G-4-DO

Thomas Ken, 1673

P-2

Genevan Psalter, 1551

Praise God from whom all bless-ings flow; Praise Him, all crea-tures here be-low;

Praise Him a-bove, ye heav'n-ly host; Praise Fa-ther, Son, and   Ho-ly Ghost.

562 No One Ever Cared For Me Like Jesus

D-4-DO
C. F. W.

I will mention the lovingkindness of the Lord . . .
according to all that the Lord hath bestowed . . . Isa. 63:7

L-4
C. F. Weigle

1. I would love to tell you what I think of Je - sus, Since I
2. All my life was full of sin when Je - sus found me, All my
3. Ev - 'ry day He comes to me with new as - sur - ance, More and

found in Him a friend so strong and true; I would tell you how He
heart was full of mis - er - y and woe; Je - sus placed His strong and
more I un - der - stand His words of love; But I'll nev - er know just

changed my life com - plete - ly, He did some - thing that no
lov - ing arms a - bout me, And He led me in the
why He came to save me, Till some day I see His

CHORUS

oth - er friend could do.
way I ought to go. No one ev - er cared for me like Je - sus,
bless - ed face a - bove.

There's no oth-er friend so kind as He, No one else could take the

sin and dark-ness from me, O how much He cared for me.

Jesus, Name Above All Names 563

*That the name of our Lord Jesus Christ
may be glorified in you.* 1 Thess. 1:12

E♭-4-MI

Naida Hearn

N-1, P-2

Naida Hearn

1. Je - sus, name a - bove all names:___ Beau - ti - ful
2. Je - sus, Lord God Al - might - y, Won - der - ful

Sav - ior, glo - ri - ous Lord,___ Em - man - u - el, God is
Couns - 'lor, Light of the world, The Prince of Peace, Hope of

with us,___ Bless - ed Re - deem - er,___ Liv - ing Word.
glo - ry, Man of Sor - rows, Lamb of God.

Follow Me

Come, take up the cross, and follow Me. Mark 10:21

564
E♭-4-MI
I. F. S.

C-13, F-3
Ira F. Stanphill

1. I trav-eled down a lone-ly road And no one seemed to care,
2. "I work so hard for Je - sus" I of-ten boast and say,
3. Oh, Je-sus if I die up-on A for-eign field some day,

The bur-den on my wea-ry back Had bowed me to de-spair;
"I've sac-ri-ficed a lot of things To walk the nar-row way;
'Twould be no more than love de-mands; No less could I re-pay;

I oft complained to Je - sus How folks were treat-ing me,
I gave up fame and for - tune; I'm worth a lot to Thee,"
"No great-er love hath mor-tal man Than for a friend to die,"

And then I heard Him say so ten-der-ly:"My feet were al-so
And then I hear Him gen-tly say to me:"I left the throne of
These are the words He gen-tly spoke to me:"If just a cup of

weary, Up - on the Cal-v'ry road; The cross be-came so heav-y,
glo - ry And count-ed it but loss, My hands were nailed in an - ger

wa - ter I place with-in your hand, Then just a cup of wa - ter

I fell be-neath the load; Be faith-ful wea - ry pil-grim, The
Up - on a cru - el cross; But now we'll make the jour-ney With
Is all that I de-mand;" But if by death to liv-ing They

morn-ing I can see, Just lift your cross and fol-low close to Me."
your hand safe in Mine, So lift your cross and fol-low close to Me."
can Thy glo - ry see, I'll take my cross and fol-low close to Thee.

He Is Lord

565

F-4-DO
American Folk Hymn

*Who is the blessed and only sovereign,
the King of kings, and Lord of lords. 1 Tim. 6:15*

C -6
American Folk Melody

He is Lord, He is Lord! He is ris - en from the dead and He is Lord!

Ev - 'ry knee shall bow, ev - 'ry tongue con - fess That Je - sus Christ is Lord.

566 Christ Returneth

*But of that day and hour knoweth no man,
no, not the angels of heaven, but My Father only.*

Matt. 24:36

Db-3,4-DO
H. L. Turner, 1878

James McGranahan, 1878

S-2

1. It may be at morn, when the day is a-wak-ing, When
2. It may be at mid-day, it may be at twi-light, It
3. O joy! O de-light! should we go with-out dy-ing, No

sun-light thru dark-ness and shad-ow is break-ing, That
may be, per-chance, that the black-ness of mid-night Will
sick-ness, no sad-ness, no dread and no cry-ing, Caught

Je-sus will come in the full-ness of glo-ry, To re-
burst in-to light in the blaze of His glo-ry, When
up thru the clouds with our Lord in-to glo-ry, When

CHORUS

ceive from the world His own.
Je-sus re-ceives His own. O Lord Je-sus, how long,
Je-sus re-ceives His own.

how long Ere we shout the glad song, Christ re-turn-eth! Hal-le-

O Father, Let Us See His Death 567

E minor-3-LA
Craig A. Roberts

But we see Jesus, who was made a little lower than the angels
for the suffering of death . . . that He . . . should
taste death for every man. Heb. 2:9

C -4, L -1
R. J. Stevens

1. O Fa - ther, bless this sol - emn day, When we as -
2. In fer - vent prayers and sa - cred hymns, We all cry
3. Then as we eat un - leav - ened bread, And drink the
4. O Fa - ther, let us see His death, And hear "for-

sem - ble, sing and pray, To hon - or Christ, Thine on - ly
out, "Re - mem - ber Him," And cry with - in, "For me He
cup, we bow our heads, And see the suf - f'ring death of
give them" on His breath, And feel His grief, dis - grace and

Rit.

Son, Who tast - ed death for ev - 'ry - one.
died, And for my sins was cru - ci - fied."
Christ -- His blood! His bo - dy! Sac - ri - ficed!
pain; O let us see His death a - gain.

568 A Soul Winner For Jesus

I am made all things to all men, that I might by all means save some. I Cor. 9:22

Bb-4-SOL

J. W. F.

S-5

J. W. Ferrill

1. I want to be a soul win-ner for Je-sus ev-'ry day, He
2. I want to be a soul win-ner and bring the lost to Christ, That
3. I want to be a soul win-ner till Je-sus calls for me, To

does so much for me; I want to aid the lost sin-ner to
they His grace may know; I want to live for Christ ev-er, and
lay my bur-dens down; I want to hear Him say, serv-ant,"You've

CHORUS

leave his err-ing way, And be from bond-age free.
do His bless-ed will, Be - cause He loves me so. A
gath-ered man-y sheaves, Re - ceive a shin-ing crown."

soul win-ner for Je - sus, A soul . . . . .
win-ner for Je-sus Christ the Lord, win-ner for

. . . win-ner for Je - sus, O let me be each day; A
Je - sus Christ the Lord,

soul . . . . . . win-ner for Je - sus, A soul . . . . . .
win-ner for Je-sus Christ the Lord, ... win-ner for

. . . win-ner for Je - sus, He's done so much for me.
Je - sus Christ the Lord,

May The Mind Of Christ My Savior 569

Let this mind be in you which
was also in Christ Jesus . . . Phil. 2:5

Eb-4-MI

Kate B. Wilkinson, 1925

C-13

A. Cyril Barham-Gould, 1925

1. May the mind of Christ my Sav-ior Live in me from day to day,
2. May the Word of God dwell rich-ly In my heart from hour to hour,
3. May the peace of God my Fa-ther Rule my life in ev-ery-thing,
4. May the love of Je-sus fill me As the wa-ters fill the sea;
5. May His beau-ty rest up-on me As I seek the lost to win,

By His love and pow'r con-trol-ling All I do and say.
So that all may see I tri-umph On-ly through His pow'r.
That I may be calm to com-fort Sick and sor-row-ing.
Him ex-alt-ing, self a-bas-ing, This is vic-to-ry.
And may they for-get the chan-nel, See-ing on-ly Him. A-men.

570 As The Life Of A Flower

All the glory of man as the flower of grass. The grass withereth and the flower thereof fadeth away. I Pet. 1:24

Bb-4-MI

Laura E. Newell

C-12

G. H. Ramsey

1. As the life of a flow'r, As a breath or a sigh, So the
2. As the life of a flow'r, Be our lives pure and sweet; May we
3. While we tar-ry be-low Let us trust and a-dore Him who

years that we live As a dream has-ten by; True, to-day we are
bright-en the way For the friends that we greet; And sweet in-cense a-
leads us each day Tow'rd the ra-di-ant shore Where the sun nev-er

here, But to-mor-row may see Just a grave in the
rise, From our hearts as we live Close to Him who doth
sets, And the flow'rs nev-er fade, Where no sor-row or

CHORUS

vale, And a mem-'ry of me. As the life of a
teach Us to love and for-give.
death May its bor-ders in-vade. As the life

flow'r,   As a breath,   or a
of a flow'r,   As a breath,

sigh,   So the years   glide a-
or a sigh,   So the years

rit.

way,   And a - las,   we must die.
glide a - way,   and a - las,   we must die.

Lord Jesus, Think On Me   571

E minor-4-LA
Synesius of Cyrene, c. 410
Tr. by Allen W. Chatfield, 1876

According to Thy mercy
remember Thou me. . . Psa 25:7

C -12, P -3
Damon's *Psalter,* **1579**

1. Lord Je - sus, think on me And purge a - way my sin; From
2. Lord Je - sus, think on me, With care and woe op- pressed; Let
3. Lord Je - sus, think on me Nor let me go a - stray; Thro'
4. Lord Je - sus, think on me, That when the flood is past, I

earth- born pas- sions set me free And make me pure with - in.
me Thy lov - ing ser - vant be And gain Thy prom- ised rest.
dark- ness and per- plex - i - ty Point Thou the heav'n- ly way.
may th'e - ter - nal bright- ness see And share Thy joy at last. A - men.

572 Wonderful Peace

These things I have spoken unto you, that in Me ye might have peace. John 16:33

A-2-SOL
H. L.

C-15, P-1
Haldor Lillenas

1. Com - ing   to   Je - sus   my   Sav - ior   I   found,
2. Peace like   a   riv - er   so   deep   and   so   broad,
3. Gone   is   the   bat - tle   that   once   raged   with - in,

Won - der - ful peace, won - der - ful peace;   Storms in their fu - ry may
Won - der - ful peace, won - der - ful peace;   Rest - ing my soul on the
Won - der - ful peace, won - der - ful peace;   Je - sus has saved me and

rage   all   a - round;   I   have peace,   sweet
bos - om   of   God,   Won - der - ful,   won - der - ful,
cleans'd me   from   sin,

peace.   Peace, peace won - der - ful peace;   Peace, peace,
glo - ri - ous peace.

CHORUS

glo - ri - ous peace; Since my Re - deem - er has ran - somed my

soul I have peace, sweet peace.
won- der- ful peace.

Can You Count The Stars? 573

F-3-DO
Johann Hey, 1837
Tr. Elmer L. Jorgenson, 1921

Casting all your care upon Him:
for He careth for you. 1 Pet. 5:7

P-5

German Folk Tune, c. 1550

1. { Can you count the stars of eve- ning That are shin- ing in the sky?
   { Can you count the clouds that dai - ly O - ver all the world go by?

2. { Can you count the birds that war- ble In the sun- shine all the day?
   { Can you count the lit - tle fish- es That in spar- kling wa- ters play?

3. { Can you count the man - y chil- dren In their lit - tle beds at night,
   { Who with- out a thought of sor- row Rise a- gain at morn- ing light?

God the Lord, who doth not slum- ber, Keep- eth all the bound- less num- ber:
God the Lord their num- ber know- eth, For each one His care He show- eth:
God the Lord, who dwells in heav- en, Lov- ing care to each has giv- en:

But He car- eth more for thee. But He car- eth more for thee.
Shall He not re- mem- ber thee? Shall He not re- mem- ber thee?
He has not for- got- ten thee, He has not for- got- ten thee.

574 The Glory-Land Way

That ye may know what is the hope of His calling, and what the riches of the glory of His inheritance in the saints . . . Eph. 1:18

G-4-MI
J. S. T.

C-12
J. S. Torbett

1. I'm in the way, the bright and shin-ing way, I'm in the glo-ry-land way;
2. List to the call, the gos-pel call to-day, Get in the glo-ry-land glo-ry-land way;
3. On-ward I go, re-joic-ing in His love, I'm in the glo-ry-land glo-ry-land way;

Tell-ing the world that Je-sus saves to-day, Yes,
Wan-d'rers come home, O hast-en to o-bey, For I'm in the glo-ry-land way.
Soon I shall see Him in that home a-bove, O glo-ry-land way,

CHORUS

I'm in the glo-ry-land way . . . . .
glo-ry-land way, I'm in the glo-ry-land way;
glo-ry-land . . . way, glo-ry-land way;

Heav - en is near - er and the way grow - eth clear - er, For
I'm in the glo - ry - land way.
glo - ry - land way.

O Lord, Help Us Remember 575

This do in remembrance of Me. Luke 22:19

E minor-4-LA
Tommy L. McClure

L -1

R. J. Stevens

1. O Lord, help us re - mem - ber, As we these em - blems take,
2. O Lord, help us re - mem - ber, The crown of thorns You wore;
3. O Lord, help us re - mem - ber That from the dead You rose;
4. O Lord, help us re - mem - ber Thou art at God's right hand;

Thy suf - f'ring death on Cal - v'ry, For our un - wor - thy sakes.
Al - tho' Thy vi - sion blood - stained, Thy love di - vine out - poured.
The pow'r of God did raise Thee Tri - um - phant o'er Thy foes.
This feast doth show Thy suf - f'ring Un - till You come a - gain.

576 Faith Is The Victory

F-2-SOL

And this is the victory that overcometh the world, even our faith. 1 John 5:4

F-1, V-1

John H. Yates

Ira D. Sankey

1. En-camped a - long the hills of light, Ye Chris - tian sol - diers, rise,
2. His ban - ner o - ver us is love, Our sword the Word of God;
3. On ev - 'ry hand the foe we find Drawn up in dread ar - ray;

And press the bat - tle ere the night Shall veil the glow - ing skies.
We tread the road the saints a - bove With shouts of tri - umph trod.
Let tents of ease be left be - hind, And on - ward to the fray.

A - gainst the foe in vales be - low Let all our strength be hurled;
By faith, they like a whirl-wind's breath, Swept on o'er ev - 'ry field;
Sal - va - tion's hel - met on each head, With truth all girt a - bout,

Faith is the vic - to - ry, we know, That o - ver - comes the world.
The faith by which they conquered Death Is still our shin - ing shield.
The earth shall trem - ble 'neath our tread, And ech - o with our shout.

Faith is the vic-to-ry! Faith is the vic-to-ry!
Faith is the vic-to-ry! Faith is the

O glo-ri-ous vic-to-ry, That o-ver-comes the world.

Soldiers, Who Are Christ's Below 577

C-3-MI
Latin Hymn, 1734

*My reward is with Me, to give to every man according
as his work shall be.* Rev. 22:12

W -1, R -3
Phoebe Palmer Knapp

1. Sol - diers, who are Christ's be - low, Strong in faith re - sist the foe;
2. 'Tis no palm of fad - ing leaves That the con-qu'ror's hand re - ceives;
3. Pass - ing soon and lit - tle worth Are the things that tempt on earth;
4. Fa - ther, who the crown doth give, Sav - ior, by whose death we live,

Bound-less is the pledged re - ward   Un - to them who serve the Lord.
Joys are his, se - rene and pure,   Light that ev - er shall en - dure.
Heav'n-ward lift your soul's re - gard;   God Him-self is your re - ward.
Spir - it, who our hearts doth raise,   Three in One, Thy name we praise.

578 The Old Rugged Cross

But God forbid that I should glory, save in the cross of our Lord Jesus Christ . . .
Gal. 6:14

Bb-2-MI
G. B.

C-17
Geo. Bennard

1. On a hill far a-way stood an old rug-ged cross, The em-blem of suf-f'ring and shame, And I love that old cross where the dear-est and best For a world of lost sin-ners was slain.
2. Oh, that old rug-ged cross, so de-spised by the world, Has a won-drous at-trac-tion for me, For the dear Lamb of God left His glo-ry a-bove, To bear it to dark Cal-va-ry.
3. In the old rug-ged cross, stained with blood so di-vine, A won-drous beau-ty I see; For 'twas on that old cross Je-sus suf-f'red and died, To par-don and sanc-ti-fy me.
4. To the old rug-ged cross, I will ev-er be true, Its shame and re-proach glad-ly bear; Then He'll call me some day to my home far a-way, Where His glo-ry for-ev-er I'll share.

CHORUS

So I'll cher-ish the old rug-ged cross, old, the old rug-ged cross, Till my

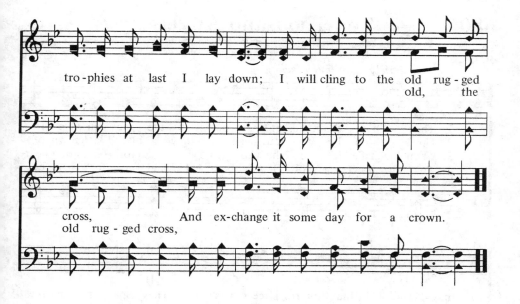

tro-phies at last I lay down; I will cling to the old rug - ged
                                                    old,   the

cross,   And ex-change it some day for a crown.
old rug - ged cross,

I Am Trusting Thee, Lord Jesus   579

Trust ye in the Lord for ever. . . Isa. 26:4

A♭-3-SOL

Frances R. Havergal, 1874

A -1, F -1

Ethelbert W. Bullinger, 1874

1. I   am trust-ing Thee, Lord Je - sus, Trust - ing on - ly Thee;
2. I   am trust-ing Thee to guide me; Thou a - lone shalt lead,
3. I   am trust-ing Thee for pow - er: Thine can nev - er fail;
4. I   am trust-ing Thee, Lord Je - sus; Nev - er let me fall;

Trust - ing Thee for full sal - va - tion, Great   and free.
Ev - ery day and hour sup-ply - ing All   my need.
Words which Thou Thy-self shalt give me Must   pre - vail.
    I   am trust-ing Thee for - ev - er, And   for all. A- men.

580 Ten Thousand Angels

Eb-4-DO
R. O.

Thinkest thou that I cannot now pray to My Father, and He shall . . .
give Me more than twelve legions of angels? Matt. 26:53

C-3, C-4
Ray Overholt

mp Slowly, with much feeling

1. They   bound the hands of Je - sus   in the gar - den where He
2. Up -   on His pre - cious head   they   placed a crown of
3. When they nailed Him to   the Cross,   His   moth - er stood near -
4. To   the howl - ing mob He yield - ed;   He did not for mer - cy

pray'd; They led Him thru the streets in shame. They spat up - on the
thorns; They laugh'd and said, "Be - hold the King." They struck Him and they
by; He said, "Wom-an, be - hold thy son!" He cried, "I thirst for
cry. The Cross of shame He took a - lone. And when He cried, "It's

Sav - ior so   pure and free from sin; They said, "Cru - ci - fy Him
cursed Him and   mocked His ho - ly name. All a - lone He suf-fered
wa - ter," but they gave Him none to drink. Then the sin - ful work of
fin - ished," He   gave Him-self to die; Sal - va - tion's won-drous

CHORUS NOTE: Chorus may be sung once after last stanza.
f *Faster*

He's to blame.
ev - 'ry - thing.   He could have called   ten thou-sand
man was done.
plan was done.

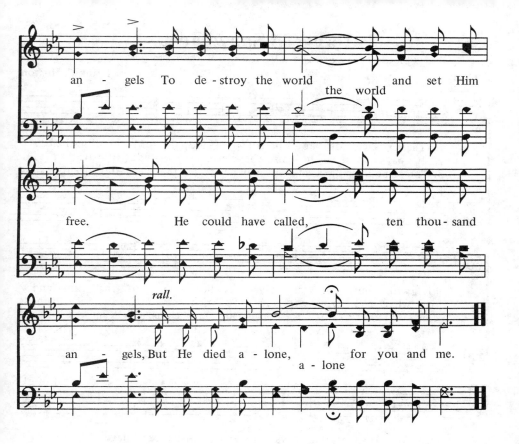

an - gels To de -stroy the world and set Him
the world

free. He could have called, ten thou - sand

rall.

an - gels, But He died a - lone, for you and me.
a - lone

O For A Faith That Will Not Shrink 581

*This is the victory that overcometh
the world, even our faith.* 1 John 5:4

A♭-3-SOL

F -1

William H. Bathurst, 1831

Arr. from Carl Glaser, 1828

1. O for a faith that will not shrink, Tho' pressed by ev - ery foe,
2. A faith that shines more bright and clear When temp- ests rage with- out;
3. Lord, give us such a faith as this; And then, what- e'er may come,

That will not trem- ble on the brink Of an - y earth- ly woe.
That when in dan- ger knows no fear, In dark- ness feels no doubt!
We'll taste e'en here the hal- lowed bliss Of an e - ter - nal home.

582 It Pays To Serve Jesus

Eb-3-SOL
F. C. H.

If any man serve Me, let him follow Me . . . him will My Father honor. John 12:26

E-1, W-4
Frank C. Huston

1. The serv-ice of Je-sus true pleas-ure af-fords, In Him there is
2. It pays to serve Je-sus what-e'er may be-tide, It pays to be
3. Tho sometimes the shad-ows may hang o'er the way, And sor-rows may

joy with-out an al-loy; 'Tis heav-en to trust Him and
true what-e'er you may do; 'Tis rich-es of mer-cy in
come to beck-on us home, Our pre-cious Re-deem-er each

rest on His words; It pays to serve Je-sus each day.
Him to a-bide; It pays to serve Je-sus each day.
toil will re-pay; It pays to serve Je-sus each day.

CHORUS

It
pays to serve Je-sus, it pays ev-'ry day, It pays ev-'ry

step of the way;
ev-'ry step of the way;

Tho' the path-way to glo-ry may

some-times be drear, You'll be hap-py each step of the way.

Take Thou Our Minds, Dear Lord 583

Eb -4-MI
William H. Foulkes, 1918

Now if any man have not the spirit of Christ, he is none of His. Rom. 8:9

P -3, D -1
William H. Monk, 1861

1. Take Thou our minds, dear Lord, we hum-bly pray: Give us the
2. Take Thou our hearts, O Christ, they are Thine own; Come Thou with-
3. Take Thou our wills, most High! Hold Thou full sway; Have in our
4. Take Thou our-selves, O Lord, heart, mind and will; Through our sur-

mind of Christ each pass-ing day; Teach us to know the
in our souls and claim Thy throne; Help us to shed a -
in-most souls Thy per-fect way; Guard Thou each sa - cred
ren-dered souls Thy plans ful - fill. We yield our-selves to

truth that sets us free; Grant us in all our thoughts to hon - or Thee.
broad Thy death-less love; Use us to make the earth like heav'n a - bove.
hour from self-ish ease; Guide Thou our or-dered lives as Thou dost please.
Thee, time, tal-ents, all! We hear, and hence-forth heed Thy sov-'reign call.

584 I Choose Jesus

E♭-2-SOL
James Rowe

For we have not an high priest which cannot be touched with the feelings of our infirmities; but was in all points tempted like as we are . . . Heb. 4:15

C-5, T-1
Samuel W. Beazley

1. When I need some-one in time of grief, Some-one my cheer to be, Je - sus I choose, for He gives re - lief, He is the best for me. I choose Je - sus When I need a friend, . . .
2. When I need some-one to guide my soul, O - ver the storm-y sea, Al - ways to Je - sus I give con-trol, He is the best for me.
3. When I need help to de - feat the foe, Some-one my shield to be, Al - ways to Je - sus in faith I go, He is the best for me.
4. When all my tri - als on earth are o'er, And the dark stream I see, Je - sus shall bear me to yon-der shore, He is the best for me. Yes, I choose my Sav-ior al-ways help-ful

CHORUS

. . . . What I need I Know that He will send;
friend, What I need I know that sure-ly He to me will free-ly send;

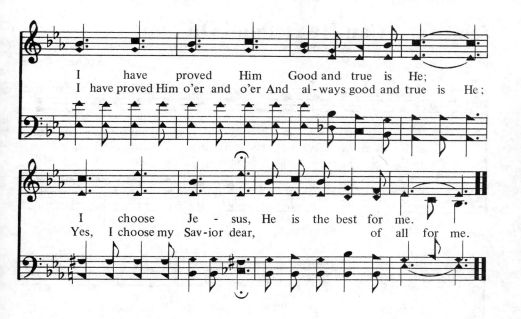

I have proved Him Good and true is He;
I have proved Him o'er and o'er And al-ways good and true is He;

I choose Je-sus, He is the best for me.
Yes, I choose my Sav-ior dear, of all for me.

Christ Is My Savior
585

D-3-DO
Dora Greenwell, 1873

Him hath God exalted with His
right hand to be a . . . Savior. Acts 5:31

C -10, T -1
William J. Kirkpatrick, 1885

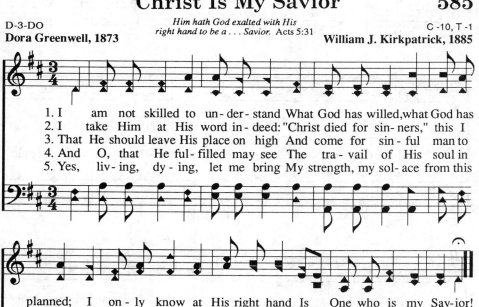

1. I am not skilled to un-der-stand What God has willed, what God has
2. I take Him at His word in-deed: "Christ died for sin-ners," this I
3. That He should leave His place on high And come for sin-ful man to
4. And O, that He ful-filled may see The tra-vail of His soul in
5. Yes, liv-ing, dy-ing, let me bring My strength, my sol-ace from this

planned; I on-ly know at His right hand Is One who is my Sav-ior!
read; For in my heart I find a need Of Him to be my Sav-ior!
die, You count it strange? So once did I, Be-fore I knew my Sav-ior!
me, And with His work con-tent-ed be, As I with my dear Sav-ior!
spring; That He who lives to be my King Once died to be my Sav-ior!

586 Can He Depend On You?

Db-2-DO
W. B.

Be thou faithful unto death, and I will give thee a crown of life. Rev. 2:10

E-1, L-6
Wilkin (Chief) Bacon

1. Je - sus the Sav - ior came down from a - bove, Came to bring
2. He from the grave on the third day a - rose, Mis - sions of
3. He is pre - par - ing in heav - en a home, For all His

mer - cy and love; "Cru - ci - fy Him" the mob scorn-ful - ly
man to dis - close; Go preach the gos - pel, all who will may
faith-ful and own; Are you pre - par - ing to stand by His

cried, So He on Cal - va - ry died; While on the
hear, Thru Him be free from all fear; Bid them be -
side, Or in that day be de - nied? Have you told

cross He prayed, "Fa - ther, for - give, For they know not what they
lieve, to re - pent and o - bey, Walk in the new-ness of
oth - ers the sto - ry of love, Show-ing them what they should

Bless The Lord, O My Soul 587

G-4-SOL
Psalm 103:1

Bless the Lord, O my soul; And all that is within me,
bless His holy name! Psalm 103:1

P-2
Traditional

588 I'll Live On

Bb-4-SOL
T. J. L.

Now if we be dead with Christ, we believe that we shall also live with Him. Rom. 6:8

C-15, T-1
Thos. J. Laney

1. 'Tis a sweet and glo-rious tho't that comes to me, I'll live
2. When my bod-y's ly-ing in the cold, cold clay,
3. In the glo-ry-land, with God up-on the throne,

on, yes, I'll live on; Je-sus saved my soul from death and
yes, I'll live on; I will meet my Je-sus in the
I'll live on, yes, I'll live on; Thru e-ter-nal a-ges sing-ing,

CHORUS

now I'm free, I'll live on, yes, I'll live on. I'll live
judg-ment day,
home, sweet home, I'll live on,

on, yes, I'll live on, Thru e-ter-ni-
and on, and on,

ty I'll live on, and on, I'll live on, and on, yes, I'll live

on,   Thru e-ter-ni-ty I'll live on.
and on,   yes, I'll live on.

As The Deer

*For He satisfied the longing soul, and filleth
the hungry soul with goodness. Psa. 107:9*

W -5, D -1

D-4-MI
Psalm 42:1-2

Martin Nystrom
Arr. by R. J. Stevens

1. As the deer pants— for the wa-ter so my soul longs af-ter You.
2. I want You more than gold or sil-ver, on-ly You can sat-is-fy.

Fine

You a-lone are my heart's de-sire— and I long to wor-ship You.
You a-lone are the real joy-giv-er, and the ap-ple of my eye.

D.S. You a-lone are my heart's de-sire and I long to wor-ship You.

D.S. al Fine

You a-lone are my strength, my shield; to You a-lone may my spir-it yield.

590 He Will Pilot Me

A♭-4-SOL

And He arose . . . and said unto the sea, Peace be still. And the wind ceased, and there was a great calm. Mark 4:39

G-3

Charles T. Bailey

Byron L. Whitworth

1. Al - tho' I can - not see the way, O'er life's tem - pes - tuous
2. Dark clouds may gath - er in the sky, And rough the sea may
3. Dear Lord, what - e'er the storm may be, I'll sim - ply trust in

sea, dark sea, I know that Je - sus is my Friend, And that He'll
be, may be; His love shall ev - er be my song, I know He'll
Thee, in Thee, Re - ly - ing on Thy love so true, To safe - ly

CHORUS

pi - lot me. By His hand He'll pi - lot me,
pi - lot me. He'll pi - - - lot me from

O - ver life's tem - pestuous sea, When my blind - ed eyes can't see,
day to day, When blind - - - ed eyes can't

Can not see the way, the way; Come what may, let
see the way; Let come what

come what may, On life's dark and storm-y sea, My dear Lord,
may on life's dark sea, My bless - -

bless - ed Lord, He will pi - lot, pi - lot me.
ed Lord will pi - - - lot me.

Lord, Increase Our Faith 591

A♭-4-SOL
Craig A. Roberts

Lord, increase our faith. Luke 17:5

F -1, E -1
R. J. Stevens

1. Lord, may our faith be like A-bra-ham's, Our path, the path he trod;
2. Like oth-er's faith, Lord, may our faith be, At work in times of fear,
3. Lord, may we be like the pa-tient man, Whose faith could long en-dure,
4. And may our pray'rs, like the faith-ful pray'rs Of pro-phets long a-go,

Our gifts from Thee, sac-ri-ficed as alms, Our name, the "Friend of God."
Pro-tect-ing men who would die for Thee On no-ble mis-sions here.
Though blessed by Thee, tried and blessed a-gain, In all, re-main-ing pure.
Call down Thy pow'r, so that ev-'ry-where, The cause of Christ will grow.

592 I Want To Be Ready To Meet Him

F-4-SOL

Be ye therefore ready also: for the Son of man cometh at an hour when ye think not.
Luke 12:40

S-2

Adger M. Pace   **G. T. Speer**

1. You may have your world-ly pleas-ures, your sil - ver and your gold,
2. You may talk a - bout your rich - es, your diamonds and your pearls,
3. There is one thing I can boast of, sal - va - tion from the fall,

You may pile up all the rich - es that this old world can hold;
You may gain the wealth for a - ges of this and all the worlds,
I'm an heir to wealth in glo - ry, my Fa - ther owns it all;

D. S.–to meet Him in the sky;

But I'd rath - er have my Sav - ior, and with Him firm - ly
But the Sav - ior is more pre - cious, with Him I'll take my
That is why I'm shout - ing hap - py and go at His com -

Oh, I want to be more like Him, and do His blest com -

stand,
stand, For I want to be read - y to meet Him in the
mand,

mand,

Fine CHORUS

glo - ry - land. I want to be read - y to
I want to be read - y

D. S.

meet Him by and by, I want to be read - y
I want to be read - y

Rejoice, The Lord Is King 593

Db-4-DO

Charles Wesley, 1746

But we see Jesus . . . crowned with glory and honor. Heb. 2:9

C -6, J 1

John Darwall, 1770

1. Re - joice, the Lord is King: Your Lord and King a - dore! Re -
2. Je - sus the Sav - ior reigns, The God of truth and love; When
3. Re - joice in glo - rious hope! Our Lord the Judge shall come, And

joice, give thanks, and sing, And tri - umph ev - er - more: Lift up your
He had purged our stains He took His seat a - bove: Lift up your
take his ser - vants up To their e - ter - nal home. Lift up your

heart, lift up your voice! Re - joice, a - gain I say, re - joice!
heart, lift up your voice! Re - joice, a - gain I say, re - joice!
heart, lift up your voice! Re - joice, a - gain I say, re - joice! A - men.

594 The Lily Of The Valley

I am the offspring of David, the bright and morning star. Rev. 22:16

F-4-MI

A-1, C-5
English Melody

1. I have found a friend in Je-sus, He's ev-'ry-thing to me,
2. O He all my griefs has tak-en, and all my sor-rows borne;
3. He will nev-er, nev-er leave me, nor yet for-sake me here,

He's the fair-est of ten-thou-sand to my soul;
In temp-ta-tion He's my strong and might-y tow'r;
While I live by faith and do His bless-ed will;

The Lil-y of the Val-ley, in Him a-lone I see
I have all for Him for-sak-en, and all my i-dols torn
A wall of fire a-bout me, I've noth-ing now to fear,

D.S.-Lil-y of the Val-ley, the bright and morn-ing star,

Fine

All I need to cleanse and make me ful-ly whole.
From my heart, and now He keeps me by His pow'r.
With His man-na He my hun-gry soul shall fill.

He's the fair-est of ten-thou-sand to my soul.

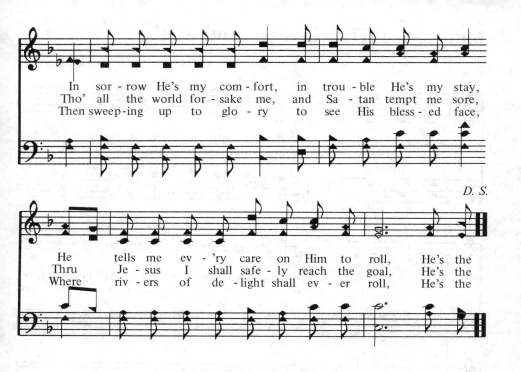

In sor-row He's my com-fort, in trou-ble He's my stay,
Tho' all the world for-sake me, and Sa-tan tempt me sore,
Then sweep-ing up to glo-ry to see His bless-ed face,

D. S.

He tells me ev-'ry care on Him to roll, He's the
Thru Je-sus I shall safe-ly reach the goal, He's the
Where riv-ers of de-light shall ev-er roll, He's the

Cross Of Jesus, Cross Of Sorrow 595

Christ also . . . suffered for sins, the just for
the unjust. 1 Pet. 3:18

F-3-MI
C -2

William J. Sparrow-Simpson, 1887

John B. Dykes, 1862

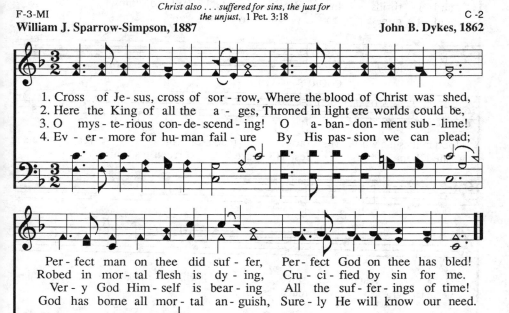

1. Cross of Je-sus, cross of sor-row, Where the blood of Christ was shed,
2. Here the King of all the a-ges, Throned in light ere worlds could be,
3. O mys-te-rious con-de-scend-ing! O a-ban-don-ment sub-lime!
4. Ev-er-more for hu-man fail-ure By His pas-sion we can plead;

Per-fect man on thee did suf-fer, Per-fect God on thee has bled!
Robed in mor-tal flesh is dy-ing, Cru-ci-fied by sin for me.
Ver-y God Him-self is bear-ing All the suf-fer-ings of time!
God has borne all mor-tal an-guish, Sure-ly He will know our need.

596 His Grace Reaches Me

C-3-MI
W. G.

That being justified by His grace, we should be made
heirs according to the hope of eternal life. Tit. 3:7

G-2, J-1
Whitey Gleason

Slowly

1. Deep-er than the o-cean and wid-er than the sea, Is the
2. High-er than the moun-tains and bright-er than the sun, It was

grace of the Sav-ior for sin-ners like me; Sent from the Fa-ther,
of-fered at Cal-v'ry for ev-'ry-one; Great-est of treas-ures,

and it thrills my soul, Just to feel and to know that His
and it's mine to-day, Tho' my sins were as scar-let, He has

CHORUS

blood makes me whole. His grace reach-es me, yes, His
washed them a-way. Yes, His grace reach-es me,

grace reach-es me, And 'twill last thru e-ter - ni-
yes, His grace reach-es me,

ty;   Now I'm un-der His con-trol and I'm hap-py in my

soul, Just   to know   that His grace reach-es me.
Just to know,

O For A Closer Walk With God   597

F-3-DO
William Cowper, 1779

*What doth the Lord require of thee . . . to walk
humbly with thy God. Micah 6:8*

F -2, D -1
John B. Dykes, 1868

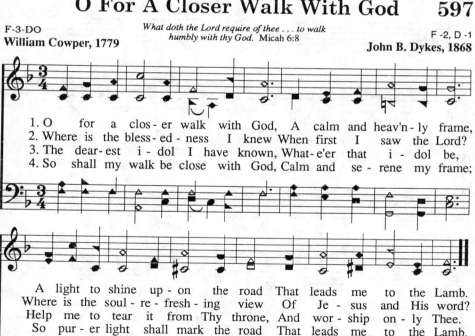

1. O   for a clos-er walk with God, A calm and heav'n-ly frame,
2. Where is the bless-ed-ness I knew When first I saw the Lord?
3. The dear-est i-dol I have known, What-e'er that i - dol be,
4. So shall my walk be close with God, Calm and se-rene my frame;

A light to shine up-on the road That leads me to the Lamb.
Where is the soul-re-fresh-ing view Of Je-sus and His word?
Help me to tear it from Thy throne, And wor-ship on-ly Thee.
So pur-er light shall mark the road That leads me to the Lamb.

598 You Never Mentioned Him To Me

S-5

Take heed unto thyself, and unto the doctrine; continue in them:
for in doing this thou shalt both save thyself, and them that hear thee. 1 Tim. 4:16

Ab-3-MI

James Rowe

J. W. Gaines
Arr. H. F. M.

1. When in the bet-ter land be - fore the
2. O let us spread the word wher - e'er it
3. A few sweet words may guide a lost one

bar we stand, How deep - ly grieved our souls may be;
may be heard, Help grop - ing souls the light to see,
to His side, Or turn sad eyes on Cal - va - ry;

If an - y lost one there should cry in deep de -
That yon - der none may say, "You showed me not the
So work as days go by, that yon - der none may

REFRAIN

spair, "You nev - er mentioned Him to me."
way, You nev - er mentioned Him to me." "You nev - er
cry, "You nev - er mentioned Him to me."

men-tioned Him to me, You helped me not the light to

see; You met me day by day and knew I

was a - stray, Yet nev - er men-tioned Him to me."

We Bow Down In Reverence 599

Thou hast heard my voice: hide not Thine ear at my cry . . . Lam. 3:56

P-3, P-2

Bb-2-SOL

G. B. S.

Glenda B. Schales
Arr. by R. J. Stevens

1. Please hear our prayer, ho- ly God, Oh let our words come to Thee.
2. Now we ap- proach in Thy love; We know Thou hear - est our plea.
3. For hum - bly now do we bow Be - fore Thy throne prais-ing Thee.

We bow down in rev - 'rence for we be - lieve.
We bow in Thy pres-ence and seek Thee in rev-'rence in Thee.

600
I Want To Be Like Jesus

D-2-MI

T. O. Chisholm

God anointed Jesus of Nazareth . . . who went about doing good,
and healing all that were oppressed . . . Acts 10:38

C-13

David L. Ives

1. I have one deep, su-preme de-sire, That I may be like
2. He spent His life in do-ing good; I want to be like
3. Oh, per-fect life of Christ my Lord! I want to be like

Je - sus. To this I fer-vent-ly as-pire, That I may
Je - sus. In low-ly paths of ser-vice trod; I want to
Je - sus. My rec-om-pense and my re-ward, That I may

be like Je - sus. I want my heart His throne to be,
be like Je - sus. He sym-pa-thized with hearts dis-tressed;
be like Je - sus. His Spir-it fill my hun-g'ring soul,

So that a watch-ing world may see His like-ness
He spoke the words that cheered and blessed; He wel-comed
His pow-er all my life con-trol; My deep-est

shin - ing forth in me. I want to be like Je - sus.
sin - ners to His breast. I want to be like Je - sus.
pray'r, my high - est goal, That I may be like Je - sus.

Psalm 113

601

G-2-DO

Tune: Lord We Come Before Thee Now

P-2

Psalm 113

Arr. from H. A. C. Malan, 1823

1. Praise Je - ho - vah; Praise the Lord; Ye His ser - vants,
2. From the dawn to set - ting sun, Praise the Lord, the
3. Who is like the Lord our God? High in heav'n is

praise ac - cord; Bless - ed be Je - ho - vah's name; Ev - er -
Migh - ty One. O'er all na - tions He is high; Yea, His
His a - bode, Who Him - self doth hum - ble low Things in

more His praise pro - claim, Ev - er - more His praise pro - claim.
glo - ry crowns the sky, Yea, His glo - ry crowns the sky.
heav'n and earth to know, Things in heav'n and earth to know.

602 O For A Child-like Heart

F-3-SOL

In malice be ye children. 1 Cor 14:20

D-1, P-3

Huey P. Hartsell

R. J. Stevens

1. O for a child-like heart in me, To serve You, Lord, in
2. The lit-tle ones are mal-ice free, I'll put a-way all
3. Their hum-ble minds speak hon-est-ly, So I will live by
4. In child-like trust I come to Thee; My way, dear Lord, I

pu-ri-ty; And hold Your hand so close each day, Till
en-mi-ty; With o-pen mind to seek Your way, I'll
Your de-cree; To feel for all hurt in life's way, And
can-not see. I'll nev-er fear the un-seen way, My

CHORUS

I'm called home with You to stay.
let Your steps lead ev'-ry day.
love all souls who are lost to-day. O for a child-like
Fa-ther will not lead a-stray.

heart in me, to serve You, Lord, in pu-ri-ty; Till by Thy

grace a crown I'll wear, for-ev-er in Your love and care.

Burdens Are Lifted At Calvary 603

F-2-MI
J. M. M.

*Surely He has borne our griefs,
and carried our sorrows.* Isa. 53:4

C-3
John M. Moore, 1952

1. Days are filled with sor-row and care, Hearts are lone - ly and drear;
2. Cast your care on Je - sus to-day, Leave your wor - ry and fear;
3. Trou - bled soul, the Sav - ior can see Ev - 'ry heart-ache and tear;

Bur - dens are lift - ed at Cal - va - ry, Je - sus is ver - y near.
Bur - dens are lift - ed at Cal - va - ry, Je - sus is ver - y near.
Bur - dens are lift - ed at Cal - va - ry, Je - sus is ver - y near.

CHORUS

Bur - dens are lift - ed at Cal - va - ry, Cal - va - ry, Cal - va - ry;

Bur - dens are lift - ed at Cal - va - ry, Je - sus is ver - y near.

604 I'm The One

Db-4-SOL
R. O.

C-3, T-1
Ray Overholt

All we like sheep have gone astray; we have turned every one to his own way;
and the Lord hath laid on Him the iniquity of us all. Isa 53:6

1. I was not in the gar-den when He knelt to God and prayed,
2. I was not at the tri-al when the crowd jeered at His name,
3. I was not on the hill-side when He gave His life that day,

I did not kiss Him on the cheek when Je-sus was be-trayed;
I did not make Him bear a cross or walk a road of shame;
I did not nail His pre-cious hands or take His robe a-way;

I could not do a sin-gle thing to hurt God's on-ly Son, But
I could not do a sin-gle thing to hurt God's on-ly Son, But
I could not do a sin-gle thing to hurt God's on-ly Son, But

ev-'ry time I sin on earth I feel that I'm the one.
ev-'ry time I sin on earth I feel that I'm the one.
ev-'ry time I sin on earth I feel that I'm the one.

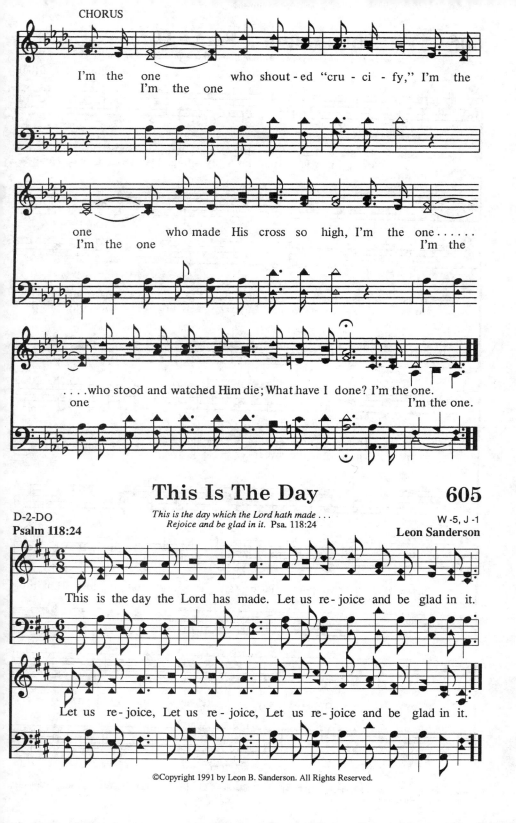

CHORUS

I'm the one who shout-ed "cru - ci - fy," I'm the
I'm the one

one who made His cross so high, I'm the one......
I'm the one I'm the

....who stood and watched Him die; What have I done? I'm the one.
one I'm the one.

This Is The Day

605

D-2-DO
Psalm 118:24

This is the day which the Lord hath made . . .
Rejoice and be glad in it. Psa. 118:24

W -5, J -1
Leon Sanderson

This is the day the Lord has made. Let us re - joice and be glad in it.

Let us re - joice, Let us re - joice, Let us re - joice and be glad in it.

606 The Longer I Serve Him

Serve the Lord with gladness: come before His presence with singing. Psa. 110:2

Ab-3-SOL

W. J. G.

W-4

William J. Gaither

1. Since I start - ed for the King - dom, Since my life He con-
2. Ev - 'ry need He is sup - ply - ing, Plen-teous grace He be -

trols, Since I gave my heart to Je - sus, The long- er I
stows; Ev - 'ry day my way gets bright-er, The long- er I

serve Him, the sweet - er He grows.
serve Him, the sweet - er He grows.

CHORUS

The long - er I

serve Him the sweet - er He grows, The more that I love Him, more

love He be - stows; Each day is like heav - en, my heart o - ver-

flows, The long-er I serve Him, the sweet-er He grows.

Psalm 25

607

Tune: Blest Be The Tie

F-3-MI
Psalm 25:1-7

P-3

Johann Georg Nageli
Arr. Lowell Mason, 1845

1. To Thee I lift my soul, O Lord; I
2. Yea, none that wait on Thee Shall be a-
3. Show me Thy ways, O Lord; Thy paths, O
4. For Thou art God that dost To me sal-

trust in Thee, My God, let me not
shamed at all: But those that wan-ton-
teach Thou me: And do Thou lead me
va-tion send, And I up-on Thee

be a-shamed Nor foes ex-ult o'er me.
ly trans-gress, Up-on them shame shall fall.
in Thy truth; There-in my teach-er be.
all the day Ex-pect-ing do at-tend.

608   The Love Of God

Eb-3-DO

F. M. L.

Who shall separate us . . . from the love of God, which is in Christ Jesus our Lord.
Rom. 8:35-39

L-5

F. M. Lehman

Arr. by Claudia Lehman Mays

1. The love of God is great-er far   Than tongue or
2. When hoar-y time shall pass a-way,   And earth-ly
3. Could we with ink the o-cean fill,   And were the

pen can ev-er tell; It goes be-yond the high-est star,
thrones and king-doms fall; When men who here re-fuse to pray,
skies of parch-ment made; Were ev-'ry stalk on earth a quill,

And reach-es to the low-est hell; The guilt-y pair bowed
On rocks and hills and moun-tains call; God's love, so sure, shall
And ev-'ry man a scribe by trade; To write the love of

down with care,   God gave His Son   to win; His err-ing
still en-dure,   All meas-ure-less   and strong; Re-deem-ing
God a-bove   Would drain the o-cean dry; Nor could the

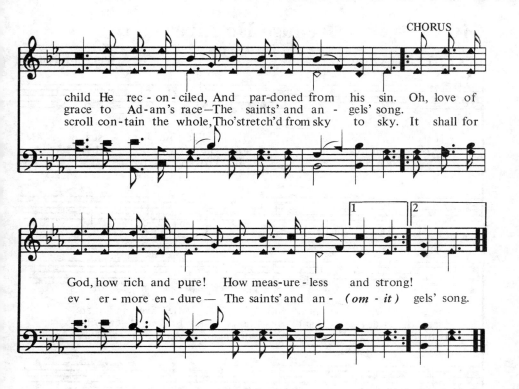

child He rec - on - ciled, And par-doned from his sin. Oh, love of
grace to Ad - am's race—The saints' and an - gels' song.
scroll con - tain the whole, Tho' stretch'd from sky to sky. It shall for

1 | 2

God, how rich and pure! How meas-ure-less and strong!
ev - er - more en - dure— The saints' and an - *(om - it)* gels' song.

Psalm 148

609

Tune: When My Love To Christ Grows Weak

C-3-MI
Psalm 148

P -2
Phoebe Palmer Knapp

1. Praise the Lord, His glo - ries show, Saints with - in His courts be - low,
2. Earth to heav'n and heav'n to earth, Tell His won - ders, sing His worth,
3. Praise the Lord, His mer - cies trace, Praise His prov - i - dence and grace,

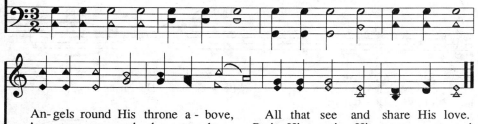

An - gels round His throne a - bove, All that see and share His love.
Age to age and shore to shore, Praise Him, praise Him ev - er - more!
All that He for man hath done, All He sends us through His Son.

610 Because He Lives

Because I live, ye shall live also. John 14:19

Bb-4-SOL

W. J. G. and Gloria Gaither

C-12, T-1

William J. Gaither

1. God sent His Son, They called Him Je - sus, He
2. How sweet to hold our new-born ba - by, And
3. And then one day I'll cross that riv - er, I'll

came to love heal and for - give; He lived and died
feel the pride and joy he gives; But great - er still,
fight life's fi - nal war with pain; And then as death

to buy my par - don, An emp - ty grave is there to prove my
the calm as - sur - ance, This child can face un - cer - tain days be -
gives way to vic - t'ry, I'll see the lights of glo - ry and I'll

CHORUS

Sav - ior lives.
cause He lives.
know He reigns. Be - cause He lives

I can face to-mor-row, Be-cause He lives all fear is gone; Be-cause I know He holds the fu-ture, And life is worth the liv-ing, just be-cause He lives.

Father Of Mercy

611

D♭-3-MI
Unknown

Lord, hear; O Lord forgive, O Lord,
hearken, and do. Dan. 9:19

P-3
Arr. from Handel

Fa-ther of Mer-cy, we bow be-fore Thee;

Bless us, O— bless us, and hear— our prayer. A-men.

612 Love Lifted Me

Bb-2-SOL
James Rowe

L-4

He was afraid; and beginning to sink, he cried, Lord, save me.
And immediately Jesus stretched forth His hand . . . Matt. 14:30,31

Howard E. Smith

1. I was sink-ing deep in sin, Far from the peace-ful shore,
2. All my heart to Him I give, Ev-er to Him I cling,
3. Souls in dan-ger, look a-bove, Je-sus com-plete-ly saves;

Ver-y deep-ly stained with-in, Sink-ing to rise no more;
In His bless-ed pres-ence live, Ev-er His prais-es sing,
He will lift you by His love, Out of the an-gry waves,

But the Mas-ter of the sea Heard my de-spair-ing cry,
Love so might-y and so true Mer-its my soul's best songs,
He's the Mas-ter of the sea, Bil-lows His will o-bey;

CHORUS

From the wa-ters lift-ed me, Now safe am I.
Faith-ful, lov-ing ser-vice, too, To Him be-longs. Love lift-ed
He your Sav-ior wants to be — Be saved to-day.

me! Love lift - ed me! When noth - ing
e - ven me! e - ven me!

else could help, Love lift - ed me, Love lift - ed me.

Come My Soul, Your Plea Prepare 613

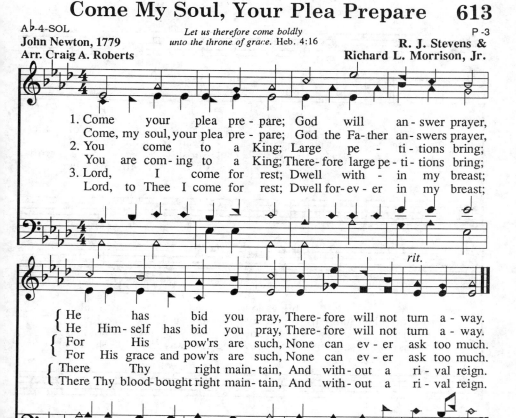

A♭-4-SOL

John Newton, 1779
Arr. Craig A. Roberts

Let us therefore come boldly
unto the throne of grace. Heb. 4:16

P -3

R. J. Stevens &
Richard L. Morrison, Jr.

1. Come   your   plea pre - pare; God   will   an - swer prayer,
   Come, my soul, your plea pre - pare; God the Fa - ther an - swers prayer,
2. You   come   to   a King; Large   pe - ti - tions bring;
   You   are com - ing to   a King; There - fore large pe - ti - tions bring;
3. Lord,   I   come for   rest; Dwell   with - in   my breast;
   Lord, to Thee I come for   rest; Dwell for - ev - er   in   my breast;

{ He   has   bid   you   pray, There - fore will not turn a - way.
{ He   Him - self has bid   you   pray, There - fore will not turn a - way.
{ For   His   pow'rs are   such, None can ev - er   ask too much.
{ For   His grace and pow'rs are   such, None can ev - er   ask too much.
{ There   Thy   right main - tain, And with - out a   ri - val reign.
{ There   Thy blood - bought right main - tain, And with - out a   ri - val reign.

614

Eb-2-DO
D. O.

The Fruit Of The Spirit

But the fruit of the Spirit is love, joy, peace . . . Gal. 5:22

E-1, H-4
Dusty Owens
Arr. by R. J. Stevens
and Margie Garrett

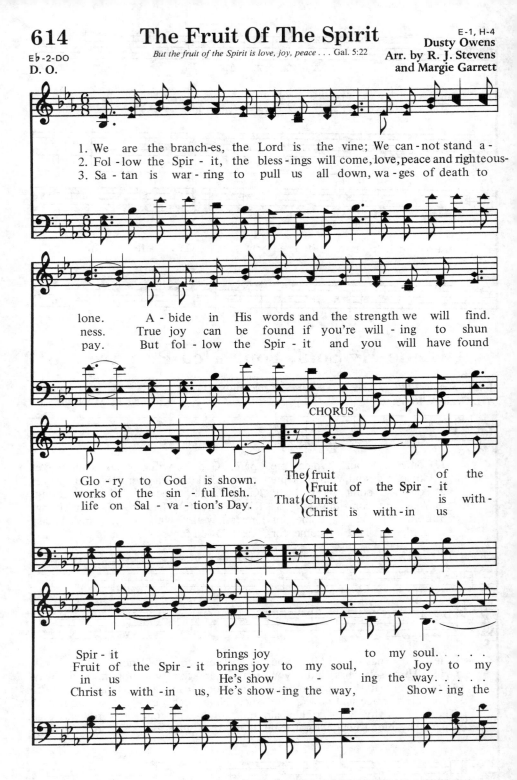

1. We are the branch-es, the Lord is the vine; We can-not stand a-
2. Fol-low the Spir-it, the bless-ings will come, love, peace and righteous-
3. Sa-tan is war-ring to pull us all down, wa-ges of death to

lone. A - bide in His words and the strength we will find.
ness. True joy can be found if you're will - ing to shun
pay. But fol - low the Spir - it and you will have found

CHORUS

Glo - ry to God is shown. The fruit of the
works of the sin - ful flesh. Fruit of the Spir - it
life on Sal - va - tion's Day. That Christ is with -
Christ is with - in us

Spir - it brings joy to my soul. . . .
Fruit of the Spir - it brings joy to my soul, Joy to my
in us He's show - ing the way. . . . .
Christ is with - in us, He's show - ing the way, Show - ing the

soul. The fruit of the Spir-it
fruit of the Spir-it, fruit of the Spir-it is

way.

how we may know E-ter-nal life He will
is how

give us, We'll har-vest the fruit on that day.

Father, I Adore You

615

The grace of the Lord Jesus Christ, and the love of God,
and the communion of the Holy Spirit, be with you all. II Cor. 13:14

F-4-DO
T. C.

H-4, P-2
Terrye Coelho
arr. by D. Shepard

1. Fa-ther,
2. Je-sus, I a-dore You, Lay my life be-fore You, How I love You!
3. Spir-it,

* Denotes round

616 Into Our Hands

G-3-SOL
But as we were allowed of God to be put in trust with the gospel, even so we speak... S-5

Mrs. Roy Carruth I Thess. 2:4 **Tillit S. Teddlie**

1. Swift-ly we're turn-ing life's dai-ly pag-es, Swift-ly the
2. Mil-lions are grop-ing with-out the gos-pel, Quick-ly they'll
3. Souls that are pre-cious, souls that are dy-ing, While we re-

hours are chang-ing to years; How are we us-ing
reach e-ter-ni-ty's night; Shall we sit id-ly
joice our sins are for-giv'n; Did He not al-so

God's gold-en mo-ments? Shall we reap glo-ry? Shall we reap
as they rush on-ward? Haste, let us hold up Christ the true
die for these lost ones? Then let us point the way un-to

CHORUS

tears?
light. In-to our hands the gos-pel is giv-en, In-to our
heav'n.

hands is giv-en the light, Haste, let us car-ry God's pre-cious

mess - age, Guid - ing the err - ing back to the right.

I Will Remember Thee 617

This do in remembrance of Me. 1 Cor. 11:24

F-4-MI

James Montgomery, 1825

L -1, G 1

Arthur Cottman, 1874

1. Ac - cord - ing to Thy gra - cious Word, In meek hu - mil - i - ty,
2. Thy bod - y, bro - ken for my sake, My bread from heav'n shall be;
3. Geth - sem - a - ne can I for - get? Or there Thy con - flict see,
4. When to the cross I turn mine eyes, And rest on Cal - va - ry,

This will I do, my dy - ing Lord, I will re - mem - ber Thee.
Thy tes - ta - men - tal cup I take, And thus re - mem - ber Thee.
Thine ag - o - ny and blood - y sweat, And not re - mem - ber Thee?
O Lamb of God, my Sac - ri - fice, I must re - mem - ber Thee.

618 Let Me Live Close To Thee

F-4-MI

For in Him we live, and move, and have our being. Acts 17:28

C-12

J. R. Baxter, Jr.

Virgil O. Stamps

1. In Thy field I would wield sick-les brave and true, In the fight for the
2. Not the crown nor re - nown that the world might see, I would work, nev-er
3. Help me bear and to share some poor pil-grim's load, Be my friend to the

right I would dare and do, Spend my days in Thy praise all the jour - ney
shirk, bless-ed Lord, for Thee, But to know where I go that my soul is
end of the toil-some road, I would sing to my King in the soul's a-

CHORUS

thru,
free, Let me live close to Thee each day. Let me live
bode,
Let me live

close to Thee, Take my hand, dear Lord, and guide me all a-
close to Thee, Guide me all a-

long the rug-ged way; O let me live close to Thee,
long the way; Let me live close to

Let me walk and talk with Thee, dear Lord, each day.
Thee, Let me walk close to Thee each day.

Speak, Lord, In The Stillness 619

Speak, Lord; For Thy servant heareth. 1 Sam. 3:9

D♭-4-DO
E. May Grimes, 1920

C -16, P -3
Harold Green, c. 1925

1. Speak, Lord, in the still-ness While I wait on Thee;
2. Speak, O bless-ed Mas-ter, In this qui-et hour;
3. For the words Thou speak-est, They are life in-deed;
4. All to Thee is yield-ed, I am not my own;

Hushed my heart to lis-ten In ex-pect-an-cy.
Let me see Thy face, Lord, Feel Thy touch of power.
Liv-ing bread from heav-en, Now my spir-it feed!
Bliss-ful, glad sur-ren-der, I am Thine a-lone. A-men.

620 Room In God's Kingdom

B♭-4-MI
J. R. B., Jr.

Whosoever shall give . . . a cup of cold water only in the name of a disciple . . .
shall in no wise lose his reward. Matt. 10:42

K-1
J. R. Baxter, Jr.

1. There is room in the king-dom of God, my broth-er, For the small
2. Just a cup of cold wa-ter in His name giv-en May the hope
3. There's a place in the serv-ice of God for work-ers Who are loy-

things that you can do; (you can do;) Just a small, kind-ly deed
in some heart re-new; (hope re-new;) Do not wait to be told,
al to Him and true; (loy-al, true;) Can't you say to Him now,

CHORUS

that may cheer an-oth-er Is the work God has planned for you. There is
nor by sor-row driv-en To the work God has planned for you.
"I will leave the shirk-ers, And the work Thou hast planned I'll do." There is

room, there's a place In the king-
room in the king-dom, there's a place in the serv-ice,

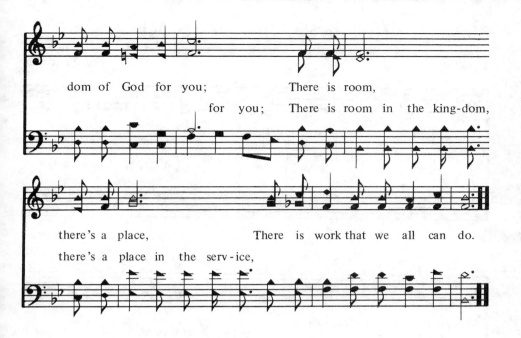

dom of God for you; There is room,

for you; There is room in the king-dom,

there's a place, There is work that we all can do.

there's a place in the serv-ice,

God, Who Touches Earth With Beauty 621

F-2-MI

He hath made everything beautiful in His time. Eccl. 3:11

C -16, P -3

Mary S. Edgar, 1925

C. Harold Lowden, 1925

1. God who touch-es earth with beau-ty, Make my heart a-new;
2. Like Your springs and run-ning wa-ters Make me crys-tal pure,
3. Like the arch-ing of the heav-ens Lift my thoughts a-bove,
4. God who touch-es earth with beau-ty, Make my heart a-new;

With your Spir-it re-cre-ate me, Pure and strong and true.
Like Your rocks of tow-'ring gran-deur Make me strong and sure.
Turn my dreams to no-ble ac-tion, Min-is-tries of love.
Keep me ev-er, by Your Spir-it, Pure and strong and true. A-men.

622 In The Service Of My King

A♭-4-SOL
T. S. T.

Serve the Lord with gladness: come before His presence with singing. Psa. 100:2

S-5, W-4

Tillit S. Teddlie

1. To the har-vest fields I will glad-ly go, In the serv-ice.....
2. Let me ev-er work with a will-ing hand,
3. Let me win some soul that his life may be,
4. Just a kind-ly word or a song or pray'r, In the bless-ed

..... of my King; With a song of love to the faint and
Guid-ed by His word, heed-ing each com-
Let me sing some song that will make me
serv-ice of my King; That the lost may turn and His glo-ry

CHORUS

low, In the serv-ice of my King! In the
mand,
free,
share, In the bless-ed serv-ice of my King! In the

serv-ice of my King, In the
bless-ed serv-ice of my King, my heav-en-ly King! In the

3

serv - ice of my King! It is glo - ry here,
bless - ed serv - ice of my King! of my King!

joy be - yond com - pare, In the serv - ice of my King!
In the bless - ed serv - ice of my King!

Psalm 145

623

A b-3-MI
Psalm 145

Tune: Jesus Calls Us

P -2
William H. Jude, 1887

1. God, my King, Thy might con - fess - ing, Ev - er will I bless Thy name:
2. Full of kind - ness and com - pass - ion, Slow to an - ger, vast in love,
3. All Thy works, O Lord, shall bless Thee; Thee shall all Thy saints a - dore;

Day by day Thy throne ad - dress - ing, Still will I Thy praise pro - claim.
God is good to all cre - a - tion; All His works His good - ness prove.
King su - preme shall they con - fess Thee, And pro - claim Thy sov - 'reign pow'r.

624 We'll Be Like Him

When He shall appear, we shall be like Him; for we shall see Him as He is. 1 John 3:2

B♭-4-MI
R. L. P.

S-2
R. L. Powell

1. When the Sav - ior comes for His chos - en ones, We'll be like
2. Let the mes-sage ring o - ver hill and plain,
3. He's the One we love, He's the One we prove,
4. Tho' He tar - ry long, this will be our song, We'll be like our

Him, We'll be like Him; When the bright day breaks and the
Send it far and wide on the
He's the One who cheers thro' the
King when He comes a - gain; Tho' the path be dim we will

dead a - wakes; We'll be like Him when He comes.
gos - pel tide; We'll be like Him when He comes.
wea - ry years; We'll be like Him when He comes.
cling to Him; We'll be like Him when He comes.
when He comes,

CHORUS

We'll be like Him, sing the glad re - frain; We'll be
We'll be like our King,

like Him when He comes a-gain; Bless-ed tho't to me that His
our King

face I'll see, And be like Him when He comes.
when He comes.

One Sweetly Solemn Thought   **625**

D-4-SOL

*For now is our salvation nearer
than when we believed.* Rom. 13:11

H -2, F -2

Phoebe Cary, 1852

R. S. Ambrose

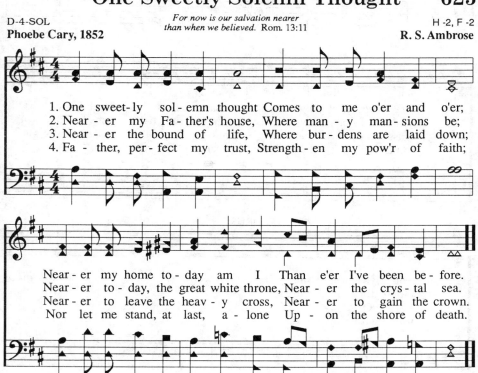

1. One sweet-ly sol-emn thought Comes to me o'er and o'er;
2. Near-er my Fa-ther's house, Where man-y man-sions be;
3. Near-er the bound of life, Where bur-dens are laid down;
4. Fa-ther, per-fect my trust, Strength-en my pow'r of faith;

Near-er my home to-day am I Than e'er I've been be-fore.
Near-er to-day, the great white throne, Near-er the crys-tal sea.
Near-er to leave the heav-y cross, Near-er to gain the crown.
Nor let me stand, at last, a-lone Up-on the shore of death.

626 It Is Well With My Soul

But God will redeem my soul from the power of the grave: for He will receive me. Psa. 49:15

D♭-4-SOL

H. G. Spafford

P-1, T-1

Phillip P. Bliss

1. When peace like a riv - er, at - tend - eth my
2. Tho' Sa - tan should buf - fet, tho' tri - als should
3. My sin— O the bliss of this glo - ri - ous
4. And, Lord, haste the day when the faith shall be

way, When sor - rows like sea bil - lows roll, What - ev - er my
come, Let this blest as - sur - ance con - trol, That Christ hath re -
tho't!—My sin— not in part but the whole, Is nailed to His
sight, The clouds be rolled back as a scroll, The trump shall re -

lot, Thou hast taught me to say, "It is well, it is
gard - ed my help - less es - tate, And hath shed His own
cross and I bear it no more, Praise the Lord, praise the
sound, and the Lord shall de - scend, "E - ven so" it is

CHORUS

well with my soul." It is well, with my
blood for my soul.
Lord, O my soul!
well with my soul. It is well,

soul,   It is well, it is well with my soul.
with my soul,

Like A Little Child   627

E♭-4-DO
Sherry Cecil

*Whosoever therefore shall humble himself
as this little child, the same is the greatest
in the Kingdom of Heaven.* Matt. 18:4

P -3, F -2
Steve Goff
Arr. by R. J. Stevens

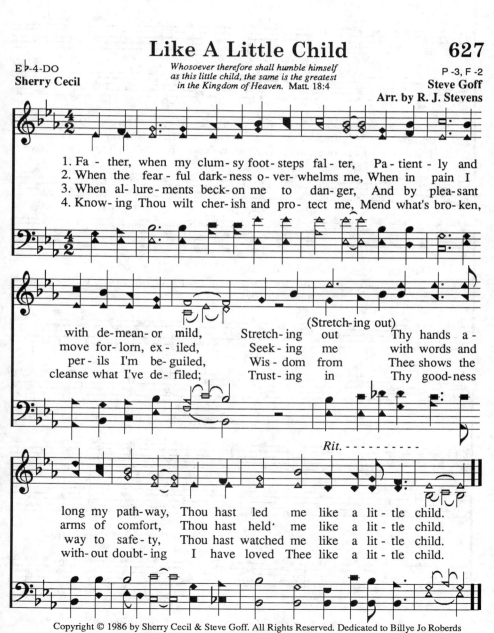

1. Fa - ther, when my clum-sy foot-steps fal-ter, Pa-tient-ly and
2. When the fear-ful dark-ness o-ver-whelms me, When in pain I
3. When al-lure-ments beck-on me to dan-ger, And by plea-sant
4. Know-ing Thou wilt cher-ish and pro-tect me, Mend what's bro-ken,

(Stretch-ing out)

with de-mean-or mild,   Stretch-ing out   Thy hands a-
move for-lorn, ex-iled,   Seek-ing me   with words and
per-ils I'm be-guiled,   Wis-dom from   Thee shows the
cleanse what I've de-filed;   Trust-ing in   Thy good-ness

Rit. - - - - - - - - - -

long my path-way, Thou hast led   me like a lit-tle child.
arms of comfort, Thou hast held me like a lit-tle child.
way to safe-ty, Thou hast watched me like a lit-tle child.
with-out doubt-ing I have loved Thee like a lit-tle child.

628
Grant Me Peace And Hope

Bb-4-MI
A. F. S.

Grace be to you, and peace from God our Father,
and from the Lord Jesus Christ . . . Eph. 1:2

P-3

Anne Finley Stevens
Arr. by R. J. Stevens

1. When I'm lost in dark-ness, light the way for me. When my
2. When I sin, Lord, par-don my in-firm-i-ty. When I've
3. When my bod-y's weak-ened, give me faith in Thee. When I've

soul's in pri-son, give me lib-er-ty. When I stum-ble,
doubt-ed, let me see the prints on Thee. When my load is
lost my dear ones, love and com-fort me. When my days have

lift me up to stand with Thee.
heav-y, lift it up for me. Grant me peace and hope, is my plea.
end-ed, take me home with Thee.

CHORUS

I am blind and of-ten lose my way, filled with sad-ness,

ter-ror, and dis-may, In our Fa-ther's house pre-pare a

place for me. Let me dwell with Thee e - ter - nal - ly.

Heaven, The Place I Long To Be   629

Eb -2-DO
Sam Binkley, Jr.

Having a desire to depart, and to be with Christ;
which is far better. Phil. 1:23

H-2
Sam Binkley, Jr.
Arr. by R. J. Stevens

1. If heav - en's a place where there'll be no pain, No sor - row
2. If heav - en's a place with its street of gold, Where saved ones
3. If heav - en's a place with its beau - ty rare, With plea - sures
4. But most— of all it's my Lord to see Who shed His

nor cry - ing ev - er a - gain; Where saints and an - gels—
shall walk and nev - er grow old; There safe from harm in the
and joys be - yond all com - pare; E - ter - nal life with the
life's blood to set my soul free; Oh heav - en means so—

sing re - frain; Then that's the place I long to be.
Shep - herd's fold; Then that's the place I long to be.
Fa - ther there; Then that's the place I long to be.
much to me; Yes, that's the place I long to be.

630 Watch And Pray

Take ye heed, watch and pray: for ye know not when the time is. Mark 13:33

Bb-4-SOL
E. B.

S-2
Elbert Bailey

1. Watch and pray, for the Lord is com-ing, Com-ing in the
2. He may come in the ear-ly morn-ing, He may come at
3. When He comes He'll re-ward the faith-ful, What a glo-rious

clouds some day; Wash your robes in the cleans-ing foun-tain,
close of day; Watch and pray, in His prom-ise trust-ing,
day 'twill be; Joy a-waits those who have made read-y,

REFRAIN

Watch, oh, watch and pray. Watch and pray,
Watch and pray, watch and pray, oh,

watch and pray, For we know not the hour when the
watch and pray ev-'ry day,

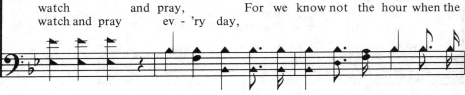

Lord shall come: Watch and pray, watch and
Watch and pray, watch and pray, oh, watch and pray,

pray, And be read-y to en-ter the soul's bright home.
ev - 'ry day,

Lord, Thy Word Abideth

631

D-4-DO
Henry W. Baker, 1861

*Lord, Thy word abideth forever, O Lord, Thy
word is settled in heaven. Psa. 119:89*

W -3
Michael Weisse's
Ein Neu Gesengbuchlen, **1531**
Arr. by William H. Monk, 1861

1. Lord, Thy Word a - bid - eth, And our foot - steps guid - eth;
2. When our foes are near us, Then Thy Word doth cheer us,
3. When dark clouds are o'er us, And the storms be - fore us,
4. O that we, dis - cern - ing Its most ho - ly learn - ing,

Who its truth be - liev - eth Light and joy re - ceiv - eth.
Word of con - so - la - tion, Mes - sage of sal - va - tion.
Then its light di - rect - eth, And our way pro - tect - eth.
Lord, may love and fear Thee, Ev - er - more be near Thee! A-men.

632 Come Unto Me

Come unto Me, all ye that labor and are heavy laden, and I will give you rest.
Matt. 11:28

C-4-MI
C. P. J.

I-1

Charles P. Jones

1. Hear the bless-ed Sav-ior call-ing the op-pressed, "O ye heav-y
2. Have you cares of bus-'ness, cares of press-ing debt? Cares of so-cial

la-den, come to me and rest; Come, no long-er tar-ry, I your
life or cares of hopes un-met? Are you by re-morse or sense of

load will bear, Bring me ev-'ry bur-den, bring me ev-'ry care."
guilt de-pressed? Come right now to Je-sus, He will give you rest.

CHORUS

Come un-to me, I
Come un-to me, come un-to me, I will give you rest,

will give you rest; Take my yoke up-
I will give you rest; Take my yoke up-on you,

633
How Long Has It Been?

*Cast all your care on Him
for He cares for you.* 1 Pet. 5:7

Ab-3-SOL

Mosie Lister

E-1, P-3

Mosie Lister

1. How long has it been since you talked with the Lord And
2. How long has it been since you knelt by your bed And

told Him your heart's hid-den se-crets? How long since you prayed? How
prayed to the Lord up in heav-en? How long since you knew that

long since you stayed on your knees till the light shone thru? How
He'd an-swer you, and would keep you the long night thru? How

long has it been since your mind felt at ease? How long since your
long has it been since you woke with the dawn and felt that the

heart knew no bur-den? Can you call Him your friend? How
day's worth the liv-ing?

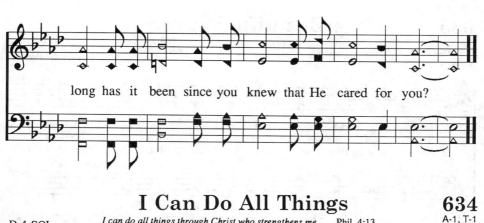

long has it been since you knew that He cared for you?

I Can Do All Things

I can do all things through Christ who strengthens me... Phil. 4:13

634

A-1, T-1

D-4-SOL

Marilyn Woolf

Marilyn Woolf
Arr. by R. J. Stevens

1. I can find safe-ty with Christ who strength-ens me; I can find
2. I can have peace— with Christ who strength-ens me; I can have
3. I can show cour-age with Christ who strength-ens me; I can show
4. I can do all things through Christ who strength-ens me; I can do

safe-ty with Christ who strength-ens me; I can find safe-ty
peace— with Christ who strength-ens me; I can have peace—
cour-age with Christ who strength-ens me; I can show cour-age
all things through Christ who strength-ens me; I can do all things

with Christ who strength-ens me;
with Christ who strength-ens me; Yes, I can, I can, I can!
with Christ who strength-ens me;
through Christ who strength-ens me;

635 A Beautiful Prayer

O My Father, if it be possible, let this cup pass from Me;
nevertheless not as I will, but as Thou wilt. Matt. 26:39

C-2-SOL
L. G. P.

G-1, P-3
Luther G. Presley

1. In the Bi - ble we read of a beau - ti - ful pray'r, A
2. You can catch the sad tone of His voice as He said, "Thy
3. As He prayed there a - lone in such deep ag - o - ny, It

pray'r (fer - vent pray'r) sent to heav - en a - bove; It was prayed by a
will (bless - ed will) not my own must be done;" As a lamb to the
was (yes, it was) a most beau - ti - ful pray'r; Just to think His great

heart that was la - den with care And filled (it was filled) with such
slaugh - ter He soon must be led To die (yes, to die) as the
heart was all brok - en for me, That He (yes, that He) my great

won - der - ful love.
Cru - ci - fied One.
sor - row must share.

CHORUS

When He was pray - ing Je - sus was
When the Sav - ior was pray - ing, ...

pray - ing There in Geth - sem - a - ne,
. . . In the gar - den of Geth - sem - a - ne, He

©Copyright 1937. Renewal 1965 by Stamps-Baxter Music.

636 The Love Of God

Keep yourselves in the love of God, looking for the mercy of our Lord Jesus Christ unto eternal life. Jude 21

D-4-MI
Laurene Highfield

L-2, L-5
Samuel W. Beazley

1. Since the love of God has shed price-less bless-ings on my head, I have
2. Since the Son of God came down with His love our lives to crown, He with
3. He who gave His love to me, that I might from sin be free, Bids me
4. While His love burns true and bright, we are walk-ing in the light, He has

made it my own; I will hide it in my
us would re-main; Great-er love there could not
share it to-day; "As I loved you," He has
shown us the road; We His glo-ry must re-

1. I have made it my own

heart, that it nev-er may de-part, It shall rule there a-
be, Je-sus died for you and me, In our hearts, He would
said, "you must serve men in My stead, As you go on your
flect, lest our dim-ness and neg-lect Keep some soul from its

It shall rule

CHORUS

lone. The love of God with-in the
reign. The love of God..........
way."
God.

there a - lone.

heart, Will kind-li-ness and warmth im-
..... with-in the heart, Will kind-li-ness ....

637 Wonderful City Of God

But now they desire a better country, that is, an heavenly . . .
for He hath prepared for them a city. Heb. 11:16

Ab-2-SOL
J. W. F.

H-2, R-3
J. W. Ferrill

1. There's a won-der-ful place we call home, 'Tis a cit-y of
2. O how sweet it will be there to dwell With the Sav-ior and
3. When the jew-els of Je-sus are brought, There to shine in that

glo-ry di-vine, It is built in the gar-den of rest, And that
Fath-er of all, In a pal-ace of dia-mond and gold, Where no
land of sweet song, What a beau-ti-ful, beau-ti-ful thought That

beau-ti-ful home shall be mine, O that won-der-ful E-den, so blest,
e-vil to us can be-fall; There no sor-row that home shall in-vade,
I shall be there in that throng; Sweetest peace to my soul it will be,

Where Je-sus, the Mas-ter has gone To pre-pare us this
And our loved ones no more there shall die; One ce-les-tial, un-
To be-hold such a glo-ri-ous sight, Where the sun and the

glo-ri-ous home. There He bids us a wel-come to come.
brok-en, sweet day, While e-ter-ni-ties' a-ges roll by.
moon nei-ther shine, But the glo-ry of God is the light.

638 Wonderful Grace Of Jesus

And the grace of our Lord was exceeding abundant
with faith and love which is in Christ Jesus. 1 Tim. 1:14

Db-4-SOL
H. L.

G-2
Haldor Lillenas

1. Won - der -ful grace of Je - sus, Great - er than all my sin;
2. Won - der - ful grace of Je - sus, Reach-ing to all the lost,
3. Won - der -ful grace of Je - sus, Reach-ing the most de -filed,

How shall my tongue de - scribe it, Where shall its praise be - gin?
By it I have been par - doned, Saved to the ut - ter - most,
By its trans-form - ing pow - er, Mak - ing him God's dear child,

Tak - ing a - way my bur - den, Set - ting my spir - it free; For the
Chains have been torn a - sun - der, Giv - ing me lib - er - ty; For the
Pur - chas -ing peace and heav - en, For all e - ter - ni - ty; And the

won - der -ful grace of Je - sus reach - es me.

CHORUS

Won - der -ful the

the match-less grace of Je - sus,

match-less grace of Je - - sus, Deep - er than the

639 He's A Wonderful Savior To Me

For the Son of man is come to save that which was lost. Matt. 18:11

E♭ - 4 - MI

Virgil P. Brock

Blanche Kerr Brock

C-10

1. I was lost in sin but Je - sus res - cued me,
2. He's a Friend so true, so pa - tient and so kind,
3. He is al - ways near to com - fort and to cheer,
4. Dear - er grows the love of Je - sus day by day,

He's a won - der - ful Sav - ior to me;

I was
Ev - 'ry
He for-
Sweet-er

so won - der - ful!

1. bound by fear but Je - sus set me free,
2. thing I need in Him I al - ways find,
3. gives my sins, He dries my ev - 'ry tear,
4. is His grace while press - ing on my way,

He's a won - der - ful

CHORUS

Sav - ior to me.

so won - der - ful!

For He's a won - der - ful

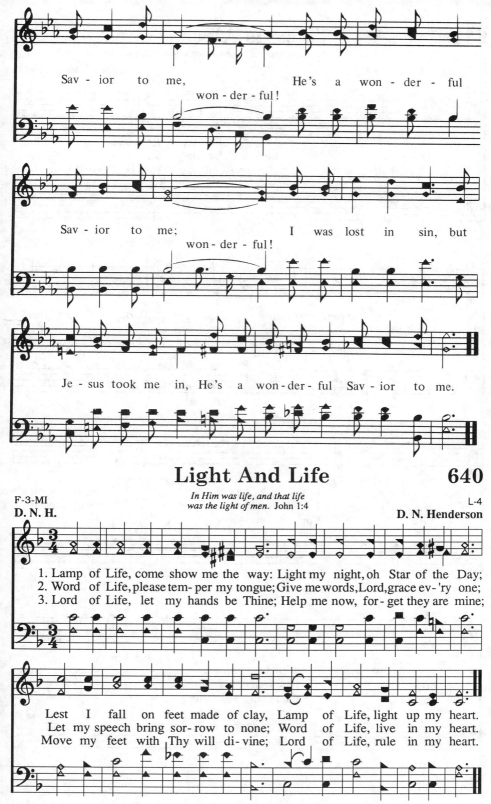

Sav - ior to me, He's a won - der - ful

won - der - ful!

Sav - ior to me; I was lost in sin, but

won - der - ful!

Je - sus took me in, He's a won - der - ful Sav - ior to me.

Light And Life 640

*In Him was life, and that life
was the light of men. John 1:4*

F-3-MI

D. N. H.

L-4

D. N. Henderson

1. Lamp of Life, come show me the way: Light my night, oh Star of the Day;
2. Word of Life, please tem- per my tongue; Give me words, Lord, grace ev- 'ry one;
3. Lord of Life, let my hands be Thine; Help me now, for- get they are mine;

Lest I fall on feet made of clay, Lamp of Life, light up my heart.
Let my speech bring sor- row to none; Word of Life, live in my heart.
Move my feet with Thy will di- vine; Lord of Life, rule in my heart.

641 There Is A Sea

Remember the words of the Lord Jesus . . . It is more blessed to give than to receive.
Acts 20:35

E♭-4-MI
L. K. Z., v. 3; vs. 1, 2 (?)

W-4
Lula Klingman Zahn

1. There is a sea which day by day Re-ceives the rip-pling rills, And streams that spring from wells of God, Or fall from ce-dared hills; But what it thus re-ceives it gives With glad un-spar-ing,

2. There is a sea which day by day Re-ceives a full-er tide; But all its store it keeps, nor gives To shore nor sea be-side; It's Jor-dan stream, Lies heavy as mol-ten

3. Which shall it be for you and me, Who God's good gifts ob-tain? Shall we ac-cept for self a-lone, Or take to give a-gain? For He who once was rich in-deed Laid all His glo-ry

1. But what it thus now turned to re-ceives it gives With glad un-spar-ing,

un - spar - ing hand: A stream more wide, A stream more
hand: A stream more wide, ...
lead; Its dread - ful name . . . .
down; That by His grace, ...

wide, with deep - er tide, Flows on, flows
. . . with deep - er tide, Flows on . . . . . .
. . . doth e'er pro - claim That sea . . . . . .
. . . our ransomed race Should share . . . . . .

rit.

on to low - er land. to low - er land.
. . . to low - er land.
. . . is waste and dead.
. . . His wealth and crown.

O Worship The Lord

O worship the Lord, in the beauty of holiness. Psa. 96:9

642

W-5

F-3-DO
Psalm 96:9; 34:3

Fanny B. Earle
Arr. by R. J. Stevens

O wor - ship the Lord, In the beau - ty of ho - li - ness.

Let us ex - alt His Name to - geth - er. A - men, A - men.

643
643
F-3-MI
Lanny Wolfe

God's Family

Be kindly affectioned one to another with brotherly love. Rom. 12:10

F-2, L-2
Lanny Wolfe

1. We're part of the fam - 'ly that's been born a - gain;
2. When a broth - er meets sor - row we all feel his grief;
3. And tho' some go be - fore us, we'll all meet a - gain;

Part of the fam - 'ly whose love knows no end;
When he's passed thru the val - ley we all feel re - lief;
Just in - side the cit - y as we en - ter in;

For Je - sus has saved us, and made us His own,
To - geth - er in sun - shine, to - geth - er in rain,
There'll be no more part - ing, with Je - sus we'll be

Now we're part of the fam - 'ly that's on its way home.
To - geth - er in vic - t'ry thru His pre - cious name.
To - geth - er for - ev - er, God's fam - i - ly.

CHORUS

And some - times we laugh to - geth - er, some - times we cry;

Some-times we share to-geth-er, heart-aches and sighs;

Some-times we dream to-geth-er of how it will be

When we all get to Heav - en, God's fam-i - ly.

Psalm 118

644

Tune: I'm Not Ashamed To Own My Lord

A♭-3-SOL
Psalm 118:22-29

T -2, P 2

Arr. from Carl Glaser, 1828

1. That stone is made head corn - er stone Which build-ers did de-spise.
2. This is the day the Lord hath made; Let us be glad and sing.
3. Thou art my God; I'll give Thee thanks. My God I'll wor-ship Thee.

This is the do - ing of the Lord, And won-drous in our eyes.
Ho - san - na Lord! O give suc-cess! O Lord, sal-va-tion bring!
O thank the Lord, for He is good; His grace will end-less be.

645 Hallelujah! We Shall Rise

For the trumpet shall sound, and the dead shall be
raised incorruptible, and we shall be changed. 1 Cor. 15:52

Bb-4-SOL

R-2

J. E. Thomas

1. In the res-ur-rec-tion morn-ing, When the trump of God shall sound,
2. In the res-ur-rec-tion morn-ing, Bless-ed tho't it is to me,
3. In the res-ur-rec-tion morn-ing, We shall meet Him in the air,

We shall rise, we shall rise! Then the saints will
Hal-le-lu-jah! I shall see my
And be car-ried

come re-joic-ing, And no tears will e'er be found, We shall rise, ...
bless-ed Sav-ior, Who so free-ly died for me,
up to glo-ry, To our home so bright and fair, Hal-le-

Fine CHORUS

. . . lu-jah! we shall rise,
lu-jah! In that morn-ing we shall rise. We shall rise! . . . Hal-le-

lu-jah! We shall rise! A-men! We shall rise! In the
We shall rise! Hal-le-lu-jah!

res - ur - rec -tion morn -ing When death's pris - on bars are brok - en,

Father Of Heaven

646

F-3-MI
Edward Cooper, 1805

The Father, the Word, and the Holy Ghost:
and these three are one. 1 Jn 5:7

P -3, G -2
Henry Baker, 1859

1. Fa - ther of heav'n, whose love pro- found   A ran - som for   our
2. Al - might - y Son,   in - car - nate Word,   Our Proph- et, Priest, Re -
3. E - ter - nal Spir - it, by whose breath   The soul is raised from
4. Je - ho - vah   Fa - ther, Spir - it,   Son — Mys - te - rious God - head,

souls   hath   found,   Be- fore   Thy   throne   we   hum - bly   bend;
deem - er,   Lord,   Be- fore   Thy   throne   we   hum - bly   bend;
sin   and   death,   Be- fore   Thy   throne   we   hum - bly   bend;
Three   in   One,   Be- fore   Thy   throne   we   hum - bly   bend;

To   us   Thy   par - d'ning   love   ex - tend.
To   us   Thy   sav - ing   grace   ex - tend.
To   us   Thy   quick - 'ning   pow'r   ex - tend.
Grace,   par - don,   life   to   us   ex - tend.   A - men.

647 The Way That He Loves

F-2-SOL
W. E. M.

Behold, what manner of love the Father hath bestowed upon us . . . I John 3:1

L-4
W. Elmo Mercer

1. The way that He loves is as fair as the day, That
2. The way that He loves is as deep as the sea, His

bless - es my way with light. The way that He loves is as
spir - it shall be my stay. The way that He loves is as

soft as the breeze, Ca - ress - ing the trees at night. So
pure as a rose, Much sweet - er He grows each day. His

ten - der and pre - cious is He, Con - tent - ed with
peace hov - ers near like a dove. I know there's a

Je - sus I'll be. The way that He loves is so
heav - en a - bove. To Je - sus I cling, life's a

thrill - ing be - cause His love reach - es e - ven me.
won - der - ful thing Be - cause of the way He loves.

Unto The Hills

648

I will lift up mine eyes unto the hills, from whence cometh my help. Psa. 121:1

Eb-4-MI

Psalm 121
Arr. by John Campbell, 1866

A -1

C. H. Purday, 1860
Arr. by Craig Roberts & R. J. Stevens

slowly

1. Un - to the hills a - round do I lift up my long - ing eyes;
   O whence for me shall my sal - va - tion come? From whence a - rise?
2. From ev - 'ry e - vil shall He keep thy soul, from ev - 'ry sin.
   Je - ho - vah shall pre - serve thy go - ing out, thy com - ing in.

1. From God the Lord doth come my cer - tain aid, From
2. A - bove thee watch - ing, He Whom we a - dore Shall

God the Lord, whom heav'n and earth have made.
keep thee hence - forth, yea, for - ev - er more.

649 All Hail The Power

649

Bb-3-SOL

Thou art worthy, O Lord, to receive glory, and honor, and power. Rev. 4:11

P-2

Edward Perronet, 1779; arr.

James Ellor, 1838

1. All hail the pow'r of Je - sus' name! Let an - gels
2. Ye cho - sen seed of Is - rael's race, Ye ran-somed
3. Let ev - 'ry kin - dred, ev - 'ry tribe, On this ter -
4. O that with yon - der sa - cred throng We at His

pros-trate fall, Let an - gels pros - trate fall; They bro't the
from the fall, Ye ran - somed from the fall, Hail Him who
res - trial ball, On this ter - res - trial ball. To Him all
feet may fall, We at His feet may fall! We'll join the

O praise

roy - al di - a - dem, O praise Him, praise Him,
saves you by His grace, O praise Him, praise Him,
maj - es - ty as - cribe, O praise
ev - er - last - ing song,

O praise Him, praise Him,

Him, Praise Him,

praise Him, praise Him, O praise Him Lord of
Him, Praise Him,

praise Him, Praise

praise Him,   praise Him,

all,   praise Him, O praise   Him   Lord   of   all!

praise . . . . Him,

. . . . .Him,   O praise Him Lord   of   all!

His Name Is Jesus   650

She will give birth to a son, and you are
to give him the name Jesus. Matt. 1:21

F-3-MI
Max Wheeler

L -4, N -1
Max Wheeler

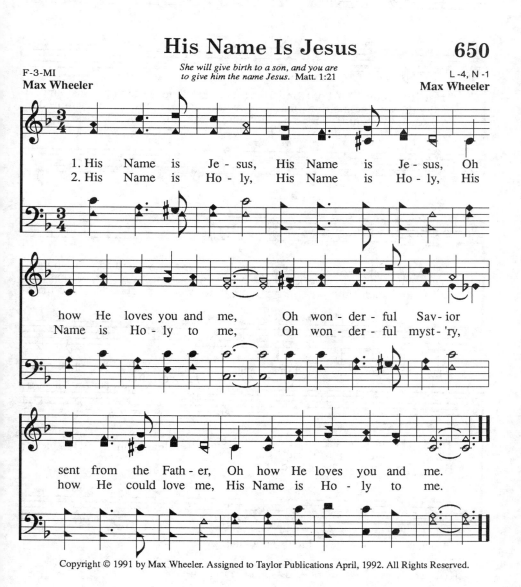

1. His   Name   is   Je - sus,   His   Name   is   Je - sus,   Oh
2. His   Name   is   Ho - ly,   His   Name   is   Ho - ly,   His

how   He   loves you and   me,   Oh   won - der - ful   Sav - ior
Name   is   Ho - ly   to   me,   Oh   won - der - ful   myst - 'ry,

sent   from   the Fath - er,   Oh   how   He   loves   you   and   me.
how   He   could love me,   His   Name   is   Ho - ly   to   me.

651 Hide Me, Rock Of Ages

But the Lord is my defence; and my God is the rock of my refuge. Psa. 94:22

G-4-SOL
B. C. G.

G-3
Brantley C. George

1. O thou bless-ed Rock of A-ges, (Rock of A-ges, I am)
2. Keep me when the storm-clouds gath-er, (storm-clouds gath-er, Keep me)
3. When my jour-ney is com-plet-ed, (is com plet-ed, Sav-ior,)

Trust-ing now dear Lord in Thee; (dear Lord in Thee I'm trust-ing)
Till the sun comes shin-ing thru; (comes shin-ing thru the shad-ows)
And there's no more work to do; (no work to do, O bless-ed)

Keep me till my jour-ney's end-ed, (jour-ney's end-ed, Keep me)
Keep me till my work is o-ver, (work is o-ver, Keep me)
Sav-ior guide my wea-ry spir-it, (wea-ry spir-it, To that)

D.S.-When the storm a-round me rag-es, (round me rag-es, Bless-ed)

Fine CHORUS

Till Thy bless-ed face I see. Hide me, O blest
Till I bid this world a-dieu. Rock of A-ges hide Thou me.
Hap-py land be-yond the blue.

Rock of A - - - ges, Till Thy
A - ges, Rock of A - ges, hide me,

D. S.

bless - ed face I see; (Thy face I see, in glo - ry)

There Is A Green Hill

652

E minor-2-LA
Cecil F. Alexander, 1848

*Wherefore Jesus also, that He might sanctify
the people with His own blood, suffered
without the gate. Heb. 13:12*

C -3, C -17
Traditional
Arr. by Dane K. Shepard

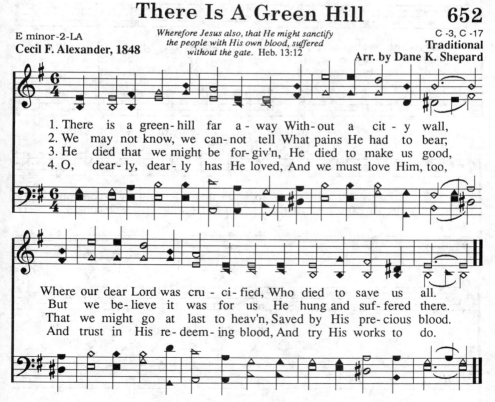

1. There is a green-hill far a - way With-out a cit - y wall,
2. We may not know, we can-not tell What pains He had to bear;
3. He died that we might be for-giv'n, He died to make us good,
4. O, dear-ly, dear-ly has He loved, And we must love Him, too,

Where our dear Lord was cru - ci - fied, Who died to save us all.
But we be-lieve it was for us He hung and suf-fered there.
That we might go at last to heav'n, Saved by His pre-cious blood.
And trust in His re-deem-ing blood, And try His works to do.

653 When Jesus Comes

Bb-4-MI

J. W. G.

Well done, thou good and faithful servant . . . enter thou into the joy of thy Lord.
Matt. 25:21

S-2

J. W. Gaines

1. When Je - sus comes a - gain to gath - er His own, And to the
2. I want to tell to all the sto - ry of love, That they may
3. I do not know the day my Sav - ior will come, But I must

true, a crown is giv'n, I want to hear Him say, "My
know His par - don free; And there be - fore His throne in
be pre - pared to go; If I am read - y He will

serv - ant, well done, Thy soul shall know the joys of heav'n."
glo - ry a - bove, Re - ceive a crown of vic - to - ry.
call me His own, And that's e - nough for me to know.

Fine

D. S.–And ev - er there with Him a - bide.

CHORUS

I want to know that He will wel - come me there,
I want to know that He will wel - come me there,

I do not want to be de - nied;
I do not want to be de - nied;

I want to meet Him in that cit - y so fair,

I want to meet Him in that cit - y so fair,

Are You Weighed Down? 654

Let us run with patience the race
that is set before us. Heb. 12:1

A♭-3-DO
Craig A. Roberts

E -1, P -5
Richard L. Morrison

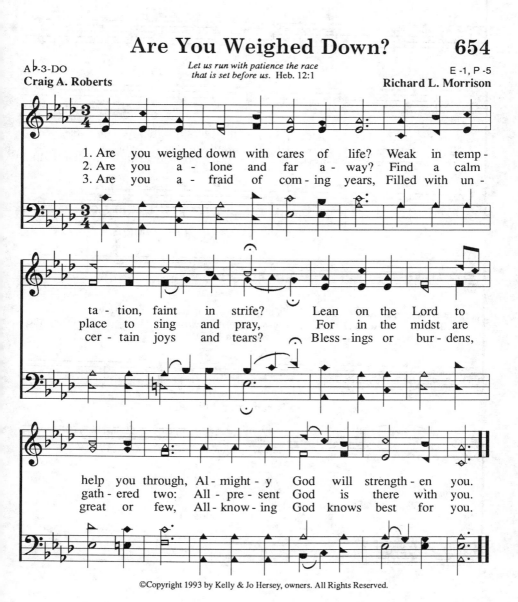

1. Are you weighed down with cares of life? Weak in temp -
2. Are you a - lone and far a - way? Find a calm
3. Are you a - fraid of com - ing years, Filled with un -

ta - tion, faint in strife? Lean on the Lord to
place to sing and pray, For in the midst are
cer - tain joys and tears? Bless - ings or bur - dens,

help you through, Al - might - y God will strength - en you.
gath - ered two: All - pre - sent God is there with you.
great or few, All - know - ing God knows best for you.

655 The Walls Came Tumbling Down

The wall fell down flat, so that the people went up into the city...
and they took the city. Josh 6:20

F-4-SOL
G. A. T.

E-1
G. A. Thacker

1. The Lord told Josh-u-a to go to Jer-i-cho, And to
2. If you are trust-ing in the pow-er of the blood, And you
3. The Lord is call-ing, sin-ner, come to Him to-day, Turn from

march sev'n times a-round; He fol-lowed faith-ful-ly the bless-ed
hope to wear a crown; Go for-ward quick-ly, and o-bey the
this vain world's re-nown; If you will fol-low Him in faith, like

Fine CHORUS

Lord's com-mand, And the walls came tum-bling down. Yes, the walls.......
ho-ly word, Walls of doubt will tum-ble down.
Josh-u-a, Walls of sin will tum-ble down.

Yes, the

D. S. And the walls came tum-bling down.

.... came tum-ble-ing down; Josh-u-a,.........
walls
Yes, the walls, yes, the walls
Josh-u-

Josh - u - a, marched sev- en times 'round, Then the
a, Josh- u - a

D. S.

Then the walls, might-y walls came tum - ble - ing down,
walls all the walls

All Life Comes From Thee 656

F-4-SOL

Craig A. Roberts

*In Whose hand is the soul of every living being,
and the breath of all mankind.* Job 12:10

P-2

Kelly R. Hersey

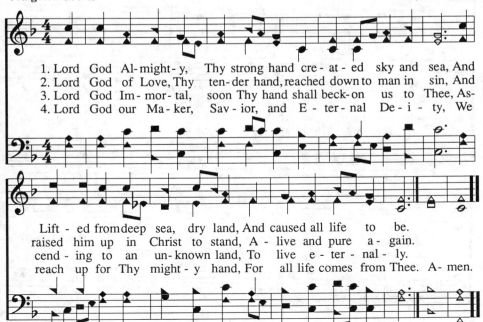

1. Lord God Al- might- y, Thy strong hand cre- at- ed sky and sea, And
2. Lord God of Love, Thy ten- der hand, reached down to man in sin, And
3. Lord God Im- mor- tal, soon Thy hand shall beck- on us to Thee, As-
4. Lord God our Ma- ker, Sav- ior, and E- ter- nal De- i- ty, We

Lift - ed from deep sea, dry land, And caused all life to be.
raised him up in Christ to stand, A - live and pure a- gain.
cend- ing to an un- known land, To live e - ter- nal- ly.
reach up for Thy might- y hand, For all life comes from Thee. A- men.

657 Heaven's Jubilee

Then we which are alive and remain shall be caught up together with them . . .
to meet the Lord in the air . . . I Thess. 4:17

S-2

G. T. Speer

A-4-DO

1. Some glad morn-ing we shall see Je-sus in the air, Com-ing
2. Seems that now I al-most see all the saint-ed dead, Ris-ing
3. When with all that heav'n-ly host we be-gin to sing, Sing-ing

af-ter you and me, joy is ours to share; What re-joic-ing
for that ju-bi-lee, that is just a-head; In the twink-ling
in the Ho-ly Ghost, how the heav'ns will ring; Mil-lions there will

there will be when the saints shall rise, Head-ed for that
of an eye, changed with them to be, All the liv-ing
join the song, with them we shall be Prais-ing Christ thru

CHORUS

ju-bi-lee, yon-der in the skies. Oh, what
saints to fly to that ju-bi-lee. What a day of
a-ges long, heav-en's ju-bi-lee.

sing-ing, Oh, what shout-ing, On that hap-py
sing-ing, sing-ing, what a day of shout-ing, shouting,

morn-ing when we all shall rise; Oh, what
when we all shall glad-ly rise; What a day of

glo - ry, Hal - le - lu - jah!
glo - ry, glo - ry, Glo - ry hal - le - lu - jah! glo - ry!

When we meet our bless-ed Sav-ior in the skies.
Sav - ior yon - der in the skies.

Into My Heart 658

F-2-MI
Harry D. Clarke, 1924
St.2, American Folk Hymn

That Christ may dwell in your
hearts by faith. Eph. 3:17

D -1, H 1
Harry D. Clarke, 1924

1. In - to my heart, In - to my heart, Come in - to my heart, Lord Je - sus;
2. Out of my heart, Out of my heart, Shine out of my heart, Lord Je - sus;

Come in to - day, Come in to stay, Come in - to my heart, Lord Je - sus.
Shine out to - day, Shine out al - ways, Shine out of my heart, Lord Je - sus.

659 Channels Only

I Will Sing Of The Mercies

660

D-4-DO
Let's Sing, 1960

S-4, T-1
Let's Sing, 1960

*I will sing of the mercies
of the Lord forever.* Psalm 89:1

I will sing of the mer-cies of the Lord for-ev-er, I will

sing, I will sing, I will sing, I will sing, I will sing of the mer-cies

of the Lord for-ev-er, I will sing of the mer-cies of the Lord. *Fine*

With my mouth my mouth will I make known make known Thy

faith-ful-ness, Thy faith-ful-ness, With my mouth my mouth will I make

known make known Thy faith-ful-ness to all gen-er-a-tions.

D.C.

661 Let Jesus Dwell Within Your Soul

That Christ may dwell in your hearts by faith . . .
being rooted and grounded in love . . . Eph. 3:17

Bb-4-SOL
Miss Vernie Prichard

E-1
D. A. Roberson

1. O will you now from sigh-ing cease? . . . . . .
2. Thro' tri-als oft your soul must go,
3. And when the hour of death draws near, ...

1. O will you now from sigh-ing

. . . . O will you seek the path of peace? . .
. . . . The Sav-ior wills this to be so, . . .
. . . . Trust Him to take a-way all fear, the
cease? O will you seek

. . . . Give Christ your heart, make heav'n your
. . . . Trust Him with all, as they of
. . . . The joys of heav'n will soon un-
path of peace? Give Christ your heart,

goal, make heav'n your
old, Let Je-sus dwell with-
fold,
make heav'n your goal, Let Je-sus dwell

662

I'll Live In Glory

B♭-4-MI
J. M. M.

H-2
J. M. Menson

The sufferings of this present time are not worthy to be compared
with the glory which shall be revealed . . . Rom. 8:18

1. I'd like to stay here long - er than man's al - lot - ted
2. I want to be of serv - ice a - long this pil - grim
3. The end I know is near - ing— by faith I look a -

days And watch the fleet - ing chang - es of life's un - e - ven
way, And lead the lost to Je - sus as fer - vent - ly I
way To yon - der home su - per - nal—the land of end - less

ways, But if my Sav - ior calls me to that sweet home on
pray; As day by day I trav - el, I'll keep Him ev - er
day; I'll cling to Him for - ev - er, and look be - yond the

high, I'll live with Him for - ev - er in Glo - ry by and by.
nigh, And live with Him for - ev - er in Glo - ry by and by.
sky, And spend the end - less a - ges in Glo - ry by and by.

663 Just A Little While

Bb-4-DO
E. M. B.

For yet a little while, and He that shall come will come, and will not tarry.
Heb. 10:37

H-2
E. M. Bartlett

1. Soon this life will all be o-ver, And our pil-grim-age will end,
2. Soon we'll see the light of morn-ing, Then the new day will be-gin,
3. Soon we'll meet all the re-deemed ones, And we'll take them by the hand,

Soon we'll take our heav'n-ly jour-ney, Be at home with Christ our friend;
Soon we'll hear the Fa-ther call-ing, "Come, my chil-dren en-ter in;"
Soon we'll press them to our bos-om, O-ver in the prom-ised land;

Heav-en's gates are stand-ing o-pen, Wait-ing for our en-trance there,
Then we'll hear a choir of an-gels, Sing-ing out the vic-t'ry song,
Then we'll be at home for-ev-er, Thru-out all e-ter-ni-ty,

Some sweet day we're go-ing o-ver, All the beau-ties there to share.
All our trou-bles will be end-ed And we'll live with heav-en's throng.
What a bless-ed, bless-ed morn-ing That e-ter-nal morn will be!

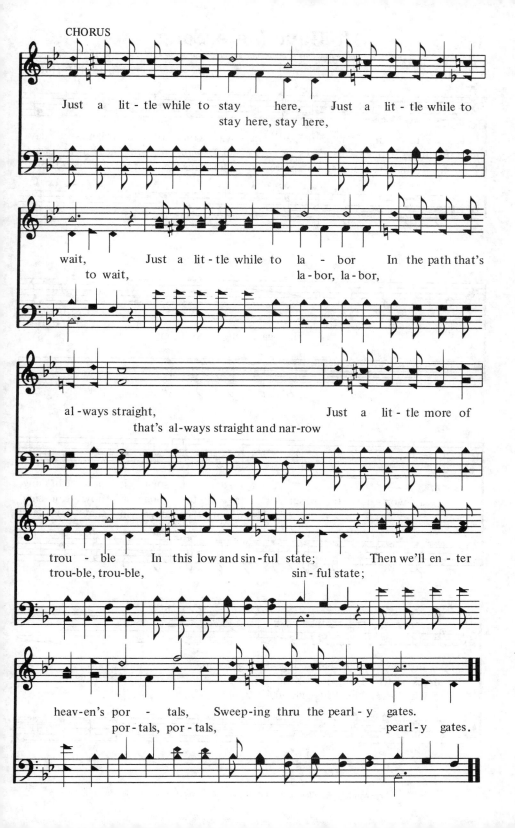

CHORUS

Just a lit-tle while to stay here, Just a lit-tle while to stay here, stay here,

wait, Just a lit-tle while to la - bor In the path that's
to wait, la - bor, la - bor,

al - ways straight,   Just a lit - tle more of
that's al-ways straight and nar-row

trou - ble   In this low and sin - ful state;   Then we'll en - ter
trou-ble, trou-ble,   sin - ful state;

heav-en's por - tals,   Sweep-ing thru the pearl - y gates.
por - tals, por - tals,   pearl - y gates.

664 He Gave Me A Song

C-4-MI
A. H. H.

And He hath put a new song in my mouth, even praise unto our God. Psa. 40:3

J-1, S-4
Alton H. Howard

1. He took my bur-dens all a-way, up to a bright-er day,
2. Bright-er the way grows ev-'ry day, walk-ing the heav'n-ly way,
3. I am re-deemed no more to die, nev-er to say "good-bye,"

He gave me a song, He gave me a song, a won-der-ful

song; a won-der-ful song; A won-der-ful song I now can sing,
And some of these days in that fair land,

in my heart joy bells ring, He gave me a song, ...
prais-es to Him, my King, He gave me a
sing with the cho-rus grand,

CHORUS

665 Walk With Me

Cause me to know the way wherein I should walk; for I lift up my soul unto Thee.

Psa. 143:8

Eb-3-DO
A. L.
2nd verse by P. J. Zondervan

C-12, F-2
Al Langdon

1. Walk with me, walk with me, Lest mine eyes no long-er see
2. Talk with me, talk with me, Lest mine ears no long-er hear

All the glo-ry, all the sto-ry of your love;
All the won-der, all the beau-ty of your grace;

Talk to me, talk to me, Like you spoke so ten-der-
Walk with me, walk with me, As you walked so lov-ing

ly, When You talked there, when You walked there by the sea.
ly, When You walked there, when You talked there by the sea.

CHORUS

Let me fol - low in the foot-steps that

666 He Bore It All

F-4-SOL

J. R. Baxter, Jr.

Who His own self bare our sins in His own body on the tree, that we . . .
should live unto righteousness . I Pet. 2:24

C-3, C-4

Virgil O. Stamps

1. My pre-cious Sav-ior suf-fered pain and ag-o-ny, He
2. They placed a crown of thorns up-on my Sav-ior's head,
3. Up Cal-v'ry's hill in shame the bless-ed Sav-ior trod

bore it all . . . . that I might live; . . . .

Free-ly bore it all I with Him might

. . . He broke the bonds of sin and set the cap-tive
By cru-el man with spear His side was pierced and
live; Be-tween two thieves they cru-ci-fied the Son of

free, All that I might in His
bled,
God He bore it all that I might live . . . . .

Fine CHORUS

pres-ence live. He bore it all that I might see His
Je - sus bore it all,

shin - ing face, Free - ly bore it
see His shin - ing face, He bore it all . . . .

all, I with Him might live; I stood con-
that I might live; . . . .

D. S.

demned to die but Je - sus took my place,
stood con-demned to die free - ly took my place,

667 I Hold His Hand

Db-2-MI

He leadeth me beside the still waters. He restoreth my soul. Psa. 23:2,3

D-1, F-2

J. R. Baxter, Jr.

W. Allan Sims

1. I hold to the hand of my Sav - ior and friend, He shields me from
2. I hold to His hand when the storm-clouds a - rise, He speaks and the
3. I hold to the hand that is stead-fast and sure, No oth - er foun-

ev - il till dan - gers all end, He'll take me to heav - en where
shad-ows roll back from the skies, 'Tis won-der - ful glo - ry for
da - tion is ev - er se - cure, I look for the home that will

CHORUS

voic - es now blend;
our hu - man eyes; I hold to the hand of my Lord.
ev - er en - dure;

I

Dai - ly I hold to the scarred hand of my dear Lord,
hold to the hand of my Sav - - -

668   The Greater Light

Eb-4-DO
Craig A. Roberts

For God, Who commanded the light to shine out of darkness,
hath shined in our hearts to give the light... II Cor. 4:6

C-12, F-3
R. J. Stevens

1. A - bove the earth and far a - way, God sta - tioned two
2. Then shin - ing down from God in Heav'n, The Great - est Light
3. O les - ser lights, we shine not bright With glo - ry of

great lights, A great - er light to rule the day, A
soon came; He burned in - to the heart of man And
our own, But we re - flect a Great - er Light— Bright

les - ser light, the night. He set them high, and
kin - dled there a flame. He said, "The light I
glo - ry from the Son! When men be - hold the

hour by hour, All men look up to see His un - seen
shine in you, Let it be shed a - broad, So men will
lives we live, They see our God a - bove; And when they

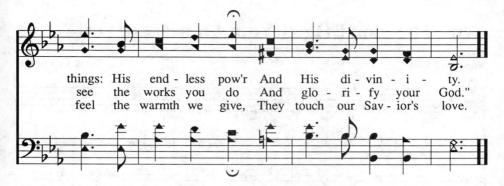

things: His end - less pow'r And His di - vin - i - ty.
see the works you do And glo - ri - fy your God."
feel the warmth we give, They touch our Sav - ior's love.

Holy Is The Lord

669

Eb-2-MI

You shall be holy, for I the Lord
your God am holy. Lev. 19:2

P-2

American Folk Hymn

Franz Schubert, c.1826

Ho - ly, ho - ly, ho - ly, Ho - ly is the Lord.

Ho - ly, ho - ly, ho - ly, Ho - ly is the Lord.

Ho - ly is the Fa - ther, Ho - ly is the Son,

Ho - ly is the Spir - it; Bless - ed Three in One.

670 The Lord Bless You And Keep You

C-4-SOL

Num. 6: 24-26

The God of all grace, who hath called us . . .
make you perfect, establish, strengthen, settle you. I Pet. 5:10

W-2

Peter C. Lutkin

The Lord bless you and keep you, The Lord lift his coun-te-nance up-on you, and give you peace (and give you peace,) and give you peace, (and give you peace,) The Lord make His face to shine up-on you and be gra - cious un-to you, be gra-cious,

The Lord make His face

and be gra-cious and be gra - cious,

The Lord be gra - cious, gra - cious un - to you, A - men.

Seven-fold Amen

(you,)

A - - - - men,

A - - - - men, A - - - - men, A -

A - - men, A - - men, A - -

men, A - - - - - - - men, A -

- - men, A - - men, A - men, ...

men, A - - men, A - - - - -

men, A - - - - - - - men, A -

. . . A - men, A - - - - - - men.

- - - men, A - - - - - men, A - men.

men, A - - - - - - - men, A - men.

671 He Carried My Sorrows

Surely He has borne our griefs,
and carried our sorrows. Isa. 53:4

E♭-4-DO
G. B. S.

R-1, C-3

Glenda B. Schales
Arr. by R. J. Stevens

1. He car - ried my sor - rows, He bore my griefs,
2. He suf - fered in an - guish, He writhed in pain,
3. De - spised and re - ject - ed, He knew no sin,
4. My heart mourns His chas - t'ning, My tears still fall,

Was pierced for trans - gres - sions, af - flict - ed for peace.
Was smit - ten, for - sak - en, a - ban - doned and slain.
Was crushed for His peo - ple, no vio - lence with - in.
My sin is the rea - son He gave me His all.

CHORUS

He knew by His stripes I am healed, thru His blood I can

kneel, For by His op - pres - sion, I wor - ship my King.
my Sav - ior, my King.

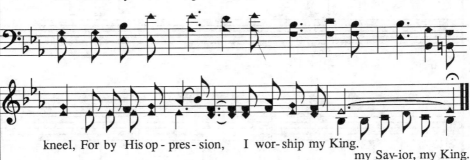

Above All, Love

672

And now abideth faith, hope, charity, these three;
but the greatest of these is love. 1 Cor. 13:13

D-4-MI
Don Alexander

L-2, L-3
Don Alexander
Arr. R. J. Stevens

1. If I speak with tongues of men and an - gels, too;
2. Love is pa - tient, love is kind and en - vies not;
3. Love pro - tects, and trusts and al - ways per - se - veres.
4. Help us, Lord, to love You with our heart and soul.

If I have the gifts of pro - phe - cy and faith;
Nev - er boast - ful, nev - er rude or filled with pride.
Nev - er fail - ing, love will nev - er pass a - way.
Teach us, Lord, to love our neigh - bors as our - selves.

If I give all I pos - sess and give my bo - dy as a
Love is nev - er seek - ing self and is not eas - i - ly pro-
In the path of love the Sav - ior walked and hum - bly gave Him-
Make us un - der - stand that lov - ing one - an - oth - er is the

sac - ri - fice; If I have no love I'm noth - ing af - ter all.
voked to wrath. Love hates e - vil but re - joic - es with the truth.
self to die. And the path of love leads straight to Cal - va - ry.
on - ly way. May our hearts be moved to im - i - tate Your love.

673 Sing Me A Song About Jesus

Sing praises to the Lord . . . declare among the people His doings. Psa. 9:11

Bb - 4 - DO

G. T. S.

L-4, S-4

G. T. Speer

1. Sing me a song a-bout Je-sus, Sing me a song a-bout His love,
2. Je-sus the won-der-ful Sav-ior, Guides me a-long the rug-ged way,

Sing with all your might, ev-'ry day and night, Make the hal-le-lu-jahs
Nev-er lets me fall, hears my fee-ble call, Makes the way so bright for

roll; Sing out the bless-ed old sto-ry, Tell how He
me; I will for-ev-er a-dore Him, I will for-

gave the vic-to-ry, Dy-ing on a tree, all for you and me,
ev-er sing His praise, He will take me home, nev-er more to roam,

CHORUS

How He came and made me whole.
Then His lov-ing face I'll see. Sing me a song a-bout

674

A-4-MI
G. B. S.

It Is Time To Build

Thus saith the Lord of host; Consider your ways. Hag. 1:4

K-1, S-5

Glenda B. Schales
Arr. by R. J. Stevens

1. It is time to build in the church of our Lord. It is time
2. Have we built our homes, have we cared for our own while ne-glect-
3. Let us ga-ther wood in the moun-tains of truth. Ham-mer faith,

to con-si-der our ways. This great work is be-fore us, the
ing the tem-ple of God? But it's time; let us work giv-ing
ham-mer hope to its frame. Now let's streng-then our hands for the

need sounds its cry to all and God seek-eth those who o-bey.
all to our bless-ed Lord, ye cho-sen, ye peo-ple of God.
work, sound the Word now as we stand on the pow'r of His name.

CHORUS

"Now have cour-age," says our Lord. "I am
"Now have faith, ne-ver fear,"

with you, My spir-it a-bides with you. Now have cour-age,
Now have faith,

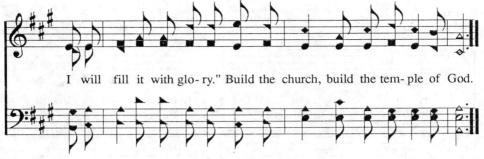

I will fill it with glo- ry." Build the church, build the tem- ple of God.

The Blessed Life
675

Blessed are the pure in heart: for they shall see God. Matt. 5:8

D-2-DO

J-1, C-16

Glenda B. Schales

Glenda B. Schales

2. (A)   Pure   in heart   we   see   that
3. (A,T)   Poor   in spir - it,   meek   and
4. (A,T,S) Per - se - cut - ed   like   our
5. (A,T,S) Rich   in bless - ings   from   our
Vr 1 - 5 Bless-ed,bless-ed, bless- ed are we, whom God has blest with mer- cy,

God   is   great   and pure   in
gen - tle,   we   are blest   with
Lord,   and   like   the proph - ets,
God,   we   hum - bly seek   His
com- fort and peace when we have hum- bly sought His name to con- fess,

1 - 4

5

ho - li - ness.
hap - pi - ness.
we'll   be   blest.
right - eous - ness.
hun- gered and sought His right- eous- ness. And we are

©Copyright 1992 by Glenda B. Schales. All Rights Reserved.

676 Resurrection

C-4-MI

Fear not ye: for I know that ye seek Jesus, which was crucified.
He is not here: for He is risen . . . Matt. 28:5,6

C-8

Homer P. Morris, 1911

Thomas B. Mosley, 1911

{ They cru-ci-fied my Lord, Laid Him in the tomb, Now lies the Son of God
The Man of grief and toil There in si-lence lies; Death has with-in its coil

in death's sa-ble gloom. }
God of earth and skies. }

But, be-hold, there was an earth-quake, For from

heav'n there came an an - gel, With a coun-ten-ance like light-ning,

And a rai-ment white as snow. When at dawn came Mar-y Mag-da-lene,

'Twas the an-gel's voice which said:
the voice which said:

"Lo! He is not here, but ris-en!"

Christ is ris-en from the dead.

He who for the world's sal-va-tion bled,

677 Jesus Paid It All

He bare the sin of many, and made intercession for the transgressors. Isa. 53:12

C-4-MI
M. S. Shaffer

C-4, R-1
Samuel W. Beazley

1. Gone is all my debt of sin, A great change is bro't with - in,
2. O I hope to please Him now, Light of joy is on my brow,
3. Sin - ner, not for me a - lone Did the Son of God a - tone;

And to live I now be - gin, Ris - en from the fall; Yet the debt I
As at His dear feet I bow, Safe with- in His love, Mak - ing His the
Your debt, too, He made His own, On the cru - el tree. Come to Him with

did not pay, Some - one died for me one day, Sweep -ing all the
debt I owed, Free - dom true He has be -stowed; So I'm sing - ing
all your sin; Be as white as snow with - in; Full sal - va - tion

CHORUS

debt a - way, Je - sus paid it all. Je - sus died and
on the road To my home a - bove, Je - sus died and
you may win And re - joice with me.

Bass to predominate

paid it all, yes, On the cross of
paid it On the cross of

678 If We Never Meet Again

And the dead in Christ shall rise first: then we which are alive and remain . . .
and so shall we ever be with the Lord. I Thess. 4:16,17

Eb-2-MI

A. E. B.

H-2

Albert E. Brumley

1. Soon we'll come to the end of life's jour-ney And per-
2. O so oft - en we're part - ed with sor - row, Ben - e-
3. O they say we shall meet by the riv - er, Where no

haps we'll nev - er meet an - y more, Till we gath - er in
dic - tions oft - en quick - en our pain, But we nev - er shall
storm-clouds ev - er dark - en the sky, And they say we'll be

heav-en's bright cit - y Far a - way on that beau - ti - ful shore.
sor - row in heav - en, God be with you till we meet a - gain.
hap - py in heav - en In the won - der - ful sweet by and by.

CHORUS

Nev - er meet this side of heav - en,
If we nev - er meet a - gain this side of heav - en

Strug - gle thru this world and its strife,
As we stru - gle thru this world and its strife, There's an-

679

Jesus, Hold My Hand

For I the Lord thy God will hold thy right hand . . . I will help thee. Isa. 41:13

Eb-4-SOL
A. E. B.

D-1, G-3
Albert E. Brumley

1. As I trav-el thru this pil-grim land There is a Friend who walks with me, Leads me safe-ly thru the sink-ing sand, It is the Christ of Cal-va-ry; This would be my pray'r, dear Lord, each day To help me do the best I can, For I need Thy light to guide me day and night, Bless-ed Je-sus, hold my hand.

2. Let me trav-el in the light di-vine That I might see the bless-ed way; Keep me that I may be whol-ly Thine And sing re-demp-tion's song some day; I will be a sol-dier brave and true And ev-er firm-ly take a stand, As I on-ward go and dai-ly meet the foe, Bless-ed Je-sus, hold my hand.

3. When I wan-der thru the val-ley dim To-ward the set-ting of the sun, Lead me safe-ly to a land of rest If I a crown of life have won; I have put my faith in Thee, dear Lord, That I may reach the gold-en strand, There's no oth-er friend on whom I can de-pend, Bless-ed Je-sus, hold my hand.

CHORUS

Bless - ed Je - sus, hold my hand, Yes I need
Je - sus, hold my hand, I need Thee

Thee ev - 'ry hour, Thru this land, this pil - grim land
ev - 'ry hour, Thru this pil - grim land, Pro -

By Thy sav - ing pow'r; Hear my plea, my fee - ble plea,
tect me by Thy pow'r; Hear my fee - ble plea,

Lord, dear Lord, look down on me, When
O Lord, look down on me, When I kneel in

I kneel in pray'r, Bless - ed Je-sus, hold my hand.
pray'r I hope to meet you there,

680 Anywhere Is "Home"

A♭-4-SOL

J. M. Henson

For I have learned, in whatsoever state I am, therewith to be content . . .
I can do all things through Christ . . . Phil 4:11,13

A-1, C-12

Homer F. Morris

1. Earth-ly wealth and fame May nev-er come to me,
   Earth-ly wealth and hon-ored fame
2. Oft I'm tossed a-bout And driv-en by the foe,
   Oft I'm tossed, am tossed a-bout
3. I will la-bor on Till I am called a-way,
   I will la-bor, la-bor on,

And a pal - - ace fair, Here mine may nev-er be;
And an earth-ly pal-ace fair,
Sad with-in, with-out, Wher-ev-er I may go;
Sad with-in and sad with-out,
Till the morn shall dawn, Of that e-ter-nal day;
Till the morn at last shall dawn,

But let come what may, If Christ for me doth care,
But let come, let come what may,
But I press a-long Still look-ing up in pray'r,
So I press, I press a-long,
Look-ing un - - to Him, Who keeps me in His care,
Ev-er look-ing un-to Christ

An-y-where is home, If He is on-ly there.
An-y-where is home, sweet home,
For it's home, sweet home, If Christ is on-ly there.
O I know 'tis home, sweet home,
An-y-where is home, If Christ, my Lord is there.
An-y-where is home, sweet home, on-ly there.

CHORUS

An - y - where is home, Let come and go what may,
An - y - where sweet home, come what may,

An - y - where I roam, He keeps me all the way;
An - y - where I chance to roam, each day;

So for His dear sake, My cross I'll meek - ly bear,
So for my dear Mas - ter's sake

An - y - where is home, If Christ, my Lord, is there.
An - y - where sweet home, on - ly there.

681 Looking For A City

For he looked for a city which hath foundations, whose builder and maker is God.

Heb. 11:10

B♭-4-DO

W. Oliver Cooper

H-2

Marvin P. Dalton

1. Here a-mong the shad-ows (liv-ing) in a lone-ly land, With stran-gers
2. In this land of dan-gers (we are) go-ing here and there, We're sim-ply

we're a band of pil-grims on the move; Thru dan-gers bur-dened
trust-ing in the bless-ed Sav-ior's love; And mer-cy tho' we

down with sor-rows, And we're shunned on ev-'ry hand, But we are look-ing
may be stran-gers, Liv-ing in this world of care, We're al-ways look-ing

CHORUS

for a cit-y built a-bove.   look - -
                a-bove. O yes, we're look-ing here and there

ing for a cit-y,   Where   we'll nev-er
Look-ing for a cit - y, Yon-der where we'll nev-er die,

die,   There   the saint-ed mil-lions,. . . . . .
nev-er die no nev-er, And up there with all the saints,   yes, with all the

. . . .   Nev - - er say good-by,
mil-lions, We will nev-er say good-by,   say good-by no nev-er, Yes, and

There   we'll meet our Sav-ior,   And
when we gath-er there,   We'll meet Christ our Savior, Glory and we know we'll meet

the saved ones too,   the saved ones,   Come   O Lord my
friends and oth-er saved ones, Now we pray Thee quick-ly come,

Sav-ior   All   our hopes re-new.
Pray Thee come O Savior, Come, O come! on Thee we call,   All our hopes renew.

682 The New Song

And they sing the song of Moses the servant of God, and the song of the Lamb . . .
Rev. 15:3

Eb-4-SOL
J. R. Baxter, Jr.

P-2, S-4
C. C. Stafford

1. It thrills my soul to hear the songs of praise, We mor-tals sing be - low,
2. The great-est joy that I have ev - er known, Is prais-ing Him in song,
3. The sweet-est song that earth can ev - er boast, Was sung when Christ was born,

And tho' it takes the part - ing of the ways, Yet I must on - ward go;
I know some day when I have old - er grown, My voice will not be strong;
Yet He who walked the Gal - i - lee - an coast, Some-times was sad for - lorn;

I hope to hear thru - out un-num-bered days, The song earth can-not know,
But if good seed for Je - sus I have sown, With an - gels I'll be - long,
He left the earth to send the Ho - ly Ghost, To guide us till that morn,

They sing in heav'n a new song, Of Mos - es and the Lamb.

REFRAIN

I want to

{ O to hear the an - gels sing - ing, To bid me wel-
{ hear an - gels sweet - ly sing, and to
{ O to see the Mas - ter bring - ing, A pre - cious life -
{ see see the Mas - ter bring, crown of

683 Sing And Be Happy

Serve the Lord with gladness: come before His presence with singing. Psa. 100:2

E♭- 2-MI
E. S. P.

J-1, S-4
Emory S. Peck

1. If the skies a - bove you are gray, You are feel - ing so
2. Oft - en we are trou - bled and tired, Sick with sor - row and
3. Oft we fail to see the rain - bow Up in heav - en's fair

blue, If your cares and bur - dens seem great All the
pain, There are oth - ers liv - ing in sin Blest with
sky, When it seems the for - tunes of earth Frown and

whole day thru, There's a sil - ver lin - ing that shines
earth - ly gain, Take new cour - age we can - not tell
pass us by, There are things we know that are worth

In the heav - en - ly land, Look by faith and
What the mor - row may bring, When the dark clouds
More than sil - ver and gold, If we hope and

see it my friend, Trust in His prom - is - es grand.
van - ish a - way Then your heart tru - ly can sing.
trust Him each day, We shall have pleas - ure un - told.

CHORUS

Sing and be hap-py, Press on
Sing and you'll be hap-py to-day, Press a-long to the

to the goal, Trust Him who leads you, He
goal, Trust in Him who lead-'eth the way, He is

will keep your soul; Let all be faith-ful
keep-ing your soul; Let the world know where you be-long,

Look to Him and pray, Lift your voice and
Look to Je-sus and pray,

praise Him in song, Sing and be hap-py to-day.

684
In The Kingdom Of The Lord

E-3-SOL

Palmer Hartsough *Now is come salvation, and strength, and the kingdom of our God. Rev. 12:10*

H-2, K-1

F. Clark Perry

DUET: Alto and Tenor

1. In the kingdom of the Lord, Dwell the good, dwell the blest, In the kingdom of the
2. In the kingdom of the Lord, Finds my tho'ts its em-ploy, In the kingdom of the
3. In the kingdom of the Lord, Thru the bow-ers I shall roam, In the kingdom of the

QUARTET:

Lord, There is peace, there is rest.
Lord, Is my hope, is my joy.
Lord, In my bright heav'n-ly home.

To that bless-ed land
Of that bless-ed land
To that bless-ed land

To that land my soul shall
Of that land so fair and
To that land are my de-

glad my soul shall fly, When this pil-grim-age, pil-grim-age is
land so fair and bright, Trav-el-ing a-long, trav-el-ing a-
Thine are my de-sires, Sav-ior's blest a-bode, Sav-ior's blest a-
fly, When this pil - - grim-age, this pil-grim-age is
bright As I'm trav - - el-ing, am trav-el-ing a-
sires, There's my Sav - - ior's blest, my Sav-ior's blest a-

o'er, Dwell be-yond the sky, dwell be-yond the sky,
long, Al-most catch the sight, al-most catch the sight,
bode, Thee, my heart as-pires, Thee, my heart as-pires,
o'er, I shall dwell be-yond the sky,
long, I can al - - - most catch the sight,
bode, Un-to Thee my heart as-pires,

With my Sav - ior blest,   blest for ev - er - more.
Al - most hear the song,   al - most hear the song,
Home-land of my God,   home-land of my God.
With my Sav - - - ior ev - er - more.
I can al - - - most hear the song.
Dear - est home - - - land of my God.

CHORUS

When the sun   is sink-ing low,   So oft I
When the sun is low,   sun is sink- ing low,

sing,   so sweet-ly sing,   O that
then so oft I sing,   then so sweet-ly sing,

land,   to which I go,
land, that bless- ed land,   land to which I go.

rit.

Where my Fa - ther is the King.
     He is the King.

685 The Lord Our Rock

Be Thou my strong rock, for an house of defense to save me.
For Thou art my rock and my fortress. Psa. 31:2,3

E-4-SOL
J. P. L.

C-9
J. P. Lane

1. O the Rock! 'tis a cleft and a strong, sure de-fense From the
2. O the Rock safe-ly shields from the foes that sur-round, Tho' the
3. O the Rock, bless-ed Rock, what a calm, blest re-treat, We will

dark gath-'ring tem-pest so threat-'ning and dense; In the
per-ils are man-y, and tempt-ers a-bound; In the
rest in the shade all se-cure from the heat; In the

Rock we are safe, we will suf-fer no fear, But in peace that is
Rock, all se-cure, from all harm we a-bide; Since He shields us and
Rock we're con-tent-ed, we're hap-py and free; Sin-ner, flee for thy

CHORUS

change-less, we rest sweet-ly here. For the Lord
keeps us, no ill can be-tide. For the Lord is our Rock,
life, O to this Re-fuge flee. For the Lord

is our Rock and is might - - y and
for the Lord is our Rock, and is might-y and strong, and is

686 Salvation Has Been Brought Down

Now is come salvation . . . and the kingdom of our God, and the power of His Christ.
Rev. 12:10

Bb-4-SOL
S-5

A. E. B.
Albert E. Brumley

1. Je - sus gave His life a ran - som yon - der on Cal - va - ry, On Mount
2. All a - lone with-out a friend He suf - fered to pay it all, Yes, He
3. There's a bless - ed home pre-pared 'way o - ver in glo - ry - land, In bright

Cal - va - ry, cru - el Cal - va - ry; Paved the way by blood that we might
paid it all, Je - sus paid it all; In His bless - ed prom - is - es sweet
glo - ry - land, bless - ed glo - ry - land; I have trust - ed in His love and

win a bright shin-ing crown, Praise His ho - ly name,
vic - to - ry can be found, bless - ed ho - ly name, sal-va-tion has been bro't
now I am heav - en bound,

CHORUS

Praise the Lord, sal - va -tion has been bro't down
down, O glo - ry. the Lord, bless-ed Lord, from heaven,

Go and shout and tell it the world a - round,
and shout, go and shout go preach it and

687 Did You Repent, Fully Repent?

Repent ye therefore, and be converted,
that your sins may be blotted out...Acts 3:19

F-4-SOL
R. S. A.

E-1
Robert S. Arnold

1. Christ the dear Lord, glo - ri - ous Lord, speaks to us gen - tly, By His great
2. Yes, He has said, tru - ly has said, how we should live now, What to par -

word that is our light each day;   Tell us the way, glo - ri - ous
take, what to a - void while here;   Do un - to those that are a -

way, we may reach heav - en,   If we be - lieve, if we re - pent,
bout a kind - ly serv - ice,   Tell them of Christ, teach them that He

CHORUS

if we o - bey.   Re - pent,   re - pent of your past
al - ways is near.   Did you   ful - ly

sins, friend,   Con - fessed   name   high?   Be -
When you   His   on   Did you

688 Paradise Valley

V. O. S. Db-2-MI

To him that overcometh will I give to eat of the tree of life,
which is in the midst of the paradise of God. Rev. 2:7

H-2
Virgil O. Stamps

1. As I trav-el thru life, with its trou-ble and strife, I've a
2. As I roam the hill-side, or I list to the tide, As I
3. Tho' your gar-den is rare, it is naught to com-pare With the

glo-ri-ous hope to give cheer on the way; Soon my toil will be o'er
pluck the sweet flow-ers that grow in the dale; A faint pic-ture is there
flow-ers that bloom in the gar-den a-bove, In the midst of it grows

and I'll rest on that shore Where the night has been turned in-to day.
of a land bright and fair Where per-en-ni-al flow-ers ne'er fail.
Shar-on's per-fect sweet Rose; 'Tis the won-der-ful Flow-er we love.

CHORUS

Up in the beau-ti-ful par-a-dise val-ley, By the
Up in par - a - dise val-ley

side of the riv-er of life, Up in the
of the riv-er of life, Up in par-

689 Master, The Tempest Is Raging

What manner of man is this, that even the wind and the sea obey Him! Matt. 8:27

C-2-SOL

M. A. Baker

C-6, P-1

H. R. Palmer

1. Mas-ter, the tem-pest is rag-ing! The bil-lows are toss-ing high! The sky is o'er-shad-owed with black-ness, No shel-ter or help is nigh; Car-est Thou not that we per-ish? How canst Thou lie a-sleep, When each mo-ment so mad-ly is threat-'ning A grave in the an-gry deep?

2. Mas-ter, with an-guish of spir-it I bow in my grief to-day; The depths of my sad heart are trou-bled— O wak-en and save, I pray; Tor-rents of sin and of an-guish Sweep o'er my sink-ing soul; And I per-ish! I per-ish! dear Mas-ter; O hast-en, and take con-trol.

3. Mas-ter, the ter-ror is o-ver, The el-e-ments sweet-ly rest; Earth's sun in the calm lake is mir-rored, And heav-en's with-in my breast; Lin-ger, O bless-ed Re-deem-er! Leave me a lone no more; And with joy I shall make the blest har-bor, And rest on the bliss-ful shore.

CHORUS

The winds and the waves shall o-

690 Matchless Love

For His great love wherewith He loved us, even when we were dead in sins . . .

Eph. 2:4,5

Ab-4-SOL
S. W. B.

Samuel W. Beazley

L-4

1. It was match-less love that found me, When the bands of sin had
2. What a ten - der lov - ing-kind - ness, That sought me in my
3. What a won - der - ful re - la - tion That I, in low - ly

bound me, It was love that planned es - cape for me When I was
blind-ness, And a mar - vel - ous re - demp-tion wro't That mor-tals
sta - tion, Am called a "son un - to God," what more Could hu-man

lost, un - done; It was love in sad plight, saw me, It was
might be free! What an act in its com - plete-ness! What a
heart de - sire? By His ten - der love o'er - shad - ed, I'll be

love that reached out for me, 'Twas the pre - cious love of Je - sus
love in ten - der sweet-ness! What a won - der - ful sal - va - tion
kept till earth has fad - ed From my sight, and I shall en - ter

CHORUS

Christ The might - y, ho - ly One.
now A - bounds for you and me! Love, 'twas love,
in To join the heav'n - ly choir.

'Twas love, 'Twas match-less

match-less love, Love, 'twas love, match-less love, Up-

love, That caused my Sav-iour there

on the cru-el cross to choose A death of

death of shame for e-ven

shame for me; Love, 'twas love, match-less love,

me; How can I e'er re-pay The

Love, 'twas love, love I owe, For His sal-va-tion

debt of love I owe,

full and free, Giv'n thro' love, love, match-less love?

3

won-der-ful love, match-less love?

691 Inside The Gate

Blessed are they that do His commandments, that they . . .
may enter through the gates into the city. Rev. 22:14

Ab-2-SOL
J. W. V.

H-2
J. W. Vaughan

1. Saved ones in glo-ry are wait-ing for me,
2. Won-der-ful mu-sic there sure-ly will be, Just in-side the gate;
3. We shall see Je-sus, O praise His dear name,

Some gold-en morn-ing their fac-es I'll see, Just in-side the gate;
All the sweet sing-ers of heav-en we'll see, pear-ly gate;
All thru the a-ges His grace we'll pro-claim,

There will be shouting and sing-ing up there, Glo-ry for-ev-er with them we shall share,
We shall re-joice while the a-ges shall roll, Joining with an-gels His name to ex-tol,
An-gels and saved ones are looking this way, Hoping to greet us some wonderful day,

When we shall en-ter our man-sion so fair, In-side the gate.
There in the beau-ti-ful home of the soul, Just in-side the gate.
When we move o-ver to heav-en to stay,

692 In The Shadow Of The Cross

Eb-2-SOL

He humbled Himself, and became obedient unto death, even the death of the cross.

C-17

Bernice M. Bronstrom

Phil. 2:8

W. H. Daniel

1. As we jour-ney on t'ward heav-en's shin-ing goal,
2. On that tree of sor-row Je-sus died for all,
3. There are souls to res-cue, there are souls to save,

We may suf-fer pain and loss;
Took up-on Him-self our dross;
On the sea of life they toss;

Bur-dens on-ly
As I see Him
May we be a

D. S. - Where the Sav-ior took your place?

By the cross He'll

bring us bless-ings if we live
there I long to ev-er live
light and teach them how to live

In the shad-ow of the

lead us to that home a-bove, There we'll see Him face to

Fine CHORUS

D. S.

cross. Are you liv-ing in the shad-ow of the cross,

face.

Were You There?

693

E-4-SOL
Traditional Spiritual

*And they bring Him unto the place Golgatha . . . and it was the
third hour, and they crucified Him.* Mark 15:22,24

C-3
Traditional Spiritual

1. Were you there when they cru - ci - fied my Lord? Were you
2. Were you there when they nailed Him to the tree? Were you
3. Were you there when they laid Him in the tomb? Were you
4. Were you there when He rose up from the dead? Were you

there when they cru - ci - fied my Lord? Oh!
there when they nailed Him to the tree? Oh!
there when they laid Him in the tomb? Oh!
there when He rose up from the dead? Oh!

Some - times it caus - es me to trem - ble, trem - ble, trem - ble.

Were you there when they cru - ci - fied my Lord?
Were you there when they nailed Him to the tree?
Were you there when they laid Him in the tomb?
Were you there when He rose up from the dead?

694 Savior, Teach Me

We love Him, because He first loved us. 1 John 4:19

F-2-MI
Jane E. Seeson

D-1, L-3
Carl von Weber

1. Sav - ior, teach me, day by day, Love's sweet les - son to o - bey:
2. With a child-like heart of love, At Thy bid-ding may I move,
3. Teach me all Thy steps to trace, Strong to fol - low in Thy grace,

Sweet - er les - son can - not be—Lov - ing Him who first loved me.
Prompt to serve and fol - low Thee—Lov - ing Him who first loved me.
Learn - ing how to love from Thee—Lov - ing Him who first loved me.

695 Savior, Grant Me Rest And Peace

Let your requests be made known to God. And the peace of God . . .
shall keep your hearts . . . Phil. 4:6,7

G-3-SOL
Grace Glenn

D-1, P-1
J. H. Fillmore

Slowly

1. Sav - ior, grant me rest and peace, Let my trou - bled dream-ings cease;
2. I would trust my all with Thee, All my cares and sor - rows flee,
3. I would seek Thy ser - vice, Lord, Lean-ing on Thy prom-ise-word;

With the chim-ing mid-night bell, Teach my heart that "all is well."
Till the break-ing light shall tell Night is past, and "all is well."
Let my hour-ly la - bors tell I am Thine, and "all is well." A - men.

He Loves Me

696

G-4-SOL

L-1, L-4

Christ also hath loved us, and hath given Himself for us. Eph. 5:2

Vana R. Raye

Arranged

1. Why did the Sav-ior heav-en leave And come to earth be-low
2. Why did the Sav-ior mark the way, And why temp-ta-tion know?
3. Why feel the gar-den's dread-ful dross? Why thru His tri-als go?

Where men His grace would not re-ceive? Be-cause He loves me so!
Why teach and toil and plead and pray? Be-cause He loves me so!
Why suf-fer death up-on the cross? Be-cause He loves me so!

CHORUS

He loves me! He loves me! He loves me this I know! He

gave Him-self to die for me, Be-cause He loves me so!

697   In Brotherly Love

E♭-3-MI

Don Alexander & R. J. S.

Let brotherly love continue. Heb. 13:1

L-2, V-1

R. J. Stevens

1. Raised up in Christ to heav - en - ly plac - es, I boast of
2. Pu - ri - fied souls with hearts that o - bey Him, Fer - vent - ly
3. Liv - ing to - geth - er with those who know Him, Spir - its that

great - ness on - ly in Him. Hon - ored to sit with fel - low be -
lov - ing, walk - ing in grace. Blest be the tie, in truth we're u -
con - quer tri - als of faith. Praise God for my dear fam - 'ly in

liev - ers, Broth - ers and sis - ters, serv - ing with them.
nit - ed, Long - ing to see our dear Sav - ior's face.
Je - sus, Lov - ing me 'til I leave them in death.

CHORUS

O what a joy to live in Christ Je - sus! I know the

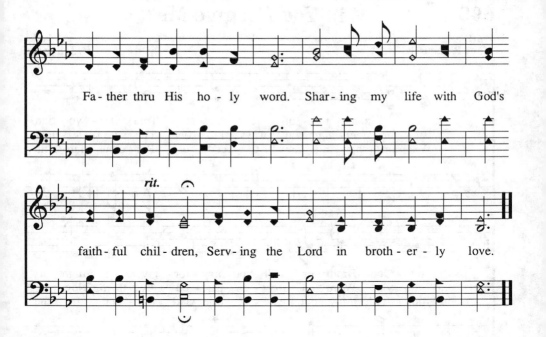

Fa - ther thru His ho - ly word. Shar - ing my life with God's

rit.

faith - ful chil - dren, Serv - ing the Lord in broth - er - ly love.

Dear Savior Of My Soul

698

F-4-DO
Bob Benfield

*For ye were as sheep going astray: but are now returning
unto the Shepherd and Bishop of your souls.* 1 Pet. 2:25

C-10, C-17
R. J. Stevens

1. Dear Sav - ior of my soul, When I see dawn's ear - ly
2. Dear Sav - ior of my soul, I do pray this day I'll
3. Dear Sav - ior of my soul, In the dark - ness of the
4. In a - go - ny, dear Je - sus, Thou hast paid the price for

light, I rec - og - nize Thy might, Dear Sav - ior of my soul.
be Ac - cep - ta - ble to Thee, Dear Sav - ior of my soul.
night Pro - tect me by Thy light, Dear Sav - ior of my soul.
me Up - on the cross of Cal - v'ry, Dear Sav - ior of my soul.

699   Will You Forgive Me?

F-4-DO   *... First be reconciled to thy brother.* Matt. 5:23-24   L-2, U-1

Huey P. Hartsell   **R. J. Stevens**

1. As I come to of-fer wor-ship, True de-vo-tion
2. Bit-ter feel-ings al-ways hin-der The sweet fel-low-
3. We are shar-ing now to-geth-er, Pre-cious kin-ship

to my God. Broth-er will you now for-give me, Aught a-
ship di-vine. We're no long-er part-ed by them, Now we
in our Lord. May our care be true and ten-der, In the

CHORUS

gainst me in your heart?
wor-ship with one mind. Let us then as one a-
har-mo-ny of love.

dore Him, Give the Lord our ar-dent praise. Broth-er will you

please for-give me, As our voic-es now we raise.

Train Your Children

700

F-4-MI
Train up a child in the way he should go. Prov. 22:6
H-5

Huey P. Hartsell

R. J. Stevens

1. Pre - cious gifts that come from God, Our dear chil-dren whom we
2. Fa - thers you must lead the way, Dai - ly teach and with them
3. Sweet - est home Christ has pre- pared, Where no tear will dim our

love. What a bless - ed priv - i - lege we have, Mold-ing
pray. And the moth - ers too with ten - der hand, Kind - ly
eye. And our faith - ful loved ones there can sing Grate-ful

CHORUS

hearts for heav'n a - bove. Teach your chil - dren! Love your
guide them lest they stray.
praise to God on high. Teach your chil-dren!

chil - dren! Train them in the way of God. What a
Love your chil - dren!

sweet re - un - ion there will be In our home e - ter - nal - ly.

701 Walk Beside Me

Show me Thy ways, O Lord; teach me Thy paths.
Lead me in Thy truth, and teach me. Psa. 25:4,5

G-3-MI
Katherine E. Purvis

G-3
James M. Black
Arr. R. J. Stevens

1. Walk be-side me, O my Sav-ior, While life's morn-ing sky is bright;
2. When the noon-tide's glow-ing splen-dor Brings its weight of toil and care,
3. When the twi-light shades de-scend-ing, Warn my soul that night is near,

Grant me now Thy lov-ing fa-vor, Flood my path with heav'n-ly light;
May Thy love, so pure and ten-der, All my heav-y bur-dens bear;
With the hues of sun-set blend-ing, Let the light of heav'n ap-pear;

Wheth-er good or ill be-tide me, Wheth-er skies be dark or clear,
In a wea-ry land, pro-vide me Shel-t'ring rock and cool-ing spring;
Thru the val-ley, Sav-ior take me, Close my eyes when night shall come;

Ev-er stay so close be-side me, I may know and feel Thee near.
When the temp-est ra-ges, hide me Un-der-neath Thy fold-ed wing.
Then bid an-gel voic-es wake me, Sweet-ly sing-ing, "Wel-come home."

Fine

D.S. Ev-er stay so close be-side me, I may know and feel thee near.

CHORUS

D.S.

Bless-ed Sav-ior, walk with me; Take a-way all anx-ious fear;

Thank You, Lord, For Homes

702

C-4-MI
Huey P. Hartsell
Arr. Craig Roberts

Therefore shall a man leave his father and his mother,
and shall cleave unto his wife: Gen. 2:24

H-5

R. J. Stevens

1. Thank You, Lord, for in cre - a - tion man was lone - ly, in - com-
2. Thank You, Lord, for faith - ful fa - thers, lov - ing, giv - ing, strong and
3. Thank You, Lord, for lov - ing mo - thers, god - ly hearts and hands to
4. Thank You, Lord, for lit - tle chil - dren, how they fill our hearts with

plete; From his rib You made a help - er suit - ed for him kind and
brave, Lead - ing hap - py house - holds on - ward, pray - ing for their homes to
serve, Priced a - bove the pre - cious ru - bies, hav - ing vir - tues all ob -
love! Hum - ble, in - no - cent, and trust - ing, like Your chil - dren up a -

sweet, "Leave your fa - ther and your mo - ther, go and cleave un - to your
save, For their dai - ly needs pro - vid - ing, will - ing to cor - rect and
serve. Chil - dren rise and call them bless - ed; hus - bands give them prais - es
bove. In our hands, as clay they're mold - ed, ev - er learn - ing morn and

wife." What a beau - ti - ful re - la - tion; two be - com - ing one for life.
stand. Oh how pre - cious are our fa - thers! How we need them in the land!
due. Who can tell of their a - dorn - ment, in - ward beau - ty, pure and true?
eve. What a her - i - tage we're leav - ing; pre - cious chil - dren who be - lieve!

SCRIPTURE INDEX

TOPICAL INDEX

To help in the selection of songs in varying keys and meters within the same category, the key and beat pattern have been placed after each title. The beat pattern will be in either simple (2,3,4) or compound (2c, 3c, 4c) times. NOTE: To aid in finding songs in the same topical category, each song has been given one or two index-guide symbols such as A-1, B-2, C-3, etc. These letters and numbers have been placed in the upper right side of each song and correspond with a specific heading in the topical index.

TOPICAL INDEX

GENERAL INDEX

NOTE: Titles are in caps. First lines are in small letters

GENERAL INDEX